D0722930

Pierre-Joseph Proudhon

Other works in the same field
by Edward Hyams

Killing No Murder
The Millennium Postponed
A Dictionary of Modern Revolution
Terrorists and Terrorism

Pierre-Joseph
PROUDHON

His Revolutionary Life, Mind and Works

EDWARD HYAMS

TAPLINGER PUBLISHING COMPANY
NEW YORK

First published in the United States in 1979 by
TAPLINGER PUBLISHING CO., INC.
New York, New York

Library of Congress Catalog Card Number:
78–72023
ISBN 0–8008–6552–9

Printed in Great Britain

Contents

Publisher's Note

EDWARD HYAMS DIED in Besançon in November 1975. He had nearly finished the typescript of this book and was doing some final research in Proudhon's birthplace. At first it seemed that the difficulty of finding someone to complete the book was going to prove insoluble but a closer examination of Edward Hyams's drafts and working notes showed how very close to the end he had got. In effect all that was required was the working up into a linking narrative of the notes on Proudhon's last ten years of life. This would form the background to the discussion of his last six major works which Edward Hyams had already completed. During these years Proudhon led a 'retired and modest' family life in Paris or in exile in Brussels and his energies were almost entirely channelled into his writing and the fight against ill health so that, in his own words, he could 'have the last word'.

The task of marshalling Edward Hyams's material for these last years was finally undertaken by Edwin Mullins, one of his closest friends, who by a happy coincidence was working at the time on the artist Gustave Courbet. Courbet knew Proudhon well and his own view of art owed much to Proudhon's ideas. We would like to thank Edwin Mullins for his skilful and unobtrusive help. Acknowledgement must also be given to George Woodcock's biography of Proudhon published in 1956 from which a number of short translated passages from Proudhon's letters and works, amounting to 300 words in all, have been taken.

Edward Hyams would probably have written an epilogue, had he lived, about Proudhon's posthumous influence on the First International, on Bakunin, on the Commune, on the Anarchist movement as a whole, and the French and Spanish working-class militant in particular. Knowing the man, he would have also allowed himself some last comments from a Proudhonian standpoint, on modern states and governments. As it is, his final words on Proudhon's final book serve well enough as an abiding impression.

Introduction

PROUDHON WAS BORN in the same year, 1809, as Charles Darwin, at about the moment when the reaction against the French Revolution, led by the old imperial monarchies and the British aristocratic oligarchy, began to triumph. That triumph was short-lived but at the time it was clear to only a very few men that Europe was facing a century of revolution.

It was in the half-century following Proudhon's birth that a number of men of talent and two men of genius, Proudhon and Karl Marx, sought to give form and practical applicability to the social, political and economic philosophy to become known as socialism. Thus Auguste Blanqui, who when not fighting the monarchy and the bourgeoisie, was in prison working out the principles of communist trade unionism and was the father of the French Socialist Party, was only four years Proudhon's senior; Alexander Herzen, the great publicist of socialism in Russia, was born in 1812, as was Louis Blanc who developed revolutionary socialism out of the idealistic proto-socialism of Saint-Simon. Michael Bakunin, the Russian anarchist and Marx's most troublesome enemy, was born in 1814; Marx in 1818 when his master, Hegel, was not yet fifty; and Engels in 1820. Lassalle, founder and master of the formidable German Workers' Party, was born in 1825.

These men and others of like mind and heart, were not the inventors of socialism, a word coined about 1820 and first used in print in the London Co-operative Society's magazine in 1827. They read and digested the works of some or all the proto-socialists and, the French using their native wit, the Germans the discipline of philosophy, sought to discover the laws of political economy considered as a science in the belief that by their means it would be possible to establish a just, egalitarian and prosperous society from which both poverty and privilege would have been eliminated. The task they set themselves had a negative and a positive side: first to analyse and criticize the existing society so as to justify and lead to its destruction by revolution; and then to discover the laws of social-political-economic evolution so as to lay down guide-lines for the new 'socialist' society.

They believed that the institution of private property in land and the means of production is unjust and responsible for degrading poverty, and that its abolition is a pre-condition for the establishment of a social justice reflecting, in its turn, 'immanent' justice. It was possible to so believe until Darwin, Proudhon's exact contemporary, drew attention to the facts of life.

This idea was given very early expression in such rhymes as 'When Adam delved and Eve span, Who was then the gentleman?' It was first given literary expression in Western Europe in More's *Utopia*. As for the folk criticism of property, I have wondered whether it reflected the memory of the time when there was, indeed, no property in land; and the knowledge that the only possible original title to real estate was occupation defended by brute force. More, like any other man of education who could nevertheless free his mind from cant, knew that communism (not Soviet state capitalism, rather the phalanstery or cenobitic form of socialism) was inherent in the primitive Christian Church; *And all that believed were together and held all things in common* (Acts 2:44). At all events the society discovered by Ralph, More's hero, in Utopia, and of which his creator approved, was communist.

In the 18th century there were a number of writings in English and French, later drowned in the flood of Marxist exegesis, which advanced ideas we should now call socialist. First (1755) came Morelly's *Code de la Nature* which argues that only a communist society based economically on social ownership could give social and political expression to immanent justice and so achieve a just society: the book inspired Gracchus Babeuf's ultra-left Society of Equals during the French Revolution and needless to say the burgesses, no more tolerant of disrespect for property rights than of aristocratic privilege, sent Babeuf and his associates to the guillotine. Ideas similar to those of Morelly were put forward by Jean Meslier in his *Testament* (1764) and by Mably in *De la Législation* (1778), while Thomas Spence (*Mode of Administering the Landed Estate of the Nation* 1775) and William Ogilvie (*The Right of Property in Land*) both foreran Proudhon in seeking the origin of property right in land, finding it in theft by armed force, condemning it as therefore unjust, and proposing that the land of England should return to the people of England, to be held in common.

Among the English proto-socialist philosophers William Godwin was outstanding. In 1793 he published his *Enquiry Concerning Political Justice* which contained two very important social discoveries: that the precondition for the establishment of social justice is economic equality, and that the pre-condition for economic equality is not only the abolition of the institution of private property – Spence and Ogilvie had already reached that conclusion – but the abolition of the state. He called the state 'That brute engine which has been the only perennial cause of the vices of mankind', because it necessarily institutionalizes social injustice. The state was to be replaced by co-operation in the economic field, and in the political field, by direct democracy decentralized down to the parish level. Had Proudhon ever read Godwin – he read Greek, Latin and Hebrew but neither English nor German – he would have discovered that the Englishman had forestalled him; but as far as I can determine, he never so much as heard of Godwin and the only Englishman among his masters was Adam Smith.

Four years after Godwin's statement of the Anarchist case came Tom Paine's *Agrarian Justice*. Of the same author's illegally published *Rights of Man*, for which Paine was forced to take refuge in France, the Prime Minister, William Pitt, master of the most powerful aristocratic oligarchy in the world, had this to say: 'Tom Paine is quite in the right, but what am I to do? As things are, if I were to encourage his opinions we should have a bloody revolution'. This admission of Paine's case demonstrates an important truth: morally, the socialist idea is unassailable and no honest man who clears his mind of cant can deny it. From the beginning, therefore, its opponents – those who were capable of reflection – have been thrown back on an argument one may perhaps call Darwinian: human nature being what it is, a particular manifestation of Nature at large, and there being no justice in nature, socialism is morally right but in practice inexpedient. Feudalism and capitalism might be unjust but they were *dans le vrai*; socialism might be just, but it was impossible because 'unnatural'. Not until Proudhon, in a critique of the economist Rossi, did any man of the revolutionary side reject the argument of the left based on morality and humanity. It was not a question of socialism having to justify itself by dragging in the moral or humane argument. Socialism – and libertarian not state socialism at that – was the only scientifically valid and viable system, virtually synonymous with sound political economy. The trouble with property (*ie* capitalism) was not that it was wicked; it was – as he demonstrated – *impossible*. Marx, long after reading Proudhon's *What is Property?*, came to the same conclusions.

The opponents of socialist aspirations and systems thought and felt that socialism was sentimental. That is the judgement which inspires such 'bourgeois' folk-wisdom as the saying that while a man who is not a socialist before thirty has no heart, the man who is a socialist after thirty has no head. They confused justice with law, believed, as they were entitled to believe, that what was lawful was just. It took a Godwin or a Proudhon to perceive and point out that since law is the defence of property and since property is theft, the law is injustice institutionalized.

Robert Owen (1771–1858) was the leader of the new thinking among the next generation in Britain after Godwin and Paine. He was a self-made mill owner who had started work at nine after receiving a primary education. He had read John Hall's book *Effects of Civilization on the Peoples of European States* which may well have been the first to indict capitalism as the exploiter of the workers who produced the wealth of society, only to be robbed of it by the extortion of profit, interest and rent (another Englishman who foreran Proudhon, Hall proposed to begin the process of setting things right by nationalizing land). His reading, his experience as a wage-earner, and his experience as an employer of labour on a large scale, had led him to two conclusions of his own: that organized religion is the root of all evil; and that character is formed by environment, at that time another original and dangerous notion. Give a man a decent wage and working conditions, and he would be a good and valuable citizen; deny him those things, and he would be prone to vice and crime. At least two pre-Freudian philosophers would have agreed with him: the American, Emerson and the Frenchman Fourier.

Owen advocated the establishment of industrial co-operatives as the ultimate solution to the social and economic problem. This solution was later known as Syndicalism, though Owen is not looked on as a Syndicalist forebear. He introduced into his own New Lanark mills, where he employed over 2000 workers, reforms far in advance of his time. He cut the working day to ten and a half hours, refused to employ children under ten, opened shops for his workers where goods of quality were sold at cost price, opened infant schools where the beating of children was forbidden; and when an American embargo on the sale of cotton to Britain closed his mills, he continued to pay his workers. Later, helped financially by Jeremy Bentham the Utilitarian, and some like-minded associates who had been impressed by Owen's pamphlet *A New View of Society*, he reorganized his business to channel profits into improvement of workers' conditions and into workers' education. His model mills and workers' villages became world famous.

From those beginnings Owen went on to establish a communist co-operative in Glasgow. In 1824 he went to America, bought a village and 20,000 acres of land in Indiana, and there started another commune, of European immigrants. It failed because a high proportion of the members did not give the commune a fair day's work. Owen consoled himself with the conclusion that his theory about the influence of environment on character was correct: these poor people had been morally ruined by oppression, exploitation and grinding poverty in the lands of their birth, and no longer had the character to carry through an enterprise.

I don't know if Owen had read Montesquieu who had long since (1748) pointed out that a democracy depends for its survival on the 'virtue' of its citizens.

Owen was largely responsible for getting the first Factory Act on to the statute book, with the help of aristocratic Tories who saw in the working-class a possible ally against the rising power of the industrial and commercial burgesses. And he inspired the London Co-operative Society in whose magazine the new social economic theories were first defined: 'Those who think that capital should be common are the communists and socialists.'

It was in the Saint-Simonien newspaper *Le Globe* that similar ideas were being put forward at the same time in France. The comte Claude de Saint-Simon, born 1760, proposed, in a number of works beginning with *Letters from a Resident of Geneva to his Contemporaries* (1802), and written and published over a period of twenty years, to reorganize society by getting rid of capitalism and substituting a planned economy managed scientifically but in the spirit of Christian moral law by an intellectual élite open to working-class talent. The change was not brought about by revolution, that is by force, but by persuasion and propaganda.

Another French proto-socialist who influenced Proudhon directly ('For six weeks I was the captive of this bizarre genius.' Proudhon, then an apprentice-compositor, was proof-reading the man's book), was Charles François Fourier who, in his *Le Nouveau Monde Industriel et Sociétaire* proposed setting up phalansteries, that is communes, of free co-operators. These would steadily spread to absorb the entire economic life of the nation. Fourier believed that crime and vice were symptoms of mental sickness caused by the repression of strong passions. In ordinary mental health man would be attuned to the 'Universal harmony' which, according to Fourier, governed the universe (our old friend, discredited by Darwin, 'immanent justice') and that state of health could be ensured only if men lived together in co-operative communes.

Pierre Leroux, editor of *Le Globe*, the Saint-Simonien newspaper, went further than his master towards socialism. It was he who coined the slogan, 'From each according to his capacity; to each according to his work', and who first identified the opposing social classes as 'Bourgeoisie' and 'Proletariat'. He advocated abolition of inheritance (a proposition rejected by Proudhon on the grounds that it would concentrate property in the hands of the tyrant state), and management of the economy and of the state by workers' co-operatives. Under his influence the silk-weavers of Lyon in the 1830s formed a trade union, which was illegal, and demanded a living wage. When it was refused the weavers rose in revolt. The revolt was put down by the army – there are glimpses of this incipient social war in Stendhal's *Lucien Leuwen*.

*   *   *   *   *

These and other proto-socialist or proto-communist ideas were the raw material out of which Proudhon, Marx, Engels, Bakunin and their contemporaries formed their socialist-economic systems. Two of these systems were to emerge triumphant: Marxism, which has conquered half the world; and trade unionism, as powerful in the other half, and especially in the English-speaking parts of it, as was the Church in mediaeval Europe.

Now both these systems, while they have greatly advanced the cause of the working-class, and increased the workers' share of the wealth which they produce, have failed to realize the equally important non-material aspect of the socialist vision. They have come nowhere near to realizing the aim of making society a free association of free men voluntarily cooperating in the management of the economy and the necessary political and social organs. They have betrayed the old socialist vision, trade unionism because of its respect for law, and Marxism because of its worship of the state.

Marxism has given us societies in which the state has become the instrument of a bureaucratic tyranny. This is precisely what Proudhon said would happen if Marx's ideas were given practical force and expression. (Lenin, in his last writings, also foresaw and repeatedly warned the peoples of the Soviet Union against the danger of this tragedy.) The tyrant bureaucracy may be more or less benevolent towards all but the dissidents among the people it rules, and may manage the people's business more or less conscientiously. The price is liberty. Moreover, like all tyrants, the Marxist bureaucracy feels itself threatened, develops a bad case of paranoia, becomes militaristic, and channels so great a proportion of the surplus value of the people's labour into military and police defence of its empire that the people are scarcely any better off than they were when that surplus was going into capitalist pockets. The people owe the improvement in their conditions more to the advance of industrial technology than to the bureaucracy's respect for social justice.

In the Western world the combination of part state-capitalism, part corporation-capitalism, liberalized by socialist philosophy, and trade unionism, is tending swiftly towards a rather similar petrification. The joint managers of Western societies, government–capital–trade unions, begin to look and to behave more and more like a Marxist bureaucracy and are far too strong, in the long run, to be held in check by the old parliaments, or the Congress. In any case, these last are 'penetrated' by the managers and progressively weakened.

The control of the means of production, distribution and exchange by the workers is not accomplished by putting them into the hands of the state: from the pure socialist point of view, nationalization of agriculture and industry is a fraud; or at very best a step, called by Lenin state capitalism, in the direction of socialism. The moral flaw in Marxism derives from the fact that Marx inherited his master Hegel's conviction that the state is a being superior not only to each individual but to the sum of all the individuals composing a society. This conviction, a direct and unavoidable consequence of a strict application of the Hegelian dialectic to politics, has inevitably made the Marxist state into a devouring monster. The self, the person, the citizen is Thesis; society – all the others, Antithesis: they are reconciled and absorbed in Synthesis – the state. But the state must be managed, the managers are the bureaucrats and technocrats. One man has already contrived to make himself Arch-Bureaucrat and in his corruption by power into a tyrant as irrational, as heartless and, finally, as cruel as any in the history of mankind, he serves as an Awful Warning. For the bureaucracy, whether it have one head or many, at once servant and master of the deified state, cannot but proclaim later if not sooner, *L'Etat c'est moi*.

In the East as well as the West, men who trouble to think about our condition at all, and who are unwilling to learn to love either Big Brother or Big Business, seek an alternative society. The search has led to absurd aberrations but that does not invalidate it. It might be as well, therefore, to take a fresh look at the life, times and thought of the most brilliant persistent and courageous exponent of libertarian, as opposed to state, socialism. If we are open to argument at all and have not lazily and wearily closed our minds, we are influenced, when listening to that argument, by two forces: the quality and power of the argument itself; and the personality and character of the man advancing it. Captivated myself not only by what he thought and did, but by the man he was, I believe that if the struggle to establish a just society is to continue, then Proudhon, who died in 1865, has a future.

Peasant and Printer

PIERRE-JOSEPH Proudhon was, throughout his life and at times self-consciously, a man of the Franche-Comté and of the Jura, the land of his birth. It has been held that nobility of heart and mind and, in general, the rugged virtues, are more often to be found and stand longer against the insidious and debilitating ease of civilization, in mountain men than in plainsmen. The Franche-Comté is for the most part mountainous country, rich in good natural pastures, in wild flowers which have long since become extinct in England, in fine woods, noble rivers and fertile valleys. It has obvious affinities with neighbouring Switzerland. At one time a part of Burgundy, later belonging to Spanish Flanders, it did not become a part of France until conquered by Louis XIV; but now, at least, it is wholly French in spirit and manners. The land is superlatively well-cared for but not exploited, the villages and towns handsome, seemly and very *paysan* and *bourgeois* respectively. And the Franc-Comtois tends to be proud of his condition and to respect the genius of his place, instead of aspiring to something other.

A notable German scholar, Victor Heyn, once divided Europe into two parts; on the one hand were the beer-and-butter countries, on the other the lands of wine-and-oil. The Franche-Comté manages to belong to both: the vineyards of its *côtes* are celebrated for such excellent wines as those of Arbois; its cooks use both butter and oil, and beer is as native as with us; indeed, Claude-François Proudhon, Pierre-Joseph's father, was himself a brewer and cooper, first a *garçon brasseur*, workman-brewer, in the rich Renaud brewery in the Moullière suburb of Besançon; and later, disastrously, artisan brewer and cooper on his own account. On both sides of his family Proudhon came of peasant and artisan stock; but they were never serfs. Free from time immemorial of the *corvée* and of *mortmain*, they owned their farm and vineyard; and most of them also practised a trade, like Claude-François who, as a cooper, could earn his living in town as well as country.[1]

Proudhon's mother, Catherine Simonin, born at Corderon in the parish of Burgille-les-Marnay on the river Ognon, '*Belle et forte fille de la campagne*', as her son describes her, was five years older than her husband, thirty-four when Pierre-Joseph was born. She was cooking for the workers at Renaud's brewery when Claude-François met her. It seems that she was a woman notable in her parish and in Besançon for her Roman-matron virtues, and especially for her strong republican sentiments. This republican spirit she had inherited from her father, known as Tornesi, after the regiment in which he had served in the Hanoverian wars; her looks were inherited from her mother Marie Gloron, celebrated throughout her countryside for her beauty. This Tornesi Simonin had been the spokesman and leader of the small farmers and artisans in all their quarrels with the nobility: he had been particularly resentful of and ready to break the game-laws which the Revolution was to abolish, and, as a formidable poacher, repeatedly involved in rows and brawls with the local great landowners' gamekeepers. It was in one such quarrel that, in the autumn of 1788, he shot a man who, before he died, confessed that the fault had been his and that Tornesi had been defending himself. Some months later, in the year locally remembered not for the fall of the Bastille – the Jura is a long way from Paris – but as 'the year of the great frost', Tornesi Simonin died as the result of a bad fall on ice.

Sainte-Beuve[2] says that Proudhon was actually born in the Moullière *faubourg* where the Renaud brewery was located; he was mistaken. In 1808 Claude-François bought a house to take his bride to, just inside the city walls in the Battants quarter of Besançon, and now known as No. 37, Rue des Petits Battants. The price was 1000 francs and as he had no savings and Catherine's little dowry did not amount to anything like so considerable a sum, he arranged to pay the balance over a period of ten months at 5 per cent interest.

It was in that house that Proudhon was born and reared. Tall and narrow, it would have been uncomfortably crowded had his four siblings – he was the eldest of five children – all lived. Claude-François' coopering and brewing shed adjoined the house and there was also room for a vegetable garden and even a house-cow; that piece of land was later built on. Whether Claude-François set up in business on his own account when he and Catherine married and moved into the house, or later, in 1814, when the Moullière *faubourg* including the Renaud brewery was pulled down to facilitate the defence of the town against the Allied armies, is not clear.

Claude-François' enterprise did not prosper and Catherine Simonin had to do a great deal of 'managing'. Sainte-Beuve described Proudhon's father as a decent sort of man but of low intelligence and not always respectable behaviour, and there is a tradition that he was a drunkard. Proudhon himself, and Daniel Halévy,[3] are kinder. Proudhon describes his father as 'a simple man who knew little arithmetic' (*un homme simple qui savait peu calculer*); he was fond of him and when he died, bitterly regretted that he had been unable, as he had hoped to do, to make the old man's last years easier.[4] It is true, however, that he did not have for his father the affectionate respect which he had for his mother.

There was, nevertheless, one aspect of his father's character and behaviour which Proudhon not only respected and admired, but which had a lasting influence on his work. When Besançon was besieged by the Allies, and in the subsequent hard times until the 1820s, the town's brewers seized the opportunity to make their fortunes by progressively raising their prices. To those friends and kinsmen who urged Claude-François to do likewise, he had only one answer: 'Not at all. So much for my raw materials plus so much for my work, that's my price.' Halévy points out, with the condescending arrogance of a man who had never been obliged to descend to the basenesses of trade, that such honesty in commerce was *néfaste*, disastrous. That honesty was of a very particular kind, however: the Proudhons and Simonins, having 'land and vineyard and workshop, owing their livelihood to nothing but their labour, and touching their caps to no man unless they felt like it',[5] were what is called in *bousse-bot*, the Franc-Comtois *patois* of which the Battants quarter was the last refuge in Besançon, *cudots*.[6] It's not easy to translate: it describes a man whose obstinacy is a product of pride, vanity, satisfaction with what he is; and is presumptuous. If there be an equivalent in England I think I'd look for it in Yorkshire: in America, one might find it in Connecticut. Throughout his life Proudhon was a bit of a Yorkshireman, a bit of a Yankee, and all of a *cudot*.

Now, Claude-François' principle in business – cost of materials plus a fair wage for work equals selling price – became the basis of Proudhonian economics: it excludes interest in any form; it excludes rent; it excludes profit. Yet even at the age of ten Proudhon realized that it was not as simple as that: 'I felt perfectly all the decency and honesty there was in the paternal method, but nevertheless also perceived the risk which it entailed. My conscience approved the former, my fears for our safety made me aware of the latter. It was an enigma.'

Proudhon's brother, Jean Etienne, was born in 1811 and Proudhon told Sainte-Beuve that he recalled being savagely jealous of the attention paid to the child, and how he had hated him. That hatred soon changed and never in all his life did he love any man or woman more than he had loved Jean-Etienne. Of the qualities which inspired such affection there is no record. We know only that when Jean-Etienne died while serving as a conscript in the army, mysteriously, and apparently after threatening to expose his captain for some kind of fraudulent misuse of army funds, Proudhon recorded: 'This captain was a thief; that death completed the work of making me an irreconcilable enemy of the established order.' There is a curious parallel here with Lenin's history: he is supposed to have turned revolutionary as a result of the judicial murder of his elder brother by the Tsarist government.

The third and fourth of the Proudhon children died in infancy: the youngest brother, in whom Proudhon never seems to have taken much interest, survived to become the Burgille-les-Marnay blacksmith, and his mother's companion in her widowed old age.

The Proudhons did not lose touch with the countryside. Claude-François earned a little extra money each year when casual labour was required in the vineyards for pruning or for the vintage. At five years of age Proudhon himself was sent to the Simonins at Burgille and until he was ten spent most of his time there, doing such jobs about the farm as a child could do, and as a rule minding the cows out at pasture. Half a century later he recalled,[7] 'For five years I was a cowherd. I know of no life which is at once so contemplative and so realistic or more opposed to the absurd spirituality which is the basis of Christian education and the Christian life.'

The anti-Christian feeling was a later development, for as a child Proudhon, like all his family on the rural side, was deeply religious. At Burgille there were frequent gatherings of all the family for prayers, a practice more Protestant than Catholic, but very Franc-Comtois, especially in the Jura. At times later in life he was a practising Catholic, despite a harshly critical attitude to the Church. Another Protestant trait – the book in which his mother taught him to read was the Bible. In choosing it she may have been demonstrating her independence of the Catholic – at that time ultra-royalist – Church; it would have been like her famous republicanism. Proudhon remained a Bible-reader for most of his life and, as will appear, by leading him to learn Hebrew and then to correct some of the Latin and vernacular translations, it finally led him to the proposition that property is theft.

At Burgille he learned that passionate love of the country which lasted all his life; but it was not, as an Englishman's or a German's would have been, a romantic love of nature. It was a cultivated countryside he loved; the hard but fundamental and honest toil of farm work; the lush pasture, the wheat fields, the vineyards. As a child cowherd he looked not for wild flowers, but for things to eat – berries, grass-seeds, mushrooms; he knew, he had good cause to know, their importance: when he was eight years old, for example, the whole region was stricken by famine and in 1817 the barley was harvested green to make a kind of bread.

If the principal influence of his Burgille kinsfolk was religious, there were others: he never forgot a saying of his ex-Jacobin maternal uncle – 'Religion is as necessary to man as bread and as pernicious as poison'; nor the old vigneron who once said to him, speaking the *langue d'oc*, 'Lou bon Dué, c'ost lou chaud,' that is, 'The good God is the sun'. He once recalled that at ten years of age the things he 'believed in' were God, Christ, Mary, nymphs, and fairies.

Thus when, at twelve years of age, Proudhon started work as cellar-boy in his father's small business, he had already been earning his own living or part of it for seven years. Yet his education was not neglected: his mother taught him not only to read but to write and calculate; and very likely a great deal more, for Sainte-Beuve says that his enquiries concerning Catherine Simonin among her fellow-Bisontins led him to the conclusion that she was altogether 'une femme supérieure'. It is at least possible that he had made a beginning in Latin, for the Battants parish priest, Father Sirebon, finding the boy as outstandingly clever and intelligent as his mother said he was, had taken an interest in him. Moreover, the rich brewer, Renaud, the Proudhon's former employer, had undertaken the systematic education of his own children, and agreed to Catherine's suggestion that her boy be allowed to attend the lessons when he could be spared from his work in the brewery-cooperage.

It would have been normal, in the family tradition too, for Pierre-Joseph to be apprenticed to a master artisan at about the age of twelve or thirteen, and he certainly would have been had not his mother again intervened. With the help of Father Sirebon and Monsieur Renaud, she procured for her son a small *bourse* which gave him access to the best education which Besançon could afford at the Collège de Besançon, a royal foundation, to which the burgesses and regional nobility and gentry sent their sons.

Proudhon was very far from happy at school: he missed the relative freedom, and the manly responsibility, of his life as a worker in both country and town. Although he had a vocation for study, it was best answered in solitude. Then, he was the one poor boy in a community of rich ones; his clothes were rustic and much patched, his feet were shod in clogs, and his manners were not those of his school-fellows. His father's business affairs were going from bad to worse throughout the years of Proudhon's schooling; his parents could not afford to buy the books he needed, and he was forced to borrow books from his school-fellows and copy out the texts he required. Moreover, he was not getting enough to eat; very often the only food in the house was milk from his mother's house-cow.

Despite these miseries, or in response to the severity of their challenge, Proudhon was among the most brilliant pupils of a school with a distinguished record. He became an excellent Latinist, a good Grecian, a good mathematician; and he read voraciously, chiefly in the town's very good public library. He recalls the times when he arrived home laden with prizes, to find that there was no dinner because no money to buy food. 'I pursued my humanities throughout my family's miserable poverty and all the disgusts which can afflict a sensitive youth bursting with the touchiest kind of pride. My father was a sick man, and as if the disastrous state of his affairs were not enough, was carrying on a lawsuit which was to be our final ruin.'

At school he was sombre, sullen, *farouche*; few of the boys befriended him, but among those few he was a leader despite his handicaps. It was because the courses there did not try him hard enough that he took to reading at the municipal library whose chief librarian, Monsieur Weiss, Proudhon's ally in many later trials, told Sainte-Beuve that his curiosity about the youngest of his readers was aroused by the boy's habit of asking for as many as twelve books at a single sitting. Weiss received a dusty answer to his, 'My young friend, what do you want with so many books at once?' Proudhon scowled at him and replied, 'What's that to you?'

In spite of his manners, Weiss and other men of sense and sensibility liked and respected the boy who was striving against such odds to get an education; and those sentiments were to stand him in good stead much later, when so many of his fellow-citizens, in common with their fellow-countrymen all over France, came to fear and detest the doctrine he was propagating.

One of the school prizes which he received when he was fourteen was Fénélon's *Démonstration de l'Existence de Dieu*. He was very eager to read it, for he was trying to overcome the disgust and suspicion aroused by the fanatical missionary preachers whom the ultra-reactionary Church of the Bourbon restoration was employing in a campaign to reconvert the French provinces (Paris was hopeless) to a blind obedience to authority. Fénélon's was the first of hundreds of works of theology and philosophy to disappoint him: he found it impossible to respect arguments so wanting in intellectual rigour, in moral integrity and, above all, so loftily indifferent to terrestrial justice. Fénélon, and the missionary preachers, between them, drove him to give up, for the time being, the practice of his religion.

*   *   *   *   *

In Proudhon's eighteenth year he was due to be 'crowned' as one of the College of Besançon's laureates. His fellow prizemen all had their parents and friends attending the public ceremony; but neither his father nor his mother could be there to see him honoured, they were in court, awaiting the judgement in his father's lawsuit, and Proudhon was obliged to stand alone, in his threadbare clothes and all his awkwardness, to receive the Rector's congratulations and accolade. When he reached home he found the family in distress and gloom: the judgement had gone against them and their ruin was accomplished. He was able to sit the baccalaureate examinations and to pass them: but as there was not a penny in the house, he could not afford the 'taxation' of the diploma; and so did not receive one.

It was now vital for Proudhon to find work, to choose a trade. He could no longer be a farmer as his ancestors had been; the moneylenders and lawyers had so plundered the family that there was no farm left. In any case, he was far from being displeased at the idea of being an artisan, or, rather, an *ouvrier*; it was, in his eyes, the most honourable condition. He chose printing as his trade, perhaps because there were openings there, perhaps because it would connect him with books. Besançon was a considerable centre for the printing industry and there were a number of firms: he was taken on by the house of Gauthier et Cie, as proof-corrector and learner-compositor.

The firm was much involved in the printing and publishing of religious books and works of theology for which, in the anti-revolutionary and reactionary last years of the Bourbon restoration, there was a good demand. The first proofs which Proudhon was given to correct were those of a law book in Latin. Millet, at that time Gauthier's *prote d'imprimerie*, master compositor, and later editor of the *Journal de l'Ain*, told Sainte-Beuve:

... After that, he was given Berruyer's *Histoire du Peuple de Dieu*. Then we were printing Fourier's *Nouveau Monde Industriel et Sociétaire*. Fourier used to call for his proofs in person and calculate the number of letters in a volume. Proudhon was already apt to slash his whole doctrine, amusing us with his outbursts. A good lad, for ever drifting in and out of the proof-correctors' room, asking how things were going among the gleaners of errors, running his hand through his hair, and then starting a conversation about history or current events.

Proudhon may have *sabrait* Fourier's doctrine; he was, nevertheless, and at least for a month or two, under the influence of his fellow-townsman, the prophet of the socialist phalanstery, or commune, in France.

At about this time Proudhon had his first love affair; we know nothing about the girl excepting that she was of his own class. It was, however, an *amour honnête*, that is to say, chaste. It is difficult, indeed impossible, to know whether Proudhon was under-sexed by our standards, which he would have condemned as lascivious and, in his own word, pornocratic; or an extraordinarily successful sublimator. This is what Sainte-Beuve believed, claiming Proudhon had an almost mystical belief in the value of chastity which, he was convinced, conserved and reinforced moral and intellectual power. Any yielding to sexual appetite even, beyond a certain point, in wedlock, was corrupting.

As will appear when I come to his unsympathetic attitude to the love-affairs and marriages of his friends, and to his *Pornocracy*, a polemical pamphlet against the emancipation of women, Proudhon remained a peasant, an ultra-reactionary of the *Kirche–Kuche–Kleine* kind in his attitude to women and sex. Confronted with a George Sand, instead of conceding that some women at least could be free spirits and creative artists, he took refuge in his opinion that the writing of novels (he might have made an exception in the case of his friend Tolstoy for whom he provided the title of *War and Peace*) was a trivial and socially worthless occupation.

At all events, this love affair of his nineteenth year had one very curious consequence: he resumed the practice of his religion. Should I, perhaps, be writing, he took refuge from his emotions and physical impulses in his religion, in that 'spirituality' of Christianity which he was later to compare so contemptuously with the realism of herding cows? The most classically cynical of 20th-century novelists, Somerset Maugham, once said that a woman who involved herself with an intellectual could expect much cry but little wolf; but in Proudhon's case there was not much cry either; he was savagely contemptuous of the romantic attitude to women. There is, in short, nothing to go on but what he said: 'I was a Christian again because I was in love.'

*   *   *   *   *

Either as a proof-corrector, or in pursuit of his own search for a God called Immanent Justice, Proudhon read the Fathers, read Lactantius, read Bossuet and Bergier. But, equally, he read such anti-religious and anti-clerical writing as he could lay hands on; he found it contemptible. What he sought was a justification for demanding of all Christians that they devote themselves to establishing among themselves a justice to match that which must surely be in nature. Or, if it was not in nature, then let mankind face the fact that the world and the flesh were of the devil. It was an almost Manichean view; it was certainly his sense of the evil of a Church corrupted by the pie-in-the-sky doctrine of indifference to terrestrial justice, which set him on the revolutionary path. He had an extraordinary flair for the phoney, especially the grand, pretentious phoney. Here he is, for example, on the subject of Châteaubriand:

It was not without intense anger that, at twenty years of age, I read the works of that phrasemaker without awareness or philosophy, whose only worth was in his fluency ... The men of '89, witnesses to feudal tyranny and sacerdotal corruption, would not have been taken in by such gaudy stuff.

The first modern author to make a positive impression on his mind was that De Bonald whose dictum, *L'art, c'est la société*, and whose socialist aesthetics were the foundation of the working philosophy of another product of the College of Besançon, and later Proudhon's friend and almost disciple, the painter Courbet. De Bonald sought natural laws of human societies which, once revealed and understood, would make possible the installation of a definitive, perfected, and therefore immutable, form of society. But still Proudhon remained critical: even as a very young man he was never fooled by the vision of Utopia; he knew that De Bonald's perfected and therefore immutable society must be a chimaera. The condition of life was change, and consequently tribulation; that was the fundamental natural law, and any human society which failed to take account of it was a nonsense. Moreover, his extremely practical mind was irritated by De Bonald's as by other socialist philosophers' lofty ignoring of such problems as the maldistribution of wealth. How about an explanation of the fact that his own father's 'So much for my raw material plus so much for any labour, that's my price', obviously both logical and honest, turned out to be ruinous? And why did all the ·thinkers he was reading shy away from the obvious truth that the Church, as presently constituted, had such a vested interest in sin, that it could certainly not afford to take up the cause of terrestrial justice?

Two of the books his firm was printing and whose proofs he was correcting at this time turned out to be important influences on his future, but for reasons which had little to do with their matter: one was the source of the first of his passionate friendships; the other led him to that proposition which was the inspiration of his first important revolutionary book – that property is theft.

The first was a Latin edition of *Lives of the Saints* for which Gauthiers were employing, as editor, a brilliant young scholar and philologist, Gustave Fallot, who had settled in Besançon when, to satisfy his vocation for letters, he had defied his family, refused to enter the family business, and been cut off without even the proverbial shilling. Reading the proofs, Proudhon found flaws and awkwardnesses in the Latin, and went beyond his brief to write suggested improvements in the margins. Far from resenting this officiousness, Fallot found the proof-reader's suggestions interesting and valuable, enquired concerning their author, and was surprised to be told, 'He's one of our workmen'. He sought the *ouvrier*'s acquaintance. The two young men very quickly became friends; and it was Fallot who put into Proudhon's mind the notion, on which he was to waste a great deal of time and thought, that the first clues to a revelation of the universal structure of the divine creation might be found in the study of primitive languages and, in general, of linguistics.

Partly in pursuit of this chimaera, partly to meet the demands of the other book whose proofs he was correcting, a Bible in which the Hebrew and Latin texts were interlined, Proudhon now set about learning Hebrew. This study, which he carried to a level far beyond that required for his present task, made the original texts of, for example, the Ten Commandments, available to him, with results which will appear in their place.

Proudhon, and Besançon, seem scarcely to have noticed the 'revolution' of July 1830. What did it matter to most Frenchmen that Charles X had been chased off the throne, to be replaced by a partnership between a crafty dullard, Louis-Philippe of Orleans; a Chamber of Deputies elected on a very limited franchise, on the English model; a Chamber of Peers on the same model; and the bourgeoisie of industry and commerce – *le patronat* – and the *haute banque*? All that was changed, for the ordinary man, was the pickpocket's hand: the object of politics became control of the budget. Not one of the aspirations which were beginning to move Frenchmen, especially young Frenchmen, were satisfied; and soon the dead and dirty hand of the *juste-milieu* bourgeoisie was clamped heavily down on working-class aspirations to a living-wage and a say in government, on their intellectual allies, on the nascent trade union movement, on all the brands of socialism.

Both Proudhon and Fallot were, however, seriously affected by the first result of the July Days: a sharp business recession with consequent widespread unemployment generating further recession, were the first consequences of the installation of the *juste-milieu* government whose social and economic philosophy was, in one word, the market. Both young men were penniless; there was nothing for them to do in Besançon when Gauthiers were forced to dismiss them along with many more of their workers. Fallot went to Paris where he got a job in the offices of the Chamber of Peers; Proudhon to the small town of Gray, not far from home and the native place of his almost-namesake the painter Prudhomme, where he got a job at a school as *maître d'études*, which sounds grand but in practice meant an usher. They kept in touch by mail, letters being rationed since neither could afford the heavy postage. Fallot tried to get his friend a job as tutor to the children of a rich Gray industrialist, Jobard by name, but over-reached himself in his letter of recommendation by making too much of the advice to overlook Proudhon's rough ways in consideration for his remarkable mind and talents: I daresay it was Madame Jobard who decided against an un-polished genius as her children's preceptor.

Gustave Fallot's letters are full of his sense of Proudhon's genius, his potential greatness as a philosopher. No lesser kind of literature was in question, for both young men agreed that French imaginative literature was suffering from 'incurable wounds' and was now in the last stage of decadence.

The *Académie* of Besançon was (early 1832) about to award a scho-larship, the first Suard *pension*: Fallot, who had all the requisite qualifications, had the idea of applying for it, and then of sharing the income with Proudhon.[8] His chief difficulty in getting his friend to Paris and helping him to realize his own potential, was in Proudhon's *cudot* insistence that he was and should remain a working man, a compositor: he now had his *livret* as *prote d'imprimerie* which was a passport to a printing job anywhere in France. What had he to do with scholarship and philosophy?

*　　*　　*　　*　　*

Proudhon's obstinate insistence that he was and should remain nothing but a printer seems to have been prompted by a kind of super-stition: it is almost as if he feared that if he avowed his real aspirations, he would be crushed by that *âte* which follows *hubris*. For, while denying that he was or could be a scholar and philosopher, he was practising both disciplines. Before losing his job at Gauthiers he had been working on the proofs of Father Bergier's *Eléments primitifs des langues découvertes par la comparaison des raçines de l'hébreu avec celles du Grec, du Latin et du Français*. It seems that this work was of little value because, able though Bergier was, he knew nothing of the work in comparative philology done by the Germans and his book was years out of date long before it was published. Proudhon was allowed to add to this edition an essay of his own, *Essai de Grammaire Générale*, in the writing of which Fallot had encouraged him. Knowing nothing of philology I have not thought it useful to read it. Apparently it suffered from the same fatal flaw as Bergier's own work: linguistic arguments based on the Bible, and on Hebrew as the proto-language, were anachronistic; Proudhon was treading a path long since abandoned as leading nowhere. He had probably never even heard of Sanscrit, knew nothing of the Indo-European roots of the European languages, had never read the German work in that field – he could not, in fact, read German, a far more serious handicap in the 19th than in the 20th century. All of which he was to realize himself years later, when studying under Eugène Burnouf, the first French disciple of the German philologists.

However, this juvenile essay in out-of-date scholarship twice had consequences of importance years later: it helped him to the Suard *pension* when at last he applied for it; and it was brought up against him fifteen years later by enemies seeking a stick to beat him with, who located some old stock of Bergier's book, put it on sale, and then attacked Proudhon in their newspapers for having written his essay tongue-in-cheek in an effort to fool the Besançon *Académie* into giving him one of the valuable bursaries in their gift. Proudhon sued for libel and lost his case. A third use was ultimately made of this first of his published works: the research he had done for it came in handy for the writing of his *Recherches sur les catégories grammaticales et sur quelques origines de la langue française*.

Fallot at last persuaded his friend to give up his deadening job in Gray and to join him in Paris, there to share with him the 100 francs per month to which the grant of the Suard *pension* had raised his income. Proudhon could not afford the coach fare, so he walked to Paris. Saint-Beuve makes too much of a similar walk to Paris which Proudhon was to make some years later, again for want of the fare, but it was a commonplace of the time: there was no other way for poor people to travel but on foot. The Paris he walked to was the old one, the city as she was before Haussman, before the outer boulevards, before the satellite villages had become faubourgs jointly forming a conurbation: there were still vineyards on the slopes of Montmartre, the Moulin Rouge was for grinding corn and there were fruit orchards on Montparnasse; and Halévy writes of it as being, in 1832, the Paris of Maturin Régnier, Diderot and Camille Desmoulins.

But Proudhon, suffering from the timidity of the provincial in a metropolis for the first time, from the Franc-Comtois *cudot* denying that even Paris could have anything worth having that Besançon lacked, took against the place. Monuments, picture galleries were all very well, but did nobody but himself notice that people were dying of starvation in the streets, that people reduced to beggary for no fault of their own were treated as criminals, that the whole city was uneasy with the tension generated by the hostility between the poor and the rich? The libraries seemed to be all that Paris had to offer this difficult customer.

Loyally and lovingly Fallot shared his room, his food and his friends with Proudhon; but this intimacy put a strain on their friendship. Fallot was romantically in love with Paris and was blind to her faults. In Proudhon's letters home he had nothing to say about Paris; but one letter to his parents throws light on his state of mind:

Holy Thursday 1832.

... For the time being I do nothing but read and write in my room, read and write in libraries. It is, I admit, a little vexing for you: this is not at all what I had given you to hope for. But in this [authorship] as in all things, one has to begin at the beginning. However, it cannot go on for more than six months. If, at the end of that time, we perceive that there's nothing I can turn my hand to, I shall go back to being a compositor and proof-corrector which I can always be whenever it suits me. It will cost me the trifling humiliation of hearing myself called an author *manqué*, but the fact is that I am faced by only three alternatives: to work at becoming an author; to die of starvation; to resume my trade as printer. The last does not much tempt me, the second even less; so for want of better I'm left with the first. What would one not do to avert death or the cholera?

Proudhon and Fallot might disagree as to whether anything at all could be done about the abominable condition in which the majority of their fellow-citizens lived, but they agreed after studying them that none of the socialist doctrines then being canvassed had the answer: the phalansteries of Fourier, their fellow Bisontin, were utopian nonsense; the Saint-Simonian vision of a morally impeccable technocratic dictatorship was repulsive; the communism of the Blanquists would end in an intolerable tyranny. Something quite else was needed and Proudhon could not fall in with his friend's opinion that there was really nothing mere men could do about the misery of the poor majority which repeatedly found expression in riots mercilessly suppressed by the soldiers of the enthroned and crowned businessman who sold their services to his partners in social crime, the merchants and money-lenders: he began to see in the search for the means to a just society and economic order, the looming shape of his life's work.

Cholera was one of the hazards of city life in mid-19th-century Europe. Paris had an epidemic in 1831/2 and Fallot caught the disease. Proudhon nursed him with a love and devotion which were almost womanly; his friend had a poor constitution and it seemed certain that he would die; he, himself, thought so and in a crisis of the disease he demanded of Proudhon, 'Swear that if I die, you will immortalize me'. Unlike Proudhon he must have had a taste for the romantic literature of the time, but it is not clear how Proudhon was to accomplish the task. He did not die, he made a slow recovery, but his convalescence was followed by news of family financial troubles which, since he felt obliged to help, so shortened his means that Proudhon realized that he had become a burden and decided to give up the Paris adventure and make a *petit tour de France* in search of work as a compositor; his *livret*, and the necessary two respectable bourgeois referees to vouch for him, enabled him to obtain the passport without which a Frenchman's travels in his own country were apt to be subject to harassment by the police.

In the spring of 1832, with 50 francs in his pocket, and his books and such clothes as he was not wearing, on his back, he set off walking south, through the vineyards of *chasselas* grapes which supplied the Paris markets, the plantations of espalier pear-trees and the market gardens, and vestiges of ancient woods where now the Rungis fruit and vegetable markets which have replaced les Halles, and Orly airport, industrialize the scene. His *tour de France* had been forced on Proudhon, but it was quite usual for young *ouvriers typographes*, provided with a *livret* in which each employer entered his opinion of the man's work and capacities, to see something of their country by walking from job to job. Proudhon's tour, recorded in his *livret*, included Lyon, Draguignan, Marseilles, and even Neufchâtel in Switzerland, in all of which places he got enough work to help finance his next move, but in none of which could he find a job which would enable him to settle. His original capital of 50 francs had shrunk to 3 francs 50 when (June 1832), shortly after the latest rising of the starving workers in Paris had been put down with more than the usual amount of bloodshed, he arrived in Toulon. He was within three and a half francs of the same case as the Paris unemployed, but being single-handed could hardly resort to violence; on the other hand he could use his superior education and address to demand what he conceived to be his rights in law under the Charter.

He went to the *mairie*, demanded to see the mayor and was granted an audience; he placed his passport on the table and addressed that functionary as follows:

Here, Monsieur le Maire, is a piece of paper which cost me 2 francs ... and which promises me that it is incumbent on the civil and military authorities to afford me aid and protection in case of need. Now, you must know, Monsieur le Maire, that I am a compositor and that all the way from Paris I have sought work and found none; and that I am now at the end of my savings. Theft is punished; begging prohibited; there remains only paid work, the guarantee of which can alone, as it seems to me, fulfill the terms of my passport. I am at your disposal.

The mayor was a short, round, bouncy little man, very self-satisfied and full of himself, and known to his friends as *Tripette*; he was one of the 'new men' of the July Days, an attorney who'd made a fortune at his trade. He took Proudhon for a refugee from the reaction to the June riots in Paris, but was perfectly polite; Proudhon says that he quite took to the little man who told him,

'M'sieur, your claim is misconceived and you misinterpret your passport which means no more than that the authorities will defend you if you are assaulted or robbed.'
'Forgive me M. le maire, but the law of France protects everybody, even the guilty whom it punishes: the policeman has not the right to strike the assassin he is arresting excepting in self-defence, nor may the prison governor appropriate the personal property of the man he imprisons. In the case of a working-man, either the passport and the *livret*, for I have both, mean more; or they mean nothing.'
'M'sieur, I shall give you an order for 15 centimes per league to get you home. That is all I can do for you, for my attributions extend no further.'

Proudhon told him that that was mere alms which he did not want. But there had been a letter waiting for him in Toulon and it contained very bad news; he had to get home: his beloved brother Jean-Etienne had been unlucky in the conscription lottery and would have to do five years' military service. Proudhon accepted the 18 francs he was entitled to and set off for Besançon.

As soon as he was known to be back at No. 37, Rue des Petits Battants, he was offered a job: a Monsieur Muiron offered him the managing editorship of *L'Impartiale*, his far from impartial Fouriériste newspaper. Proudhon accepted and had written his first leader when he learned for the first time that all copy would have to pass the censorship of the Prefect of Police; he tore up the leader and resigned. Fortunately an old mate of his at Gauthier's, Auguste Javel, also had a job for him. Javel had set up his own printing shop in Arbois, a very attractive little town of artisans and merchants selling the wine of the vineyards which surround the town. Javel had been offered a share in a considerable government contract but could only accept it if he had a good Latinist to oversee the type-setting and proof correction. He offered Proudhon a high wage, 5 francs a day (at that time a family of four could live in decent poverty, wanting for nothing absolutely essential, on 3 francs 50). Proudhon accepted, walked the thirty miles to Arbois in one day, and found lodging in the house of a retired captain in Napoleon's armies who made a modest living out of his vineyard.

But for the captain, it was a house of women, for all the young people were daughters. The 'feel' of the household as Proudhon remembered it in after years is singularly agreeable, cheerful and good-natured; in my own mind it at once evoked Goldsmith's *The Vicar of Wakefield*. Grave but kindly, the captain was very tolerant of his young people's high spirits but saw that all was kept within the limits of Christian virtue.

Proudhon was not solely dependent on Javel and the captain's family for social life in Arbois. A fellow, and subsequently distinguished, Bisontin, Monsieur Micaud, had given him an introduction to a friend of his who lived in Arbois: this was the town's chief notary public, and possibly its most conservative citizen. With him Proudhon formed a friendship which only seems improbable until one remembers that he was at heart a Tory, a Tory of the ancient kind, whose virtues were the 'Roman' ones, who was as hostile to the class of money-grabbing commercial liberals whose business interests made them the new oppressors of the workers, as to the old aristocrats and their clerical allies. At least twice a week Proudhon and his notary friend went for country walks in the evening after work, or on Sundays. Often they took a meal with them in their pockets, and when they had no more to say to each other, they would sit down in the sunshine, in the skirts of a wood overlooking a vineyard or a pasture, to eat their bread and meat and drink their wine in companionable silence. The old notary would spend an hour or two making watercolour sketches of the countryside, while Proudhon made notes towards the writing of the book which he had in his head.[9]

In his landlord's house, Proudhon either kept to his room where he read and wrote; or he joined the family in the parlour where he would persuade the captain to tell him stories of his campaigns, which the old soldier was very willing to do; sometimes he would join the girls and their friends of both sexes in a game of lotto, and the house rule was that the principal victor had to spend his or her winnings on *marrons glacés* and sweet white wine for the whole party. From time to time there would be a certain amount of flirtatious horseplay between the girls and the respectable young men who frequented the household: when that happened Proudhon would rise, bid the company goodnight and go to his room. It was the gesture of a prig, yet nobody ever accused him of priggishness and despite these rather stately manners, the girls liked him, one of them far too much for her own peace of mind. It was Josephine, the eldest, who willingly nursed him through a bad bout of quinsy; but it was the youngest, Caroline, who fell in love with him and this was no silly young girl's ephemeral infatuation: although Proudhon never gave any sign that he was aware of her feelings, and certainly did not return them, Caroline followed his career for the rest of her life, confided her love to their mutual friend Auguste Javel, twice made long journeys in vain attempts to see him and renew their friendship. Not until she heard that he had married, many years later, did she give up hope of him.

It seems to have been agreed between Javel and Proudhon that his job would last only until the work on the Latin law-book was finished. When he had seen it through the press, he took leave of his Arbois friends with kisses all round, a ceremony which the captain insisted on, and walked home to Besançon, where he immediately found work with his old firm, Gauthier et Cie. He heard from Fallot that he had obtained an interesting and well-paid post as secretary to the government commission set up by Guizot to edit and publish historical documents in the national archives. Fallot was made so uneasy by his friend's repeated insistence that a working-man he was and would remain, giving up the foolish ambition to make a great name in philosophical letters, that he wrote to his friend Weiss urging him to befriend Proudhon and dig him out of his obstinate retreat. Weiss tried to do so but recorded in his diary 'Despite all the advances I have made to him, young Proudhon refuses to see me.'[10]

For the time being he had no use for bourgeois friends; he had 'gone into the wilderness' and did not want to be interrupted in his train of solitary thought. He was touchy about, yet exaggerated, or at least emphasized, his rustic accent, appearance and manners.

At Gauthier's he was correcting the proofs of Bergier's *Dictionaire Théologique*, and of an edition of the Vulgate. He made use of his Hebrew to criticize and comment on the Latin text of this Bible; and, for his own satisfaction, entirely retranslated some passages.[11]

It seems that the Hebrew for the Commandment which in English is rendered *Thou shalt not steal*, and by an exact equivalent in the other European languages, is *lo thignob*: Proudhon's translation of this is *Thou shalt divert nothing* or, in other words, *Thou shalt lay nothing by for thyself*. In other words, again, the stock of capital is and must remain common, and it is unlawful to withhold any part of it passing through our hands, to lay up an accumulation for our private enrichment. Which comes to this: it is unlawful to get power over others by the exercise of thrift, for thrift is simply theft from the common stock.

It may seem curious today that a man should turn to the Bible for justification of a revolutionary idea, but hostile though he might be to the Church, Christ was always one of Proudhon's masters. The decline in the status of the Scriptures and the critical attitude towards them is a post-Darwinian, post-German exegesis phenomenon. Proudhon was therefore reinforcing or supporting his nascent theory of property by reference to the only known work of Divine Authority; he was making sure that God was on his side. Halévy, by the way, interprets Proudhon's translation of the eighth Commandment thus: '*Lo thignob*: thou shalt not possess; thou shalt live by thy labour; if thou livest not by labour, thou livest by theft.'

Lo thignob, then, was a seed from which in due season grew *What is Property?*

*   *   *   *   *

Proudhon's almost sullen insistence that it was his destiny to be nothing but a working printer was either disingenuous, or it was a kind of finger-crossing and wood-touching. He knew that his need, and certainly his wish, was for leisure for study; this he could get only by finding paid employment which left him much leisure, or by becoming master of a business of his own in partnership with men he could trust. Whether it was he, or his fellow-*prote* Lambert, *chez* Gauthier, who suggested that they set up as printers on their own account, is not clear. As the firm they formed was at first called Lambert et Cie, and only much later bore Proudhon's name, it may be that Lambert was the prime-mover. A small printing shop was in the market, the Montarsolo press; they bought it,[12] how is not clear, but their subsequent financial troubles can be explained most readily on the assumption that it was done on borrowed money.

His mastership of a press gave Proudhon one immediate joy: some months earlier Gustave Fallot had told him, in one of his letters, that he was having great difficulty in finding a publisher (in those days a printer-cum-bookseller) for his *Recherches sur les formes grammaticales de la langue Française au XIIIeme siècle*. Proudhon was now able to write to the friend who had done so much for him and offer to print and publish the book. The reply was unhappy: Gustave had found a publisher but he was now having great difficulty in finishing the book and doubted if he would have the strength to do so. The cholera which Proudhon had nursed him through had further weakened an already wretched constitution. Fallot's foresight was only too brutally vindicated: in 1836 he caught scarlet fever and died of it; he was twenty-nine.[13]

When the news of his friend's death reached him Proudhon felt that 'half my life and half my mind' had been cut away; he suffered a terrible sense of loneliness, of having not a single friend in the world of his own intellectual calibre, and recorded, 'That Fallot leaves behind him friends who mourn him as much as I do, I have no doubt. I have not shed a single tear, for I never weep. But since his death I have not, I daresay, passed four hours at a time without his memory, like a fixed idea, a veritable monomania, occupying my thoughts.'

As if to 'continue' Fallot, perhaps in an attempt to 'immortalize' him as he had once promised to do, Proudhon resumed the study of linguistics and, still preoccupied with Hebrew which he took to be the proto-language in which God and Adam had talked together, he came to the conclusion that it has no verb 'to be', for he translated the verb *naiah* as 'to become, to be alive, to be active'. Jehovah did not say 'God is' (I am) but 'God becomes'. So that what is usually translated 'I am He who is' should read 'I am the becoming one' (*ie* the constantly acting, the 'strong' one). Once again we have Proudhon seeking Divine Authority: life, even God's life, far from being perfect and therefore immutable, is a state of becoming *ad infinitum*, so that, even for God, there is no state which can be expressed by 'I am', since in the next infinitely small fraction of time, it is no longer true. Had Proudhon been a mathematician of genius perhaps he might have invented an historical equivalent of the differential calculus. What he certainly did perceive, and in my view never contrived clearly to express, was the fact that in the life of a human society, as in that of any living creature, the state of rest is a convention devised in order to make observation possible: it has no real existence, in the sense, for example, that it is impossible to represent an Euclidian point graphically. What has all this to do with the social and economic theories he had yet to propound? Everything: a society which does not allow fully for this one fundamental fact of life cannot for long be viable, and can never be 'just'.

Yet another Proudhonian principle emerges from this, only apparently, futile preoccupation with a science which he never mastered, and which he perhaps resumed as an act of mourning piety. If the verb 'to be' was not, as philologists said it was, the primaeval, the 'substantive' word, then what was that word? Proudhon had no doubts about that: it was 'Moi, me'. It follows that any society which entailed the diminishment of the individual, making him or her a mere element of a state, rather than making the state an extension of him, was doomed to be unjust, and in the long run unworkable, because it was flying in the face of a natural law.

In short, Proudhon's Bible and Hebrew studies contributed to his growing theory that only a society designed to obey natural laws, to allow for the endless and manifold play of its equal elements, could be a just society. His anarchism thus had much deeper, tougher, sounder roots than have been attributed to it, and it was based not simply on respect for the human personality, but respect for what he believed to be natural law and therefore divine. Only that society could be just in which every individual retains a maximum of freedom and initiative, concedes only an irreducible minimum of these not merely rights, but conditions of life, to the collective or the community, for the sake of order. A society which did not allow for the 'me continuously becoming' of all its citizens, must be unjust and must fail because it would also be against nature.[14]

The cash-flow problem was soon putting Lambert et Cie in difficulties. Besançon was a considerable centre of the printing industry and it was hard to compete with firms who had a pool of working capital. Proudhon took steps to relieve the burden of his own wage: the Suard *pension* was again 'vacant' and he decided to apply for it; meanwhile he went to Paris – January 1838 – to take work as a compositor and, at the same time, to drum up orders for his own firm.

Gustave Fallot had been the first Suard pensioner. It was a three-year bursary endowed as a memorial to her husband by the widow of the Academician Suard. It was worth 1500 francs, about £65 (gold) a year and was to be awarded to a young man, native of the Doubs *département*, who had passed his *baccalaureate*, and showed 'a particular aptitude for a career in letters, science, the law or medicine'. The *pensionaire* was to be chosen by a six-man committee of members of the Besançon *Académie*.

*   *   *   *   *

With his 'petition' to the Besançon *Académie* still to write, Proudhon arrived in Paris at the beginning of 1838 and having found a room in the

Rue Jacob, at once got in touch with Fallot's literary executor, the
Alsatian poet and man-of-letters, Paul Ackermann. It is probable that
the two men were already acquainted; whether they were or were not,
they now formed a friendship which was to be lasting, and it was
Ackermann who introduced Proudhon to another life-long friend, the
philologist Bergmann. These two were to take the place which Gustave
Fallot had occupied in his life: nothing was more necessary to him – far
more necessary than wife and child – than a friend of the mind as well as
the heart to whom he could express in talk or in letters, the ideas and
feelings which possessed him.

He was not given much time in which to ripen these friendships, for in
April he was summoned back to Besançon by the news that his partner
Lambert had disappeared. On 18 April he was writing to his old friend
Millet, now editor of the *Journal de l'Ain*, that although Lambert's body
had not been found, it was supposed that he had taken his life; he had left
a letter written in the most melodramatic language about the fatality
which was dogging him, his lack of money, and the 'desertion' of one of
his partners. At first there seemed no real reason for what Proudhon
calls, 'So desperate a resolution,' though from the letter it was clear that
Lambert was suffering from 'a profound atrabilious hypochondria',
which I suppose means a nervous breakdown. A cause soon emerged,
when it became clear that the firm's books were not in order, there were
large unexplained deficits, and Lambert had left Proudhon with a heavy
load of debt and no means of discharging it. Not until mid-May was
Lambert's body found in a wood six miles from Besançon.

With this on his mind, Proudhon had to complete his 'petition' for the
Suard *pension*; and first of all to fulfil the condition that the candidate
must hold a baccalaureate diploma. He found the money for the tax,
presumably by borrowing, and submitted a draft petition to Perennès,
the perpetual secretary of the *Académie*. Perennès was his strong sup-
porter and it was because he wanted Proudhon to succeed that he
returned the draft urging him to drop or radically modify the last
paragraph. I'll quote it because it is virtually a statement of what he
intended his life's work to be:

Born and raised in the working-class, and belonging to it in heart and mind, in
manners and in community of interests and aspirations, this candidate's greatest
happiness, should he win your suffrages – be in no doubt about this, gentlemen –
would be that of having drawn your attention to that most important section of
society, in his own person, the section so highly honoured by the designation
workers; and that of having been judged worthy to be its first representative

among yourselves. And thus, the happiness of being able to toil unflaggingly with mind and heart and will and the power of philosophy for the complete emancipation of his brothers and comrades.

It was clear to Perennès that this declaration of intent would immediately alienate a very considerable number of his members. Proudhon would not suppress the passage: he wanted the Suard *pension*, but he wanted it honestly; the most he would do was to soften its terms.

The danger of frightening some of the rich burgesses and reactionary clergy among the members was not the only difficulty: the chief purpose of the Suard *pension* was to enable the pensioner to continue and complete his studies in a particular discipline, and Perennès had to get from Proudhon a clear statement of the line of study he proposed to follow: he suggested Law. No, said Proudhon, why should he waste time on 'conventions based on conquest, slavery, force, privilege and barbarous custom?' Medicine, then? No, again: 'I have no wish to become a professional charlatan.' Then what? Philology in the service of his projected *Grammaire universelle* and his projected *Recherches sur la révélation, ou philosophie pour servir à l'introduction à une histoire universelle.*

This aspiration towards a life of pure scholarship, in conflict with his desire to serve the working-class by reforming society, was to crop up time and time again. It was nonsense; he had neither the education nor the temperament for scholarship. As Sainte-Beuve says, in this aspiration Proudhon did not know himself; or was it, rather, that he sometimes sought to evade the responsibilities imposed on him by his own conscience and his own combativeness?

The method of awarding the Suard *pension* was for the candidates to be investigated by a six-man committee which then made its recommendations to the *Académie* in full session. The members then voted for the candidate of their choice. In August Proudhon wrote to Ackermann that while all six committee-men favoured him, the result was far from being a foregone conclusion. There were seven candidates, all very active and bustling in their canvassing for votes. There was a powerful faction strongly opposed to Proudhon on the grounds that his working-class origin and sympathies made him dangerous. 'One says I'm too old; another that, albeit learned, I own an industrial establishment; a third claims I'm a Protestant: Protestant, says a fourth, you're too kind, the fellow's an atheist. It's being insinuated that I'm not the real author of *Essai de grammaire générale* which was written by someone else to do me a favour ...'

The academics, the sanctimonious bigots and the clerics were against him: he was a free-thinker, a hot-head and bound to be an awkward customer to handle. Moreover, he himself was making difficulties. He wanted, if awarded the *pension*, to remain in Besançon, partly because, as I believe, he was afraid of Paris, and partly because of his responsibilities to the printing business and to his wretchedly impoverished parents. The *Académie* insisted that the successful candidate must have no other responsibilities but study and must do his studying in Paris where he must strive to win a prominent place for himself and thus be a credit to Besançon and its *Académie*. 'What a gulf,' Proudhon wrote to Ackermann, 'between such ideas and those of an *egalitarian*!'

In his next letter to his friend, in which he announces his success in winning the Suard *pension*, there is a mysterious passage touching which I find nothing in the Proudhon papers. This is perhaps not surprising for it concerns some kind of secret society, other than the Free Masons which he joined later. The passage suggests that his friendship with Paul Ackermann dated from his earlier sojourn in Paris when he and Fallot were living together. Here it is: 'I am counting sufficiently on the friendship and esteem of the p.d.p. brothers to hope that they will regard my election as a triumph for Philadelphia.' Sainte-Beuve thought that Ackermann, Proudhon and a few others were members of 'a sort of masonic and philanthropic *cénacle*', vestige of a much earlier Franc-Comtois secret society; and it will in due course appear that Proudhon did later, briefly, entertain the idea of bringing about the revolution, in the last resort, by means of a latter-day and proletarian version of the Holy Vehm, an aberration which lasted no longer than Karl Marx's acquiescence in the conspiratorial mystique of the League of the Just.[15]

It was the practice of the Besançon *Académie* to offer an annual prize for an essay on a set subject. In 1839 the subject set, doubtless under the influence of the clerical members of the *Académie* and as a sop to the still raging reaction of the Restoration, was *De l'utilité de la célébration du Dimanche*.[16] Proudhon seized the opportunity to produce some work to justify his Suard *pension*, to give expression to some of the social theories which were taking shape in his mind, and perhaps to give the Academicians some warning of what they might expect from their awkward *pensionaire*.

The hero of the essay is Moses, founder of the Sabbath, whom Proudhon sees as a great social scientist laying the foundations of a human society based on 'natural' law.

Based upon sure foundations, this work of Moses rises like a divine creation: unity and simplicity in the principles; variety and richness in the details. Each of the articles of the Decalogue could be the subject of a long treatise; yet nothing could be added to a single one.

The essay is important because the course of his thinking for the next thirty years is already clearly mapped in it; he was twenty-three when he wrote it. For example, he shows Moses not as a creative genius *inventing* a code of laws, but as a researcher of genius *discovering* it: 'founding laws upon observation of nature and deducing them from moral phenomena, in the same way as the formulas of a treatise on physics are deduced from the behaviour of bodies.'

'According to Moses, everything which is matter for legislation and politics is an object of science, not of opinion.' For Moses, we should perhaps read Proudhon. By 1839 he had reached something like the Marxist concept of historical necessity; for what is that, if it be not a 'natural' law of human societies? At all events, the Mosaic laws are immutable – Proudhon's word – because they are no less eternal than the laws of thermodynamics. Now, it was in the search for, discovery of, and exposition of the 'natural' laws of human societies that he was to pass the rest of his life.

What Proudhon sees Moses as trying to do for the Israelites is what he himself was to try to do for the French: to lay down the rules under which all the people would come equally into a communion of love and faith, a fusion of hearts and minds for the common good. The institution of the Sabbath was not only a symbol of that communion, it was to set aside a day for rejoicing in it and giving thanks for it; and, above all, for studying those laws, and their inner meaning, by means of which it had been accomplished.

As well as the theory that valid and just societies could be founded only on the natural laws of societies, never on laws derived from the will of a political authority, the other principal concepts of his whole work were already present. Here already is his severely critical attitude to the Church and the clergy, guilty of so degrading the 'majesty' of Christianity as to seem bent upon destroying even 'that vestige of religious faith which has survived the libertinage of the 18th century'.

Here, too, is his insistence that all executive power be vested in the whole people: the Sabbath is shown as a day on which Moses assembled all Israel so that they might together make those executive decisions based on the laws which research had revealed. Legislation, the task of *discovering* the laws of societies, must be the work of a Moses, that is a 'saint, philosopher and poet': executive action lies with the people. Even this early, Proudhon eliminates political authority, government, as not only unnecessary, but as pernicious. 'The people alone have the right to constrain the people.' And even that doctrine was to be modified in favour of the individual's right to absolute freedom.

In the Mosaic law applying the total ban on work of any kind on the Sabbath to all the people without exception or distinction of class, Proudhon sees the beginning of egalitarianism. He makes a discussion of a proposal then being canvassed that the very poor – one-fifth of the entire French population – be allowed to supplement their incomes by working on Sundays, the occasion for exposing the cruel indifference of the upper classes and the Church to their sufferings. In his discussion of the manner in which the land of Canaan was divided up equally among the Israelite heads of household,[17] one can see his mind working towards a theory of equality of property as a means of eliminating both poverty and wealth, both equally pernicious.

It is one of the singularities of genius that the first work, albeit less polished, less elaborate, less rich in matter, wit and wisdom than the works of maturity, is already accomplished. The quality of the mind does not change; it grows in content. The essential Proudhon is present in *La Célébration du Dimanche*. Sainte-Beuve says of it, almost peevishly, 'He goes looking for democracy even in Mosaic theocracy,' which is true. It so offended the reactionary clerical faction in the *Académie* that although they could not prevent their more liberal lay colleagues from awarding Proudhon a commendation and a medal, they did deny him the prize on the grounds that 'The righteousness of his intention and zeal for public welfare cannot justify the temerity of the conclusions'.

*   *   *   *   *

In November of 1839 Proudhon went to Paris; he proposed to remain as short a time as possible and then, 'armed to the teeth against *civilization*', to return to Besançon and his printing-shop. With that as his base, he would wage that war against the existing social order which would, he said, last the rest of his life.

He found himself detesting Paris as much as he had expected to do: Ackermann had left it to work in Berlin, Bergmann to work in Strasbourg, and Proudhon knew nobody. His food, lodging and books cost so much that he had to ask his friends not to write too often; postage was still paid by the recipient and was very dear. 'Two francs for a letter is a serious consideration,' he wrote to Ackermann. Meanwhile, the Besançon clergy had persuaded the Prefect of Police to ban the sale of his *Célébration du Dimanche* in Besançon, and the only important newspaper to notice it, the republican *Le National*, did so only to make fun of its title and its author. Harassed and unhappy, he set about the writing of *What is Property?*, hoping to finish it in three months. Ackermann, who had criticized the style of his *Célébration du Dimanche*, urged him to pay more attention to it in his new work, and Proudhon replied:

> I am too poor and my affairs are in too bad a way to amuse myself becoming a *man of letters*. Besides, I believe that the golden age of pure literature is for ever over and done with. So long as man knows little he is obliged to talk much; the less he reasons the more he sings; and, having nothing to say, pleases his ear with his pretty babblings. I am not the man for such work. Yet I do regret not being able to express myself with facility ... I am made for the workshop, which I should never have left and to which I shall return as soon as possible.

He was, he confessed, exhausted, discouraged and altogether cast down; poor last year, this year he was a pauper, calculating that, all obligations having been met, he would, on 1 April, have 200 francs left to last him for six months in Paris. From time to time he would stand staring down at the glaucous waters of the Seine: but, resisting their temptation, decide that, for today at least, he would soldier on. Worry and anxiety drained his mental strength and half-paralysed his invention: 'I cannot work, yet work I do to avoid dying of despair, knowing that, having only hard and unhappy truths to communicate, my work will earn me only hatred and curses.' Finally, since he had very little hope of finding a publisher for his new book, he would have to publish it himself by subscription and print it on his own press. Bergmann wanted to know what, exactly, he was seeking to accomplish with the new book; he wrote: 'What I have set myself to do is to fight a duel to the death against inequality and property. Either I deceive myself, or they will never recover from the blow I am about to deal them.'

But there was, he said, no question whatever of his *inventing* anything, of constructing a system as Saint-Simon and Fourier had done. His master in method was Adam Smith. His task was one of scientific discovery and clear revelation: research to discover the natural laws of society and exposition to reveal how their correct application could not but produce a state of absolute equality, without constraint upon the individual – the natural state of man. Thus, to Ackermann:

> In all this I put nothing of my own invention. I seek; and the better to seek, I make of myself an instrument and for myself a guide. I attach a thread to the portal of the maze into which I am plunging. I never contest, never refute, but admit all opinions and confine myself to looking for their substance.

NOTES TO CHAPTER ONE

1. Details of Proudhon's antecedents and childhood are from an unpublished autobiographical note now among the Proudhon papers in the Besançon Municipal Library (B.M.L.).
2. *Proudhon, sa Vie et sa Corrèspondance 1838–48.* Paris, 1872.
3. *La Jeunesse de Proudhon.* Halévy, D. Paris, 1913.
4. Letter to Bergmann, Lyon, 22 October 1856.
5. Halévy, *op. cit.*
6. See Beauquier in *Provincialismes du Doubs*, who derives the word from *cude*, a folly, and says 'cf English *cuddy*'.
7. In *De la Justice.*
8. Letter, 11 March 1832, from Fallot to Weiss; B.M.L.
9. Some of these notebooks were subsequently printed by Auguste Javel; to me the most interesting is a note in which he drew the main lines of an argument that capitalism is inconsistent not only with liberty and human dignity, but with sound economy.
10. Unpublished; B.M.L.
11. See Halévy, *op. cit.*; and the Proudhon papers, B.M.L.
12. Weiss; unpublished diary.
13. The unfinished work was published posthumously, by his literary executor Paul Ackermann. Sainte-Beuve was not the only critic to have a very high opinion of it.
14. cf. Max Stirner's *The Ego and His Own* (1845) with Proudhon's *Du Principe Fédératif*. Stirner thought that no man could know anything whatever about anything or anybody but himself or act effectively in any interest but his own. A valid society is therefore a complex of mutually balancing egoisms holding each other in tension. But Proudhon introduces another component which Stirner would not have admitted as viable: the conscious and deliberate surrender, in the name of common sense, which tends to become synonymous with 'virtue' in the Latin sense, of a grudging minimum of freedom to the collective in order to prevent the exploitation of the weak by the strong or, equally important, of the strong by the weak.
15. According to Charles Nodier, the Philadelphia was a secret society founded and led by one Colonel Oudet whose death following the battle of Wagram was mysterious. Marx joined the communist League of the Just, a revolutionary secret society of German refugee immigrants in Paris, a couple of years later.
16. First set and printed by Proudhon himself and published Lambert et Cie, Besançon, 1839. Republished Garnier Frères with a new preface by Proudhon, Paris, 1850. Cambridge University Library has a copy.
17. His historical authorities seem to have been Berruyer's *Histoire du Peuple de Dieu* of which he had set the type; and a work by Fleury which he fails to name. He also cites Grotius, Cuneus, Spencer *et al.*

Property is Theft!

THE AUTHOR'S PREFACE to Proudhon's *What is Property?* published on 30 June 1840 took the form of a letter to the Besançon *Académie* in which he recalls that when he applied for the Suard *pension* he expressed the intention of devoting his studies to the material, moral and intellectual betterment of the poorest and most numerous class of society. It may well have been that intention which alarmed those members of the *Académie* who opposed his candidature. Most good burgesses knew by common sense, even if they had not read Say or Adam Smith, that the conditions of the poorest and most numerous class of society can be improved only at the expense of the nobility, gentry and burgesses. Proudhon's intention sounded more like a threat than a promise.

In the same letter Proudhon identified an even more specific inspiration of the book he was now dedicating to the Besançon academicians. In 1838 the *Académie* had proposed as subject for a prize essay, *To what cause should we attribute the continuously increasing number of suicides and what are the means best fitted to halt the effect of this moral epidemic?* It was clearly in his mind to establish that the institution of property, an institution which he was about to prove responsible for most of our miseries, was sufficient explanation of that lamentable social phenomenon.

Still in the same dedicatory letter Proudhon made an admission characteristic of his difficulty in compromising, or suiting his manner to his readers, a difficulty he was apt to justify by reference to the plain, blunt, but shrewd character attributed to the Franc-Comtois: 'Why,' he wrote, 'should I not admit it, gentlemen? I was ambitious for your suffrages and sought to become your pensioner in hatred of all that is established and with the aim of destroying it.' But the study incident to that purpose had calmed his mind and purged his soul: 'to cease from hating, it was enough to know.' True, he was still bent on destruction, but now with the aim of rebuilding.

Having read the work thus dedicated to them, the dedicatees hastened publicly to repudiate it: they required its author to remove the dedication from any future edition. The book laid an explosive mine under the very foundations of society – capital property. Proudhon had set out to discover the laws of, in his own words, a social system of absolute equality in which all existing institutions, *excepting that of property or the sum of the abuses of property* would not only have a place but would of themselves become means to equality. Why this down on property, that is on capital? Because, as manifest in the appalling conditions of the majority of Frenchmen, and for that matter Englishmen, and the spread of bankruptcy even through the richer minority classes, property was not only unjust, not only wicked, but was clearly 'impossible'. And why so? Because it denied absolute economic equality, the only arrangement which was socially viable.

That was by no means the only offence of *What is Property?* Another was the discovery that the experts in morality, in philosophy, in religion, in economics whom we rely on, are thoroughly unreliable. They had not even understood the meanings of such common and sacred words as justice, equity, liberty. Such were the conclusions of the research which he had embarked on with an open mind and a scientific method. Gross ignorance was the sole cause of the pauperism which was devouring society, and of all the calamities which have ever afflicted the human race.

That Proudhon really did, for the time being that is until the criticism of his work came in, really believe in the validity of his findings in the sense that Newton believed in the validity of the first law of thermodynamics, is apparent in the serene authority of his pronouncements. When the book was finished but not yet published he had written to Bergmann,

By the mercy of heaven I believe that henceforth apart from the style and a few points touching erudition, none of the propositions I have advanced can be challenged. We have a principle for social science. You must be laughing, my friend, at the spectacle of my extraordinary confidence. The fact is I know of no scientific discovery which has produced an effect comparable with that which the reading of my book is capable of producing ... let it only be read, and our old society is done for.

There is no arrogance in this; he was a scientist following where his discoveries of natural laws led him, or thought he was. As such he was not deserving of praise, for as he said, do we praise the man who happens to be the first to see the dawn?

Yet he had no reason to be surprised, even if he could not avoid being distressed, by the book's reception, especially by the fact that the most important newspapers failed to review it. He had written (22 February 1840) to Bergmann:

Unfortunately, that which will have cost me much work and great effort of mind is scarcely within the range of the common reader who prefers the diatribes of

Lammenais and company. In France nowadays nothing is understood but invective, personalities and insults. There is a thirst for calumny, spite and satire; thinking now takes those forms. The circle of the men called lettered is so narrow, that it's impossible to come to terms with them.

He had even anticipated that he would not be read at all: here he is, to Bergmann again, who had warned him that *What is Property?* would raise a storm against its author and make a martyr of him:

Is there a martyrdom more grievous than oppression by frauds and fools? Ah, if my heart does bleed from time to time, it is at the thought of my mind spent in vain ... Is it not painful to see the invalid reject the cure, the blind deny the oculist, and both skills and truth rendered useless?

For a man who feared that because he was a proletarian his voice proclaiming truths of immense value would go unheard, this was, indeed, painful. Not since Rousseau and the *Vicaire Savoyard* had any writer been so profoundly certain of the truth of his own writings, he told Bergmann.

There were problems which had nothing to do with the quality of the work or its author's want of standing among the learned and lettered. Proudhon had had such difficulty in finding a publisher that he proposed at one time to print the book on his own press. 'The fashionable publishers are *grands seigneurs* who have a singular contempt for unknown authors.'[1] The publisher he did find insisted that Proudhon cover the costs of printing the book by undertaking to sell 230 copies to his friends and acquaintances at his own risk. Publication was not even announced let alone advertised in the press. Only 200 copies were sold in the first two weeks, and Proudhon was driven to the consolation of philosophy: 'To waste six months proving things which are as clear as daylight, yet ignorance of which causes all the ills of mankind, is well designed to vex the enquiring mind and humble the proud spirit.'[2]

*　　　*　　　*　　　*　　　*

The sacred cows Proudhon attacked were by no means only those like religion – theology he defined as the science of the infinitely absurd – or monarchy. The great Revolution had rid the country of the bitterest manifestation of property, *corvée* and *mortmain* for instance; that is, it had modified the ways of enjoying property but left the principle unchanged. Between Republic and Monarchy the only difference is between the number of wills dictating the law, and under it the law still remains an expression of will whereas it should be an expression of fact. Law as an expression of will, whether one man's or ten million men's, is no more than an institutionalization of injustice.[3]

What Proudhon meant by property will presently be clear: what he did *not* mean was possessions. Authorities he agreed with make this distinction: Property is a right, a legal faculty; Possession is a fact. The tenant of house or farm, the usufructuary and the like are possessors: the landlord, the lender of money at interest, banker or usurer, the heir awaiting the death of a usufructuary to come into his own, are proprietors. Says Proudhon: 'If I dare use the comparison, a lover is a possessor, a husband is a proprietor.' Property, then is Marx's *capital*.

The distinction between possession and property gives rise to two kinds of right in jurisprudence: *jus in re*, the right to a thing; and *jus ad rem*, the right in a thing. The first is particular; the second is common. From these derive two distinct jurisprudential categories: possessory right; and *droit petitoir* which relates to ownership, not mere possession, and for which there seems to be no term in English jurisprudence, though in Scotland it is called petitory right. Proudhon says:

In writing this *factum* against Property I bring a petitory right against the whole of society. I prove that those who have nothing today are proprietors by the same title as those in possession. But instead of concluding that property should be shared among all, I demand in the name of public safety that it be abolished for all.

So much for the intention; what of the method?

The Declaration of Rights in the Charter of 1793, more generous and less cautious than the United States Constitution, recognizes *four* 'natural and imprescriptible' rights of man: liberty, equality, property and security. Proudhon, asking on what basis the legislators so concluded, discovers they had none; all they were really expressing was an opinion. Liberty is inviolable: no Frenchman can legally alienate his liberty, suffer it to be taken away from him, nor enforce nor suffer enforcement of a contract of which such alienation is a condition; equality before the law is inviolable and every career is open to talent; security is promised by the state to all citizens unconditionally in so far as it is in the power of the state to ensure it.

But property? What a difference! 'Adored by all it is recognized by none. Laws, mores, customs, public and private conscience, all conspire its ruin and death.' Then follows one of those examples which made George Woodcock[4] call Proudhon what he was proud to call himself, a man of paradox: every man has to contribute towards public expenditure by paying taxes. But why are the rich required to pay more than the poor? Because, since the rich have more, it is just. Proudhon rejoins: 'I confess that I do not understand such justice.' Does it cost the state more to fulfil its promise of security to the rich man than to the poor man? From which class is public order more in danger, the worthy burgesses or the turbulent workers? Clearly the police have more trouble with a handful of rioting unemployed than with all those 300,000 enfranchised burgesses. Does the rich man living on his rents and dividends receive more pleasures than the poor man from public spectacles or the beauty of public buildings?

No, of course. Then taxation proportional to income is iniquitous and the state should stop talking about equality of rights, which must mean that my 100,000 francs a year is as inviolable as the *grisette*'s 75 centimes a day, or it means nothing.[5] If the state takes more from me than from her, then let it give more in exchange, or cease talking about property as one of the natural rights. For otherwise the state is organizing the destruction of property; by its graded taxation it is making itself a brigand chief and as such should be haled before the justices ahead of that execrated scum of rebellious workers whom it is shooting down, presumably out of professional jealousy.

Another of his paradoxical examples to illustrate his point: the state is paying 5 per cent to 45,000 bondholders: the bonds are property; property is one of the four natural rights defended by the state. There is a general demand for conversion of the 5 per cents to 3 per cents. If it be conceded, what becomes of property as a right and the state's undertaking to defend it? Where's the justice in reducing 45,000 families to poverty by taking away two-fifths of their income? On the other hand, is it just to force 10 million taxpayers to pay the bondholders 5 per cent when they might be paying no more than 3 per cent?

In this as throughout his book Proudhon seeks not simply to show that property is wicked; much more important, it is 'impossible'; or, in Marxist terms, that capital's internal contradictions must destroy it. Marx, by the way, not only reviewed *What is Property?* favourably in the *Neue Rheinische Zeitung* but, in *Die Heilige Familie* called it 'the first decisive, vigorous and scientific examination of property'.

Since the abolition of property was essential to the establishment of a system of absolute equality, the difficult question of what Proudhon called 'innate properties' had to be dealt with; for it is by the exploitation of innate properties – memory, imagination, health, strength, will, etc. – that men of superior endowment get more than a mathematically fair share of 'acquired properties' – land, houses, plant – in short, capital. Consideration of this problem led Proudhon to a redefinition of justice; it is, he says, 'a means of restoring to equality the inequality implicit in innate properties'. One might make the point in this way: 'all men are born unequal' – which is at least nearer to the truth than Jefferson's absurd 'all men are born equal'; they can only be restored to equality by preventing the getting of acquired property by the exploitation of innate properties; that being clearly impossible, let us abolish property right.

Proudhon did not, of course, simply ignore the respected authorities in the course of his long – 120,000 words – essay which he called a *Mémoire*: he demolished them, wondering as he did so with a penetration and sharp zest as delightful to watch as a game of skill perfectly played, at the paucity of their thought. The philosophers are wretched enough, and as for the economists, '. . . one really does not know whether to believe them wanting in intelligence, or guilty of bad faith.' An example will illustrate his method.

Auguste Comte (1798–1857), the founder of Positivism, argued in his *Treatise on Property* that there could be no justifiable appropriation of things which were in inexhaustible supply, *eg* air or water.[6] Proudhon corrects him: air, water, light cannot justly be appropriated not because they are inexhaustible but because they are indispensable. But that other element, earth, the land, which Comte excludes from his category of things which must remain common, is equally indispensable, and as such common, and as such not susceptible to appropriation. For the very reason that its extent is limited, appropriation should be out of the question and its use regulated for the benefit of all. Equality of rights is proved by equality of need and where provision is limited, equality of rights can be established only by absolute equality of possession. Comte says, for example, that France, considered as a nation, has a territory which is her own (*qui lui est propre*). No, says Proudhon, the case is otherwise: France, considered as a person, has a territory which she exploits; that does not make her its proprietor. In other words the proprietor is God or the whole of mankind, and France is the usufructuary, and only the common abuse of language by philosophers who should know better attributes to her domain over the land. The right to use or abuse at will can no more, in justice, belong to a people than to a person; moreover, so true is this, that 'the time will come when a war undertaken to halt a nation's abuse of its land will be a holy war'.

Because of its relevance in our own time, I shall here try to illustrate Proudhon's argument with two examples which were not available to him, the conditions for them having been created by the growth of population and the advance of technology since his time.

It is possible by means of a device called a heat pump to draw a vast quantity of low quality (low temperature) heat from any river and, converting it into a smaller quantity of higher quality (high temperature) heat, use it to heat buildings. Whole towns are being heated by this means in one or two places. Suppose that governments, municipalities and industrial corporations along the course of a great continental river claim property right in the reaches of the river flowing through their territory, which indeed they do, and start to draw heat from them. The first law of thermodynamics being what it is, the river water gets colder and colder until at last it freezes: the fish die so the fishing interest is ruined: navigation becomes impossible so the navigation interest is ruined. Water can no longer be drawn from the river so the water-supply authority is ruined. Because the possessors or usufructuaries of the river water insist on behaving like proprietors, the river, as an instrument of production and amenity for mankind, is ruined. So not only is property right in the warmth of the river water unjust, it is inexpedient and, in the last resort, when the ice beats the heat-pumps, *impossible*.

Take an example on the global level of Comte's argument that air cannot be appropriated, and Proudhon's prediction that nations may go to war over an abuse of territorial 'rights'. We will follow Comte and allow every nation to be the *proprietor* of its land; and so allow Brazil to be the proprietor of the Amazon forests. The supply of oxygen in the atmosphere depends on the metabolism of green plants and it has been suggested that so many of the world's forests have been destroyed that if any more are lost the oxygen might fail. Suppose the Brazilians decide to clear the Amazon forests to exploit the timber and to make room for farms, people and towns, it might then be necessary for the rest of the world to stop them. In so far as, by acting as proprietors of their territory, they put all animal and human life in danger, their action would be unjust; in so far as it was suicidal, it would be, in Proudhon's sense of the word, *impossible*.

*   *   *   *   *

Surely labour, honest toil, justifies property? By no means: a man takes over a piece of wilderness capable of yielding £10 a year and by improving it makes it yield £50 a year. Should he not be rewarded? He has been – by the extra £40. His labour does not give him title to the land. If he quits it he is entitled to the cost of his improvements. Suppose him to have employed a labourer to help him make those improvements. The man is paid his living wage; but he is entitled to a share in the value of the improvements he has helped to make by the same token as his employer is. So all who have contributed to the improvements made to the world – agricultural land made out of forest and swamp; all the houses that have ever been built; all industrial plant; all machinery; all art and literature; all science – are entitled to a share in them. Neither labour nor anything else can create a right of appropriation over the things of nature; labour alone creates a right of *common* appropriation over the things labour has made.

The proprietor (capitalist) believes that he has discharged his obligation to the worker he employs when he has paid him his day's living wage; suppose he employs a thousand men all of varying skills; he still considers he has discharged his obligation to all when he has paid each. But he has cheated them abominably: for he has paid nothing for their collective effort, only for the individual effort of each. In other words to pay one man for a thousand days work is not at all the same thing as to pay a thousand men for one day's work. One man could not possibly do in a thousand days or for that matter a lifetime, what a thousand men combining their skills can do in a few hours: 'In a few hours 200 grenadiers raised the Luxor obelisk onto its plinth; could one man have done the job alone in 200 days?'

Proudhon demonstrates in a series of propositions that liberty depends on absolute equality and absolute equality on the abolition of property: here is how he answers the question – is it not unjust to refuse to reward the man who makes a superior contribution, the scientist, the doctor, the great poet, the statesman, more richly than the common labourer? In other words are not wage differentials based on skills, just? Again, no; such men are, in themselves, twofold: they contain both a worker, and the capital 'plant' in the form of knowledge and skill, which that worker exploits. But the capital component of them is not their property: it is the accumulated knowledge and skill of thousands of generations of workers in scores of trades and professions. In short it is the common property of all mankind in the same way that industrial plant is the common property of all mankind, because all mankind has contributed to its making.

There is another reason why it is, again in Proudhon's sense of the word, 'impossible' to remunerate one man more richly than any other: to do so makes economic nonsense. Any transaction whose aim is an exchange of goods or services is a commercial operation. A commercial operation is an exchange of equal values; for if the values are not equal the party who would lose by the deal declines it. One assumption has to be made here, that the transaction is between free men; a free man is one who is in full enjoyment of his reason and faculties, is not blinded by passion, constrained by fear or deceived by false opinion. A commercial operation is therefore necessarily free from inequality, for no free man knowingly makes a deal by which he is the loser. It having been shown that the things of nature cannot justly be appropriated, every commercial operation is an exchange of a quantity of labour against a quantity of a different kind of labour: which, since the exchange has been consented to, is of equal value: it follows that inequality of emolument is *impossible*.

Let Homer sing me his songs and I listen to that sublime genius by comparison with whom I, a simple shepherd and humble gardener, am as nought. What comparison can there be between my cheeses and beans, and his *Iliad*? But, if, by way of wages for his incomparable poem, Homer proposes to take all I have and make me his slave, I thank him for the offer and renounce the pleasure of his song. I can do without the *Iliad* and, if necessary, wait for the *Aeniad*. Homer cannot do without my products even for twenty-four hours.

It is all very well to prove that inequality of emolument is impossible: it exists and is justified by the economists. It exists, says Proudhon, only by reason of force or fraud, that is to say, theft: as for the economists – it is said that Cato marvelled that two clergymen could come face to face in the street without bursting out laughing; for priests, read economists.

Let us now see how, according to Proudhon, the Property system works in industry where, once again, it proves to be 'impossible'. Here are two of his parables.

Three operations are required for the production of shoes: the rearing of cattle; the tanning of hides; and the cutting out and sewing of leather. If the hide when it leaves the farm is worth one, it is worth two when it leaves the tanner's yard and three when it leaves the shoemaker's shop. Each worker has produced a degree of utility and by adding them up we arrive at the value of the article. In order to have some pairs of shoes each worker must pay first for his own work and then for that of the other two workers. So, in order to have ten pairs of shoes, the farmer must pay thirty in hides, the tanner twenty in leather: for ten of leather in the form of shoes is worth thirty of raw hide by reason of the two successive operations just as twenty of leather is worth thirty of raw hide by reason of the tanner's work. But suppose the shoemaker to demand thirty-three of raw hide or twenty-two of leather for his merchandise, then the exchange will not take place; for it would follow that the farmer and the tanner would have to buy back for eleven what they sold for ten; which is *impossible*.

Yet that is exactly what happens every time an increment of any kind is taken by an industrialist, let that benefit be in the form of rent, dividend, interest or profit. Here is a less artificial example:

In France 20 million workers in all the branches of science, art and industry produce all the things necessary to the life of man. Let us suppose the sum of their production to be 20 billion. But because of property rights – the multitude of unearned increments (*aubaines*), premiums, tithes, interest; domestic, agricultural and industrial rents; dividends – the product is estimated by the proprietors (employers, capitalists) at 25 billion. What follows? That the workers who are obliged to buy back the products of their own labour in order to live, must pay 5 for what they have sold for 4; or fast one day out of five.

If there is an economist in France capable of demonstrating that this calculation is false, let him stand forth and do so, and I undertake to retract all that, mistakenly and wickedly, I have advanced against Property.

Let us now see the consequences of this profit-taking.

If the workers' wage were the same in all the trades and professions the deduction would be felt equally by all and the cause of the evil would long since have been identified and suppressed. But since there is as much difference between wages, from those of the street-sweeper to those of the cabinet minister, as between the values of properties, there is a ricochet of spoliation off the strongest onto the weakest so that the lower the worker's place in the scale, the greater his privations, and the lowest class of people is stripped naked and eaten alive by the others.

What emerges from this is that so long as money is accumulated, bought and sold as a commodity, so long must it remain impossible to balance the national, and for that matter international, accounts. For they are permanently loaded with a debit which, since it represents no value added, is theft. All this was obvious to Proudhon in 1840.

When the legislator introduced the principle of Property into the Republic, did he first weigh the consequences? Did he understand the law of the possible? If so, why does the Code not mention it? Why was that terrifying latitude left to the proprietor to increase his property by compounding his interest?[7] Why was it left to judges to recognize and delimit the domain of property? Why was the State given latitude continuously to levy more taxes? Where is the limit beyond which the people has a right to refuse the budget, the farmer to pay rent, the industrialist to pay interest on capital? Up to what point are the idle free to exploit the workers? Where does the right of spoliation begin and end? At what point can the producer say to the proprietor, *I owe you no more?* When is property satisfied? At what point is theft no longer allowed? ...

If our Charters and our Codes have nothing by way of principle but an absurd hypothesis, then what is being taught in our law schools? What is a judgement of the appeal courts worth? What is our parliament debating? What are the meanings of *policy, statesman, jurisprudence?* And should we not rather call the latter *juris-ignorance?*

Did this mean, then, that we should have to adopt the communist alternative? No: Proudhon had studied and condemned it long before he met and argued with Karl Marx. If property could be defined as the exploitation of the weak by the strong, then communism must be defined as the exploitation of the strong by the weak; and both led either to ruin, or to an intolerable tyranny. The alternative, which does not emerge clearly in *What is Property?* which is as weak on the positive as it is strong on the negative side, had to wait upon later works. It was the substitution of scientific economic management of property, and of free associations of free productive workers for the political state. It is very clear that Proudhon, using the long, clear foresight of genius and the device of extrapolation, perceived that the state as arch-proprietor could not avoid becoming the monstrous tyrant which Arch-economist Joseph Stalin made of the Soviet bureaucracy. Stalin halted the Revolution at the stage which Lenin called state capitalism which, in Proudhonian language, means the state as proprietor, that is, as Thief.

*   *   *   *   *

Proudhon has himself questioned by an imaginary interlocutor, thus:

'You are a republican?'
'Yes, but the word tells us nothing. *Res publica* means the public thing and whoever wants the public thing, under whatever form of government, can call himself a republican. Kings, too, are republicans.'
'Then you are a democrat?'
'No.'
'What! Can you be a monarchist?'
'No.'
'A *constitutionel*,[8] then?'
'God forbid!'
'Then you are an aristocrat?'
'Not in the least.'
'Do you want, then a mixed government?'
'Less than anything.'
'Then what are you?'
'I am an Anarchist.'

So far so good, but what does it mean? For him, it means absence of master, of a sovereign; and no 'sovereign people' if you please, no 'dictatorship of the proletariat'. Who dreams of that is no better than a Marat. One king or 20 million kings, it's all one: denial of freedom by force or fraud. No; we are, willy-nilly, associates. Domestic politics? A matter of departmental statistics. Foreign policy? A matter of international statistics. The science of government should be the business of one section of the Academy of Sciences and if there has to be a prime minister it had better be the perpetual Secretary of that Academy; and since any citizen is free to address a memorandum to the Academy of Sciences, every citizen can be a legislator. But because no man's opinion should count beyond the measure of its susceptibility to practical demonstration, no man can substitute will for reason; no man is king.

It will be recalled that in *La Célébration du Dimanche* Proudhon had asserted that Moses' greatness lay in his discovery that whatever is matter for legislation is matter for science, not for opinion. In *What is Property?* he restates that case. The legislative power belongs to reason only, the reasoning to be methodically demonstrated. To attribute to any will whatsoever, single or manifold, the right of veto and sanction is the ultimate in tyranny. Justice and legality are two things as independent of our assent as are mathematical truths.

In short, for Proudhon, the only valid social law, like the only valid physical law, is one which recognizes and embodies a truth established by studious observation and repeated experiment. Any other law is no law; it is an expression and imposition of will by force or fraud; it is Theft.

NOTES TO CHAPTER TWO

1. Letter to Bergmann, 3 May 1840.
2. Letter to Bergmann, June 1840.
3. In certain cases this is obviously so, *eg* the racialist laws of the Third Reich, the law of the United States until 1865 which made chattels of black men, and the laws of most countries which, until the 1920s, made chattels of women. If law is not an institutionalization of a scientific law of social justice, such as Proudhon sought, as valid in nature as the laws of thermodynamics, then it can only be the institutionalization of the will of the monarch or the ruling class and, in so far as it protects privilege and accumulated property (theft), unjust.
4. Woodcock, G. *Anarchism*. Harmondsworth, 1963.
5. One of the demands made in the Marx/Engels *Communist Manifesto* in 1848 was for a graded income tax.
6. Grotius (1583–1645) had long before argued in *De Mari Libero* the absolute freedom on the seas along the same lines, when considering the Portuguese claim to property right in the passage round the Cape of Good Hope. It is of some interest that the maritime nations, deranged by the property madness, are now busy appropriating the sea, *ie* using law dictated by mere will yet again as an instrument of gross, and grotesque injustice.
7. In an earlier passage Proudhon has demonstrated the *effrayant* quality of this latitude to inflate the currency to one's own advantage by showing that 100 francs invested at 5 per cent to be reinvested would in six centuries reach the monstrous sum of 100,000 billion francs. The equivalent English figures are £5 and £54 thousand million. c.f. H. G. Wells, *The Sleeper Awakes*.
8. In 1870 the bishops who conformed to the revolution were called *évêques constitutionels*.

The Thieves Strike Back

Cet animal est méchant; quand on l'attaque il se défend.

SAINTE-BEUVE, who knew Proudhon, was his first biographer, and edited his letters, describes *What is Property?* as *la logique à outrance*, which one might translate by saying that the book was outrageously logical. Sainte-Beuve, of course was not converted by the book, being of Pascal's opinion that civil law and convention are good title to property, which begs Proudhon's questioning of the very basis of civil law and convention.[1] The merit he finds in the book is that it forces the reader to rethink his own position; its strength, in the probability that the same reader will find himself nearer to Proudhon's at the end. Having said which he adds wryly: 'I can hear from here his outbursts of sarcastic laughter. Perhaps after all that was all he set out to achieve.'

That last, however, was not what the great critic really believed, for he elsewhere reports that Proudhon was certain that he would inaugurate a new social era with *What is Property?* as did Sièyes with *What is the Third Estate?*, but did nothing to advance this purpose by the vein of provocative truculence in his writing.

If he had ever really believed that he could begin the transformation of society with one book, Proudhon was no longer under that illusion a few weeks after publication. He was cast down by the feeling that he had either underrated the task or overrated his powers. He had written with such assurance to Bergmann, '... the style will be rough and acrid, irony and anger will be only too manifest. An evil, but an incurable one; when the lion is hungry, he roars ...', and had ignored his friends' warnings that he would do well to use style to soften the blow he was about to deliver. But now he confessed that in the future he would pay more attention to the art of writing, and drop the foolish notion that his manner would be forgiven for the sake of his matter.

He was stricken not by the hostility the book aroused but by the indifference with which it was received by the sort of critic, the sort of newspaper, which could have made it and him famous overnight. In one of the letters written at this time he says that to perceive and to know are all of life to a thinking being. 'But how hard that life is ... No man has been given over to a sorrow deeper than mine.'

His depression might have deepened into premature despair had not rage come to his rescue, rage at the behaviour of his patron, the Besançon *Académie*: a powerful faction of its members was campaigning for his repudiation: he was to be publicly reproved, condemned, and deprived of the remaining fraction of the Suard *pension*; and ostracized by all right-thinking Bisontins. To his friend Millet he wrote that anger was accumulating and piling up in his soul:

If ever the son revolts against the mother, so that a day comes when he dares to expose the turpitude of her who bore him, then woe, woe betide her! What I have done hitherto is mere practice, what I have published is juvenilia. But the recruit will become a veteran one day, and then, I say again, woe betide the complacent and arrogant.

He returned to Besançon, ostensibly to visit his parents, towards the end of July. The *Académie* was not yet ready to deal with him: in the course of two stormy sessions, the friends and sponsors who remained to him had staved off condemnation by carrying a resolution that he should first be heard in his defence: he was, in short, to be publicly tried for publishing a work now condemned by all right-thinking people as anti-social, and an outrage against decent tradition in both matter and manner. Meanwhile he was asked to publish nothing before the end of the scholastic year 1840–1. He gave that undertaking. Meanwhile he had been able to identify his enemies:

In general they are the religious bigots, the lawyers, and the pure literature lot who have it in for me. The business-people, bankers, money-lenders, shop-keepers, are – would you believe it? – applauding me. But, then, even in Jesus Christ's time, the publicans were closer to the kingdom of God than the doctors and Pharisees.[2]

True or untrue? Sometimes his taste for paradox clouded his judgement of people, though never of ideas.

He was informed that his case before the *Académie* would not be heard until November and at the same time had a letter from Bergmann to say that he would be in Paris early in October. Proudhon, wounded in his pride, desperately anxious to talk with a friend capable of understanding him, was determined to get back to Paris in time to meet Bergmann. He was penniless, or nearly so, and could certainly not afford the coach fare – coach travel in France as in England at the time was extremely expensive – and decided once again to walk to Paris, a distance of about 240 miles. He was unable to leave Besançon until 11 October, the walk took him over a week and when he arrived his friend had gone.

Proudhon had a room in No. 16, Rue Jacob which is on the Left Bank between Saint Germain-des-Prés and the Seine. There he settled down as best he could to write his second *Mémoire* on property, *Lettre à M. Blanqui*. He was determined to get this work done while he still had some months of the Suard *pension* to run.

But he was in an unhappy state of mind: when he had first come to Paris he had detested it and believed he could never live in it. He was to reverse that opinion, but for the time being he found it a foul place, a city of stupid, arrogant, idle, chattering burgesses, and starving workers, as horrible 'as the Rome of Commodus or Caracalla'. The middle-class liberals thought they were doing enough to change it when they attended a political banquet, got on their feet and brayed some commonplaces, and then went home to bed; while the people died by hundreds in the streets and were trampled where they fell. The lucky ones were taken up for vagrancy and imprisoned. Even at that fearsome price the proprietors were not flourishing: bankruptcies were running at the rate of a thousand a year in Paris alone, with total liabilities of the order of 60 millions a year. Meanwhile the *Chambre* was about to vote the *Duc* de Nemours a wedding present of half-a-million, and half-a-million a year allowance.[3] 'O happy Property!'

Ackermann had written criticizing the harsh, uncompromising style of *What is Property?* Proudhon replied that he had indeed been at fault, and all the more so in that 'my dialectic is invincible'. But, he excused himself, when a man of nearly thirty-two is reduced to indigence through no fault of his own; when that man has just discovered as a result of his meditations that the sole cause of poverty and crime is a simple error in accountancy, a matter of faulty book-keeping; when he perceives that the advocates of property and privilege are not merely misled by their own stupidity, but activated by impudent bad faith – then would it not be surprising if his spleen were not roused and if his style bore no witness to the fury in his soul? Add to all this that he had no social life whatever, no friend nearer than some hundreds of leagues, nobody with whom he could exchange ideas, and it was no wonder, surely, 'that there are times when I fall into unutterably deep dejection'.

He tells his friend that 'old man Weiss', his old acquaintance the Besançon librarian, had also rebuked him for his style – a style in which Sainte-Beuve detected the influence of bible reading and Hebrew studies – and said to him, 'My dear friend, you injure your case by your manner of presenting it. You should remember Henri Quatre's saying that you could catch more flies with a spoonful of honey than with a hundred casks of vinegar.'

'Said I, "it's not a question of catching flies but of swatting them," which outburst made our excellent librarian, who is worth ten times the rest of the *Académie*, laugh. But I am going to reform.'

Impatiently and irritably aware that he did not *know* enough, he began to read German philosophy, beginning with Kant; to discover that Pure Reason was his divinity; to dream of a life of scholarship free from the burden of the drive to action. That was to misconceive his own temperament; restless, truculent short of physical violence which he abhorred, he was quite incapable of staying out of the fight between people and proprietors, set on trying to destroy conventions by rational thinking, and to enlighten stupidity.

The political situation towards the end of 1840 seemed to him explosive: everyone was afraid, and the republican *National* was irresponsibly exploiting their fears. Defiant workers and unemployed were singing the *Marseillaise* in the streets. Politicians and journalists no longer argued, but screamed abuse and threw mud at each other. At the top, intelligence was as wanting as were dignity and good faith. There was nothing to be hoped for from the republican party which was behaving with such folly as would probably provoke a crushing reaction; the French had become a nation of bleating sheep. The most probable outcome of all this was a dictatorship followed by a European war in which France would be beaten.

There is not much exaggeration in Proudhon's sombre account of France at the end of the first decade of Louis-Philippe's *juste-milieu* government. In France, as in England, the industrial revolution was a far more hideous spectacle, inflicted enormously more suffering on a thousand times as many people, than any political revolution until the October Revolution in Russia. There are many confirming accounts, from Louis Blanc's *Histoire de dix ans* to the picture painted with such lively wit by Stendhal, in *Lucien Leuwen*, of troops being used to put down workers in revolt against starvation wages and refusal of the right to form trade unions; of groups of *Députés* combining in the *Chambre* to form pressure groups for the sole purpose of forcing ministers to give their relations places; of the king and his ministers making use of their position to build up huge fortunes by manipulation of the *Bourse* and the telegraph.[4]

Literature was, according to Proudhon, in no better case. There were no literary journals; no greatness of ideas or inspiration among living writers; nothing but little ideas, literary pettiness, 'miniature philosophy', and flashy cleverness.[5]

I read and reread Bossuet, Montesquieu, *etc.* cannot bear the moderns. Lammenais is about to publish a grand philosophy in 3 volumes octavo; it will be no better than the *Esprit* of Helvetius or Holbach's *Système de la nature*. But the Republican party deserves no better philosopher, and as you can imagine, Lammenais's Robespierriste abstractions will be matter for sermons to them.[6]

Proudhon did not after all have to return to Besançon in November; the secretary of the *Académie* wrote to say that the hearing of his case had been postponed until 15 January 1841 when he should either attend in person or send a written defence. The secretary advised him that his only honourable course would be retraction; for indignation aroused by his 'detestable' pamphlet was still running high and not even his friends in Besançon dared to defend it. One wonders what the secretary would have written had he known what was in his *Lettre à M. Considérant,* or *Warning to the Proprietors*, the third *Mémoire* on Property, which he was working on thanks to the continuation of the Suard *pension*. It called on the proletariat to recognize that the workers and only the workers could reform society, and warned the proprietors and their servants the magistrates not to drive the workers to despair, for no police and no soldiers would be able to save them should the people be driven to their last recourse – '. . . neither assassination, nor pillage, nor insurrection, nor general strike, nor arson, nor regicide, but something more terrible and more efficacious than all these.'[7]

*   *   *   *   *

Proudhon returned to Besançon to defend his position before the *Académie* in person, and later wrote to Ackermann a facetious account of the proceedings (16 May 1841). He says that the dreadful prospect of having to emigrate to America or Russia, clearly his only course if publicly dishonoured and ruined from cellar to attics by the *Académie* of Besançon, gave him the strength to defend himself; that as he had exhausted arguments he resorted to menaces – the threat to publish his written defence and let the Bisontin public judge between him and the *Académie*. The substance of his defence was that he had invented nothing, but had merely brought to light a doctrine which millions held, albeit unwittingly until he had revealed it to them. He named by name those of his enemies whom he saw in the room, and he gave them to understand that if they were looking for a 'scandal' they were going the right way about getting one. After the Prefect had spoken on his side, about half the members found a way out of the situation which had become absurd, by laughing at the other half, and saying that 'I was a lad of talent who might go far'. He concluded, 'In short, I was *acquitted*.' The voting had been very close, sixteen for, fourteen against, and one abstention. It had been excellent practice for what was to come.

The manner in which *What is Property?* escaped public prosecution is curious. The law officers of the Crown recommended prosecution but the *Garde des Sceaux* and Minister of Justice, Vivien, insisted on reading the book himself, was impressed by the quality of the mind which had created it and, not trusting his own judgement, sent the work to the Académie des Sciences Morales with a request that they study it and answer a specific question: was M. Proudhon's work a mere political pamphlet or had it a genuinely scholarly character? The Académie requested one of its Fellows, the economist Adolfe Blanqui, brother of the militant and conspiratorial communist Auguste Blanqui, to report on the book. He did so in a paper read to the Académie which was also the basis for his review in the *Moniteur*; the substance of his answer to the Minister's question was that while M. Proudhon's work contained expressions which were extremely blameworthy, its *caractère scientifique*, scholarly character, was undeniable and worthy of respect.

*   *   *   *   *

His printing business being unprofitable and still unsold, and likely to lose what remained of the Suard *pension*, Proudhon faced the fact that he would have to take a job. Although his friends in Besançon were trying to persuade the mayor and the Prefect to find him a place in the public service which would leave him time to study and write, when a job in Paris was offered, he decided to take it. An examining magistrate with ambitions to become a *Député* had decided that the best way to draw attention to his merit was to publish a book, a *Philosophie de l'instruction criminelle*. The only trouble was that he did not know how to set about the business, a disability which too rarely discourages public men from rushing into print, and sensibly decided that he needed help. So he engaged Proudhon to write the book for him – doubtless under his guidance – at 200 francs a year plus board and lodging for a thirty-six hour week. Proudhon was to move into his employer's house, No. 18, Rue Saint-Benoît, at the beginning of February 1842.

He arrived back in Paris on 23 January but heard, on arrival, that his new *Mémoire, Warning to the Proprietors* (*Lettre à M. Considérant*), had been seized by the police on the orders of the Besançon public prosecutor; and that he himself was summoned to appear before the Doubs Assize Court in eight days' time to answer to nine charges. Moreover his printer had been raided by the police who had confiscated 500 copies of the pamphlet; a number of his friends had been questioned; his room in the rue Jacob was raided and searched on the 25th; and to add to his miseries he was suffering from bladder trouble on account of which he asked for an adjournment which was refused.

It will be recalled that but for Adolf Blanqui's intervention with the *Garde des Sceaux*, Proudhon would have been prosecuted for *What is Property?* Louis-Philippe, '*ce procureur bas-normand couronné*', as Stendhal called him (meaning to distinguish the king for low cunning), and his *juste-milieu* government, were kept in power by the industrial and commercial bourgeoisie and the *haute banque*. The *quid pro quo* was soldiers on demand to keep down the workers and a judiciary to deal firmly with reforming intellectuals and their printers. Not even Blanqui could save Proudhon from the consequences of the third *Mémoire*, in which a harsh revolutionary threat was explicit.

While he seems not to have expected prosecution by the government, Proudhon did expect the *National* to bring an action against him for the things which he had published about that newspaper in *Warning to the Proprietors*. He had not attacked the republican newspaper unprovoked, was, rather, in this case, himself the animal labelled vicious because when attacked it defends itself, as he explained in a letter to Bergmann (2 January 1842):

I was denounced by that newspaper which urged the government to prosecute me; it was I, not they, who was the offended party. Mind you, I am hoping the *National* will not overlook this blow from me; for [in court] they will have but two alternatives; either my accusations will be proved, which will break them; or they must offer an explanation, retract what they said, and profess the contrary.

Like all that Proudhon wrote, *Warning to the Proprietors* was both a demand for and a demonstration of the inevitability of absolute equality; and in it he reverted to the subject of the man of exceptional talent or ability's obligation to accept that equality gracefully, since it was, in any case the only rational course. The passage is remarkable enough to be quoted in full; and one recalls the deep distrust of 'intellectuals' which characterized the Bolsheviks of the 1920s, the East European Soviet communist colonies in the 1950s, and the USSR today, despite Lenin's warning against that very state of mind.

Talent and genius: your boasted capacities, are used to levy tribute, justified by ridiculous arguments, on the product of the workers whom, on the plea of functional inferiority, you keep in servitude. Develop the intelligence of those workers, train their natural abilities, emancipate their souls, and soon, Oh you who are morally dessicated by egoism, we shall see what your vaunted superiority is reduced to.

Typical Proudhonian truculence and just what his friends were trying to cure him of: one doesn't persuade people to behave better by abusing them.

Talent and genius! Sublime words with which mankind readily rewards the vanguard of its sons: but baleful words, too, words which have made more slaves than the word liberty has made free men. Talent and genius – at their sound the human herd falls prostrate as if God had been invoked; will is extinguished in subjugated souls; and the halting mind is paralysed by awe. 'My astounded genius trembles before his' says the hero of *Agrippinus*, yet history tells us that the cruellest of the Caesars began life as a pusillanimous child. Doubt it not, all the vile courtiers of usurped greatness, the thinkers devoid of energy, the writers without character, and the servile imitators, are the children of fear. 'We are all born originals', cries the dauntless poet of *Night Thoughts*,[8] 'How is it that most of us die copies?' I answer, because the mere appearance of a mind deprives us of sense and courage. It is this fear which renders certain epochs sterile as it makes certain States tributary. It is fear of the antique past which ushers in decadence. When tyrants seek to enslave peoples they frighten them with virtue, bawl at them that they are not the men their fathers were, so that the time for freedom is gone by. That is why every great society has had its periods of dormancy and its periods of rebirth; why, too, every manifestation of mind as of liberty, has begun in revolt. Men, at first cast down before idols which, in their imagination seem terrible, little by little take courage again; fear and respect diminish; and there comes a moment when, their hearts before their reason proclaiming equality, they stand erect again.

Do not, then, frighten the young intelligence with the scarecrow of genius, but, rather, let it grow. And cease to beg a tithe for talent while so many souls are denied spiritual nourishment. Remember that he who has not been able to compete is not to blame for losing; and that no man has a right to call him coward whom servitude has humiliated. Unbind the hands which poverty's bonds have numbed; open the cage to the captive spirit; set mankind free, and leave man self-reliant in the conditions which nature intended; and then, but only then, attack him in the pride of his youth and strength. If still, indeed he be shamefaced in the presence of his peers and humble himself before his own kind, and shrink from the noble task before him, then strike. For he is no free man, he is indeed a slave.

Never, as Sainte-Beuve commented on this passage, did any man speak against talent with more talent, or forge sharper weapons against himself. But this was a case of Proudhon the philosopher pleading for Proudhon the proletarian; and making the mistake, if it be a mistake, which is by no means clear even now, of all generous men who believe all other men are as capable as themselves of growth under the hand of education. He was sincere in this, for some years later, reverting to a conversation he had had with Karl Grün (*see below*) about Newton, Leibnitz, Kant and Hegel, he wrote that study had taught him to look fearlessly on genius, and to find it nearer to the common man than it appears to be:

I have come to believe that I, like any well-constituted man for that matter, could, by application, develop the same mental power as the men to whom you ironically compare me. To this I add that weakness of mind, imbecility, and narrowness of conception being all perturbations or *anomalies* which social progress will eliminate, the day will come when all human beings will, without being identical, be of equivalent capacities, just as they will be equals in wages.

That was Proudhon's maggot: he was to return to it on his deathbed when he completed *The Political Capacity of the Working Classes* while defying God to kill him before he had the last word. It is, of course, inconsistent with his maxim that men are born unequal in innate property. There is a way round that: although he denied that he had been a Fourieriste, it will be remembered that he had in fact, on his own earlier admission, been for six weeks under the influence of that eccentric philosopher, while he was setting the type of Fourier's *Nouveau monde industriel et sociétaire*. Now Fourier believed that the crime and vice arising from lack of capacity to deal with life normally, were due to mental sickness which would yield to therapy. It would be possible to consider the inequality in innate property, at birth, as a consequence of a curable debility.

Plants suffering from a virus disease perform unequally although physiologically identical; when phytopathologists succeed in destroying the virus, the performance of the plants becomes identically good. The 'virus' in the case of our own species may be a negative: the want of Proudhon's 'sound method or instrumentation'. It has been suggested that genius in man is no more than a manifestation of optimum performance made possible by accidents of education and experience, in a species whose performance is almost universally and consistently below the optimum because no flexible system of education has yet been devised which consistently makes the best use of the capacity of all individuals in the species.

*   *   *   *   *

The date of Proudhon's trial had been fixed at 3 February; he left Paris on 29 January, reached Besançon on the 31st, and engaged the services of an advocate whom he describes as a young man of good feeling and intelligence, but of whom he says, 'I was obliged to teach him his business or his pleading would have been a series of silly commonplaces which would have cost us the case and would in any case have displeased me.'[9] Proudhon himself did most of the work of preparing their case, working night and day to get it done in the forty-eight hours remaining to him.

The Doubs Assize Court was packed with friends, enemies and the merely curious. Feeling against Proudhon was very high in some quarters, chiefly because with the European economic crisis of the 1840s deepening, and the industrial workers everywhere being driven to truculence by desperation, *Warning to the Proprietors* inspired the middle-class and the proprietors with a terror of revolution which found expression in rage. Proudhon describes the atmosphere of the courtroom as being charged with hatred: 'I was Robespierre; worse, Antichrist.' People shrank from him as if he had some loathsome disease. There was already a rumour that he was certain to be imprisoned for at least five years.

The *Académie*, desperately anxious to repudiate him and all his works, treated him savagely in their newspaper, *Le Franc-Comtois*, in which they put his name in the list of cases for trial between that of a man charged with murder and another with infanticide; in an editorial, moreover, they called for a merely nominal fine, since Proudhon was penniless, but a ten-year prison sentence.

On the other hand there were also many in court who were sympathetic to him, and who believed that he had a perfect right to absolute freedom of expression; and in the benevolence of his intentions. He told Ackermann that had he been fined 10,000 francs the sum would have been collected among these sympathizers within two days.

There had originally been nine charges in the indictment: it had, however, been drawn up with such zeal that some of them were obviously mere duplications, and the public prosecutor and the advocate general had contracted the list to four charges: attack on the constitutional right of property; incitement to hatred of the government; incitement to hatred of several classes of citizens; offence to religion.

The strongest part of the prosecution's case was based on the passage in which Proudhon had threatened the proprietors with something more terrible than assassination, insurrection and so forth, should they drive the workers too far. When he was questioned about this, he refused to answer. Perhaps by then the idea of reviving the *Vehmgericht* in modern terms had come to seem *naïf*.

When the time came for him to speak in his own defence it took him two hours to read the paper he had prepared.[10] He later wrote to Ackermann,

Imagine the astonishment of all those curious souls, priests, women, aristocrats, etc. when instead of being confronted by a red-waistcoated republican bearded like a billy-goat, they beheld a fair-haired, fair-skinned little chap with an air of simple good nature and a tranquil countenance, who claimed that he stood accused only because of a misunderstanding in the public prosecutor's office whose zeal he nevertheless applauded.

The substance of his pleas, once again, was that his ideas were universally held; all he had done was to enable his readers to perceive clearly what they had actually always known to be true; and that these ideas, far from being a danger to the government and the Charter,[11] strengthened them. If this sounds like a disingenuous attempt to play the role of the little boy who pointed out that the emperor was naked, then that is misleading: Proudhon *was* that boy, meant what he said. There is a letter to Bergmann (3 February 1842) in which he says, '... equality and non-property are a necessary consequence of the Charter and of all institutions stemming from it, so much so that today there is no longer any question of *destroying*, but only of *developing*.' And this belief is at least implied in the letter he wrote two years later to Karl Marx (*see below*), declining to become one of the Brussels Committee's international chain of revolutionary correspondents: he told Marx he did not believe in violent revolution as a means of reforming the social-economic system.

In support of his plea Proudhon advanced learned arguments so recondite, expressed in language so technical, and in a style so metaphysical,[12] that the court found them incomprehensible. Proudhon confessed to Ackermann that this was deliberate, and called it 'judicial mystification', and 'a *pâté* of indigestible political economy'. His advocate strengthened the effect of this by opening his pleading with a confession: as he had not read all his client's writings and had not understood what he had read, he was incompetent either to accept or reject them; the implication being that the jury must be in the same case. The advocate general admitted that he was in the same difficulty but claimed that the pamphlet in question spoke for itself. The presiding judge, in his summing-up, implied that he, too, found the accused's arguments too difficult for him, thus leaving the jury '... to decide whether there was a philosophic bottom to my doctrine which rendered the appalling imprecations I had uttered against property reasonable and innocent'.

The words of the foreman of the jury returning the verdict were these:

'This man is working in a field of ideas inaccessible to ordinary people. It is impossible to be sure that he is guilty and we cannot condemn at random.'

Proudhon had seized the opportunity of the trial to advance his ideas: one of the charges was incitement to hatred of priests, academicians, magistrates and *Députés*; in short, of the scribes and Pharisees. Keeping his expression 'simple and serious' but using language full of 'salt, energy and sarcasm', he proceeded to justify his criticisms, making use of privilege to name men present in court by way of examples. 'What I was reproached for having written was as nothing compared with what I was allowed to say.'

The effect, he says, was marvellous, and I believe him. The French require above all to be amused by their public men; and whatever happens, they keep their freedom by judging politicians and publicists as the comedians they, often unwittingly, cannot but be. God help the actor who is hissed by a bored French audience. Louis-Philippe was booed off his throne as much for being a bore as for being oppressive. Stendhal shows us the banker Leuwen, as *Député*, dominating the *Chambre* – for entirely frivolous reasons – by his wit. Proudhon won his case not only by mystifying his judges but by making up for it by entertaining them.

*   *   *   *   *

Acquitted, Proudhon returned to Paris to the house in the Rue Saint-Benoît to resume work on his employer's *Philosophy of criminal investigation*, and on the preparation of his next big book, *On the Creation of Order in humanity*.[13]

In April, when the *Letter to M. Blanqui* was published, he was again reverting in letters and diary to his principal purpose, the discovery of the scientific laws of jurisprudence and politics which, by making the self-management of society's business a routine application of known rules, would be immutable because natural, and render the formal state redundant. So sure was he that such a science was possible and that he was on the right lines leading to its discovery, that he could scarcely believe that responsible men would fail to recognize it. He was excited by the way his mind was working on the *Creation of Order*: 'Sometimes one studies for a long time without any feeling that progress is being made; then suddenly the veil falls away and, after the long labour of reflexion, comes insight. That moment is divine.'

Impressed by Adolfe Blanqui's respectful treatment of his writings, Proudhon proposed to consult him about the writing of the *Creation of*

Order. Blanqui's advice was: could he not be more moderate, at least in his language? If he could, then his place as a scholar and philosopher was assured; and when there was no more reason to fear that the truculence of his writings would provoke the men of violence to make abusive use of them, then he would find himself a man of influence whose voice might be heard even in high places. No advice could have been more useless: in a letter to another of his friends, Tissot, who shared many of Proudhon's ideas but, like Blanqui, urged discretion, Proudhon had written of *felling* prejudice, *crushing* opposition, delivering up the *corrupt cowards* of the establishment to *eternal infamy*; and had concluded, 'When I shall have said all I think, I shall prepare for battle.'

It was apparently Blanqui who raised another matter with him: could he not bring himself to be kinder in his criticism of his fellow philosophers: M. de Lammenais, for instance?

Lammenais was something of a pet among liberals and radicals: he was a priest who had made a name as a Catholic apologist but moved steadily leftward through Catholic liberalism (*Parole d'un croyant*, 1834), to find himself in a revolutionary position which had caused him to be anathematized by the Pope. The Blanquiste republicans loved him. Proudhon, alone among the men of the Left, had no time for him: he called him 'morally impotent' and stigmatized his writings against belief in miracles, prophecies, original sin, and revelation as an overdone re-hash of the *Vicaire Savoyard*. And his diatribes against Catholicism and the clergy were distasteful in a man who had been a priest. 'Whatever may be said about the man, I shall always answer that I don't like apostates. Let him change his opinions by all means, but he should not wage war on his former sacerdotal colleagues; nor on Christianity which, instead of attacking he should be going into more deeply.'[14]

One of those scientific laws which Proudhon sought to uncover so that society could be run on principles as 'natural' as those of a machine (which is an intelligent application of the laws of thermodynamics), was first stated in his *Letter to M. Blanqui*: the law of historical necessity. His own gloss on it is in the letter to Ackermann quoted above: 'Society, unwittingly and by the inevitable working of providential laws, is daily demolishing the institution of property ... This historical and critical exposition of tendencies [*Letter to M. Blanqui*] ends naturally in this conclusion: that we must go the way we are going, for it is necessity which is pushing us.'

This was written one month after Karl Marx had received from the university of Jena the doctorate which the university of Berlin had refused him, for a thesis comparing the philosophies of Democritus and Epicurus; and more than two years before the two men met and talked away whole nights. Mind you, I've said nothing.

In May 1842 Proudhon made up his mind to give up his employment as soon as he could complete the work he had undertaken to do. The *Imprimerie P-J. Proudhon. Impressions Militaires*, formerly Lambert et Cie, in the Rue du College had still not been sold. Whether he did any work there when he returned to Besançon late in 1842 is not clear; among the motives which had recalled him was the wish to see his mother, and the encouragement which his friends had given him to believe that they could get him a place in the public service which would enable him to get his living at the same time leading that life of study and philosophical writing which he believed he yearned for. He wrote a critique of the biblical exegesis in use by the Church, for a local *Société d'Emulation*, which included his own translations of three Psalms with grammatical and historical analyses, and proved that the Catholic theologians were grossly ignorant of their own business. And he was alternately pleased and displeased with the *Creation of Order*. This was not published until September but it will be convenient to deal with it here by saying that it was a failure which accomplished nothing; certainly it was not what he had intended it to be, the positive complement of *What is Property*?

Sainte-Beuve, gentle with Proudhon as always, says that the book is 'a grand effort of brain rather than an achievement (*résultat*)'. Proudhon himself was, in the end, dissatisfied with what he had done; in his dedicatory letter to Bergmann he says:

I have denied religion; I have denied philosophy; yet what right have I to speak in the name of science? I must in this solemn moment confess the truth: the distractions of living, and the misfortune of an education wholly philosophical and religious have allowed me to learn hardly anything at all. My mind has been strong enough for the task of demolition, but wanting in materials for the task of rebuilding. Of all that human genius has discovered I have caught glimpses only of the smallest parts. Every line of the present work bears witness to its author's inadequacy.

Demolition, yes; yet he persisted in the belief that the local authorities who were bound to be offended by his destructiveness, would help him to continue that work by giving him a sinecure. He believed what he was told by over-confident friends, that even the Archbishop was urging the Prefect to receive him and that the Prefect could hardly refuse to give a place to a man so sponsored; he was even concerned, in advance, at the fact that having been given a place, when the *Creation of Order* appeared he would look like a monster of ingratitude. Still, it was pleasant to contemplate the idea that he would be, at one and the same time, the most advanced reformer of the age and a protégé of the powers that be.[15]

It was an extraordinary illusion, arising from his inability to believe that men of education in high places could fail to recognize and respect the truth when he revealed it to them. He, who never had the slightest intention of desisting from his work of destroying the property basis of the capitalist *juste-milieu* society, yet seems to have found nothing odd in the notion of that society helping him to the means. He knew perfectly well that the Archbishop and the Vicar General of the diocese, albeit as partisans of the old aristocracy and Bourbons, hostile to Louis-Philippe and the *juste-milieu*, were much more bitterly hostile to any form of republicanism, democracy, socialism; and took him for a new and very dangerous kind of Jacobin. Yet he seems to have believed in that tale of high clerical support even while compounding his anti-clericalism by making learned fun of the famous Jesuit preacher Father Ravignan who, that year, preached the advent sermon in Besançon Cathedral. Never, even in such late works as *The Federative Principle*, did he despair of the power of scientific truths of the kind he believed himself to have discovered, to prevail; and it never seemed to occur to him that whereas it only costs a man his belief in Genesis to accept the scientific truth from a Darwin, it is apt to cost him money in the bank, an estate in land, or in plant, to accept the same from a Proudhon or a Marx.

His life in Besançon was unsatisfactory; he had nobody to talk to; his brother he scarcely mentions; his mother he loved, respected and even admired, but only because she *was* his mother, and a paragon within the very strict limitations proper, in his view, to women.

For, in that quarter, he could scarcely have been more narrow-minded and reactionary: in due course I shall come to a consideration of his *Pornocracy, or Women in Modern Times*, but it is time to say something more about his attitude to women, and his sexual puritanism.

Sainte-Beuve's opinion is important because he knew Proudhon personally: he calls him '... a man of the old society, a very Roman, an enemy to modern innovation'. Proudhon, in other words, considered it impossible for any woman to be the equal of man. Sainte-Beuve quotes him as writing – I have not identified the letter in question – 'Do you believe that a woman, mistress or wife, is your *friend*; that [her man's] loyalty, the most perfect probity, the strictest fidelity, application to work and love of fame, the most generous sentiments, will for long outweigh in her scales those small faults which we men do not even notice?'

It reads as if he were smarting from the fact that a girl had preferred to him a young man with less talent and better manners. Perhaps not; one has to remember that this arch-enemy of property and exponent of anarchy was an old-fashioned conservative at heart. We are yet a couple of years from his friendship with the German 'True Socialist' Karl Grün, but I will quote here a letter Grün wrote about him, to his wife, for it bears on the subject:

I lunched with Proudhon today and had a lively argument with him about women. I had challenged him on that sentence in his book about property in which he says, 'Far from applauding what is nowadays called the emancipation of women, I am inclined, rather, should it come to that extremity, to put them into reclusion!' But we were unable to come to terms. He wants his future wife to be a housewife. I could do nothing with him and although I made myself very clear he kept saying that he did not understand me. Whatever you do, don't forget how to cook! If, one of these days, Proudhon pays us a visit, we shall serve him a perfect meal cooked by you in your own fashion, and then take him up on his reclusion theory. So, whatever you do, don't forget your cooking!

It is probably important to remember that Proudhon had never known a woman of education; in his attitude to women he was not only conservative, he remained a peasant whose mother, though he loved her, and his wife later, was a kind of servant. Here is Sainte-Beuve again:

His youth was chaste ... When voluptuous thoughts tormented him in the night he would rise and climb up to the attic and stand at the dormer window contemplating the moon and the stars ... and not return to bed until he was perfectly calm and serene again.

The moon and stars are not usually regarded as effective agents in neutering the importunate sexuality of a healthy and vigorous young man; maybe the cold draught from the dormer window had more to do with it.

In a letter to Ackermann (August 1838) Proudhon refers to and quotes from a letter he had written to '*mon ancienne maitresse*'. This is the girl we have already heard about but never met and it is clear that the English word would not have been 'mistress' but the innocent 'sweetheart'. I do not know who she was nor what she was doing in Lucerne where, Proudhon tells his friend, 'she is dying of boredom and perhaps love'. Perhaps she was cured of the second part of her affliction by her lover's letter:

Consider what is happening all round you: are you not sweet, gentle, chaste, industrious and honest? Why is it then that while you have barely enough to live on, a swarm of prostitutes can flaunt an insolent luxury? Let me explain this mystery. God has willed that when evil and vice have reached a zenith among mankind, it should be the good who are the first to suffer so that they may be roused to stem the tide which threatens to overwhelm them. There are a hundred thousand young men in France who, like me, have sworn to fulfill that sacred mission, and sooner or later they will vanquish, or perish in the attempt.

To put this in proportion and set it in its temporal context, I have identified one outstanding warrior in Proudhon's army of 100,000: Alexander Dumas the younger, author of *La Dame aux Camélias*, published in 1848, found it necessary to apologize, excuse and explain himself at tedious length for writing a book about a prostitute, albeit golden-hearted; and, like Proudhon, calls on the younger, his own generation to stand up against what we now call permissiveness, and dare to be virtuous.

In another letter Proudhon refers again to the young lady of Lucerne, and he describes his love as '*honnête*' which in this context must mean chaste. I have already said that Sainte-Beuve believed that this Samson was Delilah-proof. Perhaps he was: certainly he could write the most unfeeling letter to his friend Ackermann who, deeply in love, was about to be married: 'You are at that time in life when love pricks us most sharply; afterwards, this diminishes. All that is nought; what matters is to see, know and formulate the true and the beautiful.'

Here is Proudhon on another aspect of the subject writing to Joseph Garnier, the economist, who introduced him to the 'Economists Club' and to his new publisher, Guillaumin (*see below*), was a Malthusian and an exponent of Doctor Malthus's doctrine of continence in marriage as the only means of population control (February 1844).

All that has been written on this subject inspires in me a profound disgust: it is inexpressibly pitiful. So I, like you, Sir, am a Malthusian; but an ultra-Malthusian, whch is to say that reliance must be exclusively on *abstinence* in this matter of population. .... As to the future, I believe in *mores* very different from ours; in a spirituality in love such as Plato advanced, and of which Christianity has given us more than one example. I regard our present lasciviousness as wholly unnatural; all that parade of tenderness, however honourable and delicate; all those burning expressions, too, on the subject of women, which modern writing is full of, seem to me to be an expression of disordered erotic excitement rather than a symptom of legitimate tendencies ...

Proudhon was not a conventional Christian; but he was in some sort a saint. Sainte-Beuve comments on the above, 'One sees very clearly that love and what pertains to Venus was not his weakness. That abstinence

which he speaks of and which he practised could hardly be practised by
all and sundry excepting in the matter of secondary passions; it is not so
easy when it comes to what Pope calls the *dominant* passion.'

Towards the end of the year or early in 1843 Proudhon found a buyer
for his printing business, but at a price which enabled him to pay only 75
per cent of the debts which his former partner's suicide had left on his
hands, leaving him with a debt of 7000 francs on which he would have to
pay the interest until he could pay it off, which he never did.

NOTES TO CHAPTER THREE

1. The 2nd. Prop. 2, Ch. 3, *Le consentement universel ne justifie pas la propriété.*
2. Letter to Bergmann.
3. In the event the *Loi de dotation* in question was thrown out by the *Chambre.*
4. In the mid-19th century members of the French Assembly were called *Représentants*. I
have used the more familiar *Député*. A system of semaphore chains under government
control made possible the swift transmission of news and orders to and from the
capital. See Stendhal's *Lucien Leuwen*, also called *Le Télégraphe*. It was, of course, only
effective in conditions of good visibility which probably explains why it was never
really adopted in England.
5. Victor Hugo had published *Ruy Blas* in 1838; Stendhal, *La Chartreuse de Parme* in the
following year; Prosper Merimée, *Colombo* in 1840; but Proudhon was contemptuous
of novelists, and believed that all the good poetry had already been written. Louis
Blanc's *L'Organization du Travail* was published in 1839; the first part of Sainte-Beuve's
Histoire de Port-Royal in 1840.
6. Letter to Ackermann, 15 November 1840.
7. The threat is vague, but see Proudhon's letter to Ackermann of 23 May 1841. He had
in mind a revival, in modern terms and by the working-class, of the mediaeval German
secret courts of the Holy Vehm.
8. Edward Young, 1684–1765.
9. Letter to Ackermann, 23 May 1842.
10. Subsequently published as *Explications presentées au ministre public sur le droit de propriété.*
11. The Restoration constitution, flouted by Charles X and his ultra-reactionary prime
minister Polignac, but restored by the 'July Revolution' of 1830 which put Louis-
Philippe and the bourgeoisie in power.
12. The *procès verbale* can be consulted at the Bibliothèque Municipale of Besançon. The
procès verbale of the *Académie* hearing is in the possession of the *Académie des Sciences,
Belles-Lettres et Arts* of Besançon but can be seen at the municipal library.
13. *De la Création de l'Ordre dans l'Humanité ou Principes d'Organization Politique.*
14. Letter to Ackermann, 16 May 1841.
15. Letter to Bergmann, December 1842.

Businessman and Mutualist

Rejected by the Prefecture and by the Municipality; suspect in the Public Prosecutor's offices;
an object of clerical hostility, and of terror to the burgesses; devoid of assets and without credit
– such, at thirty-four years of age, is my achievement. There is now nothing for me to do in
Besançon. I have a sure and honest recourse in my trade as compositor, and my pen will procure
a little extra. By their means I shall now wait upon events and for ever renounce the role of
place-hunter.

THE FRANCE, THE EUROPE, in which Proudhon found himself thus cir-
cumstanced, were deeply disturbed. In France, Britain and Germany
the working-class had lent such strength as it had – chiefly the strength
implicit in its numbers – to the middle-class in its struggle to break the
land-owning nobility and gentry; and then found itself abandoned and in
no better case than it had been before. It was forced to the conclusion
that having no friends, it had better help itself.[1] In Britain the consequence was Chartism, of which that very shrewd judge Francis Place
had written as early as 1838:

This is a new feature in society produced by the increased intelligence of the
working people. This is the first time that desire for reform has been moved by
them and carried upwards. Until now it has always proceeded downwards and
expired when abandoned, as it always has been, by their gentlemen leaders. It
will not again expire but will go on continually, sometimes with more sometimes
with less rapidity, but on it will go.

The workers, in short, were no longer prepared to tolerate a state of
affairs in which a House of Commons majority could be returned by
151,000 middle-class votes, while they remained without a voice.

In the German states police, military and censorship were used to
prevent any effective collaboration between the radical intellectuals and
the working-class. It was the miserable poverty of the textile workers in
the Wupper valley mills, including his father's wretched wage-slaves,
which inspired the socialism of Frederick Engels. Sent by his father to the
Manchester office of the firm in 1842, and finding the condition of the
people as atrocious there as it was at home,[2] he joined the Chartists.

It was to France that the socialist leaders looked for a lead, if only
because, as Engels put it, it was in Paris that all the nervous fibres of
European civilization converged, and from which came, from time to
time, those 'electrical discharges which make the whole world tremble'.

In England violent working-class militancy had been avoided first by the legalization of Trade Unions (1824), then by the Factory Act Limiting Hours of Labour (1847), and by preemptive terrorization of the Chartists by an enormous force of middle-class special constables, of which William Ewart Gladstone and the future Napoleon III were stalwarts. Where the burgesses had refused to legalize any combination of their natural enemies, the workers had only one recourse – violent insurrection; and that could be contained only by military force. Arnold Ruge, for whose *Deutsche Jahrbücher* Karl Marx had written an attack on the Prussian censorship which, because of that censorship, was not published in Germany,[3] reached Paris early in 1842 and was immediately struck by the atmosphere of tension in the city, the sense of violence only just contained. In the *Chambre* Guizot's majority was down to three votes and it seemed to Ruge that the bourgeois monarchy was toppling; there had been attempts on the king's life. Of Louis-Philippe he wrote:

When one day I saw him driving down the Champs-Elysées, hidden deep inside his carriage, hussars before, behind and on each side, I noticed with surprise that these cavalry-men, with their muskets at the ready, served to make more manifest the state of open strife [between king and people], while giving that strife a look of burlesque. There passing before me went bad conscience personified.[4]

It was in Paris that the European revolution was expected to start, and wherever in the Continent revolutionaries were gathered together, impatiently waiting their moment, it was, said Marx, 'the crowing of the Gallic cock' that they listened for.[5]

The time was coming, however, when the German socialists would not like the sound of that crowing when it came from Proudhon: but for the moment he was in no condition to do any.

*   *   *   *   *

One of the few sons of burgesses and gentlemen who, at college, had had the heart and sense to overlook young Proudhon's ragged clothes, wooden shoes and tattered books, and to make a friend of him, and even to accept his leadership, was Antoine Gauthier, son of the merchant house of Gauthier Frères of Mulhouse and Lyon, whose interests included waterway haulage. He and Proudhon had kept in touch, they still *tutoi*'d each other in their letters, and when *What is Property?* was published Gauthier had written to Proudhon criticizing the book not simply as a 'proprietor' but from the practical business point of view. In one of his letters Proudhon, by way of dealing with his friend's objection, explains what he is about: there is, he says (the theme is one he returns to time and again), no question of *inventing* a social science, a science of politics and legislation: for that science must be there already, implicit in natural laws as immutable and reliable as those of physics or chemistry. So the task is to discover and expound those laws. This task, however, '... will take centuries to accomplish'.

But that is no reason for doing nothing or falling into despair. Once we have that science, society will run itself and Proudhon is absolutely certain that the rules, once we know them, will leave the liberty and integrity of the individual citizen absolutely intact; and the state an anachronism.

'In all reform there are two distinct stages which, all too often, are confounded: *transition* and *accomplishment*.' Present-day society has to concern itself only with transition, and Proudhon suggests the most effective immediate steps to be taken: conversion of all the Funds to lower rates of interest; reduction of the rates of return on all forms of invest- ment; reform of banking; capital issues to be limited to low interest rates; progressive reduction, to final extinction, of tariffs. In short, he proposes to attack property by attacking interests, profits, or, rather, all those kinds of unearned revenue which he calls *aubaine*.

An *aubaine* is a godsend or windfall, in other words something which you get without having done anything to earn or deserve it. Among the other forms of *aubaine* – land, house and factory or office rents, interest from money lent, and so forth – he includes salaries in excess of the average. Property is harmful in that, by loading the economy with these *aubaines*, it loads it with charges for which no work has been done, no contribution made.[6] Progressively reduce *aubaines* to final extinction and you have virtually abolished property.

This progressive abolition will, however, be no more than a negation of evil. The necessary *positive* organization must be the work of many men; and all that one man, in this case himself, could do single-handed was to discover and expound the requisite axioms:

Believe me, no man on earth is capable, as has been said of Saint-Simon and Fourier, of giving us a system complete in all its parts and which then has only to be put in operation. That is the most damnable lie which one can tell mankind and it is why I am so opposed to Fourierism. Social science is infinite and no man can know it all.

Today, of course, we know, what Proudhon was in no position to know, exactly what happens when that 'damnable lie' is taken for sober truth by a great society.

As for himself, Proudhon tells Gauthier, he is engaged in determining and publishing the elements of the required political and legislative science.

When in the spring of 1843, Antoine Gauthier heard that Proudhon was at last free of his burdensome printing business, but heavily in debt and out of a job, he offered him a job with Gauthier Frères. The title of the job, *commis batelier*, tells us nothing: in the event he seems to have been virtually the manager of the Lyon office, in charge of all correspondence, of negotiations with customers and with the authorities, and notably of all business disputes and lawsuits. He had, and was intended to have, a good deal of time for his own work. The firm had large contracts for moving coal and other goods by water, and their steam-tug, the *Dragon*, was the most powerful vessel of her kind on the Saône and associated waterways. His work brought him into continuous touch with all kinds of haulage workers, bargees, carters, stokers, with lawyers, businessmen of all kinds, industrialists and merchants. But it was on his own initiative that he sought out and associated himself with the 'Mutualist' workers in the Lyon textile mills, and I shall presently come to this very important new element in his life. To Ackermann he wrote, 'I am multiplying my observations and completing *de experto* that education in political economy which began with Adam Smith and Say.' He was impressed and distressed by the terrible consequences of applying a 'scholarly theory' – Adam Smith's – in practice, as a means of deliberate destruction – the destruction of the weaker competitors in business by the stronger. He told Ackermann that having himself been destroyed by it in his own business, he was now 'crushing others'. Able to apply some of his own theories of organization, he was making 'certain experiments on ill-intentioned competitors, in *anima vili*'.

He showed particular skill in handling Gauthier's lawsuits and in the course of the three years he worked in Lyon became known as 'Gauthier's attorney'. He attributes the consistent success of the briefs he prepared for advocates and arbitrators to the soundness of the method of argument which he had developed for his own work.

Proudhon acknowledged that by paying him a salary but leaving him free to study and write, and enabling him to go to Paris when he wanted to, Gauthier Frères had taken the place of the Besançon *Académie* as his patron. But there is no doubt that the firm got very good value for their money, and from the business ability which he displayed in their service it is clear that his own failure in business was due rather to Lambert's suicide and its financial consequences than to any want of capacity for business.

Lyon became, in more ways than one, the laboratory Proudhon needed for the practical part of his scientific search for social laws.

It was now that the master-ideas which dominated Proudhon's mind took on that substance which gave them the power to grow; or during which they crystallized and lost the power of growth. To read the *Carnets* for his years with Gauthier is to realize vividly the ordeal sustained by a man who, temperamentally and by education narrow-minded to the point of being emotionally crippled, puritanical to the point of mania, has been burdened with an understanding so swift, an intellect of such capacity, and a vision of such penetration, that everything he encounters engages first his attention and then generates an almost desperate need to put right what he clearly sees to be wrong. Morally wrong or functionally wrong, it was all one to him; an ill-designed machine was, like an ill-living man, 'unjust'. Here, indeed, is the seed of his masterpiece, *De la Justice* – Proudhonian justice being concerned as much with right functioning as right thinking and right feeling, all of which are manifestations of the same universal principle, so that injustice consists in going against the grain of nature.

That emotional crippling is manifest most strikingly, in the gross overstatement of his case against pleasure in sexual relationships, and women's claim for equality with men: man is prince, woman vassal, man is master, woman servant; no man can take serious, honourable pleasure in the company of women, for they are not and never can be at his intellectual level, and their society cannot, therefore, but corrupt men who, because of their very superiority of mind and sensibility, are more readily corrupted. Yet his sense of the honour and dignity of the role he assigns to women protects him from the worst excesses of anti-feminism. All French socialists had read Malthus and were convinced by his arguments: their prophet Fourier is supposed to have suggested that, since a clear connection had been established between female obesity and sterility, fattening up the ladies would be a means of population control. The Fourierists were advocating this, apparently quite seriously, as the best contraceptive method in a socialist society. It is easy to laugh now; it wasn't then, and Proudhon didn't:

The Fourierists are obstinate in advocating their system of fattening women, to raise an obstacle in the way of unwanted fecundity. I know nothing more ignoble, or more degrading for man, than this idea. Who can deny that fatness does, in some cases, produce sterility? But it is absurd to take Fourier's myth seriously. The true limitators of population are Work and Love, that is to say, Chastity.

Love equals Chastity: here we have Proudhon in the role of Troubador.

Was it anti-feminism which made him record in the *Carnet* for 1843 what, had it been published, would have been by far the worst notice which Rachel, the leading tragic actress of the day, ever received? It cannot have been anti-Semitism, another of his maggots, since he took her to be a gypsy. After seeing her as Roxane he was still in some doubt of her mediocrity; but, seeing her in *Phèdre*, was fully convinced that she understood nothing whatever about her roles in Racine: 'From one end of the play to the other she had given the impression of an elderly madwoman in love with a pretty fellow, and a prey to bouts of hysteria.'

Those visits to the theatre, whatever Mlle Rachel's shortcomings, inspired in him the ambition to be a dramatist, just as every contact with an art or craft or profession or trade drove him into seeing himself as a master of it: there are, in the *Carnets* dating from this period, two detailed plans for plays, *Judith* and *Galileo*. They might, as he conceived them, perhaps have been written by a Hollywood-style collaboration between Racine, Shakespeare and Sophocles. The *Galileo* project was resumed several times in subsequent years. When other projects were not going well, there was always *Galileo* and a never-completed *Course in Political Economy* to fall back on.

Lyon brought him in contact with the wholesale and retail trades, chiefly as Gauthier's agent in disputes and lawsuits about money owed to the firm. 'Character of the businessman: gain, gain, always gain. To that end, lies, lies and more lies. Exploitation, fraud, spoliation, selfishness, contempt for the general interest, and supreme ingratitude.'

That was a judgement which time was to mellow: the vices of tradespeople were not personal, nor professional, but an inevitable consequence of capitalism, and of authoritarian government.

Proudhon disliked Lyon even more strongly than he disliked Paris: it had all the nastiness of a huge city with none of the redeeming features of a capital. None the less his time there was crucial to the development of his thinking, because it brought him into direct contact for the first time with the conditions of industrial labour. Lyon was the heart of the new industrial France as well as the centre of urban working-class discontent. It was a breeding-ground of activist groups committed in one form or another to the overthrow of capitalist authority, all of them compelled through the intransigence of the law to exist as secret societies.

The largest of these groups of discontents was the Mutualists, and it was the emphasis of the Mutualists on the principle of worker-cooperatives rather than on violent revolution which drew Proudhon so strongly to them. In the workers' associations favoured by the Mutual-ists he found a practical application of many of the social ideas most dear to him, and he was fired with optimism. He felt himself at last to be at the hub of a new working-class movement which, he felt sure, would trans-form the world.

All this, believe me, will end in something, and the movement is not falling off; on the contrary, there is progress, frightening progress. If you wish to know where you stand and how the wind blows, do not ask the men of power . . . Find out the state of the whispered propaganda that occurs spontaneously among the people, without leaders or catechisms or any system yet established . . .

Here was organic socialism after Proudhon's own heart. By 1860, he predicted with bounding confidence, the entire world would be overrun by these workers' associations; and the state, all leaders, all systems of power, would have crumbled away before the self-assertion of a natural social order of things.

Proudhon's utopian frame of mind was not to last long, but his association with the Mutualists of Lyon was an experience which enriched the remainder of his life. He had discovered a new public: no longer the literary, intellectual audience to which he had previously addressed his thoughts, but an audience of working-class masses. It was Proudhon's experience at Lyon which helped make him so extra-ordinarily effective later in 1848 as the editor of the popular newspapers *Le Représentant du Peuple* and its successor *Le Peuple*. And it was his association with the Mutualists which supplied him with the practical ideas he was to expound in his last book, completed by dictation on his deathbed more than twenty years after leaving Lyon, *De la Capacité Politique des Classes Ouvrières*.

*   *   *   *   *

In the course of his visits to Paris on the firm's business and his own, Proudhon was making new friendships, some of which were to be impor-tant. He met Guillaumin, who was to be his new publisher, through Joseph Garnier, Director of the *Ecole speciale de commerce*, who had reviewed *What is Property?* in Guillaumin's *Journal des Economistes*, pointing out, incidentally, that the author might have won the readership the book deserved had he not placed his provocative conclusion – Property is Theft – on page one of his book.

In a letter to Garnier (22 February 1844) about that review, Proudhon sketched his idea of revolution as a continuous, 'natural' process: '... certain ideas destroy development.' Religion, rationalized, becomes philosophy; royalty evolves into democracy; and so it will be with property. This process he calls metamorphosis, and there is no reason why it should alarm any man of sense and goodwill. But:

There is *someone*, as the newspapers say, who does not want that fact published – *someone* who wants royalty to remain royalty, property property; who, to that end, sets public opinion working against change, making the magistracy, clergy, industrialists, teachers, the armed services and the Proprietors accomplices in his culpable pretentions. And it is to resist that *somebody* that, from time to time, I meddle in writing; and now if, under my pen, social science wears a *sans-culotte* face, whose fault is that?

Guillaumin and Garnier were members of an informal club, based on the *Journal des Economistes*, which Proudhon calls the coterie of the economists; he was soon to be gathered into that fold, but turned out to be more like a wolf than another of the sheep.

It was Proudhon who took the initiative in making Garnier's personal acquaintance: Garnier told Sainte-Beuve that one morning he was at his house in Montmartre, waiting for a workman to come and install a new stove, when a broad-shouldered man dressed roughly and wearing a flat broad-brimmed hat walked in without ceremony:

Garnier: Good day to you. I've been waiting for you impatiently. You must be the stove-setter I sent for.
Stranger: (strong Jura accent) No. I'm Proudhon.
Garnier (aside): *Sapristi!* (Aloud) You're welcome. I must apologise, but as a philosopher yourself you'll admit it is very easy to confuse a philosopher with a stove-setter.
Proudhon: Certainly, certainly ...

Garnier having introduced Proudhon to the coterie of the economists, their publisher, Guillaumin, suggested that he should write something for the *Journal des Economistes*; and that he might be interested in publishing Proudhon's next book. In moments of expansiveness, rich publishers, indulging the pleasure of patronage, are occasionally led into making proposals to authors which they later bitterly regret, and such was to be Guillaumin's fate. However, the contribution to the *Journal* was reassuring, a paper entitled 'On the competition between railways and inland waterways', a subject on which Proudhon was by then an expert. He came down firmly on the side of the waterways and pleaded the cause of the Rhone–Rhine canal. Two years later, in another connection, he was able to show that government agencies were paying up to *five times as much* for the transport of grain as they need have done; and that had waterways been used instead of railways, the price of bread all over eastern France could have been reduced by 50 per cent.

Despite all the difficulties which Proudhon had in finding publishers for his work, even late in his life, there was no grateful humility in his negotiations with Guillaumin. He required an undertaking that he would have absolute freedom to state his own opinion, and to criticize other political economists, however eminent, which meant that he would be attacking other authors on Guillaumin's list. He made one concession: he would confine himself to polite academic language; a wolf might as well have promised to bleat like a lamb.

*   *   *   *   *

It was in July 1844 that Proudhon first made Marx's acquaintance. Forced to quit Germany, Marx came to Paris and there was introduced into a secret society of German emigrant workers called the League of the Just, later to be transformed by him into the Communist League. He also took the initiative in meeting a number of French socialists. It is probable that in the course of their night-long talks during which, according to Marx, he 'infected' the Frenchman with Hegelian philosophy,[7] he made it clear to Proudhon, as he did to Louis Blanc, the prophet of cooperative socialism and author of *L'Organisation du Travail* (1839), that the Germans still looked to France for a revolutionary lead.

Their points of view were far apart, Marx being dedicated to the idea of political revolutionary action while Proudhon thought that property could be destroyed only by an economic association of the workers which, by taking the task of production away from the proprietors, would cause property to wither away of neglect. Yet each must have given the other the impression that there was enough ground common to both to enable them to work together. Marx later said of these talks that he and Proudhon formed a sort of alliance, though not a particularly cordial one; and even two years later Marx, as will appear, was inviting Proudhon's cooperation.

In October 1844 Proudhon wrote a letter to Ackermann which tells something of the degree of his involvement in the socialist movement as a whole:

What is now called the *socialist party* in France is beginning to be organized. Already several writers have set their hand to the task: Pierre Leroux,[8] Louis Blanc, several others of whom you will have heard,[9] and your friend, albeit unworthy. The people undertake to provide means and propaganda; from us they ask only that we teach them, and set the example of union. Georges Sand has wholeheartedly adopted our ideas. The makers of novels and scribblers of serials, without really committing themselves, deign to make our ideas fashionable by exploiting them. And when the contradictions of Democracy [he means parliamentary government] and *Communauté* [he means the idealistic socialism of Saint-Simon elitism, Weitling's utopianism and the Fourierist communes or phalansteries], have been exposed, and they have gone to join the Utopias of Saint-Simon and Fourier, then Socialism, raised to the level of a science, Socialism which simply *is* political economy, will seize upon society and launch it towards its ultimate destiny with irresistible force. That moment cannot be long delayed; and then France will irrevocably take its place at the head of all mankind.

That intrusion of patriotism is characteristic: Proudhon could never help feeling that France being France, obligations not laid upon the lesser breeds were laid upon her; and some of his German friends had done less than nothing to disillusion him. He was later to be accused, chiefly because of his regionalist and 'federative' ideas of being wanting in the virtue – if it be one which I doubt – of patriotism. But though he might think all peoples equal, there was never any doubt that one people was more equal than the others: France is central, the rest of the world peripheral; and in his relations with foreigners – Marx, Grün, Herzen, Bakunin – there was an element of condescension which is wholly French, and must have been irritating. He was even to claim that Hegel's dialectic was a particular, and simple, case of his own. And here is another of the temperamental differences which separated him from Marx. Marx thought, but did not feel, like a German, a freedom he probably owed to the Judaism he despised; Proudhon might try – with unhappy consequences – to think like a German; Frenchness kept breaking through. The only foreign countries he ever visited were Belgium and Switzerland, both Francophone.[10]

I apologize for the digression and get back to Proudhon's letter.

Socialism is not yet aware of itself: today it is called Communism; there are a hundred thousand, perhaps two hundred thousand Communists. I am working with all my strength to put an end to the dissidences which divide us while at the same time sowing discord in the enemy camp. In turn negotiator, economist, speculator, diplomat, writer, I seek to initiate a centralization of our forces which, if they do not evaporate in verbiage, will sooner or later manifest themselves formidably. I am sure that not half our century will have run its course before society feels our powerful influence. Moreover, all we do is now done by light of day; we no longer conspire, but make use of the measure of liberty which is allowed us.

Thus, Proudhon, like Marx, strove to unify socialism, and it had yet to become clear that their conceptions of it were irreconcilable.

He was now working on his *System of Economic Contradictions* (see p. 81) which as will appear had a Hegelian tang. On his own admission he had never read a line of Hegel,[11] but as early as 1839 there are references to his conceptions of Hegelianism in his correspondence and he was to learn more from Karl Grün (*see below*). In that same letter to Ackermann, Proudhon deplores that the French writers have no dialectic, no 'methodical and accepted' form of argument. He goes on, almost as if claiming that he had no need to read Hegel, since he had arrived at that philosopher's method independently. Well, there have been analogous cases: Newton and Leibnitz, Darwin and Wallace. But the fact is that his use of Hegel is awkward, and his emulation of the Germans he admired was a pernicious influence on his clarity.

One of the Germans to whom Proudhon refers in the above letter was Karl Grün, of the school of German idealistic socialists known as 'True Socialists'. They were about as utopian and impractical as the various schools of French *Communauté* socialists, whose ideology they had borrowed, and their socialism was wholly theoretical and confined to the middle-class. Grün and Marx were old acquaintances, for they, with the lyric poet Emanuel Geibel, had been the stars of the Bonn University Poets' Club in 1835/6, whose members were quite as interested in revolution as in poetry. In due course Marx and Engels were to make destructive fun of these utopians and of Grün himself.[12]

Grün spent a considerable part of the year 1844 systematically investigating all the brands of socialism and social philosophy; and in meeting their exponents. He did not think highly of any of them until he met Proudhon in January 1845, by the simple process of calling on him.

At the time Proudhon had a room in the Rue Mazarine, near the Quai Malaquais, and not far from the house of Victor Considérant the Fourierist prophet, in the Rue de la Seine. Grün says[13] that he had expected to meet there a hard-featured, black-haired man of forty, reserved, even suspicious, his brow furrowed by cares and by deep and difficult meditation, yet the whole countenance shedding a light of benevolence – the style is Grün's not mine. But that he was determined to get past the barrier behind which, surely, that 'wounded spirit' must have taken refuge.

For how could I suppose that the author of *What is Property?* and *Letter to M. Considérant* for which he was haled before the Doubs assizes; the sometime compositor for so long immersed in interminable study; the proletarian in search of a social conscience in the service of the proletariat and who, rewarded for his courage by prosecution, had for long years suffered the even more terrible mortification of public disdain; the thinker at once solitary, bold and ruthless – how, I say, could I suppose such a man unembittered by moral suffering?

How indeed? But happily, the supposition proved erroneous: Grün describes Proudhon as looking about thirty years of age, fairly tall, wiry, highly strung, wearing a rough woollen jacket and with his feet shod in clogs. As for his surroundings, a student's room – bed, shelf of books, copies of the *National* and an economics journal on the table. Then, as for his manner, within five minutes they were engaged in a dialogue so warm and so eager that Grün scarcely had time to realize how wrong he had been to expect reserve.

An open countenance, a brow wonderfully expressive, remarkably fine brown eyes, the lower part of the face rather heavy but altogether in harmony with the rugged and mountainous nature of his native Jura. The speech energetic, round, and often rustic by comparison with the elegant cooing of the Parisians; the language close-knit, concise, with a choice of terms precisely suited to the intention, and from a heart serene, cheerful and assured.

Proudhon, at this first meeting, offered the German one of his parables:

At the time of my first love I was, as I recall, more taken with my sweetheart's freckles than with all the rest of her person. Yet had some other girl had the same freckles I should not, therefore, have been in love with her. It is a general rule of psychology that the lover prefers in his beloved just those blemishes which contradict the laws of beauty ...

On which subject Grün, by the way, says what nobody else does, that Proudhon had a cast in one eye, and that while they talked of Hegel, Feuerbach, Adam Smith, Say, Blanqui, Wolowski, Fourier, Considérant, of List and the Zollverein,[14] of Heine and Karl Marx, he realized that the splendid sculptural line of the brow would not have looked so impressive but for that optical flaw.

Grün claims that Proudhon was the only Frenchman taking the trouble to follow the social, and philosophical developments on the other side of the Rhine. 'It was with our ideas that he charged his guns against Property,' the ideas being those of Kant and Hegel of which, alone in France, Proudhon had 'grasped the innermost meaning'. We know what Proudhon's own view of that would have been, but not even he ever claimed what Grün claims for him, that he had also reached the same conclusions as Feuerbach without ever having read a word of that philosopher.

There is an amusing contrast between this German's first impression of Proudhon and that of the Frenchman, Alfred Darimon, who became his disciple, and who was to help him both with his newspaper, *Le Représentant du Peuple* and with his People's Bank.

Proudhon, having paid a visit to his calf-country in order to see his mother, was again in Paris in the late summer of 1846, trying to obtain from the government an important contract, and 2,000 draught-horses, for his employers. Much of the wheat for eastern France was being carried by rail, a policy intended to establish the new railways on a sound economic footing in capitalist terms (a feat which, as far as I can discover, has yet to be accomplished). By making the long hauls by waterways based on the Rhone–Rhine, Proudhon claimed that the price of bread could be halved. Not even the forty *Députés* whom Proudhon won over to his side could counter-balance the weight of the railways lobby.

Proudhon also had business of his own in Paris: the publication of his *Economic Contradictions*. Darimon, a political economist from Lille, arriving in Paris early in October, saw the book in a bookseller's window and went in and bought it, for he had read Proudhon and, with some reservations, greatly admired what he had read. With the book under his arm he dropped into Baurain's restaurant in the Rue Notre-Dame-des-Victoires, for luncheon.

One of the regular *table-d'hôte* customers noticed the book and opened a conversation about it with Darimon, for the pleasure of being able to tell him that its author was also a Baurain regular, and was at that moment in the restaurant. This useful busybody offered to introduce Darimon to Proudhon.

Darimon describes him: 'A lean, powerful bony body, bottle-green *redingote*[15] reaching to his heels; knee-breeches, blue stockings, laced shoes, a flat broad-brimmed hat, and a waistcoat patterned in loud colours. The speech rough, and, at first, brusque.' Darimon considered certain opening civilities due to a celebrated author whom he admired, but Proudhon, seeing the book in his hand, cut these civilities short:

Proudhon: So you've read my book?
Darimon: No. As you see, it's uncut.
Proudhon: But you talk as if you had read it.
Darimon: That is the greatest compliment you could pay me. For it proves that I have understood you.
Proudhon: If so, you're the first who ever has.

Darimon went on to talk about Proudhon's economic theories until Proudhon, always uneasy about the impression he made as a writer, again interrupted him:

Proudhon: But you are saying nothing about my *Creation of Order in Humanity*.
Darimon: I should have preferred to avoid doing so. I confess that I find it good neither in composition nor as a whole.
Proudhon: Yes, it's a failure. I tried to write an encyclopaedia and found I knew nothing.

From this meeting developed a life-long friendship in which Darimon played the part of disciple and interpreter: his method of interpretation was to play down the scarifying and menacing aspect of Proudhon's writing while playing up and clarifying the substantial philosophical content,[16] a task at which he was so successful that a critical wit nick-named him 'Proudhon's buffer'.

Darimon must have been one of the first to learn that Proudhon had decided to give up his job with Gauthier Frères, for it was in October that he did so. He was, he told his friends, weary of being under the yoke of service and wanted to be his own master if only of 'a hut, a fishing-line and a fish-hook'. Time and again he returns to this theme, in one form or another, of the eremitic life, antithesis of the cenobitic life aspired to by the *Communautists* – for obvious reasons I cannot call them communists – whose ideas he deprecated. But there is a hint that this yearning for solitude was not the only reason for wanting to quit his job; there may have been difficulties with Antoine Gauthier, for in one of the letters written at this time he says, 'If ever again I have to bear with patronage, I shall take care to chose a stranger as my patron, who is neither my school-fellow, my disciple nor my friend; a man who never sets foot in my house, who is not concerned about me, and whose home I never enter.'

That seems to speak for itself; but it is also possible that his dealings with the Mutualist workers of Lyon may have become a source of embarrassment to his employers.

Another event which made a change in his way of life occurred in May of 1846; his father died. Writing about this loss to Ackermann, some time later, he says that it had made him give up all idea of ever living in Besançon again. His mother had returned to the village of her birth, to live with her youngest son, now the village blacksmith. Proudhon made her a regular allowance, but otherwise, 'I am now as free as if I were absolutely alone in the world and without family ties, like the High Priest

Melchizadek'. However, it was not until nearly a year later that he completely severed his connection with Gauthier Frères.

*   *   *   *   *

Another important consequence of the publication of *Système des Contradictions Économiques ou Philosophie de la Misère*,[17] was that it put an end to any question of cooperation between Proudhon and Karl Marx. In May Proudhon had received a letter from Marx, then in Brussels, in which Marx proposed that Proudhon become the French link in the international chain of corresponding revolutionary theorists designed to keep all informed of the progress and developments towards the social revolution throughout western Europe: 'This', Marx wrote, 'is a step which the social movement will have taken in its literary expression towards ridding itself of the limits of nationality. And, at the moment of action it will certainly be important for each to know the state of affairs abroad as well as at home.'

Although George Woodcock[18] says that in Proudhon's answering letter of 17 May he 'expressed his willingness to participate in the correspondence', it seems to me that Nicolaevski and Menschen-Helfen are nearer the truth in saying that he declined the offer: for the letter contains so many reservations that, as he must have known, Marx was bound to find it unsatisfactory. In the first place he deprecated the dogmatism of Marx's Brussels Committee; it was, for the time being, still the duty of all socialists to maintain the critical or dubitive attitude. In other words, there was still no agreement even about principles.

In the second place:

I heartily applaud your idea of bringing all opinions to light ... But let us not become the leaders of a new intolerance just because we are at the head of a movement, let us not set ourselves up as apostles of a new religion, though it be the religion of logic and reason. Let us accumulate and encourage protest, stigmatize exclusiveness and mysticism; never regard a question as definitively answered but even when we have used our final argument, begin again, if we must, with eloquence and irony. On that condition I shall enter your association gladly; otherwise – no.

Marx had surely made it clear during their talks in 1844 that he believed the revolution could be made only by force. Now Proudhon picked on the words 'at the moment of action' in Marx's letter, saying that while he had once been of that opinion himself and was still prepared to discuss it, his recent studies had forced him to abandon it; 'revolutionary action' being an appeal to force, is arbitrary and as such a contradiction. For his part he saw the problem as follows: 'to accomplish, by economic means, the restoration to society of that wealth which had been taken from it by economic means.'

In short, political action was the wrong way to social revolution, would in fact tend to inhibit social revolution. It cannot be denied that events have borne out this opinion.

This letter must have set up in Marx the irritation which became acute when he read *Economic Contradictions or Philosophy of Poverty*; and which inspired Marx's riposte, *Poverty of Philosophy*, written in French to ensure that it would be read in France, and published in Belgium.

The *Philosophy of Poverty* is the 'philosophy' derived from the system of economic antinomies or contradictions more familiarly known as capitalism than as 'property'. The corporation capitalism, and mixed corporation and state capitalism of the West (social democracy), and the monolithic state capitalism of the Marxist regimes of the East have, as Proudhon foresaw, continued. They have even, despite technological advances which have saved them from destruction by violence, in some ways exaggerated the evils to which Proudhon sought to put an end. The economic and political system insisted on as the only workable one by the classic economists from Adam Smith and Say onwards – that is the unrestricted 'market' economy and its antithesis, the state-controlled economy – both entailed and entail acceptance of a 'philosophy of poverty'.

Malthus had argued that in humanity's faculty for indefinite reproduction lies a permanent threat of famine; we are still very deeply in the shadow of that threat. Proudhon's contention is that Malthus was mistaken because there must exist a law of equilibrium between population and economic production, and that it is the business of the social scientist to discover it and to show how society could be reformed to conform to it.

The basic 'contradiction' of Proudhon's title, given expression in a characteristic parable, is this: under the property or capitalist regime, *fact* – the system that is – is in direct opposition to *right* – the system that should be. 'Should' in what sense? The answer to this lies in Proudhon's use of the word *droit*, right, which was to become much clearer in a later work, *De la Justice dans la Révolution et dans l'Eglise*. His judgement is not a merely moral one; or, rather, he does not separate 'rightness' in the moral sense from 'rightness' in the sense of functional efficiency. An economic and social system which does not conform to that system of reciprocal forces in equilibrium which is the universal law of the whole creation, cannot work well.

He envisages a vast building site, littered with all kinds of building materials ready for use. Workmen of all the building trades stand ready and eager to begin building. But the architect with the plans has disappeared. Can the economists help? They have a great volume of information stored in their minds: they know the origin and history of every component and what it cost to procure or to make; they know which kind of timber makes the best rafters, which kind of clay the best bricks, what has been spent on tools and wheelbarrows, how much carpenters are paid and how much masons. But they have no plan, no drawing and can only squabble over the purpose and place in the whole of each component part. Every time they try to put the parts together they find that nothing fits, until at last, made desperate by failure, they conclude by denying that there *is* a science of 'building', that is of political economy.

What, in practice, are the crippling contradictions? The division of labour and concentration of workers in factories, without which industrial production would be almost nil, results in the demoralization of the worker as a free and responsible citizen; machines, those marvels of technological ingenuity, cheapen production and at the same time result in over-production creating unemployment and thus underconsumption, a destructive cycle. Competition is essential to the reduction of production costs and to force men to overcome their natural laziness, but results in the oppression of the workers, the ruin of the weak and in its own antithesis, monopoly; taxation, the state's share, is more often than not no better than a scourge comparable in fearsomeness to fire or flood; credit has bankruptcy as an unavoidable correlative. The whole institution of property is so rotten with abuses that trade degenerates into a game of chance in which cheating is allowed.

The social edifice of Proudhon's parable has been abandoned; a mob of people has rushed on to the site, seized the materials, and, instead of a noble city, we have an agglomeration of unrelated hovels deified by property, as if they composed that glorious city.

The philosophy of capitalism is, then, really a philosophy of failure; this assertion is supported by a long series of penetrating and lively analyses. For example, his treatment of the concept of value: every product has two kinds of value, utility value, and exchange value created by trade in utility values. Utility is the condition necessary to exchange; but cut out exchange, and utility value becomes nil. Obviously, the two terms are indissolubly bound together; so where's the contradiction? A producer produces twenty units where last year he produced only ten; he is twice as rich in utility value this year as he was last year. But as exchange value is proportional to scarcity, the more utility value units he takes to market, the lower falls the exchange value. So by enriching himself in utility value the producer may impoverish, may even ruin himself. True, or untrue? Well, at the moment when these words are being written, the world's automobile industry is richer than it has ever been in utility value units, that is to say it has over a million unsold motor-cars on its hands; and is bankrupt.

Proudhon maintains that the reason why value falls in proportion to the rise in production is a 'primitive fact' which there is no point in arguing about. The only judge of utility, that is of need, is the buyer's opinion; so demand alone creates value however much material and labour have gone into the making of a product: '... three years of good grain harvests in certain provinces of Russia means a public calamity ... three years of abundance in the French vineyards means a disaster for wine-growers.'

Considering the socialist solution, he finds it won't do, unless at the price of liberty. The contradiction in question is one of the inconveniences of liberty – freedom of trade entails arbitrary prices. You could prevent this commercial arbitrariness by socialist means only by accepting administrative arbitrariness. Yet the consequences of this freedom are intolerable, including as they do trade wars, unsaleable stocks, trade recessions and slumps, import restrictions, murderous competition, wage restraint and wage-cutting, price controls which have never been known to work, enormous inequalities in wealth, and chronic poverty. From all this it emerges that we have to accept that antinomy, contradiction, is the essential character of political economy.

The most important question we have to ask as we go on from there, is this: is there no other way of arriving at the value of products in the social context? It is important because for as long as men have to work for a living and wish to work in freedom, justice in exchange must be the condition of brotherhood and the basis of any working association; but without a determination of value, justice in exchange is virtually impossible.

Value is the measure of the proportion of each element to the others in the mass of society's total wealth; the problem is to arrive at that proportion, if you reject the capitalist philosophy of poverty. Consider now, these propositions: every product represents a quantity of labour; labour being common to all products, any one can be exchanged for any other. Now subtract the element 'labour' entirely. What remains are utilities which, being unstamped with any economic character, any 'human sign', are mutually incommensurable and therefore, logically, inexchangeable. From which it follows that 'labour is the principal of the proportionality of values'.

In demonstrating the effect of the contradictions he is studying, Proudhon takes, as one case in point, the positive correlation between the growth of machine industry and the growth of poverty in England. In 1801 the population was 8,872,980 and disbursements under the Poor Law £4,078,891; in 1818 population had grown to 11,978,875 and the Poor Law was costing £7,870,801. By 1833 population stood at 14,000,000 and Poor Law payments at £8,000,000. So, then, after thirty-two years of progress in industrial technology the indigence of the unemployed poor was costing every Englishman 2 shillings and two-pence ha'penny *more* per head per annum than before that great technological advance. The richer we grow, the more poverty we have. 'Machines promised us an increment of wealth. They have kept that promise and at the same time endowed us with an increment of poverty; they promised us liberty. I shall prove that they have brought us slavery.'

When the producer is an independent artisan a tool is a useful exten-sion of his own hands; to that artisan a machine is a tool by which he is not diminished but increased, since he is stronger and quicker by the strength and quickness of the machine. But with the advent of capitalism the case is different: now the capitalist is the producer, and his tools are symbiotic creatures each composed of a man or several men, and a machine: the free artisan has been degraded to the level of a machine; he is a slave.

One may be tempted to retort that there has been progress since 1850. There has indeed: capitalism, carrying advanced industrial technology, has spread from Britain to the whole world, in certain parts of the world being transformed into the state capitalism commonly known as com-munism. It has had precisely the effect which Proudhon foresaw that it must have; it has given an enormous increment in wealth, in material well-being; by so doing it has provoked an equally enormous increase in population; and has given us an enormous, a colossal, a probably unmanageable increment in poverty and slavery. I have no fear what-ever of being contradicted when I say that there are at least ten times as many people living in misery in the last quarter of the 20th century as there were in the middle of the 19th. And where, for example in the USSR, the socialist solution, instead of going to the root of the trouble and avoiding the fatal contradictions of the system, institutionalizes it by substituting the state for the private capitalist, driving out Satan by Beelzebub, slavery, in all but name, is universal.

With the advent of the factory and of machines, Divine Right, the principle of Authority, makes its entry into political economy. Capital, the Boss, Privilege, Monopoly, Limited Liability, Shareholding – in a word, Property, these are to economy what Office, Authority, Sovereignty, Statute Law, Revelation, Religion, in a word, God, cause and principle of all our miseries and all our crimes are in the context of Political Power ...

This is a characteristically Proudhonian intrusion of God into an argument about economics. The reason for it is clear – he was attacking the whole principle of authority, by which the liberty, dignity and initiative of the individual human being is degraded and denied and of which he believed Divine Right to be the *ultima ratio*, inherited by parliaments from kings and from parliaments by soviets. What he has perceived and analysed is the phenomenon now called alienation. And the remedies put forward by the leaders of the left, by Louis Blanc and Auguste Blanqui, ranging from payment and retraining of the unemployed, to communist takeover, all had, from Proudhon's point of view, the same fatal flaw: they fell back on authority, on the state, on Divine Right:

To go cap in hand to the Government and ask them to take such an initiative is to do what our peasants do when, seeing a storm approach, they start praying to God and invoking their saints. Governments, it cannot be too often repeated, are the representatives of Divinity; I almost said, the executors of celestial vengeance.

Then there is the sacred cow called competition: 'Competition inevitably destroys competition.' Example: the French government, persuaded by the English to adopt absolute freedom of trade, refuses special measures to help the French merchant-marine to compete with the English merchant-marine in which wages and conditions are such as no Frenchman would tolerate: the result of this free competition is an English sea-carrying monopoly: cheap freight charges depress the wages paid to seamen, and in due course the English monopolist shipowners can both pay wages as low as seamen can be forced to work for, and charge freights as high as the traffic will bear. So, once again, a contradiction: competition, essential to freedom in industry and trade, is also fatal to it. And, also once again, the socialists have got the remedy wrong:

The communists in general are under a strange illusion: fanatics of State power, they claim that they can use the State authority to ensure by measures of restitution, the well-being of the workers who created the collective wealth. As if the individual came into existence after society, and not society after the individual. Furthermore this is not the only case in which we shall find the socialists unwittingly dominated by the very regime they protest against ...

The communists were not even able to dismiss the principle of competition as pernicious: all that Blanc, Blanqui and company could do was to call semantics to their aid, and rechristen competition emulation. Any readers who are sixty or over will perhaps recall the name of Comrade Stakhanov, and its significance in this context.

Competition, says Proudhon, is the only means we have of fixing the value of products, for where there is monopoly the price is arbitrary. It is, therefore, necessary as a means of calculating fair shares, and, as such, to the advent of equality. The alternative, guarantee of work and wage by the central authority, would result in 'an immense relaxation succeeding to the ardent tension of industry', a fall in real values below nominal values, and very serious inflation. Proudhon has no time at all for the theory that the nobility of labour is sufficient motive for keeping men hard at work. It is impossible to make factory-work attractive; but even if you could, it is impossible to separate the idea *work* from the concept of utility: work for work's sake is nonsense. 'When men seek in work only the pleasure of the exercise, they are not working, they are playing.'

In writing, he says, style for style's sake produces sterile literature; love for love's sake, onanism, pederasty and prostitution; art for art's sake, monkey-tricks, caricature and a cult of the ugly. Man can be persuaded out of idleness only by need, and the surest way to extinguish man's genius is to deliver him from solicitude. On all these counts, competition is essential; but, just as surely, it is destructive of liberty, can be shown reducing whole provinces to destitution, increasing instead of reducing the costs of production, substituting gambling for right; and everywhere maintaining a state of fear and suspicion among mankind.

The same element of contradiction or antinomy is as clearly demonstrated in the cases of taxation, of credit, of the growth and decline of populations. For example, in one part of Proudhon's treatment of the case of taxation, he has already asserted that a graded income-tax is unjust since it requires more from the rich than from the poor but gives them no more in exchange. But any system of taxation which is proportional to income is a monstrous injustice. He supposes that the taxpayer with an income of 1,000 pays 125 in direct taxation; that is, he pays forty-five days' work to the state. The man with 10,000 a year pays ten times as much as the man with 1,000, that is he pays 1,250 in tax, that is also forty-five days' work. In other words, both parties are taxed equally regardless of the fact that paying his taxes may cost the poor man the bread out of his children's mouths. Cruel and iniquitous but 'If the proletarian starve not to nourish Caesar, then what will Caesar eat? And if the poor cut nothing from their coats to clothe Caesar's nakedness, then who will clothe him?' Taxation of luxuries? Absurd: in the first place only the taxation of universal necessities can produce the huge revenue Caesar requires; in the second place, to tax the finest products of an advanced culture, is to tax progress in refinement, that is to tax civilization itself.

The fact is that the state, by its nature and constitution, can do nothing for the poorer classes, the great majority. It may, in theory, be the instrument of the collective power, created by society to mediate between labour and privilege; but, unavoidably chained to property, it is unavoidably directed against the proletariat and cannot help itself. Welfare legislation? It is no more than a manifestation of the social vice of pauperization. Proudhon demands for all men absolute freedom, and that means absolute independence, whereas welfare legislation creates a society of economic invalids. In no circumstances must men be left to rely on the charity, any more than they should submit to the dictates, of authority.

*   *   *   *   *

It was by this repeated return to the idea of authority, manifest as the state, as the root of all evil, the idea in which, as I have said, Godwin foreran him, that Proudhon, in his *Philosophy of Poverty*, gave the greatest offence. It should be borne in mind that in 1850 the majority of educated, as well as uneducated Europeans and Americans had and practised a religion based on the Bible, and really did believe in a personal God who had created the world about 6,000 years ago. The implications of geology, as of German criticism of the Bible, were being faced by only a tiny minority of thinkers, and Darwin's *Origin of Species* was not published until 1859. There were, of course, atheists; but Proudhon was not one of them. He refers as a matter of course, to the whole past of the human race as sixty centuries long. He did not refuse to believe in the existence of God; he hated God as man's implacable enemy, source of that authority in which all evil had its roots. No question, however, of condemning out of hand the whole political past:

Religion, consecrating by Divine Right the inviolability of the ruling power and privilege, gave humanity the strength to continue on its way and to work through its own contradictions. It was necessary that someone suffer in order that mankind be cured; and religion, consolation of the afflicted, persuaded the poor to bear that suffering.

But now the time has come for change, the medicine is working and the cure is almost accomplished:

O ye people of workers, you the disinherited, the proscribed, vexed, imprisoned, scourged, judged, executed, know ye not that there is a term even to the patience and devotion of the poor? Will you not now cease to lend your ears to those mystical orators who bid you pray and wait, preaching salvation anon by religion, now by the State, whose sonorous and vehement words hold you spellbound? Your destiny is an enigma to which neither your physical strength, nor your moral courage, nor the illuminations of zeal, nor the exaltations of sentiment, can give you the key. They who tell you otherwise deceive you, and all their fine orations serve only to delay the hour of your deliverance, now about to strike. What can enthusiasm, sentiment, vain romanticism do when at grips with necessity? To overcome necessity, look only to necessity, nature's ultimate argument, pure essence of both matter and spirit.

The ancients, says Proudhon, accused human nature of being guilty of all the evil in the world, and Christianity followed suit, damning our kind as criminal *ab ovo*. The modern philosophers, beginning with Rousseau, repudiate the charge: man is born good; society depraves him. A distinction without a difference, says Proudhon: collective man becomes the criminal. The socialist solution is to dethrone God and enthrone Man; that is, to replace Providence by Providence. The radicals may damn the Church and the Pope, yet they fall over each other in their eagerness to proclaim belief in a divine providence, or to make a new one.[19] What is the point of dethroning God, if you then replace him by the state?

Alas, in challenging his fellow-men to dispense with Providence, with an inexhaustibly rich if mysteriously whimsical Provider, and to face the prospect of fending, in complete freedom and responsibility, for themselves, Proudhon challenged them too hard. We have seen how the Russians, rid of God, deified the state, and how Marx notwithstanding, that very practical politician Joseph Stalin re-established the Church as a buttress of this new idol, thus demonstrating the truth of Proudhon's insight. If Marxism has triumphed, rather than the libertarian, responsible socialism of Proudhon, it is because men have not yet found the courage to be free. Even in the West, boasting of freedom, we dare not be free, but now treat the state exactly as we once treated Providence. We look to it for welfare (give us this day our daily bread); we talk of what we sacrifice to it of our wages and of its rightful own. We concede to it treasure (the earth is the Lord's and the fullness thereof); and power over us, colossal privileges, as to an Almighty. We allow it to regulate our morals, put us in bondage, and even to take away our lives.

Now Proudhon asks who, if man be innocent, is guilty of those economic antinomies which have resulted in an almost inconceivably terrible burden of suffering? If God exists, then God must be guilty. The atheists deny the existence of God on the very grounds that, if he existed, he would have to be so hideously wicked and cruel to have treated men as he has, that it is absurd to suppose that he *does* exist. Proudhon cannot accept that argument: the existence of a pot does, after all, imply a potter. He asks: 'Can God make a round circle and a rectangular square?' *Answer*: Of course he can. *Question*: 'Would God be culpable if, having created the world according to the rules of geometry, he put it into our minds or even allowed us to believe through no fault of our own, that a circle can be square, a square circular, with all the consequent evils?' *Answer*: Of course he would.

But that, precisely, is what God is guilty of. Man, ignorant, blind, groping wretch though he be, even man has discovered that well-being in freedom can be attained only by reconciling antinomial ideas which, being each taken as an absolute, were bound to plunge us into an abyss of misery. What even we have learnt, God must have known all the time, yet he did not warn us, did nothing to correct our judgement, abandoned us to our own imperfect logic. In short, God is the great enemy of mankind; God and Man are antinomies. 'Whatever be our crimes, it is not before Providence that we stand guilty; and if there be One who, before us and more than us merits damnation into Hell, that One is God.'

It is clear to Proudhon that there is a law, a perfect order, in the universe: and that, to that law, man is submitted and must conform. But he has first to discover its nature; and he alone can do so, nobody can help him, least of all his enemy, God. There will be hundreds of generations of struggle, man will devour man, wade through the blood of his own kind, before he is reconciled with the universe. And let no free man for a moment entertain the cringing, humiliating belief, taught by the Churches, that man cannot be expected to behave well but for fear of the Lord, or his successor, the state. So far is the fear of the Lord, of authority, from being the beginning of wisdom, that the first duty of any free and intelligent man is to put the idea of God out of his mind and conscience. For God is essentially hostile to our nature and we are in no way accountable to or dependent on His authority. If we are learning, it is despite Him; if we are moving towards a state of well-being, it is despite

Him; if we are creating a workable social order, it is despite Him. Every step forward in our progress is a victory in our war with God.[20]

Far from being impenetrable, God's ways are clear; He has constantly betrayed, insulted and tortured His creatures; God is stupidity, cowardice, hypocrisy and lies; God is tyranny; God is poverty; God, in a word, is Evil.[21]

Therefore I deny the supremacy of God over man. I reject His providential government whose non-existence is proved by mankind's economic and metaphysical hallucinations which have entailed the martyrdom of our species. I decline the jurisdiction of the Supreme Being over man. I strip Him of His titles as father, king, judge, good, clement, merciful, saving, rewarder and avenger....

So much, then, for man's point of view; but what of God's? He is anti-human, and in the game for winning which the prize is command over the universe, His cards are spontaneousness, immediacy, infallibility and eternity; while man's are foresight, reason, flexibility and finity. Man moves, God rests.[22] Thus although, in the heat of battle, Proudhon abuses the Enemy in intemperate language, he does not really blame God. He cannot help His nature; He cannot help being man's contradiction.

If I have given a great deal of attention to Proudhon's attack on the ideas of God as authority and God as providence, it is for a good reason. The revolution to liberate mankind into an absolutely just society of absolutely free and responsible men, would be impossible until two false principles had been utterly and for ever repudiated: authority and providence. Men could not possibly be just and free unless they relied on nothing and nobody but themselves, and the validity of their contract with each other. There can be no doubt at all that this lonely and tormented man was agonizingly aware of the danger implicit in authoritarian socialism, whether of Marx and his Germans, of Louis Blanc and his state-patronized cooperatives, or of Auguste Blanqui's communism. Far from liberating man, authoritarian socialism, with its insistence that the proletariat should not destroy but should take over the state and make it the agent of universal provision, would leave the workers more chained to authority and providence than ever, not free men, but irresponsible, welfare-maintained paupers, serfs to the Will of the People which could be no more than the Will of the Bureaucracy.

Because, in his letter replying to Marx's invitation to become the Paris correspondent of the Brussels committee, Proudhon had announced the forthcoming publication of his *Système des Contradictions Économiques ou Philosophie de la Misère*, Marx read the book as soon as it appeared, and immediately recognized in it that kind of anti-systematic, anti-authoritarian, anti-dogmatic libertarian socialism which offended all his deeply conservative convictions. He immediately set about demolishing it. In a letter (8 August 1847) to the German poet Georg Herwegh, he had complained that he was being reproached for writing too much in French and too little in German. But his *Misère de la Philosophie* was written in French so that it should be accessible to Proudhon's readers and published in Brussels and Paris (1847).

I confess that I find it impossible to decide whether Marx simply failed to understand Proudhon's book, or deliberately misrepresented it. He was furious at Proudhon's rejection of state capitalism as the socialist solution. He was temperamentally incapable of sympathy with Proudhon's use of intuitive insights, with his rejection of dogma, with his reliance on the value of conscientious doubts, with his fear and hatred of authority. He was equally unsympathetic to Proudhon's reliance on Mutualism – free contract between free men each conceding only the barest minimum of initiative to the complex of mutualist associations – and to his rejection of political means to revolution. To my mind the only part of Marx's criticism which has more substance than spite or latter-day scholasticism, is that passage in which he is either mocking Proudhon for not being familiar with, or accusing him of failing to acknowledge while appropriating, the socialist application of David Ricardo's labour theory of value.[23] The passage is as follows:

Whoever is even slightly familiar with political economic movement in England cannot be ignorant of the fact that nearly all the socialists of that country have, from time to time, proposed the *egalitarian* (that is to say socialist) application of the Ricardo theory.

Marx then draws Proudhon's attention to a number of English socialist works as cases in point. This is singularly unimportant, not to say petty: the fact was that a scientific discovery made for English readers by Ricardo, William Thompson, and others, was made for German readers by Robertus who later accused Marx of 'pillaging his work'[24] when he wrote *Das Kapital*. Most discoveries are the work of many men who have, over a certain period of time, been leading up to them. It is hardly surprising if they are made at about the same epoch by more than one thinker: nobody has ever suspected Newton and Leibnitz, Darwin and Wallace, of stealing from each other.

The spirit in which *Poverty of Philosophy* was written can best be conveyed by quoting briefly from Marx's foreword:

M. Proudhon has the misfortune to be singularly unappreciated in Europe. In France he has the right to be a bad economist because he passes for being a good German philosopher. In Germany he has the right to be a bad philosopher because he passes for being one of the most powerful French economists. We, in our quality of both German and economist, have felt bound to protest against this double error.

Since then no good Marxists have had to think about Proudhon. They have what is mother's milk to them, an *ex cathedra* judgement. For the essence of Marxism, as of the Christianity it succeeds, is authority.

*   *   *   *   *

A little has already been said about Proudhon's conservative, not to say reactionary attitude about women, and there is more on the subject in Chapter 13. He began his own courtship in a very strange way probably because, having always treated the passion of erotic love with contempt, his *cudot* would not permit him to admit that it ever had any power over himself. For what, but the erotic drive, can explain the conduct described below? And yet, since it is Proudhon we are dealing with, I could be quite wrong: perhaps he really was like Miss Beale and Miss Buss in the schoolgirl verses and saw in the young woman he pursued no more than the radiantly healthy, robust, simple-minded and therefore biddable, mother for the children he wanted.

Being again in Paris on business for his firm and with his publisher early in February 1847, he saw a girl in the street, followed her home, and for some days observed her comings and goings. He waylaid her one morning, apparently without alarming her, and got into conversation with her. Having learned her name and elicited some other information about her, without saying a word about himself or even telling her his name, he made her a proposal of marriage. We do not know how she dealt with it; only that she agreed to receive a letter from him by collecting it at the post office.

The girl's name was Euphrasie Piegard, twenty-four years of age, sixth and last child of artisans, braid-makers (*passementiers*), in a small and far from flourishing way of business. At a critical point in Euphrasie's education the shop had been almost ruined by a bad debt, and the girl had been taken away from school to save the fees, and to help in the workshop. Hence her lack of education: she could read and figure, and even write, but with great difficulty. Her backwardness had been aggravated by the fact that her mother had, for some reason, perhaps because she wanted no more mouths to feed when the baby was born, taken against her and neglected her: if she was not totally ignorant of cooking and housework, it was no thanks to her mother.

The letter which Euphrasie found at the post office next day must be among the most singular proposals of marriage ever made, and at the risk of losing those female readers who may still be with me, I propose to quote it at length:

Mademoiselle,

I must seem to you singularly eccentric, and you must have found my conduct of yesterday such as could hardly be stranger. To accost in the street a young person whose situation, family and name I did not know, and immediately to propose marriage! Surely, if that be not mad, it must at least be suspect. It is, therefore, as much an explanation I have now to give you, as a declaration of my feelings. . . .

In principle, then, I am resolved to marry and settle down. That being so I reasoned as follows: if I was to take a wife I should, whatever people might say, like her to be young, and even pretty, qualities which to my mind, believe me, neither exclude nor supplement the others. But I felt I had need of a companion to please my eyes almost as much as my heart and mind; and just as a silly or ill-natured woman is not, for me, a woman at all, neither is an old or ugly one.

As for fortune, out of philosophy or, if you like necessity, I hold it cheap. I know what most dowries are really worth and what obligations they impose on a husband; now, I am quite determined to make no changes in my modest ways, from which you will be able to conclude, Mademoiselle, that the woman who marries me will, like me, have to resign herself to modesty. . . . I do not believe that any man who is sure of himself need trouble to take any account of a woman's education. Whereas the working girl, simple, full of grace, naive, devoted to her work and her duties, such, in a word as I perceived the very type in you, commands my homage and my inclination.

Such, Mademoiselle, is my way of seeing in the matter of marriage; it is, perhaps, less rational than romantic, but there it is, it is my fancy and fancy is also a good, a very real good. . . . In a word, Mademoiselle, I should like to obtain from you those general indications which are refused to nobody and which will put me in a position, I do not say merely to appreciate your merits, but to know whether a suitor such as myself would have a chance of pleasing you.

You know my design, Mademoiselle; I told it to you point-blank and without preamble. I should like a wife with your figure, your face, your hair, your physiognomy, your sound of voice, your modest and intelligent air. With those advantages, the only ones which, as yet, I have been in a position to appreciate in you, it seems to me that a woman is bound to be hard-working, gentle, devoted to her husband as you are to your parents; that in all she does she will show good taste; that she will be severe on herself but indulgent to others. Above all I should wish that, the event arising, she be in a position to turn to a trade, without regrets or complaints.

What I should have to offer such a woman would be the love of a man; for me, Mademoiselle, that says all.

I have, Mademoiselle, been addressing you in language very serious, for a lover. I have had the honour of telling you my age, and my habit of mind prohibits the use of less serious language. I should consider myself wanting in the respect I owe you, and dishonour myself, were I to address you otherwise. You must by now realize that I have no intention of binding myself merely on the basis of appearance; and my expressed wish to know you better should prove that my intentions are serious and honourable.

Come, Mademoiselle, dare to tell me, of your own accord, all that I am burning to know; show yourself as you are and do not let yourself be intimidated by the eyes of a judge wholly predisposed in your favour. I have here put things on such a footing that you can without danger, without in the least compromising yourself, without falling short of your duty as a young girl, reply to my letter; and if, in a few days, I should happen to be a thousand leagues away from you, there would be no need to abandon our correspondence, it would be an extra guarantee of your safety.

Receive, Mademoiselle, the expression of my sincere homage.

My address: E. Gauthier, rue Mazarine 46.

Proudhon's reason for using his employer's name and not his own is understandable if uncandid: the man who had announced himself to be an anarchist, who called property theft and God the name of evil, was already notorious. He was afraid lest his own name scare off the girl's family, perhaps even herself. He need not have worried: it is doubtful whether the Piegards, who were not reading people, had ever heard of him.

Although Euphrasie had clearly been ready enough to prattle away with surprising freedom to the rather solemn and eccentric gentleman who had accosted her in the street, she either became much more discreet thereafter, or found the task of writing a suitable reply to his letter beyond her; at all events she let him know that her brother Auguste would answer it. A fortnight later Proudhon was obliged to write informing her that he had heard nothing, and inviting Auguste Piegard to dine with him. In the course of March there were a number of meetings, with Auguste as chaperon, during which Proudhon learned all he wanted to know, and revealed his real identity. I suspect that he was disconcerted when the sound of his name was received without any particular emotion. The Piegard family were of the kind to be impressed rather by the fact that Euphrasie's intended was a well-known writer, than to have read what he had written; and to welcome with relief, that waiver of any dowry by a suitor who was, perhaps, richer than he said he was. To do them justice, too, it is quite probable that they were more or less republican in sentiment. They were among the hundreds of thousands of small artisan-shopkeepers who were being brought to ruin by the economic depression which was blamed, with or without justice, on the king and on Guizot's administration.

There were more meetings in April; Euphrasie told Proudhon about her childhood, about the coolness between her mother and herself, and her mother's reference to him as *ta trouvaille de la rue*. His own attitude towards his prospective mother-in-law became reserved and when later in the year, he began to write Euphrasie letters, he left Madame Piegard out of the regards and respects which he sent to her brother and father respectively, until the good woman let it be known that she was wounded by this neglect. He then wrote,

I was enchanted by madame your mother's observation that in sending my respects and regards to your family, I do not mention her. I shall not say that there was some small malice in that; it would be too much of an impertinence. But I am not at all disturbed by her complaint, for it proves to me that Madame Piegard is at last deigning to take an interest in our business. Make her on my behalf all the reparation you can.

In May he had to go to Dijon where he was managing one of Gauthier's lawsuits – he had still not made up his mind to that final breach with the firm. He wrote to Euphrasie, in care of her brother Auguste, saying little about the nature of his business, rhapsodizing over the Burgundian countryside and reproving with contempt the frivolity and laziness of the Dijonais. He was back in Paris early in the summer but in August had to return to his office in Lyon. This entailed a long separation for he wrote that he would not be able to return to Paris until the New Year, being kept in Lyon by 'an important work'. That work was not simply for Gauthier: preparations for the launching of a newspaper, which was to disseminate ideas and pay his bills when he left Gauthier's, and his *Solution du Problème Sociale* were in an advanced stage and needed all his attention.

His hesitation finally to leave his employment *chez* Gauthier was due at least in part to money worries; the interest payments on the debt he had contracted when his printing firm was liquidated was – and was always to be – a burden, and whatever Gauthier paid him it did not enable him to put money by; in a letter to Bergmann written at about this time he says that he has only 200 francs in hand. The allowance he made his mother was another drain. The question was, would he be able to earn enough, as a freelance in Paris, to meet these obligations and keep not only himself, but a wife. On 19 September he wrote revealingly to Guillaumin:

I am leaving the firm of Gauthier Frères where I have been employed for four years. My intention being to settle in Paris I am going to ask you, without beating about the bush, whether you can be of any help to me. I do not know how the French public has received my latest work [*Contradictions économiques*] but a third translation has just been announced in Germany ... This leads me to expect an at least equal success for my next work, but it is a question not of foreign publishers, but of you. What might your own hopes be? Would your new terms be more favourable to me than the old ones? Oblige me by giving me a perfectly frank answer.

He went on to suggest one kind of work which he might do for the publisher: Guillaumin's printing and presentation were, he said, good, but the proof correction was not. As proof-correcting was Proudhon's own trade, and as political economy, in which Guillaumin specialized, had long been the particular subject of his study, might he not be of use there?

I am confident that being reasonably competent in the trades of typography, haulage, accountancy, political economy, literature and philosophy, I should be able to earn my living. But the last four years have left me quite out of touch, and to make my way back into the world I need friends. It is in that quality that I take the liberty of addressing you ...

That address was not in vain: Guillaumin offered to pay for the next book page by page, as the MS was delivered; and to buy from Proudhon any articles he cared to write for the *Journal des Economistes*.

As for the newspaper project, *Le Peuple*, as he wanted to call it, he wrote its prospectus – or, perhaps, manifesto is the word – late in October. It was to be:

... the first act of the economic revolution, the battle-plan of Labour against Capital, the central organ of all the operations I am about to begin against the property regime. From critique I pass to action, beginning with this newspaper and I hope that the editing and writing will be as original, as the paper's position is exceptional ...

I shall deal in detail with Proudhon's newspaper activities in the next chapter: sufficient for the moment to say that Proudhon was forestalled in his efforts to bring out a popular socialist newspaper late in 1847 by the appearance in October of a similar venture under the title *Le Représentant du Peuple*, edited by two men, Viard and Fauvety, with Mutualist convictions close to Proudhon's own. When this paper collapsed after a mere two issues Proudhon made contact with the two editors and agreed a merger between the defunct *Représentant* and his own planned publication. Thus reconstituted, the paper made its reappearance in the very month of the February Revolution, 1848, with Proudhon at the head of the board of editors, Viard and Fauvety among the others, and various of Proudhon's disciples occupying leading posts. By April the new *Représentant du Peuple* was being published daily, and immediately became the most brilliant banner of the new radical thinking in Paris, with a circulation – according to Proudhon – of 40,000 by August. But by now the paper was repeatedly being seized by the authorities, and at the beginning of September it was suppressed altogether. It was at this stage that Proudhon made plans to follow it with a new paper called, as he had always intended, *Le Peuple*.

The correspondence between Proudhon and Euphrasie went on but was one-sided: it did not take Proudhon long to understand that Euphrasie found writing difficult, and he begged her at least to acknowledge his letters by sending her card, signed with her hand, so that he could feel that she was there, and reading what he wrote. His own letters began to belie the solemn stiffness and eccentricity of the first one; they grew more affectionate, though he continued to address her as 'Mademoiselle'. Soon they were revealing something of the charm, the warmth, the capacity for playfulness which his friends knew and loved, and his children were to adore, but which his writings exclude except in some of those parables with which he demonstrated his arguments. In October he had from her, at last, a 'good and charming little letter'. I don't think he ever resented her reluctance to write; it gave him another excuse to treat her, though only on the intellectual level, like a child. This seems to have been how he thought a beloved woman should be treated. Her letter evidently said something about the pleasure she had in going to the theatre, and seeing *Le Chiffonier*. He was, he replied, glad that she had enjoyed it; for his part he was nearly always so disgusted by the reviews of plays that they prevented him from going to the theatre; but this was a fault, for when he did go, he enjoyed the play.

In the same reply to her letter, he tells her that he has finally decided to leave Gauthier Frères, settle in Paris, and live by his pen; nothing about the projected marriage, but it was not uncertainty about his ability to earn their living which restrained him. It may be that it needed her physical presence to keep his mind on what he wanted but seemed not to have time for. Or again, he was certain that the Revolution was almost upon them. The agony of mind he suffered then at the near prospect of what he had done so much to provoke was to be described in an extraordinary leader in his newspaper, two years later.

He finally quit Gauthier's, and Lyon, early in November, and went not to Paris, but to Burgille to see his mother who was dying. The Petits Battants house still belonged to the family and there he tried to get on with the work in hand. He wrote to Euphrasie that he could not remain at his mother's bedside until she died, it was imperative that he be in Paris before the end of the year. He does not enlarge on that: maybe he wanted her to think that it was for her sake that he was impatient. The truth was that not even for the old woman he loved and respected more than anyone in the world, could he neglect the revolution. He was aware that preparation to guide it had been altogether insufficient and inadequate, and feared with all his heart that it would be a catastrophe.

Characteristically, in the same letter he prescribes for Euphrasie's migraines a treatment which his mother had used to deal with hers, with all the confidence of an experienced physician: cold baths were sovereign. And with all the confidence of a fashionable hairdresser, urges her to make use of a 'regenerative water' made and sold by one Lob, an 'empiric' with a shop in the Rue Saint-Honoré, as a hair rinse. God knows how he had come by such barber's erudition, but he promises her that, should he be in Paris before she has taken this advice, he will do himself the honour of making her a present of a bottle of Lob's water.

Proudhon arrived in Paris on 12 December and had no occasion to write to Euphrasie again for two years; but it was to her he went for consolation when, five days later, his mother died. Yet he might, with Macbeth, have complained, 'She should have died hereafter'. What were the death of Mme Proudhon *mère* or the consolations, doubtless simple and sensible, of *la future* Mme Proudhon, compared with the appalling situation in Paris? Still, he found time not, indeed, to attend his mother's funeral – let the dead bury their dead – but to write her obituary in his current *Carnet*:

... a woman of brains, heart and judgement, to her I owe almost all I know ... During seventy years she was a model of devotion, abnegation and self-sacrifice ... I hope, should I marry, to love my wife as much as I have loved my mother. ...

Poor Euphrasie! And yet, I have no evidence that he ever made her feel inadequate, except perhaps when she was trying and failing to cope, as his mother would have coped, with his demands from exile. Even then he was patient with her; and aware that, before his own severe judgement, he was guilty of putting her through an ordeal for which nothing had prepared her.

NOTES TO CHAPTER FOUR

1. In France the constitution of 1830 so limited the suffrage that there were only about 300,000 enfranchised out of a population of about 25 million. In the UK, following the Reform Bill of 1832 which left 717,000 enfranchised out of a population of about 23 million, Lord John Russell, speaking for the Whigs, declared that both partisans and opponents of the measure were determined to go no further. In short, the working-class without property was to remain without a voice in government.

2. Engels, F. *Die Lage der Arbeitbenden Klasse in England*, 1845.

3. *Bemerkungen über die neueste Preussischen Zensurinstruction*; it was published in Switzerland in February 1843.

4. Ruge, A. 1846.

5. 'Zur kritik der Hegelschen Rechtphilosophie', *Deutsche-Franzoschiche Jarbücher*, February 1844.

6. Proudhon would allow, *eg*, a farm landlord payment for any work he does to put the land in condition to be farmed and so maintaining it, but nothing simply because he owns it. Similarly, the landlord of a house should be paid for keeping the house in good condition, but nothing for merely owning it.

7. Letter from Karl Marx to J. B. von Schweitzer, February 1865.

8. Pierre Leroux, editor of the Saint-Simonien newspaper *Le Globe* and originator of the slogan 'From each according to his capacities, to each according to his work', was the first to see society as divided into two mutually hostile classes, bourgeoisie and proletariat.

9. Herzen, Marx, Cabet, perhaps Lammenais though he despised him, and possibly Georges Sand.

10. See J-L. Puech and T. Ruyssen's introduction to *Du Principe Fédératif*, Paris, 1959.

11. Letter to Bergmann, 19 January 1845.

12. Engels, F. *Die Wahren Sozialisten*, 1848 and Marx notably *Die Geschichttschreibung des Wahren Sozialismus*, 1847. See, too, McClellan, D. in *The Young Hegelians & Karl Marx*, London, 1969.

13. See S-R. Taillandier's translation of parts of Grün's French reminiscences in *Revue des Deux Mondes*, 15 October 1932.

14. Customs union of the German States formed under Prussian leadership.

15. 'Frock-coat' is an unsatisfactory translation for this peculiar garment whose name derives from the English 'riding-coat'.

16. See, *eg*, Darimon, A. in *Revue Contemporaine*, 15 September 1865.

17. 15 October 1846.

18. See 'The Man of Paradox' in *Anarchism*, 1963.

19. The name of God appears forty times in L. Blanc's *Organisation du travail*.

20. I think it was Julien Benda in *Le Trahison des Clercs* who suggested that only a terrible common enemy could unite all mankind in brotherhood, and that we should recognize that enemy in God.

21. '*Dieu c'est le mal.*'

22. One is tempted to conclude that for Proudhon, God is a female: for do we not here have the Yin – dark, female and negative – and Yang – light, male and positive – of the Taoist cosmology? Proudhon was at war with, but did not blame, God or woman.

23. Ricardo, D. *Principles of Political Economy and Taxation*, 1817; 'That the value of any merchandise is solely and uniquely determined by the quantity of work required for its production.'

24. *Zur Erkenntniss Unserer Staatswirthschafftichen Zustaende*, 1842.

FIVE

1848: The February Revolution

PROUDHON'S LEADING ARTICLE from *Le Peuple*, 19 February 1849, sets the scene for the later months of 1847.

I saw the quarrel between the various shades of opinion within the great constitutional monarchy party growing more and more venomous, while below the theatre of these deplorable disputes, the gulf opening in the very body of society was continuously widened by democratic and socialist propaganda. The Château Rouge banquet, attended by the whole opposition with M. Barrot in the chair, was, for me, the signal for catastrophe.

Posted as I was at the very base of the social edifice, as one of the toiling masses, and being one of the miners who were undermining its foundations, I saw more clearly than did the statesmen arguing up on the roof both the approaching danger and the consequences of the ruin to come. A few more days and, at the slightest parliamentary storm, the monarchy would collapse and with it the old society. The tempest began to rise with the reform banquets. Events in Rome, Sicily and Lombardy further roused the ardour of all parties. Civil war in Switzerland raised feelings to a higher pitch, further inflaming irritation with the administration ...

This passage requires explanations: at the time France had no right of assembly, so that the government could, when it wished, prohibit or break-up political meetings. But a banquet could be passed off as a purely social occasion. The various oppositions to the government of Louis-Philippe organized a series of banquets in their campaign for electoral reform and to get rid of the Guizot administration; another object soon became a bill to legalize political assemblies. The Château Rouge banquet was organized as a deliberate provocation, to test the government's nerve, and to provoke a prosecution which, it was hoped, would become a test-case and lead to a change in the law.

In November 1847 the *Sonderbund* of seven Roman Catholic Swiss cantons proposed to secede from the Helvetian Federation, ostensibly over the question of the Helvetian Diet's expulsion of the Jesuits, actually for fear of the radicalism of the Protestant majority of the cantons. The united citizen armies of the Protestant cantons at once moved to prevent this secession, by force. When the Austrian government, supported by Louis-Philippe, threatened intervention, Oxenbein, the Swiss radical leader, replied that if a single Austrian soldier set foot on Swiss territory, he would invade northern Italy with 20,000 men and liberate it. Austria backed down, and when they heard, the people of Naples rose against the

Bourbons, those of Lombardy and Tuscany against Austria, the *Son-derbund* was crushed and the Revolution of 1848, which spread to the whole of Europe, was under way.

It was a dual revolution: middle-class, in that the bourgeoisie wanted to be rid of Metternich's ultra-conservative continental system, to be free to trade and make profits by becoming everywhere the masters of political power; working-class, and even socialist, in that the 'toiling masses' had by now been taught by anarchist and socialist propaganda to demand a share of that power and a measure of economic justice.

The revolution would not, of course, have been made simply for these ideas: both revolutionary classes were driven to action by the intolerable strains of a long economic depression aggravated by a series of bad harvests: there had been, on the one hand, too many middle-class bankruptcies, on the other, too much chronic unemployment and starvation. Proudhon describes the state of France at the outbreak of the revolution, in *Confessions of a Revolutionary*:

Commerce and industry, sickly and failing for several years, were now in an afflicting condition of stagnation, agriculture burdened by a load of debt, factories and workshops empty by reason of unemployment, warehouses crammed with goods for want of buyers, and the State's finances in as bad a way as those of the private sector. Despite the growth of the Budget which had risen from one billion in 1830 to a billion and a half in 1848, parliament had established that the deficit was between 800 million and one billion. The Civil Service salaries bill alone had risen by 65 millions per annum. The *Bankocrats* who, in 1830, had made a revolution for the sake of *Interest*, who had promised us *cheap* government, and who liked to call themselves economists rather than politicians, the philosophers of Debit and Credit, spent half as much again as the Legitimist government, twice as much as the Imperial government, and that without being able to balance their books.

If conditions were bad in France, in the rest of Europe they were worse: of the two 'liberal' countries, Britain thereafter remembered the decade which was coming to an end as the Hungry Forties; and in Belgium, industrially more advanced than France, unemployment consequently was worse. In the Germanies, Russia and all the nations of the Austrian empire, economic slump was aggravated by an oppressive and stupid autocracy which prevented the bourgeoisie, the peasants and the proletariat from helping themselves to better conditions.

A republican since his schooldays, Proudhon still 'shook with terror at the prospect of the Republic'. He knew that neither republicans nor socialists 'had the key to it or the science of it', so that what he foresaw was not a new and better order, but chaos followed by reaction. In all its aspects, the revolution lived up to his expectations. It was started and ended in violence, which he abhorred; he saw the working-class allow the power which they had won slip from their hands because they did not know how to use it. His own preaching had gone, at least as to its positive side, unheard, although his paper, *Le Représentant du Peuple*, the first number of which appeared on 7 February 1848, achieved popularity. And it all ended, as he had always warned that a merely political revolution must end, simply in the installation of another government to exploit and oppress the common people.

All this he foresaw, as he described in his long *Le Peuple* article:

The Revolution, the Republic, Socialism, were now approaching with giant strides ... I fled before the democratic and social monster whose riddle I could not answer. An inexpressible terror froze my soul and paralysed my mind. I cursed the conservatives who laughed at the opposition's anger, and more bitterly cursed the opposition whom I saw overturning the very foundations of society with incomprehensible fury.... I wept for the poor working people who, I foresaw, would be denied work and sunk in misery for years to come; for all those workers to the defence of whom I had vowed myself and whom I should be powerless to help. I wept for the burgesses whom I saw ruined, driven into bankruptcy, roused against the proletariat, and against whom opposition of ideas and the fatality of circumstance would oblige me to fight, though no man was more inclined to pity them than I was.

Before the birth of the Republic I wore mourning and made expiation for the Republic. Who, having the same foresights, would not have suffered the same fears?

This revolution which was about to blast the political order was the starting point of a social revolution to which no man had the key: against all experience, against that order which had hitherto been the rule in historical development, the event was coming before the idea, the act before the thought, as though Providence was this time bent on striking without warning.

There has surely never been a more transparently honest self-revelation of the state of mind of the intellectual revolutionary suddenly confronted with the crudely material, physical revolution. The prospect of facing the consequences of his own logic – though to do him justice he had never believed that you have to crack people's skulls or cut their throats in order to convince them that they are mistaken – appalled him:

... In this state of gnawing anxiety I revolted against the march of events and dared to damn the inevitable. I blamed the Sicilians for their revolt against a hated master. I was exasperated by the liberalism of the Pope who is now doing penance in exile for his flirtation with reform.[2] I disapproved of the Milanese insurrection and wished the Sonderbund well; and I, a socialist, a disciple of

Voltaire and Hegel, applauded the words of M. de Montalembert pleading the Jesuits' cause before a Chamber of aristocrats. I wished that I had a newspaper in which to wage war on the *National* and the *Reforme* and all the other organs of reformist and republican opinion; and I consigned the editor of the *Presse* to the infernal gods....

In almost every respect Proudhon's attitudes to and aspirations for the revolution, and those of Karl Marx – first in Brussels waiting for the Gallic cock to crow, then in Paris when the Prussian government bullied the Belgians into deporting him, and finally in Cologne – were antithetical. Marx wanted the workers to ally themselves as auxiliaries with the bourgeoisie from whom, at a later stage of the revolution, they would seize power for themselves. Proudhon wanted the bourgeoisie to submit to the workers' 'idea', and, as workers themselves, to accept the substitution of labour for 'Property', and confide in the good sense and generosity of sentiment of the workers' 'science and conscience'. Marx saw the social war as inevitable and creative; Proudhon saw it as avoidable and destructive. Marx saw the conquest of political power by the workers as everything; Proudhon saw it as at best irrelevant to the real revolution, at worst corrupting and self-defeating. Marx was an authoritarian, the friend of God on condition that He be called the state, and His will Historical Necessity, with which concept, borrowed from Proudhon, he replaced the implacable tyranny of the Biblical Jehovah. For Proudhon, historical necessity meant conformity with that equilibrium of contradictory tensions which held the universe together and kept all things in perpetual movement and growth; he was man's friend against the bully-boy God – Authority – State.

$$* \quad * \quad * \quad * \quad *$$

The French population in 1848 was 25 million, of whom 300,000, 1.2 per cent, were enfranchised. A very large majority of the *Députés* elected to the *Chambre des Députés* were either bought-in-advance by reason of the identity of both their interests and those of the tiny minority they represented, with the policies of Louis-Philippe and his first minister, Guizot; or bought and paid for in cash, place or favours. Lamartine, a romantic poet by trade and one of the small minority of perfectly honest *Députés*, puts it neatly thus: 'openly avowed corruption had become one of the State's powers,' a truth superlatively demonstrated in Stendhal's greatest novel.[3]

I have already quoted Proudhon on the subject of the people's economic grievances, but those Frenchmen who did have enough in their bellies had much else to complain of. They resented the king's refusal to initiate revision of the humiliating treaties of 1815; they resented his policy of subservience to London, based on the Guizot–Aberdeen entente; they resented his slow and crafty progress away from the Constitutional and towards the Divine Right sanction for his monarchy; and they resented his policy of sacrificing the interests of France to his dynastic ambitions. It was this last policy which led him finally to put at risk the two merits for which he had been tolerated for eighteen years. Set on marrying his son, the duc de Montpensier, to the Spanish *infanta*, and so securing the throne of Spain for his house, he sacrificed his long friendship with England, which had at least been good for trade and for peace-keeping, and created tensions which might lead to war. Louis-Philippe had become *trop père et pas assez peuple*. As for Guizot, in Lamartine's words, 'his character, mind, talents, errors and even sophisms were on the antique scale'. He treated the very idea that France might choose other masters as inconceivable.

Three men had hundreds of thousands of followers among the unenfranchised working people: Proudhon, Auguste Blanqui and Louis Blanc. But none of these three could have organized his disciples into an effective opposition, or had any influence whatever in the *Chambre des Députés*. On the other hand, none of the opposition factions inside that House, had anything like a real party, much less a party machine, in the country at large. In 1848 France had no Lenin, or Trotsky. Blanqui was not of that stature. Proudhon, who had the temperament for the role, repudiated it, since, for him, to lead or even to create, or allow to be created in his name, a political party, would be tantamount to leading the working-class once again into bondage; and the very idea of 'leadership', the '*führerprinzip*', was abhorrent. As for Blanc, he could have led a parliamentary labour party but never a revolution.

Among the opponents of the firm of Louis-Philippe, Guizot et Cie, for exploiting the French people, Thiers was no tribune of the people, but simply a man who wanted Guizot's job. Odillon Barrot was one of those impressive, statesmanlike political pundits who, like the latter-day British and American liberals, preach liberty without indicting its enemies, and always come down heavily on the side of order when liberty, as is often the case, proves to be incompatible with it.

Lamartine, a republican if he could be an ancient Roman, seems to have lived in the cloud-cuckoo-land proper to romantic poets. His subsequent elevation to leadership would have astonished him had he had a sense of humour. He got the job due to that French taste for apparently stagey drama in crises which, as de Tocqueville warns us, should never be mistaken for insincerity.

Among the men of mark in the *Chambre* only he refused to take any part in the banquet campaign. His personal policy, as stated by himself in his *History of the Revolution of 1848*, a book written in imitation of Latin models in which even the rascals and bores are given noble sentiments and a heroic bearing, was to give France, under God, a government equally acceptable to and respectful of rich and poor, bourgeoisie and workers, based on religion, the family, and property, and attained by a progressive extension of the franchise to produce a 'decent Democracy'. At no point, even when he was thrust into the leadership, does he show the least sign of having understood what was happening, as Proudhon, de Tocqueville and Karl Marx understood.

Berryer, spokesman for the Legitimist opposition, was a loud-voiced windbag tediously eloquent in a lost cause. At the other extreme of the Chamber, Ledru-Rollin had the makings of a leader, but only on condition of finding an organizing talent to make him effective with the people at large.

When parliamentary systems fail to function freely by reason of the predominance of party, as in Britain in the mid-1970s, then the task of real opposition – that is, opposition not to the party in office but to abusive exploitation by political and economic power – falls upon journalists. That is why governments, of whatever political colour, and as soon as they have the power to do so, put the press under censorship if they cannot go to the lengths of putting it under absolute control. In mid-19th-century France the real opposition was so closely associated with newspapers and periodicals that opposition groups were known by the names of newspapers. The *Constitutionel* and the *Courrier Français* were liberal journals which would continue to tolerate the dynasty provided the government was changed; both had done good work in bringing the fruits of the 18th-century *philosophes'* writings to the attention of a wide readership. *La Presse* probably had the largest circulation of any French newspaper until Proudhon's *Le Représentant du Peuple*, and later his *Le Peuple*, broke all records. It was liberal without being revolutionary; Lamartine says that the bugbear of its editors was 'ministerial servility', in other words it wanted the influence of the crown diminished, though Girardin, its editor, was on calling terms at the Tuileries. All the papers mentioned above campaigned for a very large extension of the franchise, and so did Chambolle, editor of the popular *Le Siècle*.

The republican newspaper which was to play a leading role in the

revolution was Proudhon's old and persistent enemy, *Le National*. Some
idea of the abhorrence in which it was held by the establishment will be
conveyed by the fact that Stendhal shows his hero Lucien Leuwen, as a
lieutenant in one of Louis-Philippe's cavalry regiments, threatened with
being cashiered when denounced by one of his colonel's spies for reading
the *National*. This being so, it is surprising to discover that the *National*
was no fire-eater; it seems to reflect the fun which intellectual
revolutionaries, what we used to call parlour-pinks, have with ideas,
rather than serious concern with social and economic facts. Marrast, its
editor, was until Proudhon's advent, the most brilliant journalist in
France, respected for his wit, his regard for logic, his subtle irony, his
horror of vulgarity, his contempt for Jacobinism; and for the literary
rather than journalistic quality of his leading articles, a quality which
must, surely, have been caviare to the general.[4]

The extreme-left, and only socialist, newspaper – Proudhon's, of
course, was anarchist – was *La Réforme*, which reflected the opinions of
Ledru-Rollin and his small group in the Chamber. But, again, one would
have thought that its style made it about as useful as a Fabian pamphlet,
in the matter of popular appeal. Lamartine says that Flocon, its editor,
was 'A man of '89' with 'the accents of a Danton, but repeated in a
political academy'. Nevertheless, it was another focus of revolutionary
violence once the revolution broke out, and the popular cry of *Vive la
réforme* acquired a double meaning.

The only paper to recognize the wholly proletarian character of the
revolution once it started, and de Tocqueville was the only contemporary observer to perceive this on the second day of street fighting, was *Le
Représentant du Peuple*, with its February 7 banner-headline WHAT IS
THE PRODUCER? NOTHING. WHAT SHOULD HE BE?
EVERYTHING. For Proudhon, the proletariat was henceforth a separate, and dominant, estate of the realm, the only one with both the
means and potentially the will to create the just, and therefore apolitical
society of the future.

When parliament reassembled late in 1847 Louis-Philippe's speech
from the throne was provocative. Confiding, like Guizot, in his bought
majority, in the impotence of the Chamber of Peers, in the 'reliability' of
the army commanded by his sons, and the steady support of the *Bankocrats* as Proudhon called them, he stigmatized the political banqueters
as either wilfully blind or hostile to good order. The 'gracious speech'
provoked an angry and aggressive reaction from the opposition parties.
Lamartine's speech stigmatized the government's foreign policy as

'Austrian in Rome, clericalist in Berne, Russian in Cracow,[5] and counter-revolutionary everywhere'. Thiers castigated Guizot for betraying the Swiss and the Italians to their Austrian enemy. And from left to right the opposition, shocked by the hint in the 'gracious speech' that force could be used against the banqueting campaign, called for an immediate bill, as a matter of urgency, to protect the right of assembly.

The immediate cause of the outbreak of revolution was the Château Rouge banquet in the 12th *arrondisement* already mentioned. The government made no immediate move to prevent this assembly, but when Ledru-Rollin called for the National Guard, the bourgeois militia established in 1789, to attend the banquet in the sacred name of the Republic, the government proclaimed the banquet an illegal assembly and warned that the banqueters and onlookers would be dispersed by force. Meanwhile, they were moving troops into and around Paris – Lamartine says 55,000, but 25,000 is nearer the mark – and manning every strategic point in the city. The officer commanding the artillery park at Vincennes received orders to prepare to move guns into position for bombarding the *faubourg* Saint-Antoine, the working-class, socialist and anarchist quarter.

Where, in all this, was Proudhon? Not at the banquets, nor among the orators – he was a very poor speaker anyway. But he and his anarchist associates, for the most part printing workers and skilled artisans in other trades, were attacking both the government and the oppositions as all equally at fault, and that in a style so biting and lively that their *Représentant* was an immediate success. Its positive message was that the only significant revolution is an economic one, and that what the workers had to do was to take their industries into their own hands, reorganize them on Mutualist lines, and simply ignore the politicians and leave them without a hearing. The fatal mistake would be to replace one government by another, for, whatever its colour, it would be oppressive and incompetent to solve any of the real problems; for that was the nature of governments.

According to the comtesse d'Agoult in her *History of 1848*, no newspaper or periodical of the epoch could compare with the *Représentant du Peuple* for talent and originality; Proudhon, she says, made more impression on public opinion from his isolation, than all the demagogues and other journals put together.

Lamartine describes the night of 22 February in a good set-piece, worth quoting:

The night was mute, as in a city which broods upon action. The morning gave no augury of the terrible day to come. None carried concealed weapons, no face expressed anger. Inoffensive crowds of the curious drifted down the *faubourgs* and gathered on the boulevards, seeming bent rather on looking than on action of any kind. Students, always the vanguard of revolution, gathered in their own quarters and then, excited by their own numbers, marched on the place de la Madeleine singing the *Marseillaise*. The people, electrified, took up the song and, following the students, their column growing as it moved, crossed the place de la Concorde and the pont Royal, forced the wrought-iron gates of the Chambre des Députés palace, still deserted, and spread aimlessly through the gardens and onto the *quais*. A squadron of dragoons advanced along the *quai*, broke into a canter, and dispersed the students without meeting any resistance. Then the infantry arrived; the artillery swung into position in the rue de Bourgogne; and the bridge was manned by troops.

The *Députés*, downcast but not uneasy, began to arrive for the day's sitting and were not interfered with. They climbed the steps of the peristyle facing the bridge, the better to observe the growing military force which the monarchy was deploying, and to watch the cavalry push back the first wave of the mob into the rue Royale. Not a shout; not a shot. Just outside the Chambre des Députés palace gates a regimental band was dispensing pacific music, and the contrast between the battle-readiness of the troops on the *quai* and this holiday music, offended the souls and produced discords in both eyes and ears of the citizens.

While Odillon Barrot, as spokesman for all the oppositions, was placing an 'act of accusation' against the government on Guizot's desk in the parliament palace, and Guizot was rejecting it with contempt, the crowds were increasing, barricades were being built, and 'committees of insurrection' were going into permanent session in the *National* and *Réforme* offices, and the secret HQs of the *Droits de l'Homme*, *Les Familles*, Blanqui's *Société Centrale Républicaine*, Barbes' *Club de la Révolution*, and other revolutionary societies. At nightfall the troops camped in the streets but no attempt was made to stop the students making a bonfire of café chairs in the Champs-Élysées. Troops had not penetrated to the republican stronghold in the narrow streets round the Cloître Saint-Mery. A group of left militants disarmed the Batignolles National Guards and burned down their post. Other groups of revolutionaries were out systematically breaking into gunsmiths' shops to arm themselves, and attacking isolated military posts. Louis Blanc and his working-class colleague Albert had nothing to do with this violence which was the work of Blanqui's communists and similar groups of revolutionary militants. Proudhon and his anarchist friends were printing posters for the revolutionary workers, and were helping to build barricades and to man them. But it was only loyalty to the embattled workers which inspired them, for Proudhon saw very clearly that the revolution had no direction, no 'idea' and would therefore accomplish nothing.

Neither the king nor Guizot would listen to the Prefect of Paris, the comte de Rambuteau, who warned that the National Guard, on whose attitude the outcome depended, was not to be relied on. The Guard would wait for what they confidently expected, and what a majority of the *Députés* now expected, the news that the king had dismissed Guizot and summoned Thiers to form a government; in that case, there was nothing to fear. Not even Rambuteau, whose contacts were all among the burgesses, had any idea of the rising anger and determination of the Paris workers, probably because they seemed to have no organization and no leaders. Late on the twenty-third a rumour that the king had capitulated ran through the city, and that night there were illuminations in some streets, cheering and rhythmic clapping, and the mood changed from suspicious watchfulness to high good humour. In fact, the king had sent in turn for Molé, least objectionable of the possible opposition leaders, Thiers, and Odillon Barrot, but, unable to stomach the policies they proposed, had decided nothing.

In any case, the rumour was simply ignored by the militant left – the groups of young men of wealth and family, inspired by republican patriotism and the thrill of a social war, the excited mobs from the working-class *faubourgs*, and from the industrial slums of Clichy, Villette, and the Ourcq canal quarter, led by members of the *Droits de l'Homme* and of *Les Familles*, or by Blanquists, Blanc socialists, Fourierists, Saint-Simoniens; but more than half of whom were Proudhonian anarchist converts.

At about ten o'clock that night, mobs of young middle-class republicans, for the most part students, and much larger crowds of workers, were being harangued by leaders of the *Réforme* group outside the paper's offices; and by Marrast, from the porter's lodge of the *National* offices in the Rue Lepelletier. There seem to have been four or five of these crowds of militants who formed themselves into columns, some of them with something like military discipline. A proportion of them were armed, and after being addressed by their journalist mentors, they moved off towards the Boulevard des Italiens to cries of *Vive la réforme!* and *A bas les ministres!* Somewhere near the Café Tortoni in the Rue Lafitte and the Boulevard des Capucines they joined forces, and, lurid in the smoking flare of many torches, the tricolour flag was raised and cheered. It was there and at that moment, though there was still much action to come, that the Second Republic was born.

The militant people were not marching at random; there was leadership, but, excepting for the somewhat sinister figure of Blanqui, it was anonymous. When the column came to the Rue de Choiseul a detachment of workers armed with sabres and pikes turned off to get round the back of the Ministry of Foreign Affairs which had been garrisoned, while the main column marched on to the front of the same building. There, the way being blocked by a battalion of infantry drawn up in battle order, and commanded by an officer on horseback, they halted.

The first serious loss of life on the revolutionary side was a consequence of bad horsemanship. The officer's horse shying and backing from the flaring torches of the crowd, bolted; the officer lost control of it, and as the ranks of infantry opened to let it pass while he fought to master it, a shot was fired. The soldiers, apparently under the impression that it had been aimed at their officer, did not wait for orders, but opened fire. At a range of a few yards, the volley was murderous. Scores of men, women and children fell, there were screams, shouts of rage, people running in all directions. The most disciplined of the people, in fear of a second volley, yet hardly able to believe what had happened, fell back as far as the Rue Lafitte and then halted uncertainly. Many of the men, as well as women, were in tears, while others screamed curses and threats of vengeance at the troops.

This was the fusillade which forced Proudhon to face the reality of revolution and to set about providing it with that 'idea' which it lacked. But this was no Bloody Sunday massacre of the kind by which the Russian autocracy tried to crush the St Petersburg revolution of 1905; Louis-Philippe was no Nicholas II, dim-wittedly ruthless in the service of the ferocious God he worshipped and of Divine Right. It was a stupid accident: the incompetent horseman commanding the troops burst into tears and sent a lieutenant to the corner of the Rue Lafitte to explain and apologize to the people; an attempt to shoot this frightened and embarrassed young man was prevented by some National Guards who had arrived on the scene. The HQ of the revolutionary crowd was now the Café Tortoni; from there someone was sent to fetch a wagon into which the bodies of the dead were loaded, and as rumours of the massacre, enormously exaggerated, began to run through the city, the crowds reformed their marching column behind the wagon, torches were relit, the tricolour, the red flag and the black flag of the anarchists, raised, and the people started a mourning progress through the city, making halts for speeches first at the offices of the *Réforme*, then at the *National*. A bolting horse and a shot fired at random had changed the goal of the

Revolution; that goal had been no more than a change of ministry, and electoral reform, now it became an end to the monarchy. Here is Lamartine again:

A man standing in the cart, his feet in blood, from time to time raised the body of a woman from the heap of dead, showed it to the watching crowds, then lowered it again to its bloody bed. At that sight the crowd's pity turned to fury and people ran to their homes to arm themselves, and the streets were emptied. Men armed with guns marched beside the wheels of the waggon as they plunged into the dark and narrow streets of the teeming heart of Paris, and made for the Carré Saint-Martin, that Aventine Hill of the people. As they went they knocked on door after door, calling the men to come out and fight for revenge. At the sight of the victims, whose deaths were blamed on royalty, the workers' quarters rose, and men ran to the churches to sound the tocsin, tore up the stone setts in the streets to arm themselves, raised and multiplied barricades. From time to time throughout the night shots rang out, as if to prevent sleep from soothing the city's anger and anxiety; and from steeple to belfry the tocsin bore warning of the morrow's insurrection to the ears of the king in the Tuileries.

Sleepless, the king heard the warning and rejected it. De Tocqueville, indeed, says that while no man was less capable of changing his opinion, none more easily reversed his conduct; and that Guizot was dismissed in two minutes without apology or thanks. But it was not so simple: rather than drop Guizot and reverse his policy, the king would abdicate, but he did not believe it had come to that. A few concessions which could always be withdrawn later should settle the matter. Not for nothing did Stendhal attribute to Louis-Philippe the devious craftiness of a Norman attorney. He sent for Molé again, who ignored the summons; he sent for Thiers who came running and, when he reached the palace, found that Guizot was still there. As if to avenge himself on Paris, Guizot had persuaded the king to appoint the army's beloved and the people's most hated Marshal Bougeaud to the command of Paris. Bougeaud, a 'hero' of the Algerian conquest, had, during the early years of the reign when there were frequent risings against the bourgeois monarchy, treated the working-class quarters of the city like besieged enemy towns. He was an exceptionally able officer and given a free hand, could have crushed the revolution within twelve hours. But Thiers agreed to try to form a government on two conditions: that Odillon Barrot, whom the king abominated, be invited to join it; and that Bougeaud be ordered to make no aggressive move against the people. Louis-Philippe gave in, but kept Guizot by his side. Before dawn Thiers had contrived to placard the city with a conciliatory proclamation, but it came too late, the people took it for a trap, and now wanted blood for their blood; the bourgeois monarchy had exhausted its credibility and, at the very reading of the terms offered, the people went out to recruit more men, to loot the gunsmiths for weapons, and to form combat columns. The students poured out of the Ecole Polytechnique and other schools, embraced the workers, and led them to the centre of the city singing the *Marseillaise* and the *Girondins*.[8]

Since dawn the barricades had been growing, encircling the precincts of the Tuileries with a ring of stone and iron and angry men, with Proudhon among the leaders. The troops waiting for orders on both sides of the Louvre, in the Place du Palais-Royal, and in the Place de la Concorde, were weary and depressed; neither they nor their horses had been fed, and the night had been cold. The National Guard began the day still in two minds; they did not yet join the insurgent people, but neither did they hinder them, and by eleven o'clock that morning some were joining in the cries of *Vive la Réforme* and *A bas les ministres*, and reinforcing the revolution with the authority of their uniforms and bayonets. De Tocqueville says that they were bewildered, and only echoed the popular slogans in 'hoarse and constrained voices'. But, by his own account, when he urged on a battalion from his own quarter that the government had been changed and all abuses would now be corrected, and that it was up to them to prevent the mob from getting out of hand, they replied that they had no intention of getting shot 'for people who had managed affairs so badly'.

In the Champs-Élysées the revolutionaries attacked each of the Municipal Guard posts and killed the guards who, as a paramilitary police intended to enforce order, were hated. An attack on the Palais-Royal, once the home of the Orleans family, forced the infantry guarding it to withdraw to the Château d'Eau to which wounded and dying Municipal Guards had been carried for refuge. The revolutionaries, having seized the Place du Palais-Royal, gave the Château d'Eau soldiers time to get themselves and the wounded out, and set fire to it, while a mob was raging through the palace smashing the furniture and works of art, but doing little or no looting.

The order, originating from Thiers, that the troops were not to fire on the people, left the soldiers no alternative but to stand and be killed, or to withdraw. While this was happening wherever people and soldiers came face to face, Odillon Barrot was out on the streets, escorted by officers of the National Guard, going from group to group and trying to use the respect in which he believed himself to be held to cool the anger of the people by assuring them that their demands had already been met. He went further, saying that if they wanted some other leader than Thiers, himself, for instance, or Lamartine, the king would consent. Lamartine says that the mob began to chant his name, as if calling on him to take over the government, but that they were merely echoing Barrot's suggestion and hardly even knew who he was.

The fact is that by this time the middle-class liberal *Députés* and journalists, unlike the National Guard, had completely lost touch with the revolution and did not understand what was happening. There were three men who did understand: Louis Blanc, who thought that a socialist ministry led by himself and Albert would alone meet the demands of the people; Alexis de Tocqueville, who, however, saw no way of checking the riots; and Proudhon, horrified by the violence, but seeing that the Revolution had now become proletarian. The people were insisting on a government which would create jobs for them, would give the workers work. He had no sympathy whatever with that demand; as he said, 'governments are not designed to give people work'. All his efforts were directed to preventing labour from clambering into the saddle from which they had flung capital. The people had it in their power to bring down the government; let them do so but let that be an end of it, an end to politics. Let them set about creating jobs for themselves by taking over their industries and trades and running them on Mutualist lines. None but the proletariat could help the proletariat, and if they did not do so as Mutualists, but replaced a bourgeois government by a government of labour, they would simply become their own oppressors.

The king and his family were at breakfast in the Tuileries when news was brought by two officers that not only the National Guard but the dragoons and infantry were drifting over to the people. The king changed into uniform, mounted his horse, and supported by the ducs of Nemours and Montpensier, his sons, went out to review the troops drawn up in the Tuileries courtyard and in the Place du Carrousel.

Louis-Philippe, neither soldier nor statesman but an enthroned businessman, had never had the majesty of royalty, but hitherto most people had been willing to behave as if he had. No longer: his troops received him sullenly, and he now heard from the ranks as many cries of *Vive la réforme! A bas les ministres!* as of *Vive le roi!* When he returned to the palace he seized his pen and wrote 'I abdicate in favour of my grandson the Comte de Paris'.

Nothing in the February stage of this revolution is more remarkable than the government's shrinking from blood-letting. Authority is based on force and to refuse to shoot down your own disobedient citizens is to

abdicate. It is extraordinary how quickly the Paris workers sensed the
government's weakness and took advantage of it. Louis-Philippe left the
palace, for refuge in London, leaving Madame d'Orleans, the boy king
her son, and the duc de Nemours, to see if they could save the monarchy
and the dynasty. The duchess, an extremely brave woman, without the
shadow of an idea what this revolution was about or of the people's
temper, set out to drive, under National Guard escort, through Paris to
the *Chambre des Députés*, believing that if she showed their new king to the
Parisians, they would receive him with cheers, and return to their 'duty'.

The *Députés* had been at their palace since eight in the morning, but
not in session: the President (Speaker) had not called the house to order
and was nowhere to be found; the old ministers had put in an appearance
but then taken themselves off. Abdication was expected, and that its
proclamation would calm the city. One group of republicans were urging
Lamartine to take the initiative and form a transitional Regency
government immediately; another was urging the same course on
Barrot. The benches and corridors were crowded, but nothing was being
done; even Thiers, when he arrived pale and frightened by what he had
seen, had nothing to say but, 'Gentlemen, the tide is rising'.

De Tocqueville claims that it was he who found Sauzet, the President,
in an office and persuaded him to take the chair and call the Chamber to
order; Lamartine, that Sauzet did so on his own initiative. A young
Député, Lafitte, rose to propose that the Chamber declare itself to be in
permanent session. The motion was carried without debate but nobody
proposed any other business. 'It was,' says de Tocqueville, 'a crowd
rather than an assembly, for nobody was leading it.'[7] This curious
paralysis can best be explained by Proudhon's observation, confirmed
by de Tocqueville's, that it was by the bourgeoisie itself that the
bourgeoisie was overthrown:

The bourgeoisie vanquished, I do not say by the people – thank God there was no
conflict between bourgeoisie and people in February – but vanquished itself,
admitted its defeat. Although caught unprepared, and full of anxiety touching
the spirit and tendencies of the Republic, it nevertheless realized that constitutional monarchy was over and done with, and that the government would
have to be radically reformed.[8]

The parliament palace was being guarded by troops under the command of General Bedeau, and de Tocqueville blames him for failing to
prevent the revolutionaries from invading the Chamber, which he was
trying to do by haranguing them. De Tocqueville sneers, 'I have never
known another man with a sword at his side with such a taste for making

speeches.' But Bedeau was both under orders to hold his fire, and suffering from that same abdication of authority which afflicted the king and the *Chambre des Députés*.

The *Députés* were still sitting on their benches wondering what they were doing there, or talking in anxious groups, or wandering restlessly about the corridors, when the duchesse d'Orleans, Nemours and the boy king, announced by an officer, entered the Chamber and were given seats. A *Député* named Dupin mounted the tribune and proposed that the duchess be proclaimed Regent: cheers from the Constitutionalists. But the business of the Chamber had by now been taken out of the members' hands. For some time individuals and small groups of working men, some of them armed, had been slipping into the palace and the Chamber from the streets: they were noisy and disrespectful but not violent or even particularly angry. De Tocqueville says that he went across the floor to Lamartine and said to him, 'We are going to ruin. You alone at this supreme moment can make yourself heard. Go up onto the tribune and speak.' To which Lamartine replied, 'I will not say a word so long as that woman and child are here.' Lamartine does not report this exchange; but he had, in fact, made up his mind that there could no longer be any question of the monarchy, and that what they had to do was to proclaim the Republic restored.

The crowd of revolutionary workers was continuously increasing. Sauzet tried to clear the Chamber, failed, then asked the duchess and her son to leave. She refused; she intended to address the house. But she was surrounded by a crowd of curious, rather than hostile, revolutionaries who made no resistance when some of her friends, helped by her National Guard escort, shoved their way through and escorted her to a safer place on the highest benches. Meanwhile Barrot was on the tribune speaking in favour of the Regency. He had scarcely done when a tidal wave of people swept in from the streets shouting *Vive la réforme!* (de Tocqueville: 'Some revolutionary balderdash or other') and carrying tricolour flags, forcing the *Députés* at floor level to clamber up to the higher benches like frightened monkeys.

As no two accounts of what happened next, least of all those of Lamartine, bent on ennobling these events, and de Tocqueville bent on exposing them as a tragic farce, are the same, it is impossible to give an exact account. A number of *Députés* tried to make speeches in the midst of uproar; many more escaped from the Chamber and made their way home. Sauzet tried to adjourn the house by the traditional gesture of putting on his hat, but inadvertently picked up the much larger hat of his secretary, thus effectively extinguishing himself. Only two speakers had anything useful to say: Ledru-Rollin, who demanded in the name of the people in arms and now masters of Paris, the immediate formation of a provisional government of the Republic; and Lamartine, who made the same demand and wanted to call an immediate general election under the rule of manhood suffrage. More people poured into the Chamber from the streets, and in sardonic good humour mockingly pointed their guns at the President and the *Députés*. De Tocqueville is certain that this was mere buffoonery, and that at no time was anyone's life in danger. The duchess and her party were hustled out by National Guards. De Tocqueville felt that 'we were staging a play about the French Revolution rather than continuing it ... a bad tragedy acted by a third-rate repertoire company.'

Lamartine, at the tribune, managed to dominate the crowd by persuading a respected and venerable member, Dupont de l'Eure, to read out a list of ministers who would form a provisional government. The names were received either with groans and insults, or by cheers: it was a sort of popular election by acclamation. But the *Chambre des Députés* was no place for a workers' government. It was tainted. There were cries of 'To the Hôtel de Ville!' which Lamartine, now a prisoner of the mob, echoed obediently.

These events confirm Proudhon's subsequent claims that the people off the streets knew very well who were their friends and who their enemies, and that they had, for the time being, the government of France in their hands. 'What happened on 24 February was the downfall of Capital; on the 25th the rule of Labour was inaugurated.' This is a reference to what we have not yet come to, the provisional government's reckless and fatal undertaking to provide work for the unemployed. De Tocqueville confirms him: he spent the afternoon of that day wandering about Paris and says that he was struck above all by the exclusively popular character of the revolution, and 'the omnipotence it had given to the people, the manual workers, over all others'.

Nothing that Proudhon could write, say or do (nothing that Karl Marx, as is clear enough from his own *Eighteenth Brumaire*, could have done) could prevent the almost immediate abdication of that omnipotence. Because of Proudhon's rejection and repudiation of the idea of organizing his followers into a political party to take office when the time came, the necessary years of preparation had been wanting.

Carried away by the governmental prejudice, the people found no task of greater urgency than that of setting up another government. The power which had fallen into the workers' hands was incontinently handed over to a certain number of men of their choice ...[9]

By his own rule, a government of any kind or colour can only be hostile and pernicious to liberty, can only institutionalize injustice and pauperism. Why then did he, in the next stage of the revolution, take a political hand?

NOTES TO CHAPTER FIVE

1. It is here obvious that Proudhon had never read Feuerbach and, despite his claims, despite his talks with Marx and Karl Grün, had a very imperfect grasp of Neo-Hegelian philosophy.
2. Pius IX, who introduced liberal reforms in the Papal states, shocking even *Punch* which said that he should be called not Pio nono but Pio yes-yes. He repented of his liberalism when the revolution drove him into exile in Gaeta, and was responsible for the not very liberal doctrines of the Immaculate Conception (1854) and Papal Infallibility (1870).
3. There is no tolerably good English translation of *Lucien Leuwen*, which throws a brilliant light on the corruption of the regime and the methods of the Orleanist government.
4. Lamartine sums up Marrast thus: *Sa révolution était le jeu d'esprit d'un coeur bienvaillant de femme*. The fact remains that his harangues on 23/24 February brought about some of the first violent clashes of the revolution.
5. 'Austrian in Rome', hostile to Italian nationalist aspirations; 'clericalist in Berne', favourable to the reactionary Roman Catholic *Sonderbund*; 'Russian in Cracow', hostile to Polish nationalist aspirations.
6. This pattern, the alliance of students and workers, with the students taking the lead, was attempted in the abortive May revolution of 1968.
7. *Recollections*.
8. *Confessions of a Revolutionary*.
9. ibid.

SIX

1848: February's Aftermath

THE PROVISIONAL GOVERNMENT was installed at the Hôtel de Ville with difficulty since it was crammed with armed revolutionaries letting off their guns in the excitement, with bodies dragged in from the streets, scores of wounded, and hundreds of municipal officials, journalists and curious idlers milling about like bees in a disturbed hive. Dupont de L'Eure accepted the Presidency of the Council of Ministers, but being over eighty and far from robust, delegated the actual work to Lamartine who took office as Foreign Secretary. The left-wing's leader, Ledru-Rollin, took the ministry of the Interior. For the rest, most are of no importance in our context. Louis Blanc, Marrast and Flocon had to be given office and were appointed 'secretaries' to the government, ministers in all but name. Blanc, virtually minister of Labour, was installed not at the Hôtel de Ville but in the Luxembourg, as chairman of the Luxembourg Commission charged with the task of solving the unemployment problem.

Proudhon asks why this government, given three months to carry out the revolutionary aims of the workers, did nothing whatever; and he answers his own question – because governments are by their very nature incapable of revolution, are 'immobilist, conservative, refractory to initiative, counter-revolutionary'.

During the first days of its life, however, the Provisional Government was in any case paralysed by popular turbulence. More than a quarter of a million half-starved, workless men and women who had streamed into the city from the *faubourgs* and the *banlieus*, besieged the Hôtel de Ville; waves of angry, suspicious workers swept like a tide into the building, even into the rooms where the new ministers were trying to work, and where they jostled each other for places from which to stare at the ministers as if they were animals in a zoo. Proclamation of the Republic, and the sight of the tricolour floating above the building, did something to calm the people, but there were angry questions: why were not Blanc and Albert, the socialist leaders, at the head of ministries? Why should not every ministry be headed by one of the proletarians who had fought for the revolution in the streets?

As this fear grew that the revolution was being betrayed, windows were smashed, doors broken down, the ministries invaded and there were demands for the immediate deposition of the Provisional Government. Blanc and Albert, while they were not stirring up revolutionary violence, were using the threat of it to force the government to undertake at once the 'organization of labour' – in other words to adopt a socialist policy of nationalization of the means of production and a planned economy. The only practical outcome of this was Blanc's assignment to establish 'national workshops' to absorb the unemployed and compete with private industry.

What, again, of Proudhon? He had helped to build the barricades, and to man them; he had been out on the streets with the people. He had been one of the crowd which stormed the Tuileries, and he had composed and printed posters for the revolutionaries. But it is impossible to escape the conclusion that he could not 'believe' in what he was doing. 'They have made a revolution without ideas. It is necessary to give direction to a movement which is already being drowned under waves of argument.' Some idea of the awe in which he was held by respectable liberals and socialists can be conveyed by quoting Lamartine again:

... Some there were who, by way of revenge for their situation in society, took pleasure in following a certain great sophist in his desperate critiques of that society. This sophist admitted his own audacity; he aspired to the utter ruin of the thinking and political world; he took delight in the prospect of present ruin and future chaos. He was the Nemesis of the old society. He was called M. Proudhon and his advocacy of ruination was at least learned: all the genius which sophism can have, he had. He played with his lies and truths as Greek boys played with knuckle bones.

Proudhon, with his loathing of all governments, must understandably have been viewed as a worm in the bud: and indeed what was he doing involving himself at all? Here, from the current *Carnet*, is his own account of 24 February, very revealing of his state of mind:

I have just been present at the devastation, for one cannot call it a capture, of the Tuileries. The people went in without a blow being struck, after a fusillade in the Place du Palais-Royal in which, they say, the Fifth Legion of the National Guard got a mawling. The king and the royal family withdrew into the chamber. The king is abdicating.

O. Barrot is preparing the regime.

The other side is proclaiming the republic. The conflict is now between the republicans (reds and crimsons), the constitutionals, legitimists etc.

The pacific democracy is offering its services.

There are no ideas in their heads. There is anxiety but the muddle is now inextricable. There's a mob of lawyers and writers, each more ignorant than the others, who will be squabbling for power. No place for me in all that.

Stupidity upon stupidity.

The republicans who've won are calling for a provisional government of fifteen men, the fifteen most suitable! All that is nothing. But the 1815 treaties torn up, republican propaganda, socialism, communism and all the utopias: it will be frightful.

There is one reliable criterion; social economy. The people have this day destroyed property to the value of several millions ... Add to that general unemployment. The 22nd, 23rd and 24th, between four and five hundred thousand men workless. The February revolution has already cost ten million. Today's victory is either the victory of anarchy over authority, or it's an illusion.

As nobody today is in doubt about his own solution, we shall go from experiment to experiment. It will be very costly. Once again the opposition's fault is enormous, incalculable; the sequel will prove it. What could and should have been done by work and study, will henceforth be demanded of the State at the expense of the Budget. What miscalculations! What follies! Who will stop us and enlighten us on this slippery slope?

The Lamartines, Quinets, Michelets, Considérants, the men of the Left, etc. Mysticism, Robespierreism, Chauvinism are in power.

They have made a revolution without an idea.

... The people of Paris is a bull which those who have seen it so often should know better. Less than ever do I believe it made for the representative regime: meetings, clubs, don't suit its temperament.

What can the republican party do? Its only hope is in universal suffrage. The republican party has no men, no abilities. Today I saw Flocon, at the *Réforme*, with nothing to offer but a quotation from Robespierre.

The intellectual poverty of the Paris bourgeois is incredible. The proclamations are meaningless. Here's a résumé of what they're asking for: abolition of the law of September, electoral and parliamentary reform, general amnesty, ... fifteen men chosen by the people for government and a heap of such poor notions. It's a case of who can say the least in the most words.

Tens of thousands of the working men who were trying to push the Provisional Government into a real social and economic revolution were Proudhonian Mutualists. Had his own doctrine of free and responsible men freely associating together for action not been the absolute limit of organization which he would tolerate, preventing political action of any kind, Proudhon would have emerged, as his disciple Michael Bakunin was to emerge, as the leader of a powerful party. As it was, the most he could allow himself to do was to call, in *Le Représentant du Peuple*, on the Paris workers to emancipate themselves without reference to government. Supported only by Charles Baudelaire's *La Tribune Nationale*, he repeatedly warned the working class not to be taken in by the confidence trick of universal suffrage, principal plank in the Provisional Government's platform. That was a device by means of which they could and would be made once again to enslave themselves.

There is, I think, only one possible reason why, in April when the

Provisional Government held a general election to a Constituent Assembly under the rule of universal manhood suffrage, Proudhon, despite his convictions, stood as a candidate. It was in the forlorn hope of being able to persuade both the Assembly and the executive to limit their own roles and leave economic organization entirely free of political interference; in other words to deny the executive the real means to power: money. And since the workers would clearly need an instrument, an economic organ, if they were to make themselves responsible for industry on Mutualist lines, at the same time as he entered politics, Proudhon set about the creation of a People's Bank.

Louis Blanc, Albert and their socialist party, at the head of the Luxembourg Commission charged with solving the problem of unemployment, were putting all the pressure they could on the Provisional Government to adopt as national policy the 'organization of labour'; as will appear, they were so bent on achieving this that they wanted the Provisional Government to hang on to its absolute power for long enough to accomplish that end before holding elections.

Nationalization of industry was the very last thing Proudhon wanted. In his *Confessions of a Revolutionary* he insists that revolution is 'an organic process ... which makes the infinite, internal, eternal constitution of a society, above political system and State constitution'. Whereas, *le pouvoir*, the exercise of political power, is a mechanical process, a matter of execution. The Provisional Government should make that distinction, and recognize the proper limitations of *le pouvoir*:

... its unique duty and only right was to invite the citizens themselves to produce, in the full exercise of their liberty, those new acts and facts on the basis of which the government might later be called upon to exercise supervision or, at need, guidance.

In other words, he wanted the government to say to the people, 'Organize yourselves into work teams, make your own mutualist arrangements for carrying on industry and trade; bring your problems to us and we will see what we can do; but do not expect us to take initiatives which are not within our province or competence.'

If the people were to do that they would, as I have said, need an economic organ to coordinate and finance their labour. Proudhon might not like the idea of the government providing even that, but there was, it seemed, nobody else with the means. He therefore put his proposal for his People's Bank to be run on Mutualist lines (see below) to Louis Blanc who, predictably, turned it down.

What, exactly, Proudhon wanted the revolutionary workers to do with the power they had grasped, in order to reconcile those antinomies revealed in his *Système des Contradictions Economiques*, will be made clear when I come to the discussion of his *Idée Générale de la Révolution*, and his *Du Principe Fédératif*. But at this point I can best give an idea of what he had in mind by drawing upon a work which was not published until after his death in 1865 and which he only just managed to finish on his deathbed – *De La Capacité Politique des Classes Ouvrières*.

Proudhon insisted that the working-classes must give a lead in utterly repudiating the existing political-economic system, and in grasping the 'idea' upon which *la democratie ouvrière*, the democracy of the producers of wealth, should be based. Fundamental to this 'idea' is the full responsibility in complete freedom of every man for himself and his family, and to the association of fellow-workers into which he enters under the terms of a contract. Also fundamental is the principle that *a day's work equals a day's work*. You are a doctor, and I am a plumber; the most either of us can contribute towards the common wealth is an honest day's work; in justice in exchange, those two days are equal. Given those fundamental principles, the economic complex consists of a federation of industrial and commercial groups cooperating under the terms of mutually advantageous contracts freely entered into. Each federated group consists of individual workers of the necessary diverse skills collaborating to their mutual advantage in their labour of production, again under the terms of a contract freely entered into. Unproductive, parasitic costs – interests of money, rent, profit – are eliminated. Central to the complex are the mutualist banks, non-profit-making administrations making a charge for the service of receiving and distributing the money circulating within, going out from, or coming into the complex, and providing free credit where it is required and justified. I emphasize that this account is grossly over-simplified for the sake of brevity and the reader is referred to Chapter 14 for a fuller exposition of how the system works. The political complex is similar, and the reader is referred to Chapter 12 for an account of it.

*   *   *   *   *

It will be obvious why Louis Blanc and Albert turned down Proudhon's application for government help in setting up the People's Bank. The state, not the people, was to be the master of France; but it could be so on authoritarian socialist lines only if the Provisional Government put through the nationalization measures before the elections. Taking into account what Blanc called 'the state of profound ignorance and moral servility' of the French peasantry and small provincial burgesses, and that 'the enemies of progress' still had command of the country's resources, it must be the duty of the Provisional Government which had been put in power by the revolutionary workers of Paris to hold and to use dictatorial powers, only to call elections 'after all the good which needed to be done, had been done'.

But Blanc, like all middle-class socialist intellectuals[1] suddenly confronted with real workers trying to put socialism into practice, lost his nerve. He learned that on 17 March, Blanqui, Raspail, Barbès and the other revolutionary leaders would lead a force of one hundred and fifty thousand workers to the Hôtel de Ville to demand that the government provide work for the workless, postponement of the elections, and withdrawal of all troops from Paris.

Like all the other Jacobin leaders Blanc was haunted by that latter-day Jacobin, that hollow-cheeked, sunken-eyed reincarnation of Gracchus Babeuf – Auguste Blanqui. Imprisoned in 1831 and again in 1836 for leading conspiracies against the monarchy, and yet again in 1838 for leading his secret Society of the Seasons in an insurrection, he was released, apparently dying, ten years later, recovered his health with his freedom, and organized the *Société Républicaine Centrale* as the nucleus of the ultra-left. It was his power over the workless masses which he might use to overthrow the authority of the Provisional Government, proletarianize the revolution completely, and set up a dictatorship of the disinherited, that terrified Louis Blanc. Proudhon commented on Blanc's revulsion from the very idea of power in the hands of the common people:

Once in power, all men are the same. Always there is the same zeal for authority, the same distrust of the people, the same fanatical attachment to law and order. Is it not amusing to observe how, on 17 March, Louis Blanc's preoccupations were the same as those which, three months earlier, had been disturbing M. Guizot?

If de Tocqueville's description is reliable, Blanqui was, indeed, the very image, out of a parlour-pink's nightmare, of a conspiratorial revolutionary terrorist: the following is from that sharp observer's *Recollections*:

It was at that moment that I saw a man mount the tribune, and though I have never seen him again, the memory of him has filled me with disgust and horror ever since. He had sunken, withered cheeks, white lips, and a sickly, malign, dirty look like a pallid, mouldy corpse; he was wearing no visible linen; an old, black *redingote* tightly clad his lean and emaciated limbs. He looked as if he had lived in a sewer and had only just emerged. Someone told me that this was Blanqui.

The native communists and anarchists were not the only people whose threat to authority, to law and order, offended and worried the conservatives, liberals and socialists alike in the Provisional Government: more than 15,000 Poles, Belgians, Germans and Italians arrived in Paris within a week of the outbreak of the revolution to join their *emigré* compatriots. The Provisional Government was not worried about the Italians, at least for the time being. But the Belgians were agitating for revolutionary military intervention in Brussels; the Germans were demanding arms with which to invade the Germanies, in the belief that, once across the Rhine, they would be joined by their oppressed compatriots in numbers sufficient to overthrow the German autocracies;[2] the Poles wanted France to liberate their country from the Russian archautocrat. Minor headaches for Lamartine and his colleagues were the lunatic fringe of the English Chartists who, having easily been cowed by special constabulary truncheons and a shower of rain at home, wanted the French revolutionaries to do their work for them; and the Irish nationalists seeking help against the Protestant English from French Roman Catholics.

Lamartine regarded the Poles as the most dangerous of all the foreigners. Their Paris colony was numerous and, as Lamartine puts it, 'characterized by heroism, turbulence and anarchy'. These Poles, having failed to persuade the French government to declare war on Russia on their behalf, had gone directly to the people, that is to the Paris militant revolutionary workers, won them over, and were using them to put pressure on the government.[3]

On 16 April, a week before the date set for the general elections in which Proudhon was standing as one of the Doubs candidates, Louis Blanc and the Luxembourg Commission's workers' corporations, the socialist and communist clubs, and the anarchists, joined in another demonstration – a march on the Hôtel de Ville and presentation of a demand for the 'organization of labour', and an end to the 'exploitation of man by man'. This could have been dealt with in the usual way, by making promises which were not intended to be kept. But both the organizers of the demonstration and the Provisional Government had, unaccountably, overlooked Blanqui. His, and the allied clubs, declared themselves in permanent session, jointly set up a Committee of Public Safety as a 'Shadow' government, and prepared to use the demonstration to enforce a purge of – I apologize for the Marxist jargon – counter-revolutionary elements.

Proudhon knew nothing of this intention until after the event, but he did not disapprove of Barbes' (of whose political club he was a member) decision to rally to the government's support. He suspected that Louis Blanc was trying forcibly to take over the government, make himself dictator, and seize all industry and even commerce for the state; in short, that he was trying to drive out the capitalist Satan by the Stateist Beelzebub, which would have left the workers worse off than ever.

All three principal leaders of the demonstration were members of the Provisional Government, Blanc, Albert and Ledru-Rollin, Minister of the Interior. Moreover, the last was, whether he knew it or not, on Blanqui's list of members designate of the Committee of Public Safety. On the morning of 16 April Ledru-Rollin sought Lamartine in his office and told him that during the night he had learned that Blanqui was planning to throw out the government, and assume the dictatorship through his Committee of Public Safety; that he would have a 100,000 men at his disposal, and would certainly attack the Hôtel de Ville. Ledru-Rollin concluded by reaffirming his loyalty to Lamartine and the Provisional Government.

He and Lamartine at once called the National Guard to arms, and sent messengers to summon the government's friends among the moderate liberal and students' clubs.

In the event, the demonstration was a flop: so many National Guards answered the call, and the number of the marchers was so much smaller than expected, that the National Guards outnumbered the demonstrators by four to one. Nevertheless, in Proudhon's opinion, this attempt, albeit abortive, to take over the government by force, set back the cause of socialism by many years and ensured a tight-centre victory in the elections. During the past couple of years the people at large had become aware of socialism as a real force for good; it was being taken seriously at last. Now Blanqui and his friends, Louis Blanc and his party, had turned it into a bogyman, a scarecrow.

... Saint-Simoniens, Phalansterians, Communists, Humanitarians and others amused the public with their innocent dreams, and neither M. Guizot nor M. Thiers deigned to pay any attention to them. They were not, then, afraid of socialism and they were right not to fear it so long as there was no question of applying it by public authority and at the State's expense. After 16 April socialism became the object of all parties' anger: an almost imperceptible minority had been seen to try to lay violent hands on the government! What makes political parties hate each other is much less ideological differences than the struggle for power. For it is power, not opinions, they are concerned with. If there were no government there'd be no political parties; and if there were no political parties there'd be no government. When shall we break out of that vicious circle?

Blanc, Albert and Blanqui and the rest had, in other words, grossly misled their people. Had the workers ignored the politicians, used their freedom to organize their industry on Mutualist lines, their efforts would have been watched with sympathy and, if successful, emulated. But as things now were, the workers had become the enemy.

All the errors, all the miscalculations of democracy derive from the fact that the people, or rather chiefs of insurrectionary groups, having pulled down the throne and driven away the dynast, are under the impression that they have revolutionized society because they have replaced the monarchy's servants with their own. They drop the sanction of Divine Right but retain the monarchy under that of the Sovereignty of the People ...

In his election address he asserted that in order to make the social revolution which must now be made, men were required who combined in themselves the spirit of extreme radicalism with that of conservatism. The triumphant workers should now offer their erstwhile employers the hand of friendship and the erstwhile employers would be very foolish to reject it. He received a respectable number of votes but was not returned: he attributed his defeat to the reaction against the 16 April demonstration. That reaction returned a Chamber which would concede nothing to the left. First Louis Blanc's fear of and hostility to Blanqui, next Ledru-Rollin's anti-socialist Constituent Assembly ... clearly, the revolution was losing both friends and impetus.

Blanqui, Barbes, Raspail and other left leaders were still demanding the 'organization of labour' and now added to their demand 'the liberation of Poland', which would have amounted to a revolutionary war against the European empires, Russia, Austria and Prussia. They organized a mass-demonstration, ostensibly in that cause, for 15 May. And as the government had done nothing about their promise to create work for the workless and find bread for the hungry, there were still hundreds of thousands of very angry people to listen to the insurrectionaries.

The new Constituent Assembly had made changes in the form of Provisional Government: five Commissioners – Arago (Chairman), Lamartine, Ledru-Rollin, Maries, and Garnier-Pagés – had been appointed to nominate ministers and then to preside over their work until the Assembly should have voted a new Constitution. The Commission received a warning that Blanqui and his friends planned to transform the 15 May demonstration into a popular rising. Twelve thousand National Guards were mobilized; *Gardes Mobiles* were stationed in reserve in the Champs-Élysées, and more troops, with artillery, were stationed in the courtyards of all the government palaces. These dispositions were completed on the morning of 15 May while the demonstrators were assembling in the Place de la Bastille, whence they set out to march to the Palais Bourbon where the Assembly was in session.

The reading of the people's petition calling on the government to undertake the liberation of Poland was on the Assembly's order paper, and members were taking turns to mount the tribune and speak in its support, when the demonstration reached the palace. The enormous number and aggressive temper of the marchers so overawed General Courtais, in command of the troops, that he did nothing at all.

The angry growling of the huge crowd, and the furious shouts of *Vive la Pologne*! clearly heard inside the palace, became so alarming, that both Lamartine and Ledru-Rollin left the Chamber, bent on trying to talk to the demonstrators and calm them down. De Tocqueville in his *Recollections* says that probably no public man was ever so loved and adulated by the people as Lamartine had been; but it is clear that his honourable attempt to hunt with the socialist hounds while running with the liberal hare had eroded his popularity. He could not get a hearing and nor could Ledru-Rollin; there were even cries of *Death to Lamartine!* although they were countered by louder cries of *Vive Lamartine!*

While he was still trying to speak, some of the leading militants climbed the iron railings which surrounded the palace grounds and got the gates open from the inside. Both the Commissioners were forced to retreat before the tide of ragged, haggard, screaming men and women which swept into the grounds and on towards the palace.

Wolowski, a relatively conservative *Député* with a bee in his bonnet about Polish nationalism, was at the tribune, urging the government to respond favourably to the petition (de Tocqueville: '... mumbling some platitude or other about Poland between his teeth ...') when the mob burst into the Chamber:

... the people suddenly demonstrated how close they were by a terrible shout which, bursting through all the windows high up in the walls of the Chamber, opened on account of the heat, fell upon us as from the sky. I should never have supposed it possible for human voices in concert to produce such a terrific noise, and even the sight of the crowd itself when it broke into the Assembly, did not strike me as so frightening as that first roar before it came into sight.[5]

The demonstrators, carrying red flags and tricolours crowned with red bonnets, burst in doors at both floor and gallery level, completely swamping the Assembly. Raspail took possession of the tribune and demanded in the name of the people an immediate declaration in favour of Polish independence. The President was ringing his bell for order, but was ignored. A member challenged Raspail's right to speak in the Assembly and was shouted down by the angry mob, while Blanqui succeeded Raspail at the tribune.

Some days earlier the starving workless of Rouen, at the end of the long patience of the poor, had risen in a riot which was put down by the National Guard with considerable loss of life. What Blanqui now demanded was revenge for the massacre which had been authority's response to the misery of the people. He also seconded Raspail's demand for an immediate vote in support of the Polish nationalists. Ledru-Rollin fought his way to the tribune but was roared down by the crowd, and forced to give way to Barbes who had been sitting in silence, his face livid, his fingers nervously twisting his moustaches. There was a sudden silence as he mounted the tribune. 'I demand that this Assembly vote immediately, at this session, to send an army to Poland; to impose a tax of one billion francs on the rich; to send all troops out of Paris; to forbid the beating to arms.[6] Otherwise, let the *Députés* be declared traitors to the fatherland.'

This provoked such an uproar of approval that not even Barbes could continue to make himself heard. Throughout these events the *Députés* sat silent, as if waiting for the revolution to go away. Louis Blanc was found, hoisted shoulder high by his little legs, and carried in triumph round the Chamber, but not allowed to speak. One of the galleries, scarcely able to bear the enormous weight of the crowd, suddenly began to sag, and in terror that the whole structure with its load of men and women was about to crash into the body of the hall, there was a breathless silence, in which the beating to arms could be heard sounding in the streets outside. Barbes shouted for those who had ordered the beating to arms to be outlawed, while others cried that the people and the revolution were betrayed. The President was dragged from the chair, Huber, a communist leader, took his place and bawled, in an enormous trumpeting voice which dominated the uproar, 'In the name of the people betrayed by their representatives, I declare the National Assembly dissolved.' As Proudhon recorded, 'The National Assembly was literally picked up and flung into the street. And for an hour all Paris believed there had been a change of government.'

Proudhon is frank about his own part in this phase of the revolution. He could not but join in with the tens of thousands whom he had called upon to emancipate themselves by throwing off the yoke of the capitalists and the state. He had no doubts that parliamentary democracy was a confidence trick. But he also saw clearly that Louis Blanc, Albert, Blanqui, Raspail, Barbès, Huber and the rest were leading the people to disaster, were forcing on a savage reaction.

In *Le Représentant du Peuple* he had opposed the 15 May demonstration, preached his economic evangel, hammered home the argument that France could not afford a ten-year revolution, that a positive resolution swiftly taken was her only salvation. 'Wasted effort,' he records sadly in his *Confessions*, '*Le Représentant du Peuple* was only a success of esteem; it won its place in the sun of publicity; but whatever it may have foreseen and forecast, it did not gain the merit of accomplishing or preventing anything.'

The two incompatible groups of parties which had made the February revolution were drifting farther and farther apart; the most obvious bone of contention over which they growled and snapped at each other, was the National Workshops.

The numerical and moral superiority of the working-class group of parties had been responsible for the Provisional Government's formal promise of the right to work; easy to make, impossible to keep. The remedy put forward by Louis Blanc and Albert, state participation in industry, was as objectionable then as it still is to the industrial and commercial burgesses; and as it was, for quite different reasons, to Proudhon.

In Paris alone there were between 150,000 and 200,000 workless. It has never been possible to work the capitalist system without a more or less large pool of unemployed, but the figure was excessive. Like all liberal parliamentary governments, the Provisional Government relied on the hope that business would take a turn for the better and so absorb the surplus of workless – surplus, that is, to the number of people required to go hungry and in rags in order to pay for the *aubaines*, that excess of money over goods in circulation represented by money-lenders' interest, rent and profit.[7] Meanwhile, also like any other liberal parliamentary government bent on defending the free market economy, the Provisional Government's supporters quietened their consciences by contriving to believe that the workless were a lot of idle rogues who did not want to work. Lamartine, for example, calls them 'an army of idlers and agitators';[8] that state of mind, very common in the middle-classes during the 1920s and 1930s, known to me as the coals-in-the-bath syndrome, or the rather earlier what-do-they-want-with-pianos? complex.

But this army of idlers and agitators had shown itself so aggressive in its demand for the work it was supposed not to want, that something had to be done. Louis Blanc had therefore been allowed to go ahead with his National Workshops. Lamartine says that this policy was never intended to last. It was in any case a fraud since no serious attempt was ever made to organize the workshops on business lines, to sort the workers into the respective trades, provide them with tools, produce and market-saleable goods. The National Workshops were no more than a means of paying the workless a dole sufficient to keep them from overthrowing the existing system in good earnest. The Paris, Rouen, Lyon and other industrial workers, on the other hand, were allowed to believe that the National Workshops represented a step forward towards the social revolution. From the moment the Constituent Assembly was returned, however, the Executive Commission was under strong and constant pressure to put an end to them. Arago and his colleagues were only too anxious to do so but were painfully aware that unless they found an acceptable way, coming up with some relatively generous Poor Law legislation and welfare schemes (unless, as Proudhon would have put it, they institutionalized pauperism on the English model) there would be another explosion of working-class violence, of bloody civil war.

Tension increased during the second half of May and the first half of June. Proudhon was elected to the Assembly in a by-election in the Seine constituency – a prophet is not without honour saving only in his own country – and could observe and take a hand in what was happening. The *Revue des Deux Mondes* commented on his election:

There are only two alternatives: either M. Proudhon, in touch with men and affairs, will retain his theories intact, in which case he will be a striking example of the impotence of radical theories; or M. Proudhon will renounce all that is excessive and chimaerical in his doctrine, to confine himself to the defence of those two principles which he holds and which will be the salvation of the future as they have been the strength of the past, liberty and credit. And the ascendancy which he has won among the masses will make of him one of the most useful men of the new regime. M. Proudhon is a man of talent and there is enough truth in his theories to justify that claim. At all events it is fortunate that the socialists have succeeded in getting the most intelligent man among them elected.
With M. Proudhon in, the experiment will be definitive.

It is, to say the least of it, a singular irony that the man on whom, according to the most influential periodical in France, the effectiveness of

socialists in the parliament was to be judged, had not an iota of faith in
the value of parliamentary institutions.

On 17 May the Chamber nominated a commission to report 'within a
few days' on the National Workshops, and to propose measures to phase
them out. The measures proposed by the Commissioners were reasonable, liberal but not revolutionary.[9] But the conservative majority in
an Assembly almost as *introuvable* as Louis XVIII's first, more-
royalist-than-the-king parliament, saw a broad highway to socialism in
any kind of intervention between management and labour, any kind of
state investment, or even credit guarantee, in industry. A new Committee was nominated to report on the proposals; it did so on 23 June and
in the sense required of it: the National Workshops were to be closed
immediately and 120,000 workers to be thrown on the streets with a
golden handshake of 30 francs, about a week's subsistence. Says
Proudhon:

Thirty francs for having founded the Republic! Thirty francs for preserving
capitalist monopoly! Thirty francs to pay for an eternity of poverty! It recalls the
thirty pieces of silver paid to Judas for the blood of Jesus Christ.[10] And to that
offer of thirty francs the workers replied with barricades.

Those between seventeen and twenty-five years of age had an alternative course: immediate enrolment in the army. 'Famine or slavery',
says Proudhon.

*   *   *   *   *

One consequence of the desperation into which the right reaction was
driving the workers, and the terror inspired in the burgesses by the
extreme left, was a revival of Bonapartism, in part spontaneous, in part
paid for by Louis-Napoleon Bonaparte's agents. He himself, as a *Député*,
could work in his own cause inside the Chamber where he first met
Proudhon and formed a high opinion of him, but who, for his part,
immediately distrusted 'Citizen Bonaparte'. The recrudescence of
Bonapartism, with its threat of military dictatorship, became so alarming that Lamartine persuaded the Assembly to apply to Bonaparte the
law of 1832 under which all members of that family were banned from
living in France. But the Assembly's resolution did not last: a Bonapartist mob was preferable to a communist mob. The memory that Citizen
Bonaparte's imperial uncle had, with a whiff of grapeshot, saved the
middle-class, the Church and the *haute banque* from the workers before,
and the magical power of the name Napoleon, in the provinces and

countryside, brought about a change of heart. Maybe the nephew would be as handy with cannon as the uncle had been. Doubtless, while Louis-Napoleon waited for the craftily spent fortune of his English mistress, Miss Lambert, and a secret Foreign Office subsidy, to do their work and put France into his hands, he was making up his mind how he would deal with Proudhon and his kind.

The Executive Commissioners were well aware, from Ledru-Rollin's agents and from a score of other sources, that neither the Paris workers nor their socialist leaders would submit tamely to the starvation of their families when the National Workshops closed. One such source is of special interest: de Tocqueville records his conversation with a lady on his left at a luncheon party given by Richard Monkton-Milnes[11] at his Paris house. His fellow-guest was what de Tocqueville, like Proudhon, abominated, a lady novelist who, moreover, 'belonged in our adversaries' camp'. This was the notorious George Sand. 'Madame Sand gave me a detailed and very lively account of the state of the Paris workers; of their organization, numbers, arms, preparations, thoughts, passions and terrible resolves ...'

Despite his prejudices, George Sand made a deep impression on him, so that he was troubled by her concluding remarks: 'Try to persuade your friends, Monsieur, not to force people into the streets by rousing or offending them; for my part, I am trying to instil patience into our people; for, if it comes to fighting, believe me you will all perish.' She was mistaken: the dog it was that died. George Sand, like all the socialist leaders, had failed to reckon with General Cavaignac, the new Minister for War.

While the Assembly was again preventing the Executive Commission from providing work for the workless and improving the country's transport system, by buying back railway concessions and resuming track-construction, at a stop for want of cash, fighting had already broken out in the streets. The railway debate was interrupted on 23 June when Cavaignac went to the tribune to report that his troops – Gardes Nationales, Gardes Mobiles, and Gardes Republicaines – were over-running the barricades and were in excellent spirits. The insurrectionaries had been driven back from Saint-Denis and the Saint-Martin quarter, and now held only the Saint-Jacques and Saint-Antoine quarters, both working-class strongholds. But general optimism was premature.

Lamartine in his *History* tries to play down the whole affair as the work of a mob of criminals and idlers; not so de Tocqueville:

It was a class struggle, a sort of Servile War, and one should note that this terrible insurrection was not the work of a few conspirators, but was the revolt of one whole section of the population against another. The women took as much part in it as the men. While the men fought, the women prepared the ammunition and brought it up to the front. And when, in the end, they had to surrender, the women were the last to yield.

He casts the blame, though not in so many words, on Proudhon:

These poor people had been assured that the property of the wealthy was in some sort the result of theft committed against themselves. They had been assured that inequalities of fortune were as much opposed to morality and the interests of society, as to nature.

Proudhon, for his part, was disastrously slow to realize where the fault lay. Like the rest of the Left in the Assembly, he was, for some days, convinced that this time the rising was Bonapartist; and that the government should be helped to resist it.

Lamartine, with flawless courage, was out trying to get a hearing for the insurrectionaries. Two colleagues with him were mortally wounded when the group came under fire. Cavaignac had shed the illusion of an easy victory; he recognized the people's mood and prepared to deal with the working men and women who had made the Second Republic as if they were foreign invaders. Large bodies of troops were concentrated in the Tuileries gardens, the Champs-Élysées, on the Place de la Concorde, at the Invalides. The general had at least one good reason for satisfaction: two of the most implacable of the revolutionary leaders, Blanqui and Barbes, were in prison awaiting trial for their part in the affair of 15 May, a fact which does something to explain Proudhon's error of judgement.

On the evening of 23 June, when he was still under the impression that he had the upper hand, Cavaignac proposed to rest on his dingy laurels until the following morning, before attacking the people in their own quarters. Lamartine, finally convinced that the people were not to be talked out of their revolution, bitterly wounded in that vanity which is so manifest in his *History*, aware, too, that something must be done to restore the Assembly's confidence in an Executive Committee suspected of lingering sympathy for the embattled workers, reversed that decision. There were four hours of daylight left in which to go over to the attack.

Lamartine himself took part in the attack, led by Cavaignac in person at the head of 2000 men, on the Temple *faubourg* barricades which were carried after some hours of battle. In three pages of his 'noble' prose he makes the affair sound like the heroic storming of a heavily garrisoned fortress defended by artillery. But so far was the fighting from being over that night that on 24 June the Assembly was on the verge of panic. The left pressed for negotiations and a truce with the insurrectionaries; the right shouted them down and called on the President to adjourn the Chamber. Cavaignac reported on the military situation. Thiers proposed to summon troops and National Guards from all over France to save Paris. A debate was started on the motion by Pascal Duprat to declare the city in a state of siege and appoint Cavaignac as dictator. The Assembly could not make up its mind; there were shouts of protest against the idea of dictatorship, and the *Députés* were still shilly-shallying when Jules Bastide, in a speech of thirty words, terrified the Chamber into voting: 'Citizens, in the name of France I implore you to vote as soon as possible. In an hour the Hôtel de Ville will have fallen.' An amendment to the motion, stripping the Executive Commission of its powers, was proposed. Affronted, the Commissioners offered their resignation. The motion was voted on and carried by a huge majority. General Cavaignac was Dictator, free to complete the victory of the army and National Guard over the Paris workers, and thereafter to offer the bourgeoisie a sweet revenge by mass executions and deportations. Proudhon:

For me the memory of the June Days will weigh for ever like remorse upon my heart. I admit with grief that until the 23rd I had foreseen, known, guessed nothing. Elected a member only a fortnight before, I had entered the Assembly with the timidity of a boy and the ardour of a neophyte. Assiduous from nine in the morning at my duties in the offices and on committees, I did not leave the Assembly until evening, exhausted by fatigue and disgust. Since setting foot upon the parliamentary Sinai I had lost all touch with the masses and, absorbed in administrative work, had lost all sight of current affairs. I knew nothing about the National Workshops, about government policy, about the network of intrigues criss-crossing the Assembly. One has to have lived in that isolation which is a National Assembly to realize that the very men who are totally ignorant of the real state of a country are always those who represent it ... Fear of the people is the sickness of all who participate in Authority; for the men in power, the people are the enemy ...

And answering, in print, the taunt of a fellow-member: 'No, monsieur Senard, I was not, in June, the coward you called me, insulting me before the whole Assembly; I was, like so many others, an imbecile ...'

In what sense had Proudhon been, as he confessed, an imbecile? In believing, as I've said, like so many of his colleagues in the Assembly, that this rising was not a socialist but a Bonapartist insurrection, fermented by Louis-Napoleon's agents. Not that this illusion lasted for very long; visiting the embattled barricades, he very soon realized the grossness of his mistake. By early July, when Cavaignac had done with mass executions and was resorting to mass transportation or sending insurrectionaries to the galleys with instructions that they were to be treated as common criminals,[12] Proudhon was doing what he could, in *Le Représentant du Peuple*, to right his mistake. The cause of the social war, he wrote, had been the misery to which 100,000 households had been reduced in Paris alone, by unemployment. 'When the people ask for work, and are offered only a mean and grudging charity, being of a proud race and refusing to accept dishonour, they rebel and shout at you.'

Cavaignac, who had resigned his dictatorial powers, returning all power to the Assembly, but who was immediately elected chairman of the Council of Ministers, that is prime minister, was now suspending the left-wing press. The *Représentant* was briefly spared only to be suspended when Proudhon used it to propose that the government should decree a reduction of one third of all rents falling due on the next quarter-day, and to call on the National Guard to demand 'work, credit and bread'. More than one *Député* mounted the tribune of the Assembly to denounce Proudhon for preaching spoliation of the proprietors, incitement of the National Guard to mutiny, and civil war.

Deprived of his newspaper, Proudhon still had his seat in the Chamber, and still, therefore, a means of making himself heard. His next move was to place before the Finance Committee of the Assembly, chaired by Thiers, a proposal for financial reform. Considering his opinion of the Committee, he cannot have been surprised when this was rejected: 'The Finance Committee never had a theory of taxation, of wages and salaries, of foreign trade, of credit, of distribution, of currency circulation, of value, or of any of those things whatsoever which comprise the science of Finance Committees.'

What Proudhon proposed was that all creditors of society be required to surrender one-third of all that had been paid to them or was owed to them over the last three years. One half of the money thus collected was to be paid to tenants and other debtors to restore them to solvency and set them working again; the other half was to be used by the state for investment in industry and commerce – not the sort of measure he normally approved of but this was a severe emergency – and thus to restore the pre-revolutionary standard of living. George Woodcock, in *Anarchism*, points out that in fact though not in form this is the now familiar device of taxation to finance reflation subsidies. Indeed, in yet another instance of Keynesianism before Keynes, Proudhon was suggesting that France spend her way out of the depression. But his proposal would have been more acceptable to monetarists than the modern versions of this device, since it did not involve the creation of new money but simply the relaunching into circulation of idle money, for a socially useful purpose.

Proudhon argued his case before the Finance Committee. He insisted that, on the public, the 'social' level, credit is a mutual exchange, and should not be considered as a mere loan. Landowners advance land to the community represented by its farmers; capitalists advance capital to the community represented by its industrialists; bond-holders (*rentiers*) advance their savings to the community represented by the state; the largest category of citizens, the workers, having neither land, houses, capital nor savings, advance their labour to society represented by all its citizens.

It is obvious that the society or community which receives is the same moral being as the society which lends; from which it follows that what the landowner calls his rents, the banker his discount, the capitalist his return on investment, the usurer loan and interest, are all, considered under a general heading, exchange *mutuum*. All the citizens are engaged, in other words, in circulating money's-worth.

What is a depression or slump? A slowing down or stoppage of circulation: the bond-holder refuses to advance his savings to the state and even sells bonds at a loss; the banker refuses to discount the businessman's bills; the capitalist refuses to invest in industry or agriculture; the merchant refuses to stock up with goods he cannot sell; for want of orders, the manufacturer ceases to produce; the worker, thrown out of work, ceases to consume. What is required to restore circulation? Something very simple: let everybody, by common consent and public convention, resume doing exactly what they were doing before the crisis. The point which Proudhon was making was that all you need to do to break out of a slump is to understand that money is not a commodity, but only a means of exchange. If *everybody* in the community agrees to do for eighty units of money what formerly he was doing for one hundred, then nobody is any worse off.[13] For the purpose of the emergency Proudhon did not at first even propose that the parasites on the community, the recipients of *aubaines* (interest, rents, etc.) be eliminated; he was to do so when he put his proposal to the Assembly.

Thiers and his Finance Committee were completely unable to understand Proudhon's argument. All he was trying to do was to reflate the economy without increasing the money-supply, but he was accused of advocating bare-faced theft, of wanting simply to seize one-third of property's revenue: 'My proposal was declared scandalous, immoral, absurd, of being an attack on the institutions of religion, family and property.' In a desperate attempt to convince the Assembly and so have the Finance Committee overruled, he defended his proposals from the tribune on 31 July. He was, by his own confession, a poor speaker, and the British Ambassador, who was present in the gallery of the Chamber to hear him, recorded that his speech was dull. Perhaps it was. But, received at first with derision, it was soon provoking rage. There were shouted threats and insults as he persisted in arguing the case for free and reciprocal credit; he was called 'Marat reborn' when he demanded the suppression of interest. His avowed aim of putting an end to the sovereignty of capital, and by the same token to governmental authority, and of making productive labour and labour in the service industries and trades paramount, was treated as the confession of an odious crime.

When he threatened that if the proprietors refused to contribute their part to the revolutionary work, that is to say, refused to consent to the progressive reduction of *aubaines* until they were extinct, then 'we our-selves shall proceed to that liquidation without you', he was challenged to say whom he meant by 'we' and 'you'. He replied that by the use of those pronouns he identified himself with the proletariat and his listeners with the bourgeoisie. Cries of 'This is class-war!'

Alexander Herzen, the man who did most to introduce European socialism into Russia and of whom I shall have more to say, was in Paris at the time, and recorded one scene of this typically parliamentary farce in his memoirs:

The parliamentary rabble greeted his speech with cries of 'To the *Moniteur* with the speech, to the madhouse with the speaker!' ... But even then Proudhon succeeded in rising to his full stature ... Thiers, in rejecting Proudhon's financial scheme, made an insinuation about the depravity of men who disseminated such doctrines. Proudhon mounted the tribune and with his stooping figure and menacing air of a stocky field-worker, said to the smiling old creature, 'Speak about finance, but not about morals; as I told you in committee, I may take that as personal. If you persist I shall not challenge you to a duel, (Thiers smiled), no, your death is not enough for me and would prove nothing. I challenge you to another sort of contest. Here, from this tribune, I shall tell the story of my life, fact by fact, and any man may remind me if I forget or omit something. And then let my adversary tell the story of *his* life!'

The smile, says Herzen, was wiped from 'the old creature's' face, and he sat silent and scowling as every eye in the Assembly was turned on him. How the *Députés* must have enjoyed that moment. But like Hamlet, in that true and tragic and repulsive scene with Gertrude, Proudhon had flaunted his virtue; and no more than Gertrude could they forgive him that. Throughout his life it was the bugbear which so terrified not only his enemies – that was to be expected – but also the men who were inclined to be his friends.

When his proposals were put to the vote not only did all the conservatives and centre deputies vote against them, but so did Louis Blanc; Proudhon called Blanc's vote the most honest one in the Chamber that day, since Blanc stood for authoritarian socialism, whereas he stood for libertarian socialism. As soon as his proposals had been thrown out, a deputy of the right rose to propose a resolution that 'the proposals of the member for the Seine are an odious attack on the principles of public morality, violate property rights, encourage scandal, and appeal to the most odious passions'. The resolution was carried by 691 votes to 2.

From 31 July I became, to use a certain journalist's expression, the One Man Terror... I was sermonised against, acted against, sung, placarded, biographied against, caricatured against; I was blamed, outraged, cursed; I was held up to hatred, ridicule, and contempt. Delivered up to the justice of my colleagues, judged and condemned by my political constituents, suspect among my political friends, spied on by my collaborators and denounced by my adherents, I was denied by my fellow socialists.

Although his speech ruined him with the bourgeoisie, the liberals and the stateist socialists, it enormously enhanced his reputation with the Paris workers and workless. Isolated in the Assembly, he was the hero of the *faubourgs* Saint-Antoine and Saint-Jacques. When on 31 August, *Le Représentant du Peuple* reappeared, with the banner-headline WHAT IS THE CAPITALIST? EVERYTHING! WHAT SHOULD HE BE? NOTHING! – its circulation soared to 40,000, a fabulous level for the times.

Proudhon and his friends did not expect to be allowed to continue to publish the paper, and the suppression of *Le Représentant* came early in September. A further two months passed before *Le Peuple*, his next paper, saw the light of day. Money had to be raked in somehow for the necessary bond. In the end Proudhon himself managed to put in 3000 francs which had come to him from sales of his own writings, and a further 6000 francs came from an unexpected source, a young Breton nobleman by the name of Baron Charles de Janzé who was a deep admirer of Proudhon. And so, with no capital and precisely thirty-five francs available towards cost of production, the first issue of *Le Peuple* made its appearance in November.

Fortunately the name of Proudhon worked magic and 40,000 copies of the first issue sold. *Le Peuple* was in business.

Le Peuple could take care of the propaganda for Mutualism, but very little that was practical could be done about it until the People's Bank was in operation and Proudhon now made up his mind that he, supported by his friends, must himself promote it.

In his *Confessions* there is an account of what the Bank was meant to accomplish, and how it was to be done, albeit brief since, as he says, he had already published a mass of writings about it. The account was written in the Sainte-Pélagie prison, after Monsieur Bonaparte, as he insists on calling the President/Prince-President/Emperor, had come to the rescue of the bourgeoisie not with a whiff of grapeshot but with a cavalry charge, and accomplished the triumph of the reaction. Proudhon's imprisonment, in conditions, by the way, unbelievably humane and liberal by our standards, was evidence of that; so was the fact that Ledru-Rollin, 'father of universal suffrage', Louis Blanc, Victor Considérant, and Cabet were all in exile; and Blanqui back in prison.

*   *   *   *   *

At the People's Bank capitalists and customers were to be one and the same: that is to say, it was to be composed of members, like a co-operative, who would put their money into it, and make exclusive use of it. It was to be a value-circulating, non-profit-making service. Its discount on bills would be nil, its investment advances free of interest. The only charge to members would be such as would cover salaries and other administrative costs, a matter of between $\frac{1}{4}$ and $\frac{1}{2}$ per cent. Thus although, as shareholders, the members would receive no dividends, as customers they would pay no interest on the money they needed.

In the second place, the Bank was designed to enable Mutualist companies of manufacturing workers, members of the Bank, to exchange the products of their labour, by means of labour-value cheques, in isolation from the conventional economic complex. These workers' companies would be linked through the People's Bank which, until such time as the whole national economy was Mutualist, would convert labour cheques into ordinary currency as and when required, with funds procured by the sale of members' products in the conventional markets.

It will be obvious what Proudhon had in mind; as more and more productive workers associated together in Mutualist companies by means of the services of the People's Bank, or a complex of Mutualist banks, capital would be left high and dry for want of labour; and the state confronted with a population of completely free and independent people who, asking nothing of it, would give nothing to it beyond payment for real services genuinely needed. In other words, the state would become a purely executive organ, taking orders from the people, not issuing orders to the people. Here was a means to complete emancipation from the God-Father complex – the semantic evocation of the Mafia image is not accidental. For the state is, cannot but be, an exploitation syndicate, a Mafia.

It may be that Proudhon's method is not perfectly clear so here is another parable, of my own invention but in Proudhon's manner. Once upon a time, on the day before all the banks in a certain town – I think it must have been Irish – were closed by a strike of all their clerks and officers, a Mr Jones, a solicitor by trade, paid his tailor for a new suit with a cheque for £100. As it happened, Mr Jones was broke; he had neither money nor an overdrawing facility at his bank, so that his cheque was a stumer. But his cheques had always been met in the past and his tailor took it for granted that this one was good. In that belief, and the absence of banking facilities, he endorsed it and used it to pay his cloth-merchant who, with the same justification and for the same reason, used it to pay his manager's wages, who, again with the same justification and for the same reason, used it to pay his son's school bill. So the cheque went on its way through many other hands until someone who had been engaged in a law-suit in which he had employed Mr Jones the solicitor used it to pay his account with Mr Jones.

The tailoring trade, the textile industry, education, and many other bits of business and society have all been kept in business by Mr Jones' dud cheque; it would make absolutely no difference if it were never presented but circulated for ever. Far fetched? Well, but is it? Your £10 note, too, is only a slip of paper. Ah, say the government's economists – and all the other economists – but the £10 is guaranteed by the Bank of England, that is, by the government. To which, animated by the spirit of Proudhon, I reply, and has that backing been worth an iota more than Jones' credit-worthiness between 1950 and 1977, when the note's value has fallen between 40 and 50 per cent?

As Proudhon asked when the People's Bank in due course ended:
Why did our economists, financiers, proprietors, industrialists, capitalists, all those lovers of order, those philanthropic advocates of trade, hard work, low prices, and progress, never conceive that idea? Why, when in the interests of production, distribution and consumption, of the workers, the business men, the farmers, of everybody, a socialist proposed it, did they all reject it? Why do they insist that the farmers who under that system could be getting long-term loans at

½%, must continue to pay 12% or 15%? ... Why, when the People's Bank, deprived of its chief, was obliged to liquidate itself, did they rejoice?

Had his question not been merely rhetorical irony, had he really been seeking an answer, he might have found it in his own declaration of the Bank's ulterior purposes. Among them was the striking of a blow at 'governmentalism' which he calls 'communist exaggerated', by providing the means for men to retain their integrity as individuals while mutually undertaking an economic initiative, ensuring work and well-being for all workers independently of the producing, distributing and exchanging community's allied enemies, capital and the state.

In September 1848 Louis Blanc published in the *Nouveau Monde* a *projet de décret*, the potential legislation which would give practical expression to the policy of the social democrats, as the men of the republican left, *La Montagne*, now called themselves. It proposed the setting up of a Ministry of Progress which would, by means of certain measures, 'gradually and pacifically' abolish the proletariat. The measures proposed included nationalization of the railways, mines, Bank of France and insurance companies; the setting up of national warehouses under state management which would receive, store, and distribute all manufactured goods, paying for them in receipts based on an expert valuation of the goods, which receipts would be negotiable as currency. Profits from these operations remaining after the subtraction of interest and amortization costs, would accrue to the workers in the form of capital to finance industrial cooperatives and agricultural colonies. These, by accumulating their own capital out of profits, would emancipate the workers by putting the means of production, distribution and exchange into their hands. The cooperatives and colonies (the latter in Algeria), would have to operate under conditions and with obligations laid down by and policed by the state.

Without going into tedious detail, it may be taken that Blanc, under the impression that he was making socialism, would in fact have been establishing a rigid state capitalism of the kind set up in Russia by the Bolsheviks after October 1917 as a stage in the progress towards communism, but which Stalin 'froze' so that it has become the Soviet establishment. Blanc's state capitalism would, however, have been considerably more liberal than that of the Soviet Union, or than that envisaged by the British Labour Party and trade-unionist left, in that the workers would have enjoyed a far greater share in both the management and the profits of industrial enterprise.

Proudhon rejected the whole package: he held the very idea of any government making a social revolution from above to be a contradiction, an absurdity. The revolution, which was no revolution if it did not uncompromisingly reject governmental authority, could only be made by the people, from below. The national purchase of the public utility services would create a huge public debt, a state of affairs which he abhorred, and which would inevitably lead to the bankruptcy of the state.[14] It was not the business of government, of the state, to be banker, haulage contractor, underwriter. To make it so would, moreover, perpetuate a crippling economic error; for both banking and insurance should be mutualist, thus excluding all question of profit which loaded their operations with a non-productive heavy charge they should not be carrying: *aubaines*. He held the state to be incompetent to become a monopoly wholesaler; above all he derided, with savage irony, the idea of the negotiable receipts. The idea of establishing the value of goods, and thereby of the receipts, by 'expert valuation' was simply ridiculous.[15] There was only one way of discovering the value of a product, and that was by putting it on to the market in competition with other goods of the same kind; only demand, only opinion, can create commercial value.

Not only did Proudhon attack the socialist plan as technically a lot of nonsense; he attacked it as socially pernicious: 'Always this communist solidarity instead of mutualist solidarity; always this government of man by man, always the same old servitude ...' And, again:

Louis Blanc, like all government men, is an enemy of revolution. It is to prevent revolution that he creates a solidarity of marble and bronze, first between all the workers in the same factory, then between all the factories in the same industry, then between all the industries. The world once thus solidified, I defy it to make the slightest movement. The People's Bank, on the other hand, seeks to regularize revolution, to establish the revolution in permanence, to make it the legal, constitutional and juridicial condition of society. We are systematically revolutionary; Louis Blanc is systematically counter-revolutionary.

Proudhon was seeking a form of organization of society which would allow it to conform with the universal growth and change and enjoy the only measure of stability possible to an organism, that of mutually balancing anti-nomial tensions, of contradictory movements holding each other in equilibrium. He sought a measure of association between men so minimal that it would allow every man to retain the optimum of individual freedom and responsibility, but sufficient to ensure an adequate process of production and exchange. Moreover, it must be as self-correcting as an organic ecosystem, as one force waned and another waxed. In other words, Proudhon sought – please see Chapter 10 – that kind of economic and social *justice* which would be so precisely because it was also *justesse*.

If all men were to be free, responsible, fully accomplished human beings, neither slaves nor masters, neither subordinates nor bosses, neither machines nor beasts whether predators on or prey to each other, then it was as vital to eliminate the vices of socialism as those of capitalism. Nothing of the least use or value to men as people, rather than as elements of the abstraction 'mankind', would be accomplished by substituting for those thieves the proprietors, that super-thief, the state.

Like all great truths Proudhon's can be stated very simply and briefly: authority and liberty, authority and fully human responsibility, are incompatible. And liberty means the government of conscience not the government of law.

NOTES TO CHAPTER SIX

1. Blanc, Louis (1811–82), b. Madrid where his father was treasury administrator during the Napoleonic occupation. Read law in Paris, suffering poverty which his mother's rich family refused to relieve. Published, 1839, *L'Organisation du Travail*, advocating cooperative industrial workshops to be financed by the state. Went into exile in England in 1849. Returned to France in 1871 and was elected a *Député* in the National Assembly of the Third Republic.
2. This project was, despite Karl Marx's agonized efforts to stop it, carried out. The German revolutionaries were wiped out as soon as they crossed the Rhine.
3. It was the passionate plea for help from the Polish nationalists to the French and British workers which led, in 1863, to the First International. This was weakened by the struggle between Marxists and Proudhonian anarchists for control of it.
4. De Tocqueville, *Recollections*. He had been returned by the Manche constituency.
5. ibid.
6. Call-up of the National Guard.
7. I am here drawing upon Proudhonian economics. To keep the economic system stable, that is free from inflation, the value of goods being produced and put into circulation must be balanced by the amount of currency in circulation. But since, under capitalism, private or stateist makes no difference, rent, profit, money-lenders' interest in diverse forms have to be paid, there is continuous inflation unless a certain percentage of the population can be confidence-tricked or forced into making good the difference by going short. Hence the need for a more or less large body of unemployed, under-employed or under-paid workers under any 'market' form of economy. This of course is Proudhon's 'philosophy of poverty' which Karl Marx singularly failed to understand.
8. *Histoire de la Révolution de 1848*.
9. The measures proposed were: aid and encouragement for workers' cooperatives; colonization in Algeria on a vast scale; conciliation boards to arbitrate between labour and management; institution of retirement pensions and public assistance funds; export subsidies and wage subsidies for industry; government orders, or financial guarantees to cover the manufacture of certain products. In short, capitalism in 1848

was already in need of the same supports by the taxpayer as it is now. The cost of the proposed measures which, it was hoped, would make it possible to close the National Workshops without provoking further working-class violence, was estimated at 200 million francs. So it was tantamount to asking the present *Chambre des Députés* to vote a special expenditure of 4 billion francs to solve the unemployment problem which no free-market economist would want to solve anyway. But the Commissioners argued that this would be a productive investment and, as such, preferable to an unemployment dole. I wonder why, in view of this report of the Commissioners to the Constituent Assembly, Maynard Keynes is credited with having invented anything.

10. 30 francs ... The French politicians of the mid-19th century did not have the benefit of advice from PR agencies.

11. Richard Monkton-Milnes, 1809–85. MP, man of letters and patron of writers. The following note on him was scribbled in the margin of the MS of de Tocqueville's *Recollections*, but not printed because de Tocqueville was not sure that it was original: 'he hurried towards anything glittering with a stupid greed reminding me of those fish one attracts by lighting a straw fire which they invariably mistake for the sun.'

12. In all some 14,000 men were either herded into pens and massacred by firing squads, or transported.

13. To anticipate an obvious objection, France was not, in 1849, dependent on imports or, for that matter, on exports, and it was possible to consider her economy in isolation.

14. Perhaps it is not necessary to point out that, by the standards of scientific accountancy, Britain, as a capitalist, is and long has been a bankrupt as a consequence of its industrial and service industry losses.

15. For Karl Marx's contemptuous analysis of the ineptitude as revolutionary leaders, of the French socialists, see his *Eighteenth Brumaire* and his *The Class Struggle in France*. Marx, Proudhon and de Tocqueville were at one in their contempt; and de Tocqueville, like Proudhon, believed that the conduct of Blanc, Blanqui, Raspail, Barbès, *etc.* had seriously damaged the socialist cause. But: 'Will socialism remain buried in the contempt which so justly covers the socialists of 1848? ... I am sure that in the long run the constituent laws of our modern society will be drastically modified. But will they ever be abolished and replaced by others? ... The more I study the state of the world ... The state of the laws and the different forms that the right of property has taken ... I am tempted to the belief that what are called necessary institutions are only institutions to which one is accustomed and that in the matter of social constitution the field of potentialities is much vaster than the people of any particular society imagine.'

SEVEN

The People's Bank and Prison

In October 1848 Lamartine informed the Assembly that on 11 December the men of France would go to the polls, and under the regime of universal suffrage allowed for by the new constitution, elect the first President of the Second Republic.

There were about 10 million voters, and it is probably safe to say that something like 80 per cent of them would recognize only one name in the list of candidates. It was the name of a man who belonged to no party, had no known policy, a shady political adventurer, a poker-faced, dead-eyed, second-rate visionary. Had he been called Monsieur Untel – Mister Such-and-Such – no rival candidate need have feared him, for not even his English gold would have enabled him to buy a majority of 10 million votes. Unfortunately Citizen-Deputy Louis-Napoleon Bonaparte bore a name which in a France weary of party strife, would have put a chimpanzee into the Presidency. Still, there had to be at least the semblance of a fight.

The governmental republicans nominated Cavaignac as their candidate: Proudhon wanted the left to support him provided he was the only other candidate, in order to make at least a credible effort to keep Bonaparte out. But the left insisted on nominating Ledru-Rollin. No, said Proudhon, in the Chamber and in his paper; if we are to have a candidate of the left let him be a socialist. And he made it clear that, if Ledru-Rollin were nominated, then he and his friends would nominate Citizen-Deputy Raspail.

Raspail had only been a *Député* for a month; and his election had been a triumph for Proudhon and *Le Peuple*; they had taken him up as their candidate, turned the paper's offices into a campaign headquarters, and proceeded to show what persistent propaganda plus Proudhon's hold over the masses of the Paris workers, could do.

The proposal to nominate Raspail infuriated the radicals, that is the non-socialist left republicans. Proudhon could not be ignored; true, the party of socialists in the Chamber of which he was temporarily, because of his influence in the streets, an ex-officio leader, were few: but if his paper backed Raspail, then their own candidate would lose hundreds of thousands of socialist votes. Proudhon was accused of splitting the left. Not at all, he replied, we accept Cavaignac. Another outcry: how could the people be expected to vote for the man who so ruthlessly put down the June insurrection? Of course the Paris workers would not vote for Cavaignac. Proudhon answered in *Le Peuple*:

Then the people would be wrong. What is here in question? The election of a President of the Republic, a chief of State. Now, the State is a bourgeois institution, therefore its chief should in good logic be a bourgeois. The most honest, the most capable bourgeois, the most honourably bourgeois bourgeois being Cavaignac, it would be judicious to choose him.

In other words, and repenting of his own involvement in politics, what the devil did it matter to the workers what the bourgeois did with their wretched state?

A means had to be found to alienate Proudhon's supporters in the Chamber and to discredit him in the streets; and a convenient means was to hand. In September Cavaignac had invited Vivien, Louis-Philippe's former Minister of Justice, to join the government. Cavaignac was never an ideologist and Vivien was a capable and experienced professional politician. Uproar from *La Montagne*: what, an Orleanist monarchist minister in the Republic's government ... monstrous outrage! All the factions of the left combined to propose a vote of censure on the government. Instead of voting for it, Proudhon abstained from voting, and when challenged to explain his treachery had a simple answer: 'I cannot forget, citizens, that in 1840 Vivien saved me from prison.'

A radical deputy, one Felix Pyat, a popular playwright and club orator, sitting on the same bench, thrust his face into Proudhon's and shouted 'Cochon!' Whereupon Proudhon rose and punched him on the nose. Roars of delighted laughter came from the gentlemen on the other side. This sort of street brawling showed up those ill-bred louts of the left in their true colours. That hilarity was mortifying: French institutions are as terrified as are Frenchmen of *le ridicule*. Something must be done to restore face by showing that the left was no more ignorant of the gentlemanly way to settle a row, than the Legitimists and Orleanists on the other side; and if it rid the Assembly of that turbulent Anarchist, so much the better. Pyat was persuaded, with some difficulty since he was not inclined to risk his life, to issue a challenge.

Proudhon was horrified: he was the last man on earth to want to take another's life, and was as reluctant as his adversary to lose his own. The affair was no joke; in 1848 the duel had not yet become a mere formality, in which nobody was in much danger of getting hurt: quite recently Emile Girardin, proprietor and editor of *La Presse*, having been called out by the political publicist Armand Carrel – it was a risk all editors in

France ran in those days – shot his man dead. There is ample evidence of Proudhon's agony of mind over this business in the *Carnets* in which he dwells on his obligations to stay alive, obligations to Darimon, Langlois, Duchêne, and all his other friends on *Le Peuple*, to his brother, to Euphrasie; and to his own mission – there was so much yet undone which he had set himself to do. But there was no doubt that to fight Pyat was a 'necessity of circumstances'.

'The necessity of circumstances,' he wrote in his *Carnet*, 'produces our judgements and forms our lives; often what we really want to do has nothing to do with the decisions which are taken to be of our own making.'

As for the outcome, either both duellists were rotten shots, or each took good care not to hit the other, or the seconds took care to see that the pistols were under-charged with powder. The *Carnet* records: 'We stood up and shot at each other like stupid brutes.' Neither was wounded.

The result of the Presidential election on 11 December was even more distressing to the left than the pessimists had feared. *Badinguet* – not that the nickname was yet current, it took the little great man a decade or two to earn it – received 5½ million votes; his adversaries shared something fewer than 2 million between them. Quatre Bras, then, was not the last of Napoleon's – the real one's – victories; from the grave he won this one and two more for his nephew – just as Proudhon had feared must happen, should the people he was trying to serve take the franchise for freedom.

There were contemporary observers so blind as to find the outcome of the election extraordinary. In his *Confessions of a Revolutionary*, Proudhon makes the point: Bonaparte was a returned exile without title to any kind of office; he had done nothing to distinguish himself; he was virtually unknown in France. To this one might add that his *Les Idées Napoliennes* (1839) had made no impression on anyone but the small Bonapartist party, that his two attempts – 1836 and 1840 – at raising military insurrections in France had merely made him look ridiculous, that his English connection was the reverse of being a recommendation, and that he was not personally prepossessing. He was not such a dullard as Louis-Philippe, but it is clear that he had no charm, and was equally incapable of majesty.

If there really be a mystery in Louis-Napoleon's success at the polls, one gets a clue to it by attaching an observation of Proudhon's to one of de Tocqueville's. That statesman tells us that the middle-class vote, including his own, went to General Cavaignac; and Proudhon, that the people make dictators and emperors to protect them against the oligarchies of nobility and bourgeoisie. The Roman plebs made Caesar, the German plebs made Hitler, and the American plebs made Franklin D. Roosevelt who came as close to the Caesarian role as any United States President yet.

But I've already said that there is no mystery about Louis-Napoleon Bonaparte's success at the polls. The names of the candidates of the left were either unknown or anathema to the majority of the French people, Lamartine was discredited and the generals unpopular.

De Tocqueville says that the politicians who supported Bonaparte's candidature did so because of his apparent mediocrity, thinking to use him while he was useful, and break him when their time came. 'In this they were greatly deceived.' He says nothing about Bonaparte's purchase of support with English money. He describes him as follows:

He spoke little and poorly; he had not the art of making others talk and establishing intimacy with them, and no facility for expression himself. ... His power of dissimulation was profound and was singularly assisted by the immobility of his features and his want of expression; his eyes were lustreless and opaque. Careless in moments of danger, his courage was fine and cool, but, as is common enough, his plans were vacillating.

One can add to all this that he had a taste for low company, was sexually greedy and promiscuous; and had been – or by the rules of that secret society still was – a *Carbonaro*. One can also add Proudhon's bitter and savage sketch, from the *Carnet* of three years later, when he had been the Prince-President's prisoner for more than two years:

The man is ill-made and physically ugly, very short in the legs, twisted and *troticulant* as Rabelais calls it, the face ignoble, the pairs of features ill-matched and out of balance, one eye higher than the other, the brow devoid of majesty and intelligence, the eyes dead. Seeing him for the first time in 1848 I had a confused feeling that I had before me a man in whom all shame was dead, or rather had never existed, like that prostitute in Martial who could not remember ever having been a virgin. That vague insight manifested itself in a pamphlet I wrote in 1848, late November, in which I depicted him as a monster of lewdness who would one day have the Republic seized by four thugs and would rape her while they held her down. It is asserted that Louis-Napoleon is so exhausted by his excesses with women, and of every kind, that his bowels are in a state of perpetual looseness. The seat of his breeches is always fouled with shit, and in his erotic orgies the filthiest ordure serves as perfume to his lusts.

A shade over-charged, perhaps; but Proudhon's horror of the idea of Bonaparte as President was such that he made himself seriously ill. First there was what his physician called a malignant grippe accompanied by ulcers in the throat, and then violent headaches with some kind of 'cerebral disturbance'. The latter part sounds like the kind of migraine which his mother had suffered from all her life and which, oddly enough, afflicted Euphrasie Piegard. But what the doctors feared was that mysterious 19th-century disease, brain-fever. For a while his life was thought to be in danger; then, as quickly as he had fallen sick, he recovered. At a guess, his recovery coincided with the moment when he found the means to reconcile himself with Bonaparte's presidency.

From the beginning, Proudhon used *Le Peuple* against Citizen Bonaparte's candidature: there could be no possible good reason for voting for a man who had no policy, no ideas, and who must be suspected of wanting to restore absolute monarchy in the form of a revived Empire. The proper course for all anarchist and socialist workers was to abstain from voting; and, in that abstention, the parliamentary left, *La Montagne*, the social-democratic republican party, should give a lead.

Proudhon's refusal to censure the government in the matter of Vivien's appointment, the Pyat duel, and his support of Raspail against Ledru-Rollin completed his isolation in the Assembly. He was beginning to realize the enormity of the mistake he had made in taking a hand in the parliamentary politics which he knew, and had declared, to be pernicious for the revolution. In *Choses Vues*, Victor Hugo, a fellow socialist *Député* and his friend, describes him in a quick sketch taken in the Chamber:

Proudhon sits beside Lagrange, in the last triangular bay on the left at the far end of the Chamber. The women in the diplomatic gallery above his head look down on him with a kind of horror, exclaiming aloud, *He's a monster*. Proudhon has his legs crossed, wears grey trousers and a brown frockcoat, and is half reclining in his seat, so that his head does not come up to the top of the backrest.

As for what was passing in his head as he sat sprawled, silent, scowling, disinclined to speak whatever the subject of the debate, scarcely listening to what he knew was not worth hearing, he wrote it down thus:

To be ruled is to be kept an eye on, inspected, spied on, regulated, indoctrinated, sermonised, listed and checked-off, estimated, appraised, censured, ordered about, by creatures without knowledge and without virtues. To be ruled is, at every operation, transaction, movement, to be noted, registered, counted, priced, stamped, surveyed, assessed, licensed, permitted, authorised, apostolised, admonished, prevented, reformed, redressed, corrected. It is, on the pretext of public utility and in the name of the common good, to be put under contribution, exercised, held to ransom, exploited, monopolised, concussed, pressured, mystified, robbed; then, at the least resistance and at the first hint of complaint, repressed, fined, vilified, vexed, hunted, exasperated, knocked-down, disarmed, garroted, imprisoned, shot, grape-shot, judged, condemned, deported, sacrificed, sold, tricked; and, to finish off with, hoaxed, calumniated, dishonoured. Such is government! And to think that there are democrats among us who claim there's some good in government!

The translation is literal: in Proudhon's French the use of alliteration and assonance makes it much funnier. Halévy comments: 'It is as if Rabelais had returned to our midst to guide Proudhon's pen.'

After the election which made Louis Bonaparte President of the Republic, Proudhon repented of his opposition: it was impossible that $5\frac{1}{2}$ million Frenchmen could have been wrong, therefore it was he, Proudhon, who had been wrong. 'I believed, poor wretch that I was, that I was opposing the Empire; whereas I was obstructing the Revolution.' An astonishing conclusion based on Bonaparte's own: 'France elected me because I belong to no party' which Proudhon translated as, 'France elected him because France wants no more government.'

With the Presidency of Louis-Napoleon Bonaparte begin the funeral rites of *le pouvoir*, of central political power. The old France was dead, rotted away by all the evils of the Orleanist bourgeois monarchy, that regime of corruption institutionalized. The task which history had assigned to Bonaparte was to bury the corpse. By the extremism of the reaction he would lead, he would complete the work of destruction of *le pouvoir* for ever. By taking all that *pouvoir* into his own hands, which he was sooner or later bound to do, he would make it possible to destroy *le pouvoir* in the person of a single man, and so odious would he have made it that never again would Frenchmen tolerate it. Thus, Bonaparte would serve, as could no other man, the cause of the revolution, and those $5\frac{1}{2}$ million voters had been right to put into the supreme office a man who could be relied on to render it intolerable. From all of which it followed that the correct course for all socialists was that of aiding and abetting the President to commit political suicide and therefore the death of *le pouvoir*, while simultaneously making a frontal attack on capitalism and the principle of authority.

President Bonaparte had two great allies: capital, and the Church resurgent. (De Tocqueville bears this out; he actually warned Bonaparte that his favouring of the Church and the Jesuits was alienating many people.) Proudhon identified these as two manifestations – *le pouvoir* being the third – of the same unique enemy of humanity: authority. The justification of *Le Peuple*'s policy and anti-presidential campaign, is in a single paragraph of the *Confessions*:

The economic idea of Capitalism, the political idea of government, the theological idea of the Church are three identical ideas reciprocally convertible. What Capital does to labour and the State to liberty, the Church does to intelligence. This triple alliance of absoluteism is necessary, in philosophy as in practice. For in order to oppress the people efficaciously you must load body, soul and mind with chains, all at the same time.

For a while Proudhon contrived to believe that his exposure in *Le Peuple* of the Usurer–Jesuit–Politician triad as the early incarnation of Beelzebub, was succeeding in its purpose; some of the other journals of the left were taking up the idea, in milder terms. It would take time for real results to show, but at least now the workers knew their enemy and had their 'idea'. 'Capital will never regain its preponderance; its secret has been unmasked. Let it now celebrate its last orgy, for tomorrow it will have to incinerate itself, like Sardanapalus, on a funeral pyre of its treasures.'

But Bonaparte was President, had about him a clique of army officers, was filling the streets of Paris with marching and countermarching soldiers: there was a nasty smell of empire in the air. Well, President he might be, he would not be emperor, not yet, not if Proudhon could help it. During that month of sickness when even his friend and physician Crétin had despaired of his life, he had not touched a pen; but there was no stiffness in the hand which wrote the long challenge, the burning defiance of the enemy which, quite forgetting that he should be helping not hindering the Prince-President to kill off *le pouvoir* by rendering it insufferable, he published in *Le Peuple*. It was the final paragraph of this virtuoso performance which gave the law officers of the republic the opportunity, which their predecessors of the monarchy had allowed Blanqui and Vivien to snatch from under their noses, to put this outrageous agitator in his place:

Ah, sure if the People, like the monkey in the fable unwittingly taking the name of a port for a man's name, elected the bear Martin or the ox Dagobert President of the Republic, they were misled by the resonance of name. It is not a Bonaparte they've elected, it's a bear or an ox, a poor beast of Circus or Carnival.

Perhaps even that jeer would have been shrugged off in the case of a man who enjoyed parliamentary privilege; what was intolerable was the roar of delighted laughter all along the boulevard from Tortoni's café to the théâtre Odeon, and the growl of approval which rose from the slums of Saint-Antoine and Saint-Jacques.

If I have given the impression that *Le Peuple* was Proudhon and only Proudhon, that needs correction. Sharing the risks of confiscatory fines and terms of imprisonment were half a dozen men who, Beslay excepted – he was briefly governor of the Bank of France two decades later – dedicated themselves to the cause and got nothing, not even glory, from their devotion. There was, of course, Alfred Darimon, in this as in all things with Proudhon until they quarrelled ten years later; and Duchêne, economist turned journalist, who was to suffer more even than Proudhon at the hands of the law. There came a day when, brought from prison for a fresh prosecution and by then knowing the form all too well, he wearily interrupted the presiding judge's partial summing-up with, '*L'addition, s'il vous plaît!*' He got it, too: ten years. Langlois, another friend until death, was a Breton, and an ex-naval officer; Ramon de la Cerna, a Spanish Mutualist come to serve under 'the master of us all'; Crétin was as much involved with the paper as with Proudhon's health; Chevet, a regular contributor, was by vocation a musician. As for Louis Ménard who was to die obscure in miserable poverty, he should, according to Halévy, have been a member of three major academies had he had his deserts; as a chemist he was the inventor of collodion, of vital importance to the development of the new craft of photography; as a philosopher, the inventor of pluralism; as an historian, of Hellenism. His *Prologue d'une Révolution*, a study of the 'June Days', suppressed in book form by the authorities, was serialized in *Le Peuple*. Finally, neither Pilhes nor Vasbenter, the paper's business managers, escaped fines and imprisonments.

Another impression which may need correction: although *Le Peuple* was a popular paper it must not be thought of in terms of today's debased popular press. With a net daily sale of about 40,000 and a readership of about 250,000, for the most part working-class, only Girardin's *La Presse* had more readers.[1] Yet its articles, written in a prose of classic correctness, often ran to more than a page, and were at a very high level of intelligence. Its attitude was serious, and its probity famous: what you read in *Le Peuple* you could rely on as true. The paper reported all major parliamentary debates in full and without political bias, as it did all major law-court proceedings of public importance. Its foreign news, chiefly of the progress of the revolution, was thorough. In short, it was what we should now call a 'quality newspaper'; it is one measure of the failure of our society that we now have to make this distinction.

This, then, was the organ with which Proudhon, having done with that aberration into politics, now set about making the social revolution. This was the way which he had always known was right, outside politics with which the working-class should have no truck, but without recourse to violence. The workers were to accomplish the revolution negatively by repudiating and withdrawing from the bourgeois state – his proposed campaign of civil disobedience and passive resistance is discussed below – and positively by organizing themselves into workers' industrial and commercial associations or companies, thereby not only depriving the capitalists of labour, but ruining them by efficient competition.

To what or to whom were the workers to look for an organizational focus, and for finance in setting-up their companies? Clearly, the time had come to incorporate the People's Bank and begin a practical experiment in free credit. A group of Bisontins, enthusiasts for the Proudhonian doctrine, had, in November 1848, sent him 20,000 francs, say a million in modern money, towards the realization of his project, so that he had starting money. On 5 February 1849 *Le Peuple* carried what must, I suppose, be called the bank's prospectus. It is, in the field of business, as singular a document as was his letter of proposal to Euphrasie Piégard in the field of love. Here are the essential parts of its introduction:

I take my oath before God and men, on the New Testament and the Constitution, that I have never had or professed principles of social reform other than those set forth in these presents. ...

I now declare that, in my innermost mind these principles with all their consequences are the be-all and end-all of socialism, and that all the rest is utopian and chimaerical.

The People's Bank is no more than the financial form, the translation into economic terms, of the principle of modern democracy.

I protest that in writing the critique of property, or more precisely of the complex of institutions of which property is the pivot, I have never had in mind, nor attacked, the rights of individuals established by anterior statutes, nor contested the legitimacy of acquired possessions, nor sought to provoke an arbitrary sharing-out of assets, nor obstructed the free and regular purchase of real estate; nor even sought by interdict or sovereign decree to suppress interest on capital or rent for land.

I consider that all these manifestations of human activity should remain free and optional to all, and that they should not be subject to modifications or restrictions other than those which naturally and necessarily result from the universalization of the principle of reciprocity and the law of synthesis which I propose.

My sole aim in putting diverse parts of the social system through the melting-pot has been to attain, by long and laborious analysis, to those overriding principles whose mathematical formula is enunciated in these presents.

This is my life and death testament. Should I be mistaken, public argument and trial will soon have disposed of my theories and nothing will remain but for me to disappear from the revolutionary arena.

If ever there was a published document which could be qualified by the *bousse-botte* word *cudot*, this was it. True, he had never called for the arbitrary, that is violent, elimination of interest, of rents, of capital: he had simply exposed them as theft, that is as criminal, and then put forward an alternative economy which would, by its functional and moral superiority, cause them to disappear.

Every newspaper in Paris reproduced this act of faith; it was as amusing to watch that pig-headed Franc-Comtois peasant tilting at the *haute banque*, as to watch him tilting at the Prince-President. Proudhon's personal manifesto of commitment was followed by the business prospectus: the bank was being incorporated, in suitably modest premises, with a capital of 5 millions in 5 franc shares which could be bought in ten monthly instalments of 50 centimes. As soon as there were 50,000 francs in hand, the issue of *bons de circulation* would begin, that is of what was to be virtually a currency, between subscribing mutualist individuals, groups, associations and companies. The circulation of that currency between members by way of the bank, members who would be worker associations in industry and commerce, farmers, individual artisans and shop-keepers, would tend to isolate a progressively larger number of people from the capitalist complex.

Twenty-seven thousand was the number of groups and individuals who responded to the prospectus. Free credit was a reality, and on 14 March there appeared in *Le Peuple* yet another example of Proudhon's Jurassic insolence:

Citizens disposed to assist the Workers' Associations already organized or in course of organization, with their savings or their capital are requested to write to the offices of the People's Bank which will register their adherence and put them in touch with its adherents. All workers' associations are functioning successfully; there is no lack of orders or work and there is promise of continuous increase in sales outlets. This is, at the present time, the safest and most advantageous investment.

It was a challenge or warning to men with both a skill and some capital to invest, to get on to the Mutualist band-wagon before it was too late.

*   *   *   *   *

In an effort to put a stop to the one-man revolution which half Paris was watching with cheers and the other half with fear, the state's law officers mounted a campaign of prosecutions with the aim of ruining *Le*

Peuple and getting its editors behind bars. Passages in Ménard's *Prologue d'Une Révolution* which were in fact an appeal for pity for the disinherited and oppressed, were interpreted as incitement to hatred, one of the most useful charges in the procurator's repertoire; Vasbenter was prosecuted both as manager and contributor and sent to prison; Darimon was heavily fined for one of his articles. *Le Peuple* paid the fines; and its readers turned their casual buying of the newspaper off the streets, into subscriptions, so as to keep it in funds. New subscribers continued to send their money into the People's Bank, and in mid-March the paper printed a sort of hymn of the workers' bank, each verse of which ended:

'Merchants of money, your reign is over!'

It reads like a contribution sent in by a zealous young reader, but characteristically, metre and rhyme are correct.

Then came the blow which all Proudhon's enemies had been waiting for: he came up for trial and was found guilty.

In attacking Bonaparte I had thought myself legally well within my rights. . . . To my very great surprise I found myself accused . . . 1) Of stirring up hatred against the government; 2) Of provocation to civil war; and 3) Of an attack on the Constitution and on Property.

Had the Minister of the Interior taken it into his head to charge me, on the evidence of an article about Louis-Napoleon Bonaparte in *Le Peuple*, with the crimes of infanticide, rape and counterfeiting money, he might just as well have done so; the accusation would have passed unchallenged and I might have been just as judiciously convicted. On its honour and conscience, before God and men, the jury, by a majority of eight to four, found me guilty of whatever they were required to find me guilty of, and I got my three years.

That would teach him to call the Prince-President Ox Dagobert or Bear Martin. Even his enemies of the left and centre, often so much more implacable than those of the right, even the men of the *National*, were shocked and called the sentence harsh. Such was the feeling that had any attempt been made immediately to execute the sentence there would would probably have been riots – in Proudhon's own constituency alone he had 100,000 men who, had he been a demagogue, would have fetched him out of the hands of the police, or tried to. But in fact no such attempt was made; the authorities were waiting for him to rid them of his presence by doing as Louis Blanc and others had done, take refuge in exile.

He did not at once go: *Le Peuple*, after some days of hesitation, carried an announcement that since Proudhon would be unable to direct the business of the bank, its operations would be suspended preparatory to liquidation. All subscribers would receive their money back, and nobody should suppose that this was the end of free credit. The bank would be back in business as soon as that became possible.

The day of the bank's reopening never came: could the bank, could Mutualism in industry and commerce, have worked within the matrix of a hostile, rich and very powerful capitalism, frightened into truculence by the spectre of economic justice, and hand-in-glove with the state? It seems unlikely, yet who knows? Had the 'necessity of circumstances' permitted Proudhon to extend his extraordinary powers of instilling the masses with courage, hope and spirit without losing a jot of his integrity, from Paris to Rouen, to Lyon, to all the great cities in which he already had a following, Mutualist industry fed by free credit might have grown too strong to crush, as the British trade unions at last grew too strong to crush, though God knows the other side tried hard enough to do it. It is impossible not to wonder what some of his associates, cool heads like Darimon, thought of the enterprise. The only one who ever published an opinion, and then only some years after Proudhon's death, was Langlois: 'Proudhon's system would have done all that was expected of it had every man in France subscribed to it and not one of them ever failed to meet his obligations.'

Before sentence had been pronounced on him Proudhon had said that he would be prepared to serve a prison sentence of up to six months, perhaps even a year. Three years were too many; and he could not for too long try the patience of the police by putting off the moment of exile. Leaving Darimon in charge of *Le Peuple*, he saved the authorities from having to seize the person of a member of parliament – though for that matter the Assembly cheerfully and with relief betrayed him by waiving privilege – by pulling his hat over his eyes, wrapping a muffler round the lower part of his face, calling himself Dupuis, and crossing the Belgian frontier.

Impossible to know whether he ever intended to go into exile, or merely to seem to do so; at all events, a week after Proudhon's flight Darimon received a mysterious message to go to a certain small and cheap hotel in the Rue de Chabrol near the Gare du Nord, to a room on the second floor. Going up the stairs he had to stand aside to let two ladies, a strikingly handsome blonde girl and a woman who was obviously her mother, make their way down. Curious he watched them out of sight, very much taken with the girl whom he described as '... a lovely creature, radiant with strength and health, with magnificent fair hair'. He went on up and there was Proudhon, the door of his room open, waiting for him. Darimon was very worried and very angry. What possible reason could there be for taking such a risk? The direction of *Le Peuple*: rubbish, Darimon was perfectly capable of handling that, and with the admirably swift mail service between Brussels and Paris, Proudhon was not barred from making his contribution as usual. The liquidation of the People's Bank: very well, it would take ten days or a fortnight, let him accomplish that from his hiding place and then take the first train to Brussels. Proudhon, cornered, then told his friend the truth: 'I see that I shall have to tell you everything. I want to be married. The presence of a wife at my fireside has become necessary to me. Otherwise I shall turn cannibal. I returned to Paris to see if I could carry out that plan, a plan I have nourished for two years.'

Thus were explained the ladies on the stairs; Darimon had no more to say.

The late Mme Suzanne Henneguy, Proudhon's grand-daughter, editor of the published *Letters* to his wife, pictures him in Belgium as utterly cast down by his failures, by the miscarriage of the revolution, by the contemptible conduct of most of the left, by his betrayal by the Assembly and by the reproaches of his friends, turning the more eagerly to the cherished dream of hearth, home and wife, and above all, fatherhood; and now in trembling doubt whether Euphrasie, neglected for her terrible rival *Marianne*, would yet consent to marry a man proscribed by the state, execrated by the respectable burgesses, hunted and penniless. That was the family tradition, at least on the distaff side; the picture is partial. It is true, by his own admission to Darimon, that it was the thought of marriage, of Euphrasie, which had drawn him back to Paris; but it was equally true that he could not bear to keep his hands off his beloved newspaper; nor could he bring himself to trust any man but Proudhon so to liquidate the bank that no man could ever reproach him for losses or find his books out by so much as a *sou*.

One thing in all this is curious: why Madame Piégard accompanied her daughter on that necessarily secret visit to Proudhon in the Rue Chabrol. It is unlikely that she had dropped her hostility to her future son-in-law at the very moment when she might be expected to say I-told-you-so; and a Paris working-girl of twenty-six scarcely needed a chaperone. On the other hand, the persecution of the government honoured rather than disgraced him, and it could not be denied that he was a great man whose name was a word of power in the Paris streets; or she may have been won over to make amends to the daughter she had been unkind to; or have come to like and respect Proudhon himself. There is just the bare possibility that she wanted to make quite sure that

Proudhon did indeed marry her daughter, if one accepts a *canard* current
later, that he had been 'living in sin' with Euphrasie for two years before
the position was regularized by marriage.

*   *   *   *   *

Proudhon's 'repentance' for his fierce opposition to Citizen
Bonaparte, in the *Confessions*, which were written in prison, is a jewel of
irony. He confessed that his immoderate aggressiveness towards the
Chief of State was unjust, for the President had in his very first measures
made a fine start on his task of rendering his office odious and its
functions abortive. Why resort to invective against a man who, the tool of
fate, should rather be applauded for his diligence? Had he not always
known that all government is by its nature counter-revolutionary; and
what better provocation to the resumption of revolutionary militancy
than counter-revolution? 'In charging him with reaction and trying to
prevent that reaction, it was I who was the reactionary.'

What was to be insisted on now by all good socialists was the Constitution, all the Constitution, and nothing but the Constitution. The
Constitution required the separation of powers: good, for the consequent
venomous strife between legislative and executive would both discredit
and cripple *le pouvoir*. The Constitution provided for 'legal resistance' to
le pouvoir; then let that right be invoked. What he meant by this will
presently appear. Was he right or wrong in his estimate of the state of
France which, he held, was ripe for the next stage of social revolution?

Writing of the state of the nation just before he became its Foreign
Minister in June 1849, when the nerve of the conservative right had been
shaken by the election result, de Tocqueville says that everybody wanted
to get rid of the Constitution, some by socialism and the rest by monarchy, a state of affairs which offered President Bonaparte the chance to
fulfil his Proudhonian 'manifest destiny' of finally rendering *le pouvoir*
insufferable. As for Bonaparte himself, '... It was clear that the only
support he could count on to keep us in his confidence was the jealousy
and hatred he felt of our common adversaries ... We wanted to make the
republic live; he wanted to inherit from it. We offered him ministers
when what he needed was accomplices.' It would seem, then, that de
Tocqueville was very much of Proudhon's opinion.

Day after day *Le Peuple* printed Proudhon's attacks on the government,
written from his hiding place in the Rue Chabrol. Léon Faucher, an
ex-journalist, now Minister of the Interior, was driven to counter-
attacking in the conservative *Le Moniteur*. With quite exceptional venom

Proudhon describes Faucher, in his *Confessions*, as '... that being, over-flowing with bile, whom heaven created even more hideous than his caricature, and who has the singular mania of trying to be worse than his reputation'. Faucher did his work of blackguarding Proudhon and the left so grossly that Proudhon prayed that he might continue in office – increasing the circulation and enhancing the credit of *Le Peuple* – for at least another three months; alas, the minister's criminal interference with the left's electioneering, by means of forgery, a sort of Watergate affair, led to his forced resignation. Had he had more time in which to discredit his master then, according to Proudhon, '... the street urchins of Paris would have been escorting Bonaparte back to the fortress of Ham'.[2]

One of the revolution's gains had been the right of assembly and the consequent legalization of political clubs which, under Louis-Philippe, had been proscribed and therefore clandestine, and consequently con-spiratorial. The first Odillon Barrot administration, which was the first of President Bonaparte's governments, alarmed by the growing strength of the left in the country and the intransigence of the opposition in the streets, decided to suppress this new liberty. The 'atrabilious' Léon Faucher tabled a draft law prohibiting the political clubs, the only foci of popular resistance to the reaction. A parliamentary committee charged with the task of examining and reporting on the measure to the Chamber, reported (21 March) that it would be a violation of the Constitution and that, consequently, the committee must refuse to join in any debate of it: 200 members withdrew from the Chamber to consider their position. This beginning of resistance to the Bonapartist reaction inside the Assembly, seemed to all the men of the right and centre so dangerous, that it was decided to tolerate Faucher's proposed violation rather than leave the opposition in the streets the means of following the lead of the parliamentary left, and then taking that lead into their own hands.

On 22 March *Le Peuple* had summoned the Paris workers to their own defence: if the Assembly adopted Faucher's project and debated it with a view to making it law, then the citizens must rise in resistance. In this summons Proudhon was not calling for a breach of law: the *Conventionel* Declaration of 1793 had recognized a right to insurrection. But Proudhon was not even advocating recourse to that right. Since the social and political debate is carried on as often with arms as with words, and a score of now respectable governments owe their office to civil war and even to terrorism, the argument he did use is of interest.

The right to insurrection is that right by virtue of which a people can reclaim its liberty from the tyranny of a despot or aristocracy by armed force. Where universal suffrage has been established there should, in theory, be no need of that right, so that when, in the year two, the Convention established it, it was providing against a danger that no longer existed. When the 1848 Constituent Assembly wrote into its Constitution (Article 110) that 'the Constitution and the rights it consecrates are entrusted to the care and patriotism of all Frenchmen', it was, again, by implication, establishing a right to insurrection.

In principle, let me repeat, universal suffrage abolishes the right to insurrection. But in practice, antagonism between the separated powers, and the absolutism of majorities can revive it ... There is one case in which the right to insurrection could legitimately be invoked by a minority against a majority: this would be in the event of a majority seeking to perpetuate its despotism by trying to abolish or restrict the exercise of universal suffrage. In such a case, I say, the minority has a right to resist even by force of arms.

The first recourse of the minority denied a voice, or an effective voice, by a majority, should be 'legal resistance', by which Proudhon means, as will appear, civil disobedience. The minority still being oppressed, then it ceases to be a political and parliamentary party of the opposition and becomes a proscribed group, and is virtually outlawed. Now, that oppression of the minority by the majority is of itself illegal under the Constitution and the majority has thus put itself outside the law.

In a considerable number of modern cases this argument has been followed and these rights claimed and used. Only the politically cretinous few who believe that the might of a majority confers all the rights, deny that in all such cases, the oppressed have had a moral right which takes precedence of the law. For, if one does not believe this, one is forced to admit that the Nazis had all the 'right' they needed, conferred by their overwhelming popular majority, to rid their country of non-conforming minorities by means of cyanide gas chambers; that Mary Tudor had a perfect right to persecute Protestants; and her successors both Puritans and Catholics, for not being of the Church of England. This is a special case of the Proudhonian doctrine 'justice is not established by laws'.

Proudhon went on from his general argument to assert that a government, to wit President Bonaparte's, which ruled that the cry in the streets or the Assembly of 'Long live the democratic and socialist republic', was factious; which denounced the democratic and socialist left in the Assembly and the country as being composed of thieves (*malfaiteurs et pillards*); which even caused them to be tried and condemned as such; a government which, when it pronounced the word 'order' meant the extermination of democratic public opinion; a government which, not daring to attack the revolution in Paris, sent an army to destroy it in Rome – that such a government was clearly and openly bent on the destruction of a minority in defiance of the Constitution. The implied conclusion was that the left now had the right to insurrection.

But it was not insurrection that he was calling for in *Le Peuple*; it was civil disobedience. He calculated that the opposition to the reaction, in the country, was about one-third of the population. There had, indeed, been a swing to the left as a result of the government's high-handed and reactionary conduct of affairs; and the reports which the government was receiving from its Prefects and police agents confirm this calculation. Proudhon called on that opposition to refuse to pay taxes and refuse military service: the results of that civil disobedience would have been far more effective than any conceivable insurrection. The socialist press, however, was as hostile to this campaign in *Le Peuple* as was the political and journalistic Establishment; Proudhon explains their hostility as follows:

If, said they, the people once refuse to pay their taxes, they will never consent to do so, and government will become impossible. Always this preoccupation with *government*! ... In short, the counter-revolution was admirably defended by the organs of the revolution ...

*   *   *   *   *

As a result of the unexpectedly large number of left republican *Députés* returned to the Legislative Assembly, the government was forced to resign; but Bonaparte asked Odillon Barrot to form a new one. Most of the ministers were the old lot in new places, but Barrot was able to introduce three new conservatives of a more conciliatory temper than Faucher and his friends, among them de Tocqueville as Foreign Minister. After his first cabinet meeting under the President's chairmanship he recorded:

One could not be in close contact with him for long without noticing a vein of madness which ran through his good sense. ... He owed his success more to this madness than to his good sense; for the world's stage is a strange place and sometimes the worst plays are the ones which succeed there. Had Bonaparte been a wise man, nay a genius, he would never have been President of the Republic.

Proudhon, in *Le Peuple*, was now insisting that the election results, so promising for the left, offered the Social Democrats a chance to give

France a socialist government: the Constitution was so worded that it could be all things to all men, conservative if interpreted by conservatives, socialist if interpreted by socialists. The left should now declare themselves to be the party of order and the Constitution, and indict the President and his ministers as un-Constitutional, even anti-Constitutional; in other words a mere gang of adventurers plotting against the liberty of the French people. An impeachment, supported by the opposition in the streets and by a civil disobedience campaign, would result in Ledru-Rollin becoming the first social-democratic president of the republic.

There were, in fact, good grounds for such an impeachment: on 7 May, just before the dissolution, the Constituent Assembly had passed a resolution specifically forbidding the government to intervene militarily in Rome to check the progress of Mazzini's republicans in the Papal States. Bonaparte and his ministers simply ignored it and sent an army to intervene. Furthermore, the outlawing of the Clubs was also in breach of the Constitution.

De Tocqueville says, in his *Recollections*, that the President's 'flouting of the law' made the conflict which all dreaded inevitable. Letters pouring in from the Prefects of the Departments, and from the chiefs of police, painted an extremely alarming picture of unrest, discontent and a marked leftward drift. He did not believe that armed revolution was imminent but it was a possibility; if civil war developed out of the political struggle then the state of Paris would be terrible indeed, for the cholera was raging again and people dying of it in hundreds. His first contact with the Legislative Assembly, as minister, confirmed his fears:

Within its walls one felt that one was breathing the air of civil war. Speeches were abrupt, gestures violent, the phrases used extravagant, insults outrageous and direct. We were meeting, for the time being, in the old chamber of deputies which was designed for 480 and now with difficulty held 750. One's body touched one's hated neighbour's for we were crammed together despite the loathing which held us apart, which discomfort stoked our anger. It was like fighting a duel in a barrel. How could the Left contain themselves? Their numbers had made them feel very strong in the nation and the army ...

Perhaps, had Ledru-Rollin, leading the left, taken Proudhon's advice in whole and not just in part, by firmly declaring his to be the party of law, order and the Constitution, bent on bringing the delinquent executive to justice, before taking an aggressive line, he might have brought the President down. What he did do on 11 May, following a news leak that a French army was fighting before Rome and doing badly, was to go to the tribune to demand the impeachment of the President and the former cabinet on the grounds of violation of the Constitution and to threaten that the left were prepared to take up arms against the government if this were not done. By this blunder he terrified the centrist liberals in the Assembly and the hesitating don't-knows in the country. They might well have been prepared to use Proudhonian civil disobedience to get rid of the King Stork they had imposed on themselves by universal suffrage combined with universal ignorance; but they were sick and tired of blood-letting.

May, 1849: general elections. Proudhon had no intention of standing again for his Seine constituency. In the first place he wanted no more to do with parliamentary politics; they were for the bourgeoisie and, as he confessed, he should never have meddled with them in the first place. In the second place, he was in much the same case as John Wilkes in the Middlesex elections of 1768: as a man proscribed he would not have been allowed to take his seat in the Chamber, even had he not been what he also was, a fugitive from justice. In the event he was given no choice: the left republicans, including the socialists, knowing his name worth 100,000 votes, overcame their detestation and nominated him. Informed of this by Darimon, he sent that faithful friend to tell them that he refused the nomination. He suggested a substitute; the committee rejected the suggestion. Proudhon was a candidate *malgré lui*.

This insistence by the left is the more surprising in that Proudhon was alone against all of them in his refusal to join in the noisy opposition to the government's intervention against the Italian unionist republicans who, as I have said above, had seized Rome from the Pope. He had never favoured Italian unity and was to write copiously against it; the proper way for Italy was a loose federation of seven small republics based on ethnic and geographical integrity. The Italian unionist republicans had murdered Rossi, Proudhon's disciple and principal Italian advocate of Federalism; Proudhon washed his hands of them.

He was returned to parliament with a majority increased by over 20,000 votes: of that victory he neither would nor could make any use. What would have happened had he tried to take his seat? The new Assembly would have had to waive privilege before the police could seize his person; no doubt they would have done so as cheerfully as their predecessors. The case did not occur. On 4 June while taking exercise away from the cramped conditions and stale air of his hotel room by walking in the purlieus of the Gare du Nord, he was recognized by a renegade Polish revolutionary turned police-informer, bundled into a cab, and driven to the Prefecture of Police. This was not the normal course: he should have been taken directly to the Conciergerie, but there were special standing orders concerning him. It so happened that the Prefect, Carlier, had a special regard for him, and even saw in him a kind of ally of the right against the centre.

Carlier received him with marked civility: a gentleman by birth and a former Legitimist, the Prefect admired Proudhon's prose and Proudhon's spirit. He informed his prisoner that he would be comfortably lodged and given all possible privileges, including freedom to write what he liked. He was allowed to go, on parole, to collect his papers and clothes from the Rue Chabrol and report himself at the Conciergerie for the night; on the following morning he was moved to Sainte-Pélagie.

As a result of these events Proudhon lost control of *Le Peuple* for several critical days. His editorial collaborators, excited like the whole of the left by Ledru-Rollin's call to arms, dropped his pacifist line and enthusiastically summoned the workers to insurrection in defence of the Republic and the Constitution. That was on 12 June; but on the same day, Ledru-Rollin and his friends, belatedly taking *Le Peuple*'s earlier line, either because they had realized they would not receive sufficient support in the streets, or because they lacked the nerve for action, backed down. When it was proposed to debate in the Assembly the proposal for impeachment, Ledru-Rollin objected that first the evidence in the case had to be tabled.[3] But that retreat into 'moderation' came too late: the leaders of the opposition in the streets snatched the initiative from the parliamentary opposition and, by their aggressive attitude, more or less forced the parliamentary leaders to resume their militant pose or lose control entirely. As it happened, the second thoughts which had obliged Ledru-Rollin, Victor Considérant, Raspail and the rest to abandon their militancy in the Chamber were the wise ones.

For, despite the call to arms of the whole left-wing press, following *Le Peuple*'s lead, by eleven o'clock on the morning of 13 June only about 8,000 men had turned up at the assembly point, the Château d'Eau, for the projected march on the Chamber of Deputies. By that same hour the ministers were with the President who was wearing uniform and ready to lead the troops against the people; and General Changarnier was explaining the disposition of his troops.

As a result of a delay in composing the order paper for 13 June, the Assembly began the day's session late. By noon most of the men of the right and centre were present, but so few of the left that de Tocqueville concluded that debate had ended and civil war begun. At three o'clock the Minister of the Interior, Dufaure, arrived to ask the Assembly to declare a state of siege. The only opposition to the motion came from the Christian Socialist Pierre Leroux; he was followed at the tribune by Cavaignac, whose exceptional and quite uncharacteristic eloquence convinced the waverers. The state of siege was declared, but very shortly thereafter came the news that the President and General Changarnier had led a cavalry charge against the column of workers, cut it in two, and scattered the marchers. They had also captured the insurrectionary HQ in the Conservatoire des Arts et Mètiers, and arrested all the leaders they could find there. In all the major cities the same fizzle-out occurred, excepting in Lyon where there were five hours of bloody battle before the troops got the upper hand. Bonaparte's triumph was marred by only one flaw: Ledru-Rollin and Victor Considérant both escaped from the Conservatoire, and got across the frontier into asylum in Brussels.

One of the insurrectionist moves which the government had been afraid of was a possible storming of Saint-Pélagie in order to release the political prisoners. Proudhon, among others, was therefore hastily moved to the Conciergerie and was a witness to the government's victory over the people, as a stream of new political prisoners began to flow into the prison. Among them were his friends Langlois and Pilhes who were able to tell him that the *Le Peuple* offices had been raided by a detachment of the National Guard who had scattered the type and smashed the printing presses: he had lost not only his liberty but the favourite part of his vocation.

In the Conciergerie he was very uncomfortably lodged: his cell, which had been Marie-Antoinette's, was running with damp; it got into his bones and he caught a cold which settled on his chest and started that catarrhal infection from which he was never again free. The associations of the place were depressing: dating from the 14th century, and once the residence of the Concierge, that is Master of the King's household, during the great revolution it had housed 1200 prisoners who went from there to the Tribunal and thence to the guillotine. From the Conciergerie the Girondins overthrown by Danton, then Danton and fifteen of his party overthrown by Robespierre, and then Robespierre and twenty of his faction, and at last Fouquier-Tinville who had prosecuted them all, together with the judges who had done his bidding, went to their deaths. That did not prevent Proudhon from working, nothing but death could do that, and he began his *Confessions of a Revolutionary*. Some say it was a result of a visit from the prison chaplain offering to hear his confession, to which offer he replied politely that he would rather write it. On 30 June his work was interrupted by the news that a constituency left republican party had nominated him as their candidate in a by-election. Having now no paper of his own, he wrote to Emile Girardin asking him to publish in *La Presse*, his absolute refusal of the candidature. At the same time he offered Girardin an alliance: *Le Peuple*, which he had every intention of reviving, and *La Presse*, working together while retaining their independence of each other, would be a formidable force for reform. 'You know me,' he wrote, 'as a revolutionary who is profoundly conservative; I know you as a conservative who is profoundly revolutionary.'

No doubt it was Proudhon's notice in *La Presse* which gave rise to the rumour along the boulevards that he was writing unsigned articles for that newspaper. Girardin picked it up and denied it, in print, continuing as follows:

Others besides myself have had talks with M. Proudhon. Louis Bonaparte was anxious to meet him the moment he returned to France; M. Proudhon was in my office when he was sent for to be driven to the Boulevard des Italiens where the prince was then living. And can it be unknown that some time prior to 24 February M.le comte de Chambord conveyed to M. Proudhon his wish that he would come to him at Frohsdorf, there to expound and discuss means to improve the lot of the working-classes and to extinguish, or at least diminish, pauperism.

Prince Louis Bonaparte was the Prince-President's cousin; he is not to be confused with that other cousin, Prince Napoleon, also known as Prince Jerome, with whom Proudhon was to have business dealings concerned with railway concessions. The comte de Chambord, living in German exile, was the Bourbon heir-pretender to the French throne, and faint white hope of the Legitimist opposition.

Proudhon wrote a letter for publication in *La Presse* in which he quoted his *Carnet* record of his meeting with Prince Louis:

26 September 1848. Called on Louis Bonaparte. The man seems well-meaning. Chivalrous face and heart; fuller of his uncle's fame than of personal ambition. For the rest, a mediocre mind. I doubt whether, seeing him closely and knowing him well, one would expect him to make a great showing. Moreover, beware. It's the way of all claimants to begin by seeking out the leaders of parties.

As for the comte de Chambord, Proudhon denied, in an amusing passage too long to quote, that he had ever received that invitation; had he done so he would have accepted it, for when the sons of kings started asking guidance of the sons of coopers, there was hope that capitalists would start asking guidance of working-men.

Not until the end of September was Proudhon restored to Sainte-Pélagie. There he had a large room, thirty feet each way and very lofty, with two windows, one overlooking the Jardin des Plantes and the other the hospital La Pitié: a much better room than the one he rented in the Rue Mazarine. He was allowed to supplement the prison diet with meals sent in by a neighbouring restaurant; but the prison bread was excellent and the prison cellar furnished him with a wine at 60 centimes the litre, which was better than the one he was buying from his own merchant at 1 franc 50. He was allowed as many visitors as he wanted to receive, all his books, newspapers and periodicals.

Every Monday afternoon the prisoners held what one can only call a *salon*, in one of the common rooms, to which friends and relations and even casual visitors were invited. Proudhon found old friends, including Charles Beslay, a *Le Peuple* contributor, at Sainte-Pélagie; and was making new ones, the most important of them being the young painter Courbet who crowned a turbulent revolutionary career by engineering the overthrow of the Vendôme column, during the Commune, twenty years later. Proudhon dominated the *salon* conversations by, above all, '... his pitiless and laughing contempt for the pretentions to eternity of all kinds of dominion ... and by identifying in each that immanent contradiction which sooner or later would be the death of it ...' The words are Giuseppe Ferrari's, author of the best history of the 19th-century Italian revolutions, and a frequent guest at the prisoners' *salon*. From much of that acute observer's remarks about Proudhon, I extract what follows:

He knew Latin, to make fun of it; philosophy to attack the Sorbonne; history, to stay out of the Institut; literature to mock the immortals of the Academy ...

And a brilliantly terse *aperçu* of Proudhon's social aims:

Above all, beware of trying to make up to him by a parade of liberalism, by expressing a wish to see the lot of the working people bettered by turning the working-man into a kind of bourgeois by giving him the right to a free hospital bed and free medical care. Proudhon stands foremost among the enemies of that slow progress which would denature and disanimate the worker, would repaint his chains, and would have no other effect but that of reinforcing the old society, his enemy.

NOTES ON CHAPTER SEVEN

1. Proudhon called Girardin (a brilliant journalistic adventurer, fore-runner of Northcliffe), the inventor of the popular press. *La Presse* was so influential in getting votes for Bonaparte in the presidential elections, that Proudhon spoke of Girardin as having 'made a president of the Republic'.
2. 'Your internal administration is vexatious, provocative and high-handed, being employed to favour certain local ambitions and local grudges. All these vices will be

further increased under Faucher's control. Such a way of ruling not only continually alienates friends, it drives those of pinkish-tendencies into the arms of the Reds and menaces us with the prospect of a revolutionary election.' De Tocqueville in a conversation with L-N. Bonaparte, 15 May 1851.

3. 'What was their object in putting off the debate like that?. . . Did they hope to use the interval to set men's minds on fire, or secretly intend to make time to calm them down? It is certain that their leaders, more used to talking than fighting, more passionate than resolute, did on that day show, for all the intemperance of their language, a sort of hesitation not apparent the day before. Having half-drawn the sword they seemed to want to sheath it again.' De Tocqueville. *Recollections*.

Marriage and *The Voice of the People*

DESPITE THE LOSS OF *Le Peuple*, of Duchêne, and of all the money invested in the paper, Proudhon was not to be silenced:

The indomitable gladiator, the stubborn Besançon peasant, would not lay down his arms, but at once contrived to publish a new journal, *La Voix du Peuple*. It was necessary to find 24 thousand francs for the guarantee fund. Emile Girardin would have been ready to give it but Proudhon did not want to be dependent on him, and Sazonov suggested that I should contribute the money. I was under a great obligation to Proudhon for my intellectual development, and after some consideration consented, though I knew that the money would soon be gone.

Thus Alexander Herzen in his memoirs.[1]

Proudhon's reluctance to accept backing from Girardin is understandable. It was one thing to envisage an alliance with him, in which each would keep his independence; quite another to submit to the control which a financial backer of Girardin's calibre would insist on. Thus Herzen's offer came as a boon. But I have yet to explain the need for a 'guarantee fund'; it had nothing to do with the actual financing of publication. It was under Louis-Philippe that the French authorities devised this means for silencing those newspapers which flouted them. The press was free, of course – *Vive la liberté!* — but to provide against irresponsible journalistic attacks on institutions and officers of the state on which and on whom the health, wealth and happiness of the French people was, of course, dependent, there had to be certain press laws. And, to provide for fines following breaches of those laws, newspaper publishers were obliged, before receiving a licence to publish, to deposit a sum of money with the authorities.

Herzen describes how this was used to ruin troublesome newspapers. The guarantee fund was exhausted by a series of prosecutions which invariably ended in prison and a money fine. The fine being paid out of the fund, the fund had to be made up again to the statutory level before publication could continue. As soon as the deficit was made good, a new prosecution was started. This device was always successful because the legal authorities were always hand in glove with the government in political cases.

That, then, was how both *Le Représentant du Peuple*, and in due course, Proudhon's other newspapers were disposed of, as well as dozens of other socialist and republican journals. The governments of the Second Republic and Second Empire saw no reason to change an arrangement which had worked so admirably as a suppressor of the truth under the Orleanist monarchy: the system even made a substantial profit.

At the time when Herzen agreed to put up 24,000 francs – equivalent to at least £30,000 of our money – he scarcely knew the man in whose mission he believed and to whom he was thus acknowledging his debt of gratitude. He had met Proudhon only twice, both times at the lodgings which Bakunin, Proudhon's greatest Russian disciple, was sharing with the musician Adolf Reichel, in the Rue de Bourgogne on the Rive Gauche. Proudhon often visited those lodgings, to listen to Reichel playing Beethoven and to Bakunin expounding Hegel. Bakunin had taken refuge in Paris when the German communist Weitling, in whose conspiratorial goings-on he was involved, was arrested and expelled from Switzerland by the cantonal police of Zurich. Of all the revolutionary thinkers he met in Paris, including Karl Marx and Pierre Leroux, Proudhon was the one who made the strongest impression on him, did most to shape his own thinking, was, as he put it, 'the master of us all'.

Herzen was aware that he had not made much of an impression on Proudhon, for on the occasions of both encounters he had modestly held his tongue and let the others talk. But he was determined, if they were to work together, that Proudhon should not regard him as a rich dilettante and should take him seriously: moreover he had his own uses for the projected newspaper, uses less narrowly French than Proudhon's were bound to be. He therefore made three conditions for his support: he must have the right to print his own articles in the paper and those of his Russian political friends; he must have supervisory control over the foreign news and views section of the paper; and he must insist on the payment of foreign contributors. French editors were altogether too apt to consider that the honour and glory of getting their stuff into a Paris paper should be sufficient pay for foreign journalists.

Proudhon reluctantly agreed, pointing out that this meant that the paper's success would depend on substantial agreement between the two of them on the policy to be followed. That agreement was achieved, largely thanks to Herzen's respect for Proudhon, and his diplomatic gifts: *La Voix du Peuple* was an immediate and astonishing success. Great editors are born, not made, a fact of life which I learned when studying Kingsley Martin of the *New Statesman*;[2] and nobody has been able to define the quality which makes them. Whatever it is, Proudhon had it, and knew that he had it, for nothing in his life did he relish more than his journalistic work, and success in it. Herzen says that '... from his prison cell he conducted his orchestra in masterly fashion. His articles were full of originality, fire, and that exasperation which is fanned by imprisonment'. Street sales soared to 40,000 on an ordinary day; and on the days when the leading article was by Proudhon, to 60,000 so that, the last edition being sold out, on the following morning copies of the paper changed hands at twenty times the paper's price of 5 centimes.

There is a *but*, an *however*, to all this: in his leaders Proudhon was courting disaster by flouting and taunting the Prince-President and his government, so that receipts from sales even at the rate of 1500 francs a day net were scarcely sufficient, and finally insufficient, to keep the guarantee fund, repeatedly depleted by fines following prosecutions, at the statutory level.

Busy as he had been with his new newspaper and his *Confessions*, Proudhon neglected Euphrasie, and in October more or less confessed it in a short letter of explanation that was the last to begin 'Mademoiselle'. The next, written in December, begins '*Ma chère Euphrasie*' and ends '*Je vous embrasse!*' Some time between those two letters they had agreed, or she had persuaded him or he her, that prison or no, they should be married. It is possible, but given her gentle nature, unlikely, that she had pointed out that for two years she had been turning down other offers.

In that same December letter he apologizes for being unable to go and buy in person the present he wants to give her, so that he is obliged to ask her to do it herself. It was a dress, in the cut and fashion of which he took an interest: it was to be made *à ma guise*, 'to my taste', and she was to spend as much as 60 francs. Three sovereigns would buy a good bedstead in those days, or a dozen plain wooden chairs, so that he was being generous. He had by then given her money for the decorating and furnishing of the flat they had found, and hints playfully that she is more interested in wallpapers than in him; but she is to spend the money as she likes, he wants no accounting for it. That was not simply kindness: it was good sense: she was the hard-minded, shrewd shopper that he never had the time, as he reckoned the value of his time, to be.

In the matter of the flat they had been lucky: at No. 9, Rue de la Fontaine he had found rooms which were not only immediately opposite to Sainte-Pélagie, but the windows of which were immediately opposite that of Proudhon's prison room. Proudhon saw the new flat, furnished, for the first time on the afternoon of Christmas Day 1849: it was one of his parole days and he had eaten his Christmas dinner with old acquaintances and colleagues, at the journalists' and compositors' political banquet at Charenton. It is, to us, well nigh inconceivable that a political prisoner regarded as dangerous should have been allowed out to attend a political banquet; but there it is.

On the last day of the year he was allowed out again: he met Euphrasie and her family at the *mairie* of the old 5th *arrondisement*, and they were married at last.

Proudhon announced his marriage, just before or just after the event, in a number of letters to friends. In several of them he took such pains to assure his correspondents that he was not in love with his wife, that one seeks an explanation of this unlikeable assertion: for, true or not, and as Daniel Halévy was the first to ask, why mention this at all? It was discourteous to the young woman and no business of anybody's but his own and her's. But surely the reason is obvious: he had all his life made such a parade of his contempt for the romantic attitude to women, that he had, whether true or not, to exclude love from the explanation of his marriage. It does him, in our eyes, no credit, but in his own was certainly nothing to be ashamed of. He had always been an ancient Roman. Whether his method of doing it was, given the erotic romanticism of the times, unkind to the girl, is difficult to know. Euphrasie, unable to read the novels of Sand, Hugo or Stendhal, might or might not have been susceptible to that Romantic climate. That method is best exemplified in a letter to his brother, Charles:

You will know that for all my forty-one years and the extinction of amorous feelings, I am about to contract a marriage. It is not that I am in love or, I assure you, the brisk and eager bridegroom; you can see for yourself that I am busy with quite other matters than amorous trifling. It is a piece of necessary business which I am concluding, moreover business I have had in mind for a long time. The wife I am taking is twenty-seven years and two months old, so no chicken you see. She has known poverty in her life, which I find very useful in forming a woman's character. The one thing she understands is work, from six in the morning till midnight. Her family are working folk, I find an analogy between her and your wife; she has never read a word of what I've written and never will. In the matter of intellectual pretensions and attitudinising, I've nothing to worry about. I've every reason to believe that she will not be demanding, if you follow me!

Vasbenter is being released from Sainte-Pélagie this morning; it was either sometimes his mother or his wife who came to do our cooking for us. Which leaves us, Duchêne and me, without help ...

My intended is blonde, of medium height, and although a Parisienne, robust and with a clear, fresh skin. She does not look more than twenty-two or three. She has a horror of worldliness, noise and commotion, and politics. In short, I am taking a wife for the commodity of my poor existence, and not to parade before my friends or the public. You know that although I have audacity in my ideas, and stand up and defy the powers that be and public opinion, in my private life I like to keep myself to myself, and permit no idlers to get their noses past my door. In that I am sure of being served to perfection.

When I was at a French school we had a way of insulting those whose manners or conduct offended us; a way as infuriating to the offender as it was unjust to the worthiest order of men: *Quel paysan!* But then, Proudhon was.

The *Carnat* entry is curt: '31 December, 1849. Married to Euphrasie Piégard, twenty-seven. My only regret is that I did not marry four years ago. When the wife is good, better get the children sooner than later.'

Proudhon's French biographers are all reluctant to accept as a fact that he married to get a housekeeper, cook and mother for his children, and nothing more; and indignant at his want of *politesse* towards the poor young woman. I have given a reason why he might have lied about this, but found no evidence that it was not quite simply true. That he came to love, respect and be grateful to his wife is certain, and that he made her, as they say, a good husband; that he was ever 'in love' with her or any other woman is not.

For the next five weeks they saw each other every day: either Euphrasie brought their dinner across the road in a covered basket; or, on parole days, he ate it with her in their flat, often entertaining a member of her family, or one of his friends.

*   *   *   *   *

The Prince-President and his government were far from being the only targets for Proudhon's polemical sniping from the pages of *La Voix du Peuple*: his campaigns against the old republican left and the Blancist social-democrats were as harsh and sustained as his attacks on the government party. It was not he who started the fight, and he might have spared them and thus not become the initiator of a bitter struggle which continued for a century and which may be resumed at any time. The fact is that the *Voix du Peuple* was forced to defend itself for, as Proudhon complained in its columns (23 November 1849), Louis Blanc in *Le Nouveau Monde* and Pierre Leroux in *La République du Dimanche* were defaming him and his paper by calling them defectors from and renegades of socialism. What was the prime reason for this bitter hostility to the anarchist line?

The ancient Romans, being polytheists, made a god of each Caesar in his turn. The modern communists, being by heritage of the monotheistic persuasion, deify the state as supreme and eternal.

The state-worshipper's reaction to the idea of freedom was, in 1850, exactly what it still remains: grief and rage, at the spectacle of the Supreme Being being denigrated, exposed as a fraud and a tyrant, fulminated against as evil, denied and defied; in a word, blasphemed against. What terrible echoes of that fury, as terrible as even the Church's against heretics, we have heard since Louis Blanc and Karl Marx first gave it expression in their struggle against Proudhon and Liberty. The strife, which split and destroyed the First International, for long remained merely wordy. But when, following the Congress of Russian anarchists at Nabat in 1919, the disciples of Bakunin whose master was Proudhon resolved to have no more to do with the Soviets on the grounds that they had become, '... purely political organs, organized on an authoritarian, centralist, Stateist basis', the Bolsheviks set about suppressing them. The last flare-up of Russian anarchism was at Kropotkin's funeral in 1921 when the black flags followed the coffin. Soon after that the executions began. Leon Trotsky, the most brilliant military commander of the century, although engaged with half a dozen 'White' armies of counter-revolutionaries, found the time and strength to wage a war to the death against the Ukrainian anarchist general, the Hetman Nestor Makhno, who had driven the Austro-German armies *and* two White-Russian armies out of his country. And still the hate continued; in the Spanish Civil War of 1936–9, so intent were the Communists on wiping out the most fervent of the Spanish anti-Fascist soldiers, the anarchist legions, that they threw away the victory they might have had.

Proudhon's crime in the eyes of all the factions of state-worshipping socialists was his persistence in pointing out that the state itself, not the mere wielders of its authority – king, oligarchy, democracy or bureaucracy – was the arch-enemy of liberty, responsibility, self-respect, and a decent prosperity.

Here is Proudhon in *La Voix*:

Just as, in the economic field, we have been up against vested interests, so in the political field we are up against the resistance of ambition and pride. Men who are not attached to capitalism either philosophically or because they are greedy, are attached to the idea of political power either as a consequence of philosophical illusions or because of their antecedents as public men. There is the secret of the hostility to *La Voix du Peuple* manifested by citizens Louis Blanc and Pierre Leroux ... We accuse citizens Louis Blanc and Pierre Leroux of obstructing the Revolution by defending, as they now do, the governmental system, last stronghold of monopoly capitalism. ...

And again (3 December):

Revolutions know no leaders; they come when the time is ripe and halt when the mysterious force which initiates them is exhausted. They can be pushed, but not pulled, which is proved today in the example of those men who, greedy for power and popular favour, have harnessed themselves to the revolutionary wagon under the illusion that it will stop when they stop pulling. But the uncontrollable machine rolls forward, sweeping aside both those who try to stop it, and those who think they are dragging it their way. O ye shrewd ones, would you avoid being crushed under its wheels? Then get behind it and, when you see it begin to gather momentum, jump on the tail-board.

Pius IX had tried to use the revolution and then to halt it at the point when he thought it had gone far enough; it ran him over.[3] Now Louis Blanc was trying the same dangerous gamble for power. This, from *La Voix*: 'Halt!' cries he, 'I am the Secretary of State for Progress, and let no man take a step forward without my permission. Down, down you anarchists, individualists, egalitarians! Men of the people, honour the State, for the State is you ...' *L'Etat, c'est vous*.

Blanc, says Proudhon in *La Voix*, is under the illusion that the February revolution was made in order to realize his 'organization of labour' plan; give him an inch of power, and to realize that ambition and satisfy his pride, he will take the ell of a despot. He had, in fact, tried to do just that, felt it his revolutionary duty to do just that, when he tried to force the postponement of a Constituent Assembly election (an example which Lenin was to follow). As for Pierre Leroux, the Christian socialist, who was arguing in *La République du Dimanche*, that to abolish government would entail abolishing religion, '... that holy man aspires to replace the Pope as the vicar of Christ on earth; and some there be who claim that he remembers having once *been* Jesus Christ ...'

Demagogue and mystagogue respectively, the two socialist leaders were counter-revolutionaries because it was not the organization of credit and reform of taxation of the kind to render political government superfluous, which they were working for. Revolution meant the disappearance of state as well as of capitalism: for the state could never be the servant of the people; it must always be their master.

Early in February there occurred a curious scene which Herzen, calling on Proudhon in his room in Sainte-Pélagie, witnessed; its sequel greatly hastened the ruin of their newspaper. Herzen found Proudhon scowling his way through some recent editions of the paper. One of his

visitors, the comte Edmond de Lignières, alias D'Alton-Shée, a Legitimist notorious for his declaration that he was not a Christian nor even a
deist, was pointing out that they were filled with poor, feeble stuff, while
the other two, both members of the *Voix du Peuple* editorial board,
watched and listened in nervous silence and, apparently, had nothing to
say for themselves. Proudhon rounded on them and growled,

> What is the meaning of this? You take advantage of my being in prison to fall
> asleep back there in the office. No, gentlemen, if you continue like this I shall
> refuse to have anything more to do with the paper, and I shall publish the
> grounds for my refusal. I will not have my name dragged in the mud. You need
> someone to hang over you and supervise every line you print. The public takes
> this for *my* newspaper! No, I must put a stop to this. Tomorrow I shall send an
> article to cancel the ill effects of your scribbling, and I shall show you what *I*
> understand to be the proper spirit of our paper.

The reason for that reference to his name being dragged in the mud is, I
think, clear. Only a sustained high level of ferocity in the paper's attacks
on the government could convince the men of the socialist and communist left, when they read his attacks on them, that there was nothing in
the accusations of Blanc and Leroux that he was a renegade.

It is probable that when his editorial colleagues received the promised
article they wished that they had the power and the courage to refuse to
print it; for it must have been clear to them that the consequences of
publication might well be the ruin of the paper. But they had no choice:
published on 5 February, entitled *VIVE L'EMPEREUR!* the article was,
in Herzen's words, '. . . a dithyramb of irony, frightful, virulent irony'.

> VIVE L'EMPEREUR! You will allow us, will you not, Citizen-President, to hail
> your joyous advent: VIVE L'EMPEREUR! You want the people to acclaim you,
> you do not want to keep the celebration to yourself? We shall all be there, city,
> *faubourgs* and *banlieu*, to serenade you. VIVE L'EMPEREUR! and down with the
> National Assembly! VIVE L'EMPEREUR! and down with taxation! VIVE
> L'EMPEREUR! and down with usury and debts! VIVE L'EMPEREUR! and
> down with priests, Jesuits and friars! VIVE L'EMPEREUR! and death to the
> tyrants!

Death to the tyrants: the mere idea of Napoleon *le Petit* in the European
revolutionary role of Napoleon *le Grand* was acid ridicule; but ridicule
was not Proudhon's only weapon in this 'dithyramb':

> Two years ago when we were the masters we wanted only two things which no
> society has the right to refuse: work and bread. We were given blood and lead. An
> end to hypocrisy and mercy! Make your *coup d'état*, the workers will support you.
> No need to provoke them by cutting down the trees of liberty under their very

eyes. Liberty is in the heart of the proletariat, not hanging from your greasy poles. All you have to do is to appear on the Tuileries balcony in imperial costume, and society, which was to have been reborn out of the steady development of its institutions, will begin its regeneration in chaos.

Thus did he compound the felony of accusing Louis Bonaparte of plotting to enslave the people of France. His worst crime, in official eyes, was to have penetrated by intuition and insight the secret mind of the Prince-President. One of de Tocqueville's conversations with Louis-Napoleon, reported in his *Recollections*, makes it sufficiently clear that Bonaparte was, indeed, already thinking in terms of the *coup d'état* which Proudhon foresaw and forecast. All the Prince-President had to do to make himself emperor was to act upon Proudhon's own theory that a people who can be gulled into accepting the institution of universal suffrage as a substitute for liberty, will make a Caesar of any man bold and crafty enough to offer himself convincingly as their protector against the greed and oppression of the patrician or bourgeois oligarchy.

It can hardly have endeared Proudhon to Bonaparte that all Paris was chattering, chuckling and laughing aloud, as copies of that day's *Voix du Peuple* were snatched from the hands of the news-boys crying it in the streets as they ran.

As a result of these indiscretions, the governor of Sainte-Pélagie was ordered to cut his mischievous prisoner off from the outside world by denying him visitors. He wrote to Euphrasie on the seventh telling her to avoid appearing at her window, to keep it shut and the curtains drawn over it. If they were caught making signals to each other, his enjoyment of other privileges would be withdrawn and he might even be moved. Waste of ink – he was moved into a cell with boarded windows and a sentry placed before the door. She was to deliver his meals in a basket at the prison office: 'I embrace you and beg you, nay order you, to accept this little setback with firmness and patience, as I do, and to take good care of yourself.' He did not at first expect to be kept for long *incommunicado*. He caught a glimpse of Euphrasie at her window despite his orders, and wrote anxiously to say that she was looking ill and drawn and was to let him know at once what was wrong with her: 'You will not serve my peace of mind by withholding anything, whatsoever it be'. He had also to tell her that their separation might be longer than he had anticipated: he suspected that the authorities hoped, by cutting his communications, to cripple the *Voix du Peuple* whose enormous circulation, up now to 60,000, with a readership of more than 250,000, depended on his leading articles. He urged his wife to see people, go to the theatre, amuse herself: 'Come, dear child, courage! The wife of Citizen Proudhon must show no weakness.'

On 21 February Proudhon was moved to the Conciergerie prison, and Euphrasie was allowed to see him again; it was there that she told him she was pregnant, and where he recorded in the *Carnet*:

I have learned from my wife that she is pregnant. The news is very sweet to me. No bachelor whatever his experience of love, can possibly imagine what conjugal and paternal love mean! I am a prisoner, yet I am happy.

He had given Carlier, the chief of police, an undertaking to write no more political articles and for some weeks there was peace. But it was impossible for him to keep his undertaking. On 19 April Proudhon published a hectoring article in support of a left-wing republican candidate, the novelist Eugène Sue. 'Vote with the people, vote with the workers, for I tell you – and I knew it twenty-two months ago when I was alone in taking up their defence – the proletarians are our strength.' With the weight of Proudhon's support behind him, Sue was elected to the Assembly along with a number of other republican candidates; meanwhile Proudhon had betrayed his undertaking to the chief of police, and on the day after publication of his article in *La Voix du Peuple* he found himself transferred from the Conciergerie prison to the Citadelle of Doullens, a hundred miles north-east of Paris, the jail normally occupied by long-term political prisoners. Here Proudhon was placed in solitary confinement and allowed no books or papers. The only activity permitted him was to keep his diary and write letters.

From Doullens he wrote to Euphrasie telling her to call on his friends at the *Voix du Peuple* for help in appealing to the Minister of the Interior for permission for both her and his brother Charles to visit him at the Citadelle; and on Garnier for money, 200 or 300 francs, to cover their expenses. Permission was granted and they saw Proudhon on 26th April; while they were with him he gave Charles a letter to the *Voix du Peuple* which he was to smuggle out. Proudhon should have known better, for poor Charles never succeeded in anything he did; he was searched in the prison guardroom on the way out and the letter discovered, and on the following day the prison governor made a noisy and humiliating scene in front of his wife, cancelled her right to access, and consigned Proudhon to a solitary confinement cell.

The reader in this year of grace will learn with astonishment that the prisoner was neither tortured, set to some exhausting and degrading task, put on starvation rations, beaten up by police thugs, used as a guinea-pig by psychiatrists, or otherwise punished for flouting author-

ity.[4] He was even allowed to write letters and on 30 April asked Euphrasie who had gone back to Paris to make another appeal to the Minister,
to let him know as soon as she possibly could, how long he was to be kept,
'against all law and all rules' in solitary confinement, so that he could
provide himself with the requisite measure of patience.

In at least one respect solitary confinement seems to have been a relief:
the ordinary rule at Doullens was easy, unlike that of the Conciergerie,
and the prisoners were free to mingle and talk in the courts and common
rooms as much as they pleased. A similar rule in Sainte-Pélagie had been
a blessing because the company had been distinguished. Doullens, on
the other hand, was crowded with boulevard dissidents, café Tortoni
loudmouths swept up by the police in their systematic raids and patrols
which were designed to extinguish all overt opposition. There is a vivid
sketch of the sort of bistro-pink Proudhon found himself forced to consort
with, in Guy de Maupassant's *Boule de Suif*.

Disgusted with his company Proudhon records in the *Carnet*:

What I see here desolates and afflicts me without remission. If the people do not
belong to the Jesuits they must be handed over to demagogues. After the
charlatans, the sectaries! What a life! O what was I about, to get myself into this
galley? I have produced a lot of ideas, done some good, conscientious work: all
thrown away. Mankind wants to be ruled; ruled it will be. I am ashamed of my
species.

The state of mind which this reveals goes far to explain the resignation,
almost relief, with which he accepted the extinction of *La Voix du Peuple*. It
should be remembered that the winter cold and damp of the Conciergerie had left him in a state of ill-health; even breathing was an effort.
The so-called catarrhal infection was, no doubt, bronchitis, or the
annunciation of that asthma which was to wear him out in his fifties. Nor
were his spirits lightened by the one fellow-prisoner whom he found he
could respect, if only in the way one would doubtless respect the Angel of
Death if one met him at one's club. Auguste Blanqui, the man whom de
Tocqueville describes as if he were some foul scarecrow-corpse risen
from the grave to ferment the dyspepsia of terror in the capon-filled
bellies of the burgesses, was in Doullens fortress. It had suited de
Tocqueville to omit from his evocation the fact that the man was quite as
schooled in the arts and sciences, and as deeply read, as his respectable
brother; only, not all men digest their education to the same effect. No
doubt it's a matter of how much spleen is flowing or, on the other hand, of
clarity or foresight. Proudhon – this is another *Carnet* entry – saw him
thus:

Blanqui is the man of black fatality. Pessimist and misanthropist, always putting things at their worst and backing up his opinion with intelligent and inexorable reasons, he desolates and appals you. He himself is appalled at his own judgements. He fears everything, scarcely hopes at all, sees the Republic as lost, the Revolution aborted, the proletariat for ever in chains, mankind irredeemable. I myself have somewhere made the sinister prediction that if the bourgeois coalition be achieved, we are done for. I fear it too: it frightens me ...

Meanwhile he had seen in the *Moniteur* that an edition of the *Voix du Peuple* had been seized, on a pretext which was ridiculous, and made up his mind that it was no use trying to carry on with it; neither he nor his colleagues on the paper would have a moment's peace until the paper was liquidated, since the government had both the clear intention and the means, by fines and seizures and suspensions, to ruin it. He was allowed to work in his cell, and tried to get on with a textbook, a *Course in Political Economy*, which Garnier had commissioned.[5]

Despite his distaste for the social life of the prison, Proudhon found solitary confinement such an ordeal that, swallowing his pride he decided to petition the governor for release. His petition coincided with an order from the Ministry which Euphrasie had obtained with the help of their friends, for his 'restoration to the freedom of the prison' as he put it. Euphrasie returned to Doullens and was allowed to see her husband every day until near the end of May when they both returned to Paris again: she none too soon, for her pregnancy was tiring her, to their flat; and he to the Conciergerie so that he could be taken, in custody, to his trial on charges arising out of his 19 April *Voix du Peuple* article. The charges were numerous, varying from the customary to the ludicrous. 'Excitement to hatred and contempt' was to be expected, but 'provocation ... to bring about devastation and pillage ...' was absurd. Had he been found guilty on all charges brought against him, Proudhon could have found himself in prison for a further fifteen years. At the very least he anticipated a sentence which would lengthen his term of imprisonment; but pleading his own cause, in the event he was acquitted.

*   *   *   *   *

Back in the Conciergerie, Proudhon now petitioned to be moved back to Sainte-Pélagie. This was refused, but Euphrasie was allowed unrestricted access to him, and his three days per month parole outings were restored. He was not required to spend time and spirit liquidating the *Voix du Peuple*, the authorities did that for him. This was as well since, despite its sales, fines and seizures had been so costly that the Herzen fund was exhausted.

Early in June Herzen, who was being expelled from France, called on him in his prison[6] to take leave. It was a mournful parting for the near future held no shadow of hope for their causes. Proudhon sat in gloomy silence; both men's minds were full of thoughts, but of what avail to voice them? In his memoirs Herzen recorded:

I have heard a great deal of his roughness, *rudesses*, and intolerance; I had no experience of anything like it in my own case. What people call his harshness was the tense muscle of the fighter; his scowling brow showed only the powerful working of his mind: in his anger he reminded me of a wrathful Luther or of Cromwell ridiculing the Rump. He knew that I understood him and knowing also how few did so, appreciated it. He knew he was considered an unde-monstrative man; and hearing from Michelet of the disaster that had overtaken my mother and Kolya[7] he wrote to me from Sainte-Pélagie, this among other things: 'Is it possible that fate must attack us from that direction too? I cannot get over this terrible calamity. I love you and carry your image deep here in this heart which so many think of stone.'

Notwithstanding his feeling that he could accomplish no more by journalism, he found it too hard to give up the pleasure which its practice afforded. Somehow Darimon, Langlois and Duchêne scraped together the money for the guarantee fund and a weekly, reviving the old *Le Peuple* title, was started. To the customary burden of fines – one prosecution was for 'incitement to civil war' – was added the new stamp-duty on newspapers and periodicals designed to give the *coup de grâce* to France's free press. The weekly *Le Peuple* lasted only four months.

Deprived at last of the newspaper press, Proudhon turned again to the writing of books. The *Confessions of a Revolutionary*, published in 1850, and on which I have drawn in chapters five and six, is, with good reason, considered to be his best work from the purely literary point of view, and was both a commercial success and a *succes d'éstime*. Daniel Halévy, writing nearly a century after Sainte-Beuve, like that critic calls the book one of the masterpieces of French literature.[8] Cuvillier-Fleury of the *Académie Française*, writing in the *Journal des Débats*, repelled by the contrasting sombreness and fire of the book, was deeply impressed by it as a work of art, quoting from it at length. Camille Pelletan, writing in Emile Girardin's *La Presse*, publicly apologized to Proudhon for having formerly calumniated him and gave the *Confessions* such a review as authors dream of. This cannot be attributed to the fact that *La Presse* and *La Voix du Peuple* had been supporting each other's political and economic proposals, Girardin supporting Proudhon's cheap money policy, and Proudhon backing Girardin's proposal to recast direct taxation into the form of a national insurance system. Also when Girardin used *La Presse* to propose a capital levy, virtually a wealth tax, Proudhon declares that it would have effects as beneficial as his own People's Bank. Pelletan had nothing to do with any of this.

The only paper which maltreated Proudhon's book was, predictably, Leroux's; that mystagogic Christian socialist declared that Proudhon was neither a republican, nor a democrat nor a socialist, but a wicked man and an atheist to boot.

The second book of his prison years, far more difficult to read, is also far more important: this is his *Idée Generale de la Révolution au XIXeme Siècle – General Idea of the Revolution in the 19th Century*.

His purpose in writing it was to set forth his vision of the revolution as it must be, not because revolutionaries willed it to be thus or otherwise, but because it was a permanent and continuing process governed by the laws of human societies – not the made laws but the 'natural' laws. His definition contains his whole faith: *Revolution is, in the order of moral facts, an act of sovereign justice proceeding from the necessities of things. Consequently it is self-justifying, and it is a crime for any statesman to oppose it.*

He finds the 'necessities of things' in a thorough study of the conditions of the working-class; the depressed state of industry and trade; the chronic mismanagement of credit by the credit institutions, including usurious rates of interest; and the unjust principles of taxation. A single statistic taken from the figures published by the Christian socialist economist Charles-François Chève demonstrates Proudhon's method of putting the negative side of his case. In round figures, France's GNP in 1849 was 10 billion (*milliard*, thousand million) francs: this was the total value of the products of industry and agriculture. Of those 10 billion no fewer than 6, that is 60 per cent of the whole, were creamed off by society's parasites – the various categories of money-lenders, rent-receivers and other recipients of *aubaines*, and the state.[9] Thus the workers with hands and brains, the actual producers of wealth, received only 40 per cent of their product. Clearly, the first revolutionary problem was to relieve the productive workers of this burden of parasitism. The solution which Proudhon put forward was ultra-radical and ultra-libertarian.

The several socialist solutions on offer are, he says, either mere utopianism, rejected by the people who have too much native good sense to believe in such stuff; or they are reactionary in that they seek only to change the personnel of government, and not to abolish it. In any case, the task is not to dogmatize – Proudhon had, it will be recalled, long since come to that conclusion during his exchanges with Karl Marx – but to seek to orient ourselves correctly, to find that point of view from which society's natural tendency to evolve towards 'justice' can be seen, and therefore followed. As will be made clear when I come to an appreciation of a later work, *Of Justice in the Revolution and in the Church*, Proudhon's social justice, and the 'rightness', in the sense of organic efficiency, of things, are indistinguishable: beauty, truth, justice are manifestations of organic equilibrium, that is of functional efficiency. The revolutionary's urgent task is to drag society out of the dangerous path on which it is set, back onto the high-road of common sense and well-being which is the true way.

Proudhon is as critical and suspicious of communes, and of workers' cooperatives within communes, as Marx himself:

It is to be feared that we have not yet done with communal utopias. Association [in communes and artisanal cooperatives] will long be, for a certain class of preachers and idlers, a pretext for agitation and an instrument of charlatanism. Considering the ambitions they give rise to, the envy disguised as devotion to a cause, the instincts of domination which they arouse and serve, they will for a long time yet remain one of the vexatious preoccupations which obstruct understanding of the revolution.

Even the Parisian workers' companies, justly proud of their successes inspired by competition with capitalist companies, yet with the evidence that they are beginning to stand for a new power in society, going to their heads, are in serious danger of turning into petty tyrants or even, by reason of exorbitant ambition leading to gigantic mergers, big tyrannies. It must never be forgotten that those who, like Louis Blanc, substitute ideology for ideas, make socialism an enemy of commonsense. These social ideologists, afraid of the logical conclusion to the revolutionary idea, seek to reinstate political, statist authority. The 'logical conclusion' thus being evaded is the really radical one: abolition of the central, authoritarian state.

The social democrats and Christian socialists are putting forward the idea of *direct* democracy, *direct* legislation, *direct* government to deal with the unavoidable vice of representational democracy: that it invariably becomes a party oligarchy. But the arguments used by these people against representational democracy are valid only in so far as they also apply to direct democracy; they are the *reductio ad absurdum* of the governmental idea. That this is so, that direct democracy, 'the only kind of government which, in view of social, technological and economic progress, now appears fair and just,' also happens to be impossible, reveals that society is being forced to abjure any kind of government whatsoever. The spirit of the people and the times is rejecting the notion of authority in favour of the notion of consent followed by contractual obligation, as the only law.

Proudhon derives the idea of political authority from the immemorial one of paternal authority; and realizes that because of its venerable pedigree, there are very great psychological difficulties in getting rid of it. It is because of political authority's deep root in paternal authority that revolutionary thinkers, while recognizing that government is a scourge and a chastisement to humanity, still insist that it is a necessary evil. Therein Proudhon finds the explanation of the fact that all revolutions end in the reconstitution of tyranny. Thus the English revolution put the people under Cromwell's major-generals; Calvin ruled Geneva ruthlessly; Luther became an ally of the princes against the starving peasantry; the American democracy became the greatest slave-owning society in history; the French Revolution ended in Napoleonic imperialism, the Russian in Stalinism, the Chinese in Maoism.

History, says Proudhon, demonstrates that always and everywhere the government, however popular in its origin, ranges itself shoulder to shoulder with the class which is the richest and best educated, against the class which is the poorest and most numerous: 'The history of governments is the martyrology of the proletariat.' Universal suffrage cures nothing, neither does the dictatorship of the proletariat. It would seem to be clear that the democracy, the socialism, which retains the governmental principle, the sacrosanctity of authority, is doomed, sooner or later, to fall under the authoritarian heel.

If, then, we are to be free, Proudhon reasons that what he calls distributive justice – the 'justice' dispensed by the will of the monarch, the oligarchs, or the polyarchs – must give away to what he calls commutative justice based not on a social contract between citizen and state, but on mutual contract between man and man. The opposite of authority is *le libre examen*, free thinking, free judgement; condemned by the Church, it establishes the authority of reason instead of the authority of will. Reason Proudhon defines as 'a pact between insight and experience'.

The place of the whole complex expressed in the idea 'government', is to be taken by commutative justice, the reign of contract, the 'economic or industrial reign'. It is emphasized that the Proudhonian contract has nothing whatever to do with Rousseau's 'social contract' which Proudhon describes as a fraud.[10] Rousseau, given the enormous influence of his writings on the men of '89, is held directly responsible for the betrayal of the true principles of revolution, to wit, negation of govern-

ment, as first glimpsed by Morelly and by Gracchus Babeuf (see
p. 2). What remains when authority, by its own internal contradictions, has destroyed itself, is socialism – the installation of mutual
contract. Common sense or, at the highest level, philosophy, replaces
law; contract replaces compulsion. The destructive force at work on
authority is 'the necessary and inevitable harmonization of economic
tensions'.

There is one passage in *L'Idée Generale de la Révolution* which would
serve as a manifesto for libertarian socialism, or anarchism:

The sovereignty of reason having been substituted for that of revelation; the
notion of contract succeeding to that of compulsion; economic critique revealing
that political institutions must now be absorbed into the industrial organism; we
fearlessly conclude that the revolutionary formula can no longer be direct
government or any kind of government, but must be NO MORE GOVERN-
MENT.

Proudhon's definitions are equally vivid: for example, he defines laws
as 'the limits set to the absolute power of the prince, conceded to popular
pressure'. It will be recalled that R. W. Emerson believed that no good
man should be over-zealous in obedience to the laws, for he can be so
only at the expense of his integrity. Proudhon went further: what, he
asks, has a free man who thinks for and is answerable only to himself, or
for that matter the man who would be free and feels himself fit to be so, to
do with laws?

I am ready to treat, but I want none of your laws. I recognize none and I protest
against *any order whatsoever* imposed upon my freedom of judgement by a political
power which merely claims to be 'necessary'. Laws! We know what they are and
just what they are worth: for the rich and mighty, gossamer; chains which no
steel can cut for the poor and weak; and, for governments, fishing-nets.

But should not the citizen, nevertheless, obey the laws of his country,
since they are there? Certainly not: the man who abrogates his absolute
freedom of judgement for any cause whatsoever, is a slave:

The law is made without my participation, despite my absolute dissent and to my
prejudice. The State does not treat with me, it offers nothing I want in exchange,
it simply holds me to ransom. Where, then, is the bond of conscience, reason,
passion or interest which puts me under an obligation to obey?

It matters not to Proudhon whether the authority of law be vested in a
prince, a Church, a social class, or the whole people: authority is universally corrupting and a people vested with it become the prince, and a
damned bad prince at that. Direct legislation by the people emancipates

no man but brings all to servitude; an excellent definition, surely, of a People's Democracy. Liberty and equality, without which no man is whole and respectable, are simply not compatible with authority and, that fact once grasped, we are bound to conclude that the era of politics is over and done with and the era of economics begins, in which the self-management of society becomes a matter of good house-keeping on rational lines, and the same self-discipline as makes family life possible.

Marx saw as historically necessary the succession of class to class as top dog, the process ending with the dictatorship of the proletariat producing a classless society. The state, and government, remain; as I've said, the state becomes the Supreme Being, and the government its hierarchy of clergy. Lip-service is paid to the idea of the ultimate with-ering away of the state; but Marxists seem to treat this not as an article of faith but as a pious belief, not to be taken too seriously. The adoration of the state necessarily leads to the hive, the ant-hill, the territory; sub-stitution of 'socialist' for 'capitalist' servants of the state, changes nothing fundamental. Proudhon will have none of such reactionary, counter-revolutionary half-measures.

We must return to his idea of contract as the only tolerable bond between free men. Something of what he had in mind at the industrial level can be gained by glancing at his intervention in the great railway controversy. In mid-century, France was building railways and cutting canals. As an expert in the haulage business, he opposed the building of railways between centres linked by waterways, waterway carriage being up to 80 per cent cheaper. He took the side neither of the bourgeoisie who wanted private enterprise to have the railways in the form of concessions, nor of the socialists who wanted the railways built and managed by the state. Yet he demanded that the construction and operation of the railways be entrusted to workers' mutualist companies bound together, and bound with society, by contracts freely negotiated and subscribed.

The whole economy was to be organized on this same basis of recip-rocal contracts or, in juridical terms, on the basis of commutative justice, that is the justice inherent in mutual engagement without refer-ence to statute.

I want the revolution to be pacific but I want it to be prompt, decisive and complete. I want the regime of poverty and oppression to be succeeded by the regime of well-being and liberty; the constitution of political power, by the organization of economic forces. I want every citizen to be bound into society only by his free, contractual undertaking, instead of by subordination and obedience ...

The intellectual snobbishness of the peasant who had educated himself to graduate level without having had the benefit of the university
discipline which enables the student to keep the philosophers in their
place, kept Proudhon half-fascinated by the German philosophers whom
he could not read, knew only at second-hand, and probably never
understood. This sometimes led him into a pretentious use – Marx and
his other enemies said abuse – of metaphysics. Sainte-Beuve, his first and
indulgent biographer, smiled at, understood and forgave this. But just as
that friend of Doctor Johnson's failed, for all his efforts, to be a
philosopher because cheerfulness kept breaking through, so Proudhon
failed to be a philosopher because his Gallic commonsense kept breaking
through. So it is with *L'Idée Generale de la Révolution*:

Any two productive workers have the right reciprocally to promise and guarantee to each other the sale or exchange of their respective products.

The same reciprocal contract can be made between any number of producers.

Producers therefore have the right to come to an understanding for the joint
formation of means of distribution, guaranteeing to exchange by sale or otherwise all kinds of provisions in guaranteed quantity and quality and at the lowest
possible prices – provisions which mercantile chaos now sells them at exorbitant
prices.

By the same token citizens have the right to found a bank for the financing of
their operations.

The object of private enterprise banks, in which they are abetted by the
national banks, is high revenue. But is it the business of a bank to make large
profits, or to facilitate industry and trade? If the former, then interest rates
must be high; if the latter, low, as low as a mere service charge of $\frac{1}{2}$% or even
$\frac{1}{4}$%.

Is it really that simple? Yes, until we come under the pernicious
influence of economic-capitalist or Marxist pseudo-science. It is in this
clarity of vision that Proudhon's genius resides: he sees that the
emperor's new clothes are really an illusion, that imperial majesty really
is stark naked. Management of the means of exchange, money, bus-
tickets, is a technical skill to be paid for like any other: gardening, mining
coal, casting steel, cooking meals or dressing hair. But the moment the
money-managers become merchants of money, charge not simply for
their services, but for the tokens they are paid to circulate and which are,
in themselves, worthless, then what results is theft.

The banker who charges for his services as a professional manager of
the distribution of the means of exchange is a labourer worthy of his hire;
the banker who charges not only for those services, but for the means of
exchange themselves as an article of commerce, is a blackmailing

extortioner and a thief; for what he sells is not his to sell, but is something in the public domain which has been withdrawn from circulation. You object that what he does is perfectly legal, is even regarded as honourable and is very richly rewarded by society; and that if, accusing him of blackmail, extortion and theft, you refuse to pay him his 10, 12, 15 per cent over and above the face-value of what you have borrowed, then the government, in the person of its judges, will allow him to distrain on your goods, or send you to prison. What does that prove? Precisely what, since the writing of *What is property?*, Proudhon had been claiming: that in any society based on property, the law is *necessarily* the institutionalization of injustice.

The law-makers of the ancient Israelites, emulated by both their Christian and Moslem successors, were fully aware of all this and made the lending of money at interest not merely a crime, but a sin.

I revert to Proudhon: 'Progressive reduction of interest rates to vanishing point is in itself a revolutionary act, since it is destructive of capitalism.' But what about the socialist solution – nationalization of the banks? The answer is terse: nationalization of the banks would constitute '. . . democratic and social consecration of the principle of spoliation,' or, in other words, the exploitation of the citizens by the state instead of by the usurers. What, then, is the alternative? The state, before its extinction, reduces the interest rates on all its bonds in line with the People's Bank; or, itself borrowing at $\frac{1}{2}$ per cent from the People's Bank, redeems them, leaving the former bond-holders with an enormous total of money which they can use only in one way, by themselves becoming mutualist worker-capitalists.[11]

The Proudhonian revolutionary policy is summed up in six words: convert and amortize down to extinction. He anticipates the outcry at this treatment of the sacred *rente*:

I know full well that bond-holders, stock exchange gamblers, the whole money pack, will scream – Spoliation! For the State, instead of operation on the *principal*, which is the normal practice on the stock exchange, would operate on the *interest*. Now marvel at Bankocratic morality! Speculation which exaggerates or depreciates the value of invested capital while keeping interest at the same level, is regarded as legitimate; yet a sovereign decree annulling interest, the unstable and abusive value, while repaying the capital, the principal, in full, is called theft! And that by people who call themselves economists, moralists, men of law and order, statesmen – there are even some who pass themselves off as Christians. So be it! For far too long have I disputed with that rascally riffraff, and for that patience I ask pardon of all mankind. The scoundrels are in the seats of the mighty; but . . . patience –

What Proudhon proposes is not expropriation. Public and private debtors are to repay the money-lenders – that is all capitalists, whether banks, other credit institutions and investors, or private usurers – in annuities over ten years for debts up to 2000 francs, over twenty years for larger debts. Furious, the money-lenders will demand immediate payment; how, then shall we answer them? By reference to the total amount of money in circulation by comparison with the amount which the capitalists are demanding as their due:

You reclaim from us eighteen billion francs; how is it, then, that there are only two billion in existence? How, with two billion francs have you contrived to make us your debtors for eighteen billion? You answer us – by the circulation of currency and the renewal of loans. Then, by the circulation of currency and the renewal of annuities shall we discharge our debt to you.

Housing was to be municipalized, with repair and maintenance contracts let to Workers' Companies on a competitive basis, the companies being financed by the People's Bank charging a service fee of $\frac{1}{2}$ per cent. The bank was to have an agricultural loans department whose object would be the disappearance of the landlord and tenant and their replacement by a land-owning peasantry. The return, over and above the farmer's subsistence, on agricultural land is reckoned to be 3 per cent: the bank buys the farm from the landlord or redeems it from the mortgagee, and sells it to the farmer who, by paying to the bank his 3 per cent annual profit plus $\frac{1}{4}$ per cent service charge, redeems the debt in thirty-four years. Thus the following major injustice would be done away with:

A tenant rents for 1200 francs a year a farm valued at 40 thousand. By good farming he improves it so that it becomes worth 60 thousand. The landlord, who has done nothing towards the improvement, increases the rent to 1800 francs. The tenant, having created 20 thousand francs of plus-value not only gets nothing out of it, but is forced to pay 600 francs more in rent. By his good farming he has made nothing but a rod for his own back.

Proudhon rejects nationalization of the land as decidedly as he rejects agricultural capitalism. Certainly, it would eliminate capitalist exploitation of the farmer, but it would entail state autocratic exploitation, that greatest of all evils. And it would deprive the farmer of eminent domain, so that his very plough would rise up and say to him, 'I know thee not; thou art nought but a slave of the Fisc'. Moreover, it is as foolish as it is undemocratic to fly in the face of the countryman's feelings: the peasant, even the socialist peasant, demands to be his own landlord. It will be remembered that the Bolsheviks produced a catastrophic famine in

Russia by ignoring that piece of common sense; and that the country which was a great grain exporter before the revolution has, since then, imported grain on a colossal scale.

Proudhon, of course, had in mind the old family-farm and, ancient Roman that he was, he believed the life of the free, land-owning yeoman to be the noblest and most wholesome open to man. How he would have applauded Oliver Goldsmith's *Deserted Village*:

> Ill fares the land, to hastening ills a prey,
>   Where wealth accumulates and men decay:
> Princes and lords may flourish, or may fade;
>   A breath can make them, as a breath has made:
> But a bold peasantry, their country's pride,
>   When once destroyed, can never be supplied.

The farm-land sold to working farmers only, was to be alienable only as farming-land and only at a price based on its return on farming: thus it could not become an object of speculation, was free from the vices of landlordism, and could change in value only in the measure of its change in productivity.

If the nation's agriculture was to be entrusted to a class of yeomen, it had to be otherwise with industry. Industries are necessarily collective undertakings: to meet the revolution's requirements – liberty and equality emancipated both from capital and the state – they had therefore to become associations of workers bound together by reciprocal contracts. But since such associations might put undesirable constraints on the liberty of judgement and action of the individual and become, from the anarchist's point of view, oppressive, such associations must be as relaxed as possible:

I mean that the degree of solidarity between the workers must be directly proportional to the economic relationship which unites them; where that relationship ceases to be appreciable or remains insignificant, no account need be taken of it: but where it is of predominant importance and necessarily subjugates the individual will, it must be fully recognized as a priority.

He does not like associations of a formal kind because they must tend at best to sap the independence and discourage the individual initiative or, at worst to become tyrants over their members. As the only acceptable alternative to the 'immorality, tyranny and theft' which is capitalism, they must, however, be tolerated.

The industry to be operated, the work to be done, are the common and indivisible property of all the participant workers. The concession of mines and railways to companies of capitalists, exploiters of the bodies and souls of their wage-earners, is a betrayal by the government, a violation of public rights, and an outrage on human dignity and personality.

Throughout the book Proudhon persists in saying that he is inventing nothing but simply revealing a natural law of social economy: 'the laws of social economy are independent of the will of man and law-maker; our privilege is to recognize them; our dignity in obeying them.'

Proudhon's revolution is establishing what we should now call an alternative society. There are no social classes; at the base of the economic pyramid are the yeomen farmers and the workers' companies of primary producers; the whole industrial complex is in the hands of workers' companies and the circulation of money, the medium of exchange, is managed by the People's Bank of which the workers are both the owners and the customers. The class of skilled artisans is still there, individuals or small groups owning their own tools and workshops ... 'the volunteers of trade and industry ... the most flexible and mobile of people, preferring their incomparable independence even to sovereignty over the soil, and native wherever there is work for their skills'.

It is the responsibility of the workers' associations to provide schools and teachers for their members' children, and technical instructors for associates at all levels, for every associate must have the opportunity to prepare himself for the more difficult and responsible tasks. The companies' rules must be passed by assemblies of all associates and every associate must subscribe to them in complete understanding of what he is doing. Managers are to be appointed by election. Every associate accepts a share of the trading risks and receives a share of that part of the trading profit available for distribution to the associates, both proportionate to the importance of function. No wages or salaries are paid; the associates get revenue from their joint industry in the same way as an artisan from his personal industry; they are, in short, self-employed. An associate leaving a company is entitled to receive his share of the company's increment, in cash.

Here there is one very big change in policy, produced by Proudhon's experience of business and industry since writing *What is Property?* ten years ago. He has abandoned absolute equality of reward in favour of differentials proportional to function, talent and responsibility. Presumably the differentials would have been relatively small.

Proudhon makes the point that this purely economic and contractual, wholly apolitical organization of industrial society would fuse together bourgeoisie and proletariat in a classless society: and this is important because, for want of higher education and experience, the working-class is lacking in men with the skills required for the management of large enterprises.[12]

Competition, it will be noted, is retained: the workers' companies within any particular industry compete with each other for orders, and this ensures that the price of products will be kept down to the lowest possible consonant with quality. Proudhon does not believe that there is any way but this of arriving at the correct price of manufactured goods. On the distributive side, he leaves the greatest possible margin of freedom. A wholesaler or retailer may be a family business or it may be a more or less large workers' company: but the merchants, having met their overhead, must pay themselves no more than a fair reward, established by agreement or contract with producers and consumers, for their labour. The element to be eliminated is what Proudhon calls *agiotage*, 'commercial arbitrariness', charging as much as you can get regardless of the real cost of the article and your own labour.

The dictionary meaning of *agiotage* is 'gambling with stocks or commodities'. It is wholly pernicious, a legalized form of theft and fraud. In its commonest form, the trader seizes the chance of a short-fall in supply to raise his price though he is paying no more himself and doing no extra work. In its extreme form it is the cornering of the market in a particular commodity. Both forward buying and forward selling of commodities are *agiotage*. Because it is practised in competition, and, like horse-racing or any other kind of gambling, entails a risk, Proudhon calls it 'reciprocal fraud', but, also, 'the most active principle of spoliation'. It is an obvious fact that the commodity jobber is, to any society, a costly and burdensome parasite, contributing nothing in exchange for his living. But Proudhon also points out that under capitalism *agiotage* is 'the necessary compensation for insecurity ... an excusable vice of the system which will disappear with the system'.

From brass-tacks to a specimen of Proudhonian flights of fancy. From time immemorial societies have been ruled by authority whose first term is DESPAIR and whose final term is DEATH. Yet slowly and secretly society has been evolving 'its own proper organism' whose elements are perfectibility of the individual and the species, dignity of labour, equality of destinies, identity of interests, decline of antagonisms, universality of well-being, sovereignty of reason, absolute freedom of the individual. We hasten the advent of this society by revolution in the direction of its evolution: we replace social classes by industrial categories; military armies give way to the collective force of workers' companies; commerce, the concrete expression of contract, replaces law; equality of exchange becomes the rule; competition remains the spur; legitimate self-interest replaces obedience; equilibrium of values and properties is established.

The new society rests upon human rights; it excludes arbitrariness and, essentially objective, excludes party and sect and therefore sweeps away the political regime. For there is an absolute incompatibility between the principles of central authority, and local initiative; between democracy and bureaucracy; between majority-right and the principle that no man owes obedience to laws to which he has not directly and personally consented. Any publicist or politician who claims to reconcile these incompatibilities is a miserable charlatan.

In place of government – Industrial organization.
In place of law – Contract.
In place of political power – Economic forces.
In place of classes – Industrial categories.
In place of public force – Collective force.
In place of standing armies – Workers' companies.
In place of police – Identity and equality of interests.

Who are the enemies of the revolution of which the 'general idea' is set forth in this book? God and King; Church and State; not until he came to the writing of his greatest work, *De la Justice dans la Révolution et dans l'Eglise*, did Proudhon develop to the full his concept of God as the great enemy of mankind. Now he merely identifies God (whether he exists or not is beside the point), as the source of all authority. But, he cries, courage, brothers, courage and patience: for Christianity as a force in public life has probably not more than twenty-five years to live, and perhaps not more than half a century will pass before priests will be prosecuted as frauds for the exercise of their ministry.[13] He holds belief in God to be the eternal, primary source of superstition, spoliation and tyranny; he also holds that no man should be denied the right to the rites of his religion if he wants them, on condition that he pay for them out of his own pocket: 'Trade in holy commodities must be as subject to the law of supply and demand as that in any other commodity ...'

The next most dangerous enemy of the just society, after God and his Church, is the 'Justice' of statutes and law-courts, since it is nothing but an 'emanation of Authority'. What he means is this: law officers of the crown or of the state, including judges, are concerned solely with what is legal, and not, excepting coincidentally, with what is just. For example, in the USSR it is, today, a crime punishable by committal to a lunatic asylum to criticize the officers or policy of the Communist Party. In Britain and America it is a crime to be 'without visible means of support'.

'Society has a right to defend itself when attacked. It may even, at the risk of reprisals, be in its interest to avenge itself. But I deny to any authority whatsoever the right to judge and to punish.' Here one must recall Proudhon's axiom that law, being the will of the prince, or the concession made to the people as heir presumptive to principality, or the will of the people-as-prince, is in any case an expression of fact; so that it has nothing to do with justice. You say that law is the expression of the sovereignty of the people; Proudhon would answer: I know no sovereign, sovereignty is anathema and therefore, '... so long as I have not willed your law, have not consented to it, have not personally voted for it and endorsed it with my signature, it does not command my obedience – *ne m'oblige pas* – and, for me, does not exist.' Let the punishment meted out to law-breakers be known by its name: vengeance, often 'the most iniquitous and atrocious vengeance'.

The only man who can do justice on the wrong-doer is himself; and it is to be expected that he will do so in a society in which every man has freely contracted to undertake certain obligations clearly defined and understood. In that case justice, proceeding from absolute liberty, will no longer entail, or be, vengeance, but only reparation;[14] for there will no longer be opposition between society's law and the individual's will.

We have, then, no need of judges and lawyers, those servants of anathemized authority: accused, accuser, witnesses, and the arbitration of fellow-workers, that is all the lawcourts we need.

*   *   *   *   *

L'Idée Generale de la Révolution appeared in June 1851 and was well received both by the press and the reading public. Proudhon owed the *visa* of the censorship bureau which licensed publication, to Carlier, his gaoler but always his friend.

During the year which had elapsed between his undertaking the book and its publication, there had occurred an event which seems in some respects to have been of deeper importance to Proudhon than the birth of any book: the birth of his first child, his daughter Catherine, on 15 October 1850, more or less coinciding with the death of the weekly *Le Peuple*. Fashions in names are hard to explain: there were objections from family and friends to the name Catherine. In 1850 it sounded ridiculous enough to raise smiles, but Proudhon insisted on it; it had

been his mother's name. The importance he attached to family continuity, to retaining the family as a social unit, in all his writings, was by
no means simply an outcome of his social theorizing: it derived from a
very strong personal conviction, from feeling rather than thinking. There
is a remarkable *Carnet* entry, inspired by the fact of being a father at last,
and as he had long wanted to be, which reveals the depth of his feeling on
this subject:

14 December. *Register, family chronicle.* This is the most moral of all institutions.
Every family should have one, signed and stamped by the mayor, simply by way
of authenticating each registration.

We live like animals, knowing nothing about ourselves or the environment we
live in; our own lives are unknown to us; we forget our fathers and do not think of
our children.

I shall assemble the materials of this chronicle for myself – My testament will
have no other object. As soon as my current book is finished I shall take it in hand
and send a copy to my brother for himself and his children.

This institution must be generally adopted. Without it the spirit of family, of
civism fades away and finally dies out. And men fall back into communism.

Is it not shameful, unworthy, immoral that a citizen should keep the books of
his trade with the utmost care, and yet have no family book? The payments made
by a rogue are entered up, but not the births of one's own children. There are
probably not a hundred thousand people in all France who know their antecedents (limiting genealogy to, say, two centuries), who know their kin and the
family alliances, and who are concerned with what their heirs and successors will
do after their deaths. All of which is brutish, ignoble. We have exterminated the
great lords, burned their castles and their cartularies: but we have remained
villeins. Now, let this be known: nobility was the exact contrary of egotism.

The last book Proudhon wrote in prison, *Philosophie du Progrès*, was not
intended for publication in book form, but was written in the form of two
long letters, respectively dated 26 November and 1 December 1851, in
reply to 'a learned critic', M. Romain Cornut, who had addressed some
questions to Proudhon. They were intended for publication in *La Presse*,
but were not, in the event, published in that journal, nor in book form
until 1855. The reason can be given in two words: *Deux décembre*.

2 December 1851, was one of the days when Proudhon was allowed out
of prison on parole. Considering what was happening in Paris, it is
perhaps surprising that his outing was not cancelled; but probably the
prison authorities themselves knew nothing of the event until it was too
late, for had Louis-Napoleon's *coup d'état* not been prepared in secret, it
could hardly have succeeded so smoothly.

The Constitution limited the President's term of office to four years; he
was determined to rule France until he died. He tried to get a

Constitutional amendment extending his term to ten years, as a step towards his ambition, but failed. The Assembly, knowing the strength of his support in the country, in May 1850 passed a new electoral law which imposed conditions to be satisfied before a citizen could be enrolled as a voter; although the appearance of universal suffrage was retained, this law, in practice, disenfranchised about 3 million men, the majority of them working-class. He had secret consultations with some of the politicians whose opinion he respected, including de Tocqueville, who candidly told him that his government was vexatious, provocative, high-handed, and too dependent on the support of the ultra-Catholics and priests. He further advised him that, if he wished to remain in power, he would have to use his popular support in the country against the Assembly, by demanding the restoration of universal suffrage which, in any case, was the only sanction for the legality of his rule. Bonaparte decided on a *coup d'état*, arbitrarily to extend his presidency to ten years. His strength in the country rested largely on his ability to make it appear that not he but the Assembly were responsible for all that was objectionable in the administration, that is, in posing as the champion of the people against the parliament.

Having prepared for the *coup* by taking into his confidence and winning over his minister for war, the general commanding the Paris garrison, and the Paris chief of police, in November he made quite sure of popular support by calling upon the Assembly to restore universal suffrage without delay or conditions. This being refused, as he had known it would be, on the night of 1/2 December his military and police officers arrested all the leaders amongst his political opponents while Paris was plastered with a proclamation restoring universal suffrage and making Louis-Napoleon Bonaparte dictator pending a referendum. (That referendum gave him the ten-year term he wanted.)

At dawn on 2 December the militant leaders of the socialists and anarchists called their people to arms. Fighting between the people and the troops broke out, but this had been anticipated, and the insurrection was put down with 'exemplary' ferocity: those of the captured left leaders who were not shot out-of-hand, were transported to Algeria.

Before the death of the weekly *Le Peuple* – Proudhon once said, 'I've had four newspapers shot under me' – Proudhon had addressed in it an article to the French socialist exiles in London, in which he called them, and the leaders of the left in general, nothing but a lot of humbugs, probably about the only thing on which he and Marx still agreed. And he had concluded, not in that article but in the *Carnet*, that only by

experience would the people discover what price it cost to take such
humbugs and idiots for their leaders and place reliance on the words of
charlatans.

He doubtless recalled that sour conclusion when, leaving Sainte-
Pélagie for his day out on 2 December, he saw a crowd gathered round an
official notice pasted to a wall. It informed the public that Prince-
President Louis-Napoleon had dissolved the Assembly and taken all
powers into his own hands. The *coup d'état* which Proudhon was in prison
for forecasting, had happened; the Empire was one step nearer; liberty
was dead; the price of choosing idiots and charlatans to lead the revolution was being exacted.

The news depressed but did not surprise him. Instead of going straight
to his rooms he set out walking to see what was happening. In the event
he saw nothing of such resistance as there was. He walked up the
Montagne Sainte-Geneviève to the Place du Panthéon where he found
the doors of the great national schools closed and strongly guarded by
armed police. He walked on and, in the Rue Soufflot ran into the sculptor
and fellow-revolutionary, Etex, one of whose subversive letters printed in
Le Peuple had once cost that paper a heavy fine. Together they walked to
the Hôtel de Ville, always the focus for revolutionary demonstrations;
but there, too, all was quiet, the doors closed and guarded. There they
parted, Proudhon to walk to Emile Girardin's, for if any man had news,
he would. But when Proudhon reached Girardin's apartment, he found
nobody at home; it crossed his mind that Girardin might have been
arrested: the Dictator would now be able to deal with the press as he
pleased.

Proudhon walked back to his rooms where Euphrasie must have been
anxiously waiting for him, and there a messenger found him. He heard
that all the left Deputies had been arrested, and all the leading left
journalists, by police who had come knocking at their doors at dawn
while they were still in bed. The messenger summoned Proudhon to a
meeting to be held that afternoon at the house of one of his political
friends: Michel de Bourges and Victor Hugo, two men he liked and
respected, would be there. But he sent word to say he would not go;
instead either de Bourges or Victor Hugo was to meet him at a place he
appointed on the embankment of the Saint-Martine canal.

It was Hugo who kept the appointment, and fortunately left an
account of it:

I found Proudhon at the appointed place, pensively leaning his elbows on the
parapet, and wearing the same broad-brimmed hat in which I had often seen him

pacing the Conciergerie courtyard. I went up to him and said, 'You have something to say to me?'

'Yes.'

He took and pressed my hand. The place we stood at was deserted. On our left was the long place de la Bastille shrouded in darkness. We could see nothing but were aware of the presence of many men: regiments were there, drawn up in battle order, not camped but ready to march; you could hear the dull sound of their breathing and the *place* was alive with the gleam of bayonets in the night. Above that tenebrous gulf towered the Juillet column. Proudhon said:

'Here it is, I've come to warn you, as a friend. You're deluding yourselves. The people have been taken in. They'll not rise. Bonaparte will win. This nonsense of restoring universal suffrage is bait to catch the simpletons. Bonaparte's taken for a socialist; he said, *I'll be the emperor of the rabble*. Insolence, but insolence can succeed with that . . .' Proudhon nodded towards the sinister gleam of bayonets . . . 'with that at its beck and call.'

He went on:

'Bonaparte has a goal. The Republic made the People; he wants to turn the People back into a populace. He will succeed and you will fail. He has brute force, cannon, the people's error, and the Assembly's folly on his side. The handful of men of the Left of whom you're one will not overreach the *coup d'état*. You're honest men and he has the advantage over you of being a scoundrel. You have scruples and he has the advantage over you of having none. Believe me, give up resisting. The situation is hopeless. We must wait; for the time being, to go on fighting is madness. What can you hope for?'

'Nothing,' I said.

'Then what will you do?'

'Everything.'

From the tone of my voice he understood that it would be useless to persist.

'Goodbye,' he said.

We parted; he plunged into the darkness; I have not seen him since.

Proudhon reported himself back at Sainte-Pélagie; some days later Victor Hugo, facing as Proudhon was later to face a choice between prison and exile, chose exile, in the peace and quiet of the Channel Isles which the French call *les isles Normandes*.

There is one distinction, as far as I know the only one, which one cannot deny the Emperor Napoleon III: that of having driven every man of genius or talent in his reign into prison, exile, or into writing that satire which purges the guilt of not having resisted wholly. The sole exception was Baron Haussmann. And, even as I write I seem to hear, wafted towards me from politicians at every point of the compass, and making a kind of susurrating chorus in my ears, *How right he was*. Those of that motley – white, black, brown and yellow – crew who can read and have, remote contingency, a conscience, can always exorcise their guilt, by quoting Plato, as the devil is said to quote Scripture.

With his arch-enemy now in supreme almost autocratic power, Proudhon decided that this was no time to draw attention to himself by publishing his two letters to Monsieur Cornut. The responsibility of being a *père de famille* was, no doubt, moderating his truculence. He describes his own state of mind;[15] he is 'sick with grief and anxiety'; his nights are 'like those of a man condemned to death'. He expects to hear at any moment the order for his transportation to Algeria or the Islands. Ill-informed about what was happening, constantly disturbed and alarmed by the rumours going the rounds of Sainte-Pélagie, he does not know what to believe. 'Why is Monsieur Bonaparte having the republican people shot down when, far from supporting their representatives, they have so readily, and even with such cowardice, accepted the *coup d'état*?' The horror of that crime, he wrote to Macher-Montjau, 'oppressed my mind, day and night and I was devoured by it. So many outrages, so many shameful acts, and so much stupidity . . .'

Three weeks later, once more in control of his nerves, he had come to a different conclusion concerning the *coup d'état*. The democracy, as yet too 'crude' and still too 'depraved by servitude' would, had the rising against the Prince-President succeeded, have involved the country and itself in disaster by trying to force the pace of social and economic reform. By preventing this, Monsieur Bonaparte had given the revolution more time in which to mature, morally and intellectually, so that, when, eventually, its time came, it would reshape society in a spirit of 'calm, discipline and conciliation'. Meanwhile, however severe the interlude of reaction, it could be only an interlude: for nothing on earth or in heaven could halt it in its course.

NOTES TO CHAPTER EIGHT

1. Herzen, A. *My Past and Thoughts* trans. Constance Garnett, revised Humphrey Higgens, London, 1968.
2. When writing *The New Statesman, a History of the first 50 years*.
3. Joseph Stalin was more successful because – it is a question of dates and technology and place – able to be ruthless. But to believe that the revolution can never be resumed in the massively conservative USSR, though the revolutionary initiative has perhaps now passed to the West, is to despair of mankind.
4. Penal degeneration has been progressive: Herzen complaining – '. . . these measures, unseemly for the correction of a naughty boy of seven, were taken . . . against one of the greatest thinkers of our age . . . This disrespect for genius is a new phenomenon that has reappeared during the last ten years.' Before that, he says, a man of genius might be persecuted and killed, but not humiliated in such petty ways.
5. He was still to be working on it ten years later; it was never to be finished.
6. Herzen says in Sainte-Pélagie; but in fact it must have been the Conciergerie.

7. Drowned at sea in November, 1851 on a passage from Marseilles to Nice when their steamer sank.
8. Halévy, D. *Le marriage de Proudhon*. Paris 1955.
9. In 1850 very little of the budget went into expenditure on what we now call Welfare. Most of it went into paying for military services, police forces, and bureaucracies, so that the taxpayer was obliged to support his worst enemies. But if, today, you were to call up Proudhon at a seance and point out that now a large part of the budget goes to pay for education, pensions, health services, supplementary benefits and subsidies; and for paying interest on loans, he would dismiss that defence of taxation in two words: *pauperization; theft.*
10. It is beside the point of his argument that he had the utmost contempt for Rousseau: 'Never was there united in one man such a measure of spiritual pride, cold-heartedness, baseness of inclination, depravity of habits and heartless ingratitude; never did passionate eloquence, ostentation of sensibility and effrontery of paradox cover such worthlessness.'
11. At no point does Proudhon consider the pensioner. Reason: he retains the family – it is the duty of children to support their aged parents. All welfare sources are stigmatized as 'pauperization'.
12. Lenin was to make the same point in his writings on Cultural Revolution.
13. This forecast was accurate, and until that one-time seminarist Joseph Stalin discovered that he had, after all, a use for dispensers of the 'opium of the people', the Bolsheviks prosecuted and persecuted the clergy. What Proudhon did not foresee was this return of the Raven to *Animal Farm*; but he was thinking of real revolution, not the state capitalist counter-revolution.
14. There are, of course, ancient precedents such as the blood-money with rates regulated on a class basis, of the Anglo-Saxon and other Germanic tribes. As to judgement by one's fellow-workers – that is by public opinion – George Orwell, among others, pointed out that it can be very dangerous, more merciless than that of the courts. It is possible that Proudhon would have accepted this and even approved of it. The 'justice' of the People's Courts in communist countries is not a case in point since, of course, it is merely an expression of the will of the bureaucracy and has even less to do with justice than that of our own courts. One can perhaps find examples in the trials of aristocrats under the Terror during the French Revolution; in Commonwealth England; in Geneva under Calvin; and in New England under the influence of Cotton Mather.
15. In letters to Mathay, 9 December, 1851; Emile de Girardin, 11 December, 1851; Michelet, February, 1852; and Macher-Montjan, February, 1853.

NINE

The Quiet Years

IN THAT LONG REPLY to M. Cornut which became Proudhon's *Philosophie du Progrès*, he implied that an identification of the unifying idea which bound together all his works and made of them the substance of a coherent doctrine, would be useful. More than that, it was necessary, because, as he had confessed elsewhere,[1] he had too often been guilty of contradicting himself, and even more often of seeming to do so. He was sorry for it, but not ashamed of it: all men err from time to time, and the very nature of his doctrine made self-contradiction a hazard.

The unifying idea is, then, consistent affirmation of progress combined with consistent denial of the absolute. I have written *progress* for *progrès*; but I am going to change over to 'progression'. In the first place, it is nearer to his meaning; and in the second place the word *progress* has been debased in English to mean technological advances when used by journalists, and nothing whatever when used by politicians. The opposition between progression and the absolute is the key to all Proudhon's polemics.[2] Here is how he defines these two concepts:

Progrès, in the pure usage, *ie*, the least empirical, is intellectual movement, *processus*, which is innate, spontaneous, of the essence, uncoercible and indestructible; as weight is to matter, progression is to the mind. It is chiefly manifest in the march of societies, that is, of history.

Mind in a condition of stasis is an impossible concept. The essence of mind being intellectual movement, the truth, that is the reality of things, is essentially *historical*, subject to progression, conversions, evolutions, metamorphoses. There is nothing fixed, finished, eternal, excepting the laws of movement itself, the study of which is the object of logic and of mathematics. Material progress, what we commonly mean when we use the word, is given its proper importance by Proudhon but it is not the process itself; it is only one of the products of *progrès*, progression.

So, his progression is the universal motion or state of ceaseless change; it is, therefore, the negation of all such concepts as immutability, immovability, impeccability; and, I suppose, the antithesis of the concept 'ideal' in his *Principes de l'Art*.

Now, for the Absolute: there is, in Proudhon's universe, no anchor, no anchor-man, no anchor-God; the only eternal state is flux. The Absolute is everything which progression denies. It is the search, utterly vain, whether in nature, in society, religion, politics, economics, morality, etc. for the eternal, immutable, perfect, definitive, incontrovertible. The search is vain because, by the very principle of the universe, the Absolute cannot be. Looking forward from *Philosophie du Progrès*, Proudhon was to say, in *De la Justice*, that if there be a God, He, too, must be in a state of for ever becoming, never finally being.

The Cartesian version of the 'rock of ages' is as unreliable as the Judeo-Christian (and therefore monarchic, authoritarian, government-al) one. Descartes thought he had found an unshakeable and eternal foundation for the fabric of philosophy (*aliquid inconcussum*) in the pro-position, 'I think therefore, I am' (*cogito ergo sum*). Proudhon does not agree. *Cogito*, I think – a *processus*, nothing still or immutable about it; and even the word *sum*, *to be*, in the most 'primitive' sense known to him, the Hebrew *haiah*, expresses not the static 'I am' but the dynamic 'I am becoming' or 'I become'. Descartes should have said, *moveor ergo fio, Je me meus, donc je deviens*, I (my mind, my me) is in movement, therefore I become. 'That which changes, is susceptible to progression, is the truth. That which appears as fixed, entire, complete, unchangeable, refractory to synthesis, is false.' Proudhon's *progrès* and Proudhon's *révolution* are, as near as makes very little difference, aspects of the same process.

This concept of progression furnishes us, according to Proudhon, when it comes to forwarding the revolution, with a means of choosing between that course which it is useful to undertake and persist in, and that which is dangerous and likely to lead us into trouble.

All those ideas which are exclusive, absolute and acted upon as such, are false, that is to say contradictory and irrational. All are true, that is susceptible of realization and usefulness, which are in evolution and can be combined in synthesis with others.

So, if the political idea you have adopted is based on dogma and is exclusive, Marxism, for example, you can be sure that it is erroneous. The criterion must always be evolution – the occurrence of continuous change in a functionally, socially, morally, economically favourable sense. Social progression – at this point our word *progress* becomes synonymous – is a process of continuous syntheses.

These definitions enable Proudhon to identify the cause of political, economic and social confusion and strife. On the one hand we have key men and key institutions still wedded to the idea of an absolute, a definitive, a final solution; and on the other the historical process, interminable change, the revolution-in-permanence, conflicting with that idea. Apply this to, *eg*, the history of the USSR. Stalin, at a certain moment, says: halt, this far but no farther, now we go by the book. Result, atrocious oppression at every level of activity. Not that Stalin was doing anything new: the British liberals tried to do the same thing after the first Reform Acts and engendered, in due, slow course, the Labour Party which destroyed them. Robespierre and Napoleon, in their different ways, even went to the length of reinstating the God whom the revolution had dethroned, to give the political stasis which suited them the old divine sanction.

Progression, progress, implies, of course, direction, movement from A to B; but it is vital to the Proudhonian argument to realize that A and B, start and finish are, in social economy as in modern physics, useful fictions that enable us to grasp the idea of movement, of from–to, of becoming. Really there is no start and no finish; all there is, is movement.

In respect of these definitions, *Philosophie du Progrès* restates Proudhon's 'serial law' of history which was worked out in *La Création de l'Ordre dans l'Humanité* (1843); its use entails a kind of differential analysis in which the events composing history are 'point-events' in the sense of having no magnitude in time. His claim in the *Philosophie* is that this notion of *progrès*, which seems in his thinking to have almost the same sense as *ordre*, is inherent even in his earliest works. Had he not, in 1840, written 'I am an anarchist, that is, the negation of the absolute'? And when he wrote of authority, he substituted economy: a synthetic and positive idea and the only one capable of leading to a rational and practical conception of social order. 'In the order of politics progression is synonymous with liberty, that is to say with evolution leading to the progressive participation of all the citizens in sovereignty and government, from an initiative freely taken by an individual or a collective.'

But, if we fail to understand that the *only* acceptable object of government is to guarantee the freedom of procedure and 'exchanges' of wealth to ensure a just distribution of that wealth; and if, with that in mind, we fail to change the whole 'organism' of government so as to substitute contract for law, then the participation of all the citizens in government results in nothing but a perpetual round of vain revolutions alternating with tyrannies.

*   *   *   *   *

Nothing on earth could stop the revolution in its course; if that were so, then the Bonapartist *coup d'état* must somehow be seen as advancing the revolutionary cause. We have already witnessed one intellectual somersault by means of which this could be done: Bonaparte, last manipulator of the power of the state machine, was to render it so odious that the people would destroy it and for ever dispense with it. Now came another Proudhonian act of paradox; he seems to me to apologize for it by himself protesting its singularity too much in a letter to Menard, almost as if he were going through the act of 'discovering' gold in a place in which he had 'salted' it himself. Supposing one were to take the Prince-President's 'democratic' and 'socialist' pretensions at their face value? The people had made him emperor in all but name (a year later another triumphant referendum corrected that omission). Might one not assume that, as trustees for the revolution, they knew what they were doing? After all, it is, by his own analysis, always against the grasping and greedy bourgeoisie that the people erect their Caesars. True, the Caesars then betray them; but might not this new Caesar be persuaded to accomplish the mission which history had entrusted to him?

At this stage there is a revealing letter to Michelet whose *Histoire de la Révolution Française* influenced all that Proudhon wrote after 1850. After thanking Michelet for the visit which he had paid him in Sainte-Pélagie, he tells of his complete recovery from the shock of the *coup d'état*, which had made him so ill, which had so stricken his heart but not, by his own account, touched his mind: *quel cudot!* But here is the passage in question:

... now I laugh, I whistle and what's more am working as if nothing had happened. All things considered, what has happened had to happen and our country had need of this shock, this sharp lesson. Only thus do peoples ever learn. If, then, you will allow me to, if I can be sure of finding you neither moribund nor in despair, if misanthropy has not cowed and withered your strong, proud spirit, I shall call on you to discuss the historical and moral usefulness of this crisis, and my own projects for the future ...

The project he had in the forefront of his mind was the new somersault, the project of giving a paradoxical twist to the Vive L'Empereur theme which had cost him so much. He proposed to demonstrate that revolutionaries must welcome the *coup d'état* because it could not fail to advance their cause. He would need a censorship *visa* – there was little point in writing a pamphlet which could never be published – and once again he had recourse to that patient policeman, Carlier.

Carlier was, by then, in no position to help him directly. Prudent and wholly professional, he had served under Charles X, under Louis-Philippe and under the Second Republic, but found that he had no mind to serve under Napoleon the Little. He had resigned ten days before the *coup d'état*. But he had not lost interest in the most remarkable of his detainees. He received Proudhon on the morning of 28 December, heard him out, and advised him to see the Minister of the Interior, M. Morny – soon to be duc de Morny. Still better, he arranged the meeting for that same afternoon.

For what transpired at the meeting between Proudhon and Morny I rely on a letter which Proudhon wrote to his friend Charles Edmond on 1 January 1852, to wish him a happy new year. But first a word about Morny. He had been, to Napoleon *le Petit* in the *coup d'état* of 2 December, more or less what Louis Bonaparte had been to Napoleon Bonaparte in the *coup d'état* of *Brumaire* 1799. He was Louis-Napoleon's half-brother, being the bastard son of Hortense de Beauharnais, Queen of Holland (Joseph Bonaparte's wife), and the comte de Flahaut. De Flahaut in turn was a bastard son of Talleyrand and therefore half-brother of Delacroix. From 1830 to 1838 Morny had served with the army in Algeria, and distinguished himself at the siege of Constantine. He made a very substantial fortune in the sugar trade, was a *député* from 1842 to 1848 and again in 1849. He became Minister of the Interior after the *coup d'état*, Chairman of the *Corps Législatif* in 1854 and a Privy Councillor in 1858. It is not without significance for what follows that he consistently sought to liberalize his half-brother's regime, and promoted the foundation of credit institutions to compete with the established commercial banks and force down the rate of interest. On the other hand, as a notorious *bon viveur* and *coureur*, he was extravagant, and in an effort to increase his fortune went in with the banker Jecker in the business of the Mexican loan. This made him use all his influence with the Emperor to launch the disastrous Mexican campaign which originated as an attempt to collect the money-lenders' dues for them, and ended in the shooting of Maximilian von Hapsburg by one of Benito Juarez's firing squads.

It seems Proudhon told Morny that whereas the revolution had been checked in its course between 24 June 1848 and 2 December 1851, on that day of the successful *coup d'état*, it had resumed its course again. What he wanted was a licence to publish a pamphlet to be called *The Social Revolution demonstrated by the coup d'état*, to be based on the proposition that '... the government of Louis-Napoleon Bonaparte is condemned by the seven and a half million votes which absolved it, to do great things and, one way or another, to introduce all the reforms demanded by socialism'.

The 7½ million votes refer of course to the electorate's endorsement of the *coup d'état*. Proudhon demanded that Morny leave him free to attack 'the Jesuits', that is Church influence on the Prince-President. Morny agreed to license the pamphlet, which is hardly surprising. The Prince-President's position was not yet as strong as it looked: he had the people and the police, but General Changarnier had the army and the National Guard, and was the man of the right-wing republicans, the big industrialists, and the *haute banque*. The Bonapartists could not do without allies. Not even all the members of his own family were on Louis-Napoleon's side. The son of Jerome Bonaparte, once the very inept and incapable King of Wurtemburg, who was known sometimes as prince Napoleon and sometimes as prince Jerome, although Jerome was not one of his four names, had sat on the extreme left, with Proudhon, in the Chamber of Deputies, was nicknamed *prince de la Montagne*, and consistently, if ineffectually, opposed his cousin. (His sister, princess Mathilde's *salon* was to be the most 'advanced' and distinguished in the Paris of the Second Empire.)

Can Proudhon's conduct be justified? Halévy tried to do it by pointing out that although the pamphlet was the worst thing Proudhon ever wrote, it was not at all 'false': Bonaparte was, he says, too much of a man of his century not to have been tempted by 'the great socialist adventure'. I daresay, but among the things which Proudhon had consistently condemned as fatal to the true revolution were reforms imposed from above, and universal suffrage in a representative democracy – the means used to persuade the people to bind on their own chains. The men to whom Louis-Napoleon might turn for advice had been young when Saint-Simon was the patron saint of rebellious youth in the great schools. It was of Lucien Leuwen's latent Saint-Simonianism that his father, that delightfully frivolous millionaire banker, was afraid. He saw it as the most dangerous enemy of his campaign to make his son rich and happy *à sa façon*.[3] To be a Saint-Simonian was to be a socialist, if you like, but a Platonic one. It was just conceivable that Louis-Napoleon like Plato, Saint-Simon, and Lady Catherine de Burgh, might adopt the policy of bullying the cottagers into health and prosperity by giving them soup and good advice. But that was hardly the kind of social revolution which Proudhon had in mind.

All the same, I think that Proudhon can be excused, if only because he did not, in his pamphlet, kowtow; he compromised, for once, his good sense, but not his independence. Listen to this:

As for the men, I am ready to believe in their good intention, but even more readily in their proneness to errors of judgement. In the Psalms it is written, 'Put not thy trust in princes, in the sons of Adam', that is in men whose thinking is subjective because salvation is not with them. I believe that, unfortunately for all of us, the revolutionary idea, ill-defined in the mind of the masses, ill-served by its vulgarisers, leaves the government, as to its policy, with all its options open. I believe that the political authorities are surrounded by impossibilities which they do not perceive, contradictions which they do not know, traps hidden from them by universal ignorance. I believe that any government can survive and endure if it will, by affirming its historical reason, and setting its course according to the interests of those it is called upon to serve; but I also believe that men scarcely change, and that if Louis XVI having launched the revolution tried to stop it, if the Emperor, Charles X and Louis-Philippe preferred their own downfall to its continuation, it is hardly probable that their successors will so soon and so readily become its promoters.

Publication, which meant much-needed money coming in, of *La Révolution Sociale démontrée dans le Coup d'état*, coincided with Proudhon's release from prison, his term fully served, on 4 June 1852. He recorded the event in the *Carnet*: 'What have I lost? If I strike the balance meticulously I should say -- nothing. I know ten times more ten times better than I did three years ago. I know positively what I have gained; and truly, I do not know what I have lost.'

All the same, his release was celebrated: Darimon, Courbet, Langlois, his father-in-law and other friends were waiting for him and, knowing what he yearned for, off they went, leaving Euphrasie to look after the children, of course, for a whole day's walking and talking in the Meudon woods, a twelve-hour outing which included '... two long meals. This immense orgy cost us 100 sous a head.'

I suspect that M. Piégard was only there to represent Madame Proudhon and felt a bit out of things; but, to Proudhon's way of thinking, it would have been impossible to have a woman of their company. Still, her turn came: on the next day he set out with her and the two little girls for a holiday at Burgille, the village on the river Ognon where he had spent so much of his childhood. I can imagine poor Euphrasie, dyed-in-the-wool Parisienne as she was – their later exile in Brussels nearly killed her – sighing, 'Oh, well ...' But the whole family benefited from the mountain air, although the season was unusually wet, especially Catherine who was a rather sickly child.[4] Proudhon fished the streams for crayfish 'as big as small lobsters', and for gudgeon. They all had huge appetites but provisions were much cheaper than in Paris. Proudhon made the rounds of old friends and the few remaining members of his family, introducing Euphrasie. They liked and made much of her. They also paid a visit to Besançon.

Early in August Proudhon left Euphrasie and the children in Burgille and went to stay with Antoine Gauthier in Lyon. The Gauthiers were considering setting up a new linked maritime and inland waterways shipping line and there was a possibility of a job for Proudhon: he needed one badly. Neither Garnier nor any other French publisher would publish his *Philosophie du Progrès* (eventually published in Belgium, it was banned in France), and even newspaper editors were afraid of the man who had made an enemy of the Dictator.

Antoine Gauthier, Proudhon and one or two other men associated with the big shipping project, travelled down the Rhône from Lyon to Avignon in the company's steamer *Le National*, and from Avignon went on to Marseilles by train, for business talks. Nothing came of them, and Proudhon was left facing the fact that his now very unpopular pen was his only resource.

Ever since leaving prison in June Proudhon had nursed a longing to return to journalism: the question was – how? What he had in mind was, not a popular daily newspaper this time, but a bi-monthly review which would scan a broad field of activities including economics, philosophy, science, literature and history. By December 1852 his plans were far enough advanced for Proudhon to announce that he hoped to bring out the first issue on 15 January the following year 'unless there are unexpected obstacles'. Obstacles there were: on 28 December Proudhon's application to publish his new review was rejected by de Maupas the minister of police, who is reported to have commented 'Let M. Proudhon go and make his request to the Emperor'. In fact, Proudhon did write not to the Emperor but to his cousin prince Napoleon, and his letter of 7 January 1853, revelas very clearly where he felt he now stood in relation to the powers-that-were and indeed how isolated he felt in a France which had changed so much while he was in prison.

... I learned quite recently that you had deigned to show some interest in a *Revue* which was to have appeared under my management, but which the minister of police refuses to authorize. How many reasons for me, Prince, to convey to you the tribute of my gratitude ... [but he does not want the Prince to get Maupas to reverse his decision] I am not even seeking any longer to obtain the all-powerful word of the Emperor as a passport for my ideas ... Why? ... My conduct is known ... always setting social institutions above political forms, and placing the *raison révolutionaire* above the *raison d'état*, I am sworn foe to any kind of abstention as to any kind of despair ... I have no thought in the face of the accomplished fact but to make the best that can be made of the new situation ... but ... Yes, Prince, for the first time in five years I am afraid ... In the face of the bourgeois, monarchist, and clerical counter-revolution which during the last 13 months has been organized around and under cover of the President and Emperor; confronted by the circle of treasons which surrounds him like a fortress ... I foresee

all too well to what furies a solitary and inopportune protest would expose me ...
I no longer find in myself the courage to become the victim of an anachronism.

Now that the counter-revolution at home and abroad is crushing us, it is time
for republicans and imperialists to come to terms. ... Is it even known in the
Tuileries that the clergy are seething with hatred for Napoleon III? Is it known
that such is the intolerance of priests that there is talk on all sides of a second
revocation of the Edict of Nantes; and that in three months the whole of the
protestant population has been alienated from the Emperor?

The *Credit Foncier* is nothing but an institution of privilege, inaccessible to
three-quarters of our small landowners and without any possible action on the
national economy; the *Credit Mobilier* is considered as no better than a vast
bucket-shop ...

People hold back, skulk, or rather, thanks to a too urgent appeal for them to
rally round, grab at places: they get themselves concessions for railways, canals
and mines, banks and privileges; they flock to fill the places in the administration, the tribunals, the general staff ... We are back in the very Philippist
monarchy, or real bourgeois government. And one can say today, of Louis-
Philippe, as was said of Voltaire, that *if he has not seen all that he has done, he has done
all that we see* ... In today's conditions Henri V [Orleans] only is logical; and since
whatever is logical sooner or later asserts itself, Henri V will return ...

I declare that I am resolved, until a fresh political change, to abstain voluntarily. I will not expose myself to the daggers either of reds or whites by having
it said that I am the Emperor's scarecrow, stuck up alone to halt the counter-
revolution ...

Perhaps the Emperor trusts in the immense strength derived from his 8 million
suffrages ... The more votes the people have given him, the more, even in the
judgement of the republicans, the people have shown themselves incapable,
incompetent.

In the months during which Proudhon was still hoping that by some
miracle of officialdom his review might be licensed (it never was), his
domestic circumstances at least took a brief turn for the better. He
dashed off a strange compilation for Garnier called *The Stock Exchange
Speculator's Manual* made up of statistics and a digest of his current views
on economics. Over the years it made him a steady sum; one wonders
what its purchasers thought they were getting. In April 1853 Proudhon
found a new place to live and work in peace. It was a ground-floor
apartment on the edge of Paris at No. 83, Rue d'Enfer (now Rue
Denfert-Rochereau), near Montparnasse: it had a spacious garden, it
faced south, and Proudhon was delighted with it. And it was here in the
garden with his two children and his books that Courbet depicted him in
the celebrated portrait which the artist painted after his friend's death,
having never been able to persuade Proudhon to sit for him during his
lifetime.

Euphrasie, whom Courbet also painted, was now pregnant again, and in September she gave birth to their third daughter, Stephanie. 'The triad is victorious,' Proudhon wrote to his friend Dr Maguet. 'In fifteen years I shall have a complete workshop, and, with my career ended and my daughters installed, I shall go into retirement and keep their books.' A letter to Bergmann in March 1854 echoes this resigned and passive mood.

The literary career is now more or less closed to me. No printer, no bookseller in Paris would dare publish or sell anything of mine. All writings bearing my name have had to disappear from the bookstalls and catalogues. There remained as a last resort a bookseller with whom I had come to terms over an important historical work; he was ruined and has just gone into liquidation. For the time being I am, while still following my studies, busy on some editorial work for certain private interests kind enough to make use of me, and even they take great care to dissimulate the suspect agency they have the courage to employ. I tried here and there to get work in business; wherever I went I was rejected with alarm; it seems that Society, really convinced that I am its greatest enemy, has excommunicated me. *Terra et aqua interdictus sum*!

For the rest, my life is serene; I have no harassments. The Police, for their part, know what kind of man I am: as contemptuous at bottom, of the Jacobin party as of the Legitimists, indifferent to the political form, sceptical as to all authority, and much more concerned with the task, the work, of the tenants of power than with their titles. It follows that this scepticism of which I have given every proof, mortal to all parties and sects, is at once my security with the Government, and the source of the implacable hatred of its adversaries.

You will doubtless have heard that I married for money. I think you are sensible enough to know that I was not up to that. You will perhaps also have been told that I obtained a railway concession. The fact is that I took a hand, as every citizen has a right to, in a matter of that kind ... The concession was given to another company.

This rail concession was for a line between Besançon and Mulhouse and Proudhon had managed to get the backing of prince Napoleon. Those who did win it afterwards offered, at the prompting of the prince, a sizeable sum in compensation to the consortium of which Proudhon was a member; Proudhon turned down his share in spite of what it could have meant to his family.

In the summer of 1854 disaster overtook the family. There was an outbreak of cholera in Paris, they all went down with it, and their little daughter Marcelle died. Euphrasie, ill herself and nursing her sick husband in the neighbouring room, at first could not bring herself to inform him. When he was well enough to be told, Proudhon felt the blow agonizingly. 'I was attached to that child who, more than her sisters, reproduced the paternal type ... It is thus that we are punished for our vanities.' His own health, already weakened by prison conditions, never fully recovered from this attack of cholera, and illness was now to dog him for the remainder of his life. In 1855 he suffered a bad attack of dysentery, and another in 1856. By now Proudhon had given up all alcohol including wine, and was drinking only water.

Although many of the left in France during these years saw the Crimean War as a crusade against the arch tyranny of the Tsar, Proudhon would have none of it. 'The old European Society is in the same state as Turkey; it is very sick, on the way out.'[5] Therefore the alliance of the two to preserve the *status quo* was only natural. To the end he saw it as an adventure contrived for the benefit of reaction and absolutism.

Proudhon spent part of the summer of 1856 at Besançon. The Petit Battants house had been sold, and his ties with his native city were now virtually broken. None the less he felt a longing for a base outside Paris. In a letter to Euphrasie on 11 June Proudhon confessed to feeling homesick, and hoped that if only he could make some money from his writings they might move to the country. It was as if he already felt himself to be semi-retired; and the following summer he again expressed the hope that in future the family might spend the summers outside Paris – preferably in Franche-Comté. Unexpectedly, the course of the Proudhon family life was soon to take a much more dramatic turn.

NOTES TO CHAPTER NINE

1. Letter to Langlois, 18 May 1850.
2. There is in the *Philosophie du Progrès* a strong foretaste of Karl Popper's contributions to the philosophy of science and to the criticism of Marxism, over the last forty-five years.
3. Stendhal, *Lucien Leuwen*.
4. She lived to be ninety-seven, dying in 1947.
5. Letter to Charles Edmond, 9 July 1854.

TEN

'Justice' and Exile

WHAT ABRUPTLY CHANGED the retired and modest course of Proudhon's life since 1852 and drove him into four years of exile was the publication of his greatest book. Not that the reception of this work can have come wholly as a surprise: the storm was gathering well before the work was in the bookshops.

The MS of *De la Justice dans la Révolution et dans l'Eglise* had been for some time in Garnier's hands, and Bourdier, Garnier's printer, had most of it in type when, in November 1857, both printer and publisher received a sinister visit. Police-Commissioner Gaillard of the Ministry of the Interior's press licensing department called on both firms and, with the authority of the Minister, Delangle, demanded to know if it were true that the work by M. Proudhon which they were known to be about to publish was entitled *Le Bon Dieu au XIXe Siècle*. Garnier indignantly denied this and asked to be given the source of this information: Gaillard could or would tell him only that 'the denunciation' came from a German source.

Garnier was worried: whatever the impression made by the book as a whole, there were long passages, among them the denunciation of God as the eternal enemy of mankind, which would certainly give offence to the Church whose influence at court was paramount. Proudhon may have been worried; he was certainly very angry. He immediately wrote to Delangle protesting against what he called an attempt at pre-emptory censorship which was illegal even in the France of Louis-Napoleon. If, when the book was published, it was found to break any laws, the Minister had his remedy: he could prosecute. But until then there was no statute which gave him the right to interfere.

It is probable that the book's singular antecedents had something to do with this officious insolence. In 1855 a hack, de Mirecourt by name, was publishing a series of libellous biographies under the general title of *Les Contemporains*. It is probable that de Mirecourt, or his publisher Gustave Havard, was subsidized by the Church which, with the Emperor's compliance egged on by the *dévote* Eugenie, was striving by every means in its power to extinguish the libertarian and revolutionary spirit and restore the old order of unquestioning submission to the joint authority of Church and state. Mirecourt had already published libels on four of the Church's *bêtes noires* and dangerous enemies, Victor Hugo, George Sand, the spoiled priest Lammenais, and Thiers, before turning his attention to Proudhon.

For information about Proudhon's family, youth and antecedents, the libellist turned to Proudhon's old enemy Mgr Mathieu, Cardinal-Archbishop of Besançon, to whose ready cooperation he owed such passages as:

The foundation of his character is irritation and bitterness against society from which he felt himself banished by reason of his family's distress. Having, by the strength of his mind, been enabled to study deeply albeit narrowly, he erected a pedestal on which to stand and receive the homage of the universe at the expense of God Whom he regards as a rival. Proudhon is not an atheist; he is God's enemy.

Stung by the Cardinal's treachery, Proudhon began an address of reproach and apologia to Mathieu, which grew, as such writings were apt to grow under his hand, into a major work – *De la Justice*.

He used a dictum of Paul-Louis Courier as the point of departure of his statement of the book's purpose: 'Ever since humanity entered upon the period of civilization, as far back as we can remember, the people pray and pay.' His statement then followed:

They pray for their magistrates, their exploiters and their parasites; they pray, like Jesus Christ, for their executioners; they even pray for those who, by profession, should be praying for them. And then they pay for those they pray for; they pay for government, judiciary, police, Church, nobility, Crown, the Funds, the proprietors and the bum-bailiffs; they pay for their every attempt to be heard; they pay for the right to come and go, to sell and buy, to eat, drink, breathe and to warm themselves in the sun; they pay for being born and they pay for dying. They even pay for the right to work. And then they pray to heaven to give them, by blessing their labour, the means to pay even and ever more.

The people have never done anything but pray and pay. We believe the time has come to make them philosophise.

This book is by far the most powerful attempt on Proudhon's part to state the master-principle of social organization by revealing the master-law of the universe and how and why only conformity with it would make the organization of a just and free society possible. *De la Justice* is also the most impressive and moving confession of his own faith. Opposing a wholly lay morality equated with right reason, to revealed religion interpreted by theology, he argues that the only revelation we need in order to be just in all things can be found in every man's own conscience. But to understand it every man must learn how to think about the relationship between the self, and the not-self, the universe of things and of other men. There is, he says, no reason why we should not all do so: there is no mystery about philosophy, it is a derivative of common sense and above all a matter of observation.

Reflecting upon Proudhon's opinion of the common man's capacity for philosophical thinking, Gabriel Séailles, the anarchist author of *Philosophie du Travail*, quotes an old proverb: 'He who works, prays'; and adds that it is at least as true to say that he who works, and pays attention to what he is doing, philosophizes. That is more or less the line which Proudhon takes in that preliminary part of his book in which he persuades the ordinary working man that he is as capable as any man of education of following the arguments he is about to set forth. Work is an education, for whoever reflects upon the nature of his work, on the implications of the operations he is performing, and on the general truths involved in them, will find in such reflections a just notion of the relationships between thought and all nature, subject and object, the actor and the acted-upon. But has the artisan, factory hand or peasant, the requisite education to think analytically? Proudhon insists that he has and for this reason, that, 'The quantity of knowledge adds nothing whatever to the philosophic quality of knowledge.' He means, for example, that all mathematical certitude is contained in the proposition $2+2=4$.

If it be true, as Proudhon insists, that philosophy simply continues and develops common knowledge, and takes its departure from observations of phenomena, it must be essentially practical, even utilitarian; as such it is not only accessible to all, but 'democratic and social'. The philosopher seeks to do universally what an artisan does when working at his trade; that is, by becoming wholly aware of what he is doing, he discovers what he is. The universe is a great workshop in which there is no real distinction between speculative and practical reasoning. There are in his argument, premonitions of both Wittgenstein and the modern Existentialists.

Now the problem which all men, as philosophers, find themselves facing is this: 'By what criterion are our observations to be measured; and according to what plan, in view of what ends, shall we raise the edifice of our knowledge?' Proudhon offers guidance in the search for that master-rule: every idea is a relationship in which there are two terms, me and non-me, subject and object. It follows that the master-idea, the master-rule implicit in all ideas whatsoever, and which coordinates them, must itself be a dualistic notion in which the primordial relationship between subjects and objects is expressed. What is that master-idea? At first we are inclined to see in the subject, action; in the object, passivity. But looking deeper we find that just as there is in any organized being a common *sensorium*, an integral life, so there exists in nature a spirit of the universe which, though it does not act outwardly, as ours does, since there *is* nothing outside it, and all is contained in it, acts inwardly, in itself, the reverse way to ours and manifests itself by creating a vast organism of which we are a part.

In the above context I think that the word 'spirit' is misleading; Proudhon's own word is *âme*, but I could not bring myself to write soul, a word without a generally acceptable meaning; both words introduce an element of the transcendental and mystical which was the very last thing, as will appear, that Proudhon intended. I think that what he refers to is that integrity which is implied by, for example, the equilibrium attained by the complex of tensions and tolerances which maintains all the members of a biological eco-system in that state we call the 'balance of nature'. The reasons for so thinking will presently be clear.

Since, in his argument, all relationships, *rapports*, between subjects and objects have a common element, the master-principle of universal relationships, one way in which we can seek to identify that master-principle is by examining the relationship between 'I' and another 'I' who is not me; that is, between man and man. The master-principle is, then, no longer a metaphysical abstraction, but a real, living and sovereign duality. From man to things there is continuity:

The law which governs subjects as between each other is logically presumed also to govern objects, since otherwise the subordination of object to subject would be impossible, and there would be antinomy, contradiction, between nature and mankind. So the philosophy of speculation becomes practical, or rather the two kinds merge into one: the rule for action, and the guarantee of judgement, are identical.

The supreme idea, the master-principle which governs the world of things and the world of men, is the idea *Right or Rightness* (*Droit*) in all its meanings. Proudhon now starts to use the word *justice* as synonymous with *droit*. It is curiously difficult to translate *droit* into English. But the obvious word is *right*; and as in English, it refers to both a material state – straightness, directness, uprightness, correctness, accuracy – and a moral state – the same words as above but also in the sense of 'I have a right to . . .' What is right is righteous. The difficulty of translation arises in the case of another usage of *droit*: a French law student would describe himself as studying *droit*, not *loi*. In English we are happily free from this confusion: I say 'happily' because it is very important to grasp that this

Justice has nothing whatever to do with the commodity sold by lawyers or imposed by judges in law-courts and which is merely the enforcement of the will of the prince or of the equally authoritarian sovereign people. Proudhon's justice is very nearly synonymous with another word from the same root, that is *justesse*, by virtue of which things hold together, are the shape they are, in English, *right*.[1]

Proudhon's justice is the rightness of things. It is the master-principle of the universe: in the order of Nature, it is manifest as equilibrium, as ecological balance; in the order of intelligence it is manifest as logic, as mathematics, as equality or equation; in the order of mechanics it is thermodynamic efficiency; in the order of imagination, it is the ideal or what we mean by beauty; and in the order of conscience it is what we commonly mean by justice (again carefully excluding the abuse of the word in the context of statute and law-court law), the rule governing our rights and obligations. From all this one can justify the Proudhonian assertion that 'the separation of science from conscience, as of logic from right (*droit*) is only a scholastic abstraction'. This is to say that knowing rightly and feeling rightly are identical. The word science has been demoted, in our time, to mean 'natural' science or, all too often techno-logy. Proudhon, like any Englishman of his day, uses it to mean 'know-ledge', 'learning' in general.

Science is of equal quality in all minds, however different be the quantity from mind to mind. (The proposition $2+2=4$ is of the same quality as the proposition $E=MC^2$, the latter merely implying an enor-mously larger quantity of science). The same is true of conscience, a fact which is recognized by the revolution when, taking account of the equivalence of judgements, it makes all men equal before the law and seeks to make all men legislators and justices. 'Democracy of intel-ligences and democracy of consciences, such are the two great principles of philosophy, and the two articles of faith of the Revolution.'

Justice as right reason and justice as right feeling being identical and in accord with the master principle of the universe, we have no need whatever of God, of religion, of theology, of mystifications of any sort, in order to know how to behave justly. All we need to do is to identify, and take our niche in, the universal ecosystem of mutually balancing tensions and tolerances which compose the justice which keeps the stars in their course, the planets in their orbits, the grass growing and the cows eating it, and people keeping their obligations to each other.

An, as it were, *post hoc* confirmation of Proudhon's synthesis of moral and physical rightness can, I think, be found in the modern conservationist's thinking and feeling. To upset the balance of nature is not only *thought* to be unwise; it is *felt* to be wrong, that is contrary to justice. There is a distinct feeling of which most of us are aware, that to upset the balance is immoral as well as foolish. The theme of Proudhon's whole life was the revolution, but what he meant by it only emerged during the course of a lifelong meditation, exposed in the procession of his writings on that theme. It is in *De la Justice* that he at last clearly understands himself and enables us to understand him.

Revolution is the movement, implicit in the conscience of the people, towards a closer and closer equivalence with justice; to make it explicit, men must use their intelligence and use it in absolute liberty constrained only by contract freely entered into. Only in those conditions can we create a society within which individuals are in equilibrium with each other and with all nature. The equilibrium is created and sustained by the ceaseless, mutually balancing movement of thought and action which governs the universe. The revolution is a permanent, ever-lasting process and can never end. Accord with universal justice is more and more closely approached; it is never quite attained. The echo of Plato here is not fortuitous: Proudhon had studied him.

* * * * *

How does this justice in the revolution compare with justice in the Church?

The Church, and indeed all higher religions, derive all righteousness, all justice, from God. We are incapable of even knowing what it is excepting by grace of revelation interpreted by theology. In the Church, justice is exterior to man, transcendent, supernatural. According to the Church there can be no justice without a higher authority to hand it down; and without that revealed justice there can be no society. Still more terrible, since God is justice, and yet there is sin in the world, the culprit is man. The doctrine of Original Sin, says Proudhon, was invented to explain the presence of evil in the work of a just creator; and having once fallen, man can be saved only by Divine intervention. Take away the Church, and the consequence must be the reign of evil.

Proudhon, speaking for man and the revolution, utterly rejects this dismal view, and passionately pleads not guilty on our behalf. Justice is innate in man; immanent, yes, but only in the sense that the universe is a complex of things and beings held in equilibrium, that is in justice. Now, man is a social animal, an integral part of a collective being; therefore he feels his integrity, his dignity as Proudhon calls it, not only in himself, but also in his kind and thus finds in himself a morality which can rise superior to self. This conscience is sufficient unto itself and has no need whatever of a mystical, revealing authority. So society has no need of a Church to supply its ethic, its morality. It has its justice built-in, and will, by means of the revolution for ever sustained, give it increasingly valid expression.

The revolution, then, can be defined as autonomy of conscience; and justice, as the essence of humanity. But, 'What has it been since the beginning of the world? Almost nothing. What should it be? Everything. The question now lies between justice according to the faith; and justice according to liberty.'

*   *   *   *   *

The revolution does not go forward steadily and always on course; it strays, for we are fallible and choose pilots who, misled, mislead. Proudhon considers the two then contending manifestations of militant socialism, communism and anarchy, as means of attaining to revolutionary justice.

Communism he defines as the total subordination of the individual to society. Far from being new, he finds it in, for example, the oriental tyrannies,[2] in Caesarism, and in the absolutism based on Divine Right. Society and state become one and the same. One makes a distinction without a difference when one says that, under communism, society, the state, is the people's thing, not merely *res publica* but *res populi*, and its dictator the proletariat. The individual is just as degradingly subordinated to it, as under the tyranny or despotism of the prince, and the only really effective law is, just as surely, constraint. We are in an even better position to know the truth of this observation than Proudhon was.

At the other extreme is anarchy; and here, though he doesn't say so, Proudhon has the anarchy of Michael Bakunin in mind.[3] Anarchy seeks to solve the social question by absolute liberty without constraint. The implied hypothesis is a natural harmony of interests in social living, which is precisely, indeed, what another anarchist, Peter Kropotkin, believed he had discovered.[4] But oppositions of interests, even to the point of bitter violence, exist? Yes, say the anarchists, and they are provoked by the imposition of authority. But for that criminal interference, all man's interests would fall into harmony, for virtue is simply egoism properly understood.

This extreme anarchist solution Proudhon rejects with the dry remark that such a measure of optimism is not in accord with the observed facts.

There are, also, the idealist or utopian socialists: they are dismissed as no better than neo-mystics seeking to replace God by some other, equally arbitrary, authority – the commune, the phalanstery, or the state. For they too, in their fashion, believe in Original Sin, believe that man's nature is bad. Proudhon, again, will not have it: rules for right conduct are not to be found in authority or in revelation by God and His bureaucracy or by the sovereign people and their bureaucracy, but in that individual conscience and science innate in all free men and which are one and the same. Seek not the principle of evil in man; seek it in degrading poverty, in ignorance, in superstition, in bad economics and bad government. If God exists, then He, not man, is to blame for evil. The time for praying, the time for guilt, the time for breast-beating, is over; it is now time for salvation through work, time for labour to accept its responsibilities. What Proudhon called for can be put into eight words: stop praying, stop paying; start thinking – and working.

Since property (capitalism), political government in any form, authority celestial or terrestrial, idealistic or communistic or anarchic socialism, are all rejected as means to the realization of justice, where lies our remedy? In Proudhonism, of course, in its familiar elements derived from his passionate and unshakeable belief in the conscience and 'science' of the common man. It is in *De la Justice* that I find his most arresting and most impressive assertion of that faith:

> To feel and assert human dignity, first of all in what is proper to ourselves, then in the person of our neighbour, without lapses into selfishness and without reference to divine or communal authority, that is righteousness. To be ready, in all circumstances, to assume the defence of that dignity, if need be against our interest, that is justice.

Yes, but we have already seen Proudhon denouncing God as evil for requiring us to love our neighbour as ourselves while allowing us to establish institutions which make obedience to that rule impossible. He now says that there is 'an idea of mankind' in which all men share, from which it follows that 'the essence being one and the same for all men, each of us is aware of himself both as a person and as a species'.[5]

The basis for free but ordered society, then, is contract: equal and reciprocal respect between persons, service for service, guarantee for guarantee. All of which produce equilibrium, which is justice. Society, an association for mutual benefit between free and reasonable men looking to their consciences for guidance, comes to this: a concert of liberties, accord being established by voluntary transactions and reciprocal undertakings. Outside that concert, society does not exist, is not above or outside individuals. It results from, and exists only as long as, reciprocal acts and finds its only expression in contract freely entered into.

Any doctrine which submits the individual to an outside law, to an authority not his own, denies the dignity of man and denies morality:[6]

Justice is respect, spontaneously experienced and reciprocally guaranteed, for human dignity, in whatever person and circumstances it be compromised, and whatever the risk we take in defending it.

*   *   *   *   *

De la Justice was published on 22 April 1858: Proudhon was still sanguine. 'Will there be a prosecution?' he wrote to one of his friends, 'Not, I think, by the government. It's possible that certain discontented persons, such as the archbishop of Besançon, will have fault to find with me; that is what I expect ...' Garnier had printed an edition of 6500 in three volumes and, within a few days, sold 4000. Proudhon was delighted; he needed a success, evidence that he had allies in his long battle with the authorities of both right, left and centre; needed, too, a financial success, for he was still carrying the burden of his old debt, and he was trying to put money by for the dowries which his daughters would one day need. His joy was short-lived: six days after publication the police raided Bourdier's warehouse and Garnier's offices and confiscated all they could find of the edition, giving Garnier a list of six reasons for confiscation. Proudhon's book, 'Reproduced, in bad faith, false news likely to cause a breach of the peace;[7] was an incitement to hatred of citizens by citizens; was an attack on family rights; was an outrage on public and religious morality; attacked the respect due to the laws; and defended acts qualified in law as crimes and misdemeanours.'

Proudhon was never in any doubt that this blow to his hopes came from Cardinal Mathieu, but it was not the only blow, for the reception of his book by the press was almost unanimously hostile. The *Observateur*, having grossly prejudiced the case by calling the book an 'outrage against public morals', smugly announced that it would withhold comment in order not to prejudice any proceedings which the authorities might bring against the author; but that if the magistrates who were the guardians of public morals failed to condemn it, then the *Observateur* would do the job for them. The *Revue des Deux Mondes* dismissed Proudhon's ideas as 'crack-brained extravagances'. The *Siècle*, he was told, was preparing to demolish him in its next number; and he records in his current *Carnet* (1 May) that Curilier-Fleury of the *Débats* had told him he would be doing likewise but for the confiscation of the edition and the pending prosecution: presumably he didn't want to appear on the same side as the enthroned adventurer nicknamed Badinguet by the faubourg Saint-Germain. The *Réveil* and *Nord* reviewers slaughtered the book and damned its author. And it was particularly irritating that this bad press was precisely of the kind which would have ensured the dowries of Stephanie and Catherine, had not Garnier been prevented from reprinting. Then, as since, there's nothing more certain to sell a book than its damnation on moral grounds.

His friends' feelings about the book were mixed. Perhaps Alexander Herzen's, which he did not live to read, were representative: he is deeply depressed by it, partly because it paints so sombre a picture of the state of France and of Europe, partly because he finds that Proudhon is no longer 'free' but is writing to a predetermined end; doing so with that intemperance of language for which his friends had been reproaching him since *What is Property*?

'Towards the end,' Herzen writes, 'I was watching over him as Kent watched over King Lear, expecting him to recover his reason. But he raged more and more – there were the same fits of intolerance, of unbridled speech as in Lear ...' On the other hand:

Latin thought, religious in its very negation, superstitious in doubt, rejecting one set of authorities in the name of another, has rarely gone further, rarely plunged more deeply *in media res* of reality, rarely freed itself of all fetters with such dialectic boldness as in this book. In it, not only the crude dualism of religion but the subtle dualism of philosophy is cast off. The mind is set free not only of heavenly phantoms, but from those of the earth, it strides beyond the sentimental apotheosis of humanity and the fatalism of progress, and has none of the invariable litanies of brotherhood, democracy and progress which are so pitifully wearisome in the midst of wrangling and violence. Proudhon sacrificed the idols and the language of revolution to the understanding of it, and transferred morality to its only real basis, the heart of man, recognizing reason alone and none other gods but reason.

But after much more in that vein, comes renewed complaint:

What chaos! Proudhon emancipated from everything except reason wished to remain not only a husband after the fashion of Bluebeard, but also a French nationalist, with his literary chauvinism and unlimited paternal authority; and therefore, behind the strong, vigorous mind of the free man one seems to hear the voice of a savage greybeard dictating his will and wishing now to preserve for his children the tottering edifice which he has spent his life undermining.

Here, Herzen's distress carried him too far: he was, of course, right enough about Proudhon's conservatism; Proudhon himself never denied it. Had he not written to Girardin: 'I am a revolutionary who is profoundly conservative'? Add to that, a remarkable exchange in conversation with prince Napoleon:

'Then what sort of society *do* you want, Monsieur Proudhon?'
'One in which I should be guillotined as a conservative, Prince.'

But Herzen went astray when he called Proudhon a French nationalist: he was never a nationalist of any kind, he had opposed the union of Italy with all his might, and he did not give a fig for the political unity of France. He was a regionalist, a Franc-Comtois; and a French chauvinist only in the sense that he hoped and believed that France would continue to be what she had been since 1789 – mankind's revolutionary pathfinder.

The distress induced by Proudhon's powerlessness to get the book into the hands of the thousands who wanted it, was compounded by those Job's comforters, any polemical author's barrister friends, who were assuring Proudhon that a 10,000 franc fine and a five-year prison sentence were the least he could expect from Louis-Napoleon Bonaparte's bought-and-paid-for judges.

Here's the *Carnet* entry for 6 May:

Appeared before the examining magistrate. For some days I've been made unpleasantly aware of the spiteful spirit of this so-called moderate republic and its rabble of lawyers. I'm told that the least I can expect is a five-year prison sentence, and that the verdict is as good as pronounced. To me they seem like people coming to my funeral; surely, they wish me dead. The deplorable thing about this despotism is that it favours the growth of intrigue, corruption, injustice and parasitism.

There is, in this complaint, a singular, but characteristic, simple-mindedness: a virtuous man can think, but cannot feel in his heart that the others are not virtuous.[8]

At his second session with the examining magistrate Proudhon produced a certified copy, obtained from Mirecourt himself, of the Cardinal's letter to that pamphleteer, proving that when he accused Mgr Mathieu of complicity in libel, he was telling the simple truth. He believed that he had, in that letter, a bargaining counter; that the government would want it suppressed, overlooking the fact that the magistrate trying his case could, if so ordered by the Minister, clear the court and exclude the press for *raison d'état*. Three days later, on 11 May, he desposited with the Senate a petition protesting against the seizure of his book as illegal, in the form of a *mémoire* which he published, compounding

his crime by printing more than the licensed 500 copies. He seems to
have believed that the lower courts could not try a case of which the
Senate was already seized. Nobody else believed this and his friends were
urging him to flee the country. This he refused to do; it would be an
admission of guilt. On 19 May he received the expected *assignation* to
appear before the *Tribunal* of the *Police correctionelle* on 2 June.

Bad though it was, the outcome of the trial could have been much
worse, for he himself worked out that the magistrates could, because he
was a *récidiviste*, a second offender, have inflicted a fine of 12,000 francs
and sent him to prison for ten years. In the event the fine was 4000 francs
and the prison sentence three years. Garnier was fined 1000 francs and
given a prison sentence of one month; Bourdier was fined 1000 francs and
given two weeks in prison. Proudhon immediately decided to appeal:

There is [he wrote to his friend Maurice] no animosity against me in high places,
nor do I believe that the public prosecutor is out for my blood. But the Church is
involved and for the time being it does not suit the emperor's government to
allow the Church to be maltreated; hence my conviction.

He meant by this that the country was in such a state and the
government so unpopular that they needed any ally they could be sure of.
He also believed that had his book been published before the Emperor's
nerve had been shaken by Felice Orsini's attempt on his life, he would
have been allowed to get away with it.[9]

As for Proudhon's opinion that the state of the nation obliged the
government to avoid offending its ally the Church, his account of France
in 1858 is sombre:

Ours are twilight times. Business is in an ever deepening depression, and
everywhere there is anxiety, disgust and despair. As much fear is generated by
the silence of the press today as by its clamour in 1848. Every government in
Europe is arming, yet nobody knows why, but the English blame France, that is,
the emperor. The clerical party, everywhere ultramontane and directed by the
Jesuits, meddles and intrigues and, in connivance with certain governments,
seeks to extinguish all revolutionary ideas. The Orleanist party is gaining ground
by making mischief. The weather and harvest look like being magnificent, for
want of confidence and security poverty is on the increase. Poor France ...
The end of the 19th century will be appalling.

The appalling event did not wait for the end of the century and had he
lived only five years longer than he did, he would have watched with
horror the Emperor blunder into and lose the war with Prussia.

The fact is that, *petit bourgeois* as Marx had accused him of being, and as
in many respects he was, yet he was losing faith in the good sense and

goodwill of the French middle-class; in one outburst in a bad moment he declared that just as the only hope of revolution in ancient Rome had been the slaves, so in Paris it must now be *les catins et les grecs*, the whores and crooks.

Half-way through June he was writing to Charles Edmond:

I am being showered with sinister warnings and repeatedly urged to leave the country. But I've taken it into my head to go to prison. These craven fears of the public and my personal friends hurt me, I really suffer. Is this how, in France today, we back up our friends? Like Bonaparte on the bridge at Arcole, I bear forward the standard against the enemy, only to find that I have nobody at my back. I'm admired as if I'd performed an act of conspicuous gallantry, and then left to deal with the consequences alone. What a generation! What a France! I am so disgusted, so horrified to find myself living in such a world, that frankly I'd almost rather be in prison ...

That bitter resolution, if it was ever more than an outbreak of petulance, did not last. He was, meanwhile, working on his appeal *Mémoire* and doing it as if he were sure of winning. Bergmann had written to say that at least, in *De la Justice*, he should have avoided such intemperance of language; he'd been giving the same advice since *What is Property?* Proudhon rejected that criticism, claimed that he had a *right* to use the strongest language in such a case. When Sainte-Beuve told him that, for the taste of artists and writers, his tone was 'too moral', that seemed only to confirm him in his view of the decadence of the arts, and of a Church which, in return for submission to its authority, had given up the unpopular duty of requiring a severe virtue of the faithful.

What finally drove him to take refuge in Brussels pending his appeal was not fear of prison but the refusal of Chaix-d'Est-Ange, the Procurator Imperial, to license an edition of more than twenty copies of his appeal *Mémoire*; and the refusal of all the printers he approached to set the work in type. There were two French-speaking places where he could print it: Switzerland and Belgium; Belgium was nearer to Paris.

Although his principal aim now was to vindicate both the opinions expressed in *De la Justice* and his right to publish them, he also had some hopes of profiting financially from the book's success by persuading a Belgian or Swiss publisher to publish a new edition. There was a brisk demand for the book, it was changing hands at 50 francs a copy, the *cabinets de lecture* were renting it out at 50 centimes per day per volume, and the case of a gentleman paying 200 francs for a copy had been reported. Garnier estimated that Swiss sales alone would have been

20,000, which would, as Proudhon wrote to a friend, have provided a substantial start to the fund for his daughters' dowries.

There were other considerations in favour of exile: his legal advisers did not share his confidence that they would win their appeal: in that case he would go to prison. If he recalled that claim made when he was leaving Sainte-Pélagie in 1852 that his three years in prison had gained him more than he had lost, he probably knew in his heart that there had been a good deal of mere *cudot* in that boast, and whatever he might now say in moments of bitter disgust with the world, he did not really want to lose another three years of freedom, that most precious of all rights. Above all, he was no longer willing to submit tamely to persecution, by a man and a government and a Church which he regarded as all equally despicable.

He left Paris for Lille, by stage-coach on 17 July, there hired a carriage which got him to Tournai late at night, started off again the following morning early, and on the eighteenth wrote to Euphrasie to announce his safe arrival in Brussels. There he found, among the French politicals in exile, a few friends – Madier-Montjou, Joly, Victor Considérant, his old German friend Karl Grün – and many of his enemies of the republican left, among whom the Marxists, as they were not, of course, then called, were the most implacable.

On 20 July he wrote again to the Rue de l'Enfer household to tell his wife that for the time being he was passing as one Dufort, a teacher of mathematics, to give her his address and to beg her to write to him and to ask Gouvernet to write; he was already suffering the melancholy of exile. Moreover he was facing the fact that return to France might be impossible. In the same letter he discusses the pros and cons of exile in Brussels as compared with what he would have preferred, Geneva. Finally, he instructs Euphrasie to let Gouvernet, Pilhes, Beslay and Chaudez know his decision to remain in exile rather than go to prison; but the rest of their acquaintances are to be allowed to believe that he intends to return to Paris as soon as his appeal *Mémoire* is printed.

The French exiles in Brussels numbered about a hundred; Proudhon neither sought nor avoided them, and behaved with careful discretion, although he could hardly overlook the fact that their newspaper, the exiles' version of the *National*, had repeatedly maltreated him and his works in its columns; and that their review, *Libre Récherché*, had savaged *De la Justice* and its author in the current number.

Still, it was heartening to find himself well-known to the Belgians, welcomed, treated with respect, and by some with warmth. He envisaged an 'international' of like-minded men. He began to feel that Brussels was a city in which he could do good work, though the climate did not suit him. Geneva would have been more congenial but was too far away. At times he felt dejected; he missed his favourite Stephanie, missed his wife and her care of him; and his stomach was upset by the Belgian beer which was a poor substitute for the wine he was used to. In his letter of 24 July to Euphrasie he tells her to ask their friend Foucon who is about to travel to Brussels, to take advantage of the Chemin-de-Fer du Nord's twenty-kilogram luggage allowance to bring him a case of good wine, because very bad 'blue' wine costs 1 franc 50 a bottle in Brussels.

His first task in Brussels was to regularize his position with the authorities, for he was in the country without permission, that is illegally, and without the *permis de séjour* which foreigners were required to carry. He called on Verheyden, the Director of Public Security, and frankly laid the full facts of his case before him. Verheyden referred him to the Minister of Justice and on the following day, again setting out the full facts, Proudhon delivered a letter. His letter concludes:

As you see, *M. le Ministre*, I am not exactly a political refugee but, rather, a refugee philosopher. I ask your leave to philosophize in your country as Spinoza philosophized in The Hague, Descartes in Stockholm, Voltaire at Ferney. And I shall be very surprised if the imperial government, ashamed of waging war on ideologists, does not sooner or later invite my fellow-refugees and myself to return and do our philosophizing in Paris.

Cudot; there was no possibility, but he knew that the Belgian government was afraid of Louis-Napoleon, and he was by no means sure of a favourable response. It would require a cabinet meeting to decide whether he was to go or stay; the Belgian government was well aware that Louis-Napoleon would not have forgiven the man who had furiously denounced his ambitions in speech and print.

Proudhon was able to let his wife know on 27 July, that he had been given provisional permission to remain; he had been slowly and reluctantly making up his mind what to do if allowed to stay in Brussels: when he received his *assignation* to appear before the appeal court in Paris, he would answer to the summons only if Chaix-d'Est-Ange agreed to an adjournment to allow him time to get his *Mémoire* printed, allowed copies of it to cross the frontier and circulate in France, and guaranteed him absolute freedom of speech in his defence and full publicity for the trial. If he did not receive those assurances, with sufficient guarantees, then he would not surrender to the *assignation*.

He had good reason for anxieties: his numerous enemies of the French republican, anti-anarchist left in Brussels were capable of making all the mischief they could, and of making his life in the Belgian capital impossible. He lived very modestly and quietly, held his tongue in their presence, busied himself with his *Mémoire*, and in investigating the cost of lodging and living for a small, humble family. He wrote to Euphrasie that they could get a house with a bit of garden for less than in Paris, and thought they could manage as well there on 200 francs a month as on 300 francs in Paris. 'The Belgian capital offers no amusements but the ladies' *toilettes* are more luxurious and elegant than in Paris.' From time to time he was taken out of himself by Belgian friends and admirers who dined and wined him. He was delighted to receive a little letter from Catherine.

Then came the news that his *permit de séjour* had been granted; and, five days later, that, without summoning him to appear, the appeal court had confirmed the sentence of the police *correctionelle* tribunal (30 July), and had struck at the nearest victim, Garnier, by increasing his sentence to four months and a 4000 franc fine. Crémieux, Proudhon's advocate, raised such substantial objections to these arbitrary proceedings that Chaix-d'Est-Ange was forced to agree to a second appeal hearing in November; in fact the case was not heard until February 1859 by which time Proudhon had lost interest and no longer cared what happened. But meanwhile he was having his *Mémoire* printed with the November hearing in mind, and was a prey to a new anxiety: there was a possibility that the court might order a distraint on all his poor worldly goods in his home in the Rue de l'Enfer. He wrote to Euphrasie urging her, in that event to lock herself and their children into the house, and to refuse to yield to anything less than force.

He was, by this time, facing the fact that his conditions for making a personal appearance before the court in Paris would not be met; and was beginning to make the best of the prospect of settling in Belgium for some years; he wrote as much to Euphrasie on 28 August, saying that, as for money, he hoped that a Belgian publisher would bring out a second edition of *De la Justice*. In a letter to his friend Doctor Crétin written in September, he says:

I believe that the public which remains to me in Belgium, Switzerland, Piedmont etc., all that one means by Europe, reads French and welcomes my writings; I believe, I say, that this public will suffice to keep my pen busy and so enable me to cover the expenses of my household. We shall scarcely be rich, but we should be able to make ends meet, and since I can no longer write in France, I shall resign myself to a cosmopolitan audience. That modest existence will at least be more worthwhile than living useless in prison!

And two weeks later he was writing to Gouvernet, asking him to prepare Euphrasie for the necessary move, and to urge her to resign herself to it: 'Today she is widowed of her husband; soon, I believe, she will be widowed of Paris and all her friends.' She, meanwhile, had sent him a present with which he was delighted: a daguerreotype of herself and the children;

Your eyes are smiling as you look at me and it is above all by the slightly malicious expression of that smile and your look that I *am* so aware of you. Thank you for your pretty gift and kiss our daughters for me; that photograph is not as good of them; far from it.

There were, as usual, elaborate instructions: Lebègue, his Belgian publisher, was coming to Paris and would bring back the papers he wanted: Euphrasie was to get everything ready; all the letters which had arrived for him were to be opened and the signatures obliterated before they were forwarded. As for his health, he could give no good report of it: constant pains in the head, and two hours reading paralysed half his brain and half his face. There were other sources of worry: Catherine was not making satisfactory progress in reading and writing; some of his mail was being tampered with by the French post office ...

In the last week of September 1858 he set off for a walking holiday in the Belgian Ardennes with his friend Delhasse. They were in Spa when he heard that his last hope of a return to France must be abandoned: his *Mémoire* had been banned by the French police. That night he sat down and wrote to his wife for whom, as he knew, exile would be a worse ordeal than for himself:

Dear wife. Greatly do I fear that hard times are now beginning for you. You want to rejoin your husband; and I do not yet know how I am to earn our living in this foreign land. Of course, there are ways and means but the perils are great and the difficulties far from trifling. I hope that you will sustain me as you always have done and that your heart will not let you reproach me.

Back in Brussels he found that she had picked the ripe pears in their little garden and sent them to him; '... do you not know that I would much rather you and our girls had eaten them?' He had no need of such reminders of her affection.

Last night I dreamed that I was sitting in my big easy-chair; Stephanie had clambered onto my shoulders, Catherine was standing on one thigh, and you were sitting on the other so that I was embracing all three of you together.

There is a very understandable but very uncharacteristic lapse into self-pity in a letter to Charles Bellet (5 October):

Forgive me, dear friend, if I sometimes have moments of sadness and anxiety. I have only too much reason to be downcast. One ought to be not more than thirty years of age to carry on a struggle like this, and I shall soon be fifty. I already feel the cold touch of age and weariness, and after so much effort, so long striving, now see myself reduced to getting my own and my family's daily bread, painfully and uncertainly, in a foreign land. Of course, I shall manage here, somehow; but it will mean working twice as hard and being twice as prudent. A man of my age does not find it easy to change his whole environment, and for a man of letters it is much worse.

He misses the calm routine of his home life, misses his wife and children, dwells with regret on all they have now lost, misses his friends. For the first time in his life he realizes the vanity of his own youthful strivings, the absurdity of believing that mankind could be saved by common sense and goodwill drawing upon innate virtue; he broods on hopes unfulfilled or betrayed; on the appalling gulf separating the happy, morally and intellectually noble France of his dream, and the actual France, servile and corrupt under the heel of a crafty and contemptible adventurer. The concluding passage of a letter to the *ami de la maison*, Gouvernet, is moving:

Farewell, dear friend; believe me, I miss you very much indeed; and if I may judge by my own feelings for you, it seems to me that my absence must leave an empty place in your heart. Our evening chats were always so pleasant to me. You relaxed my mind, and so often saved me from importunate visitors who would have overstayed their welcome. For me you were always the complement of my family, for there can be no family circle without a good family friend. All this is at an end and here we are reduced to letters.

Towards the end of September he had sent a parcel of twenty-five copies of his *Mémoire*, now a book of 160 pages entitled *La Justice Poursuivie par l'Eglise*, to Paris, addressed to Garnier Frères at their offices in the Rue des Saints-Pères; and, at the same time, a letter to the Minister of the Interior informing him of this dispatch and asking him to issue orders to the customs offices that, under Article 23 of the law of 17 May 1819, the book must be allowed free entry into France in such numbers as the author pleased. The letter was not answered but Garnier Frères were given a warning that if they sent to claim the parcel at the customs office, they would 'compromise' themselves. Later, Proudhon was informed that in future no work of his would be allowed into France. He protested about both of these acts in an enormously long letter quoting chapter and verse of the law to prove the legality of his own conduct and the illegality of the Minister's, and threatening a civil suit for damages. I don't suppose anyone bothered to read it, and there was really nothing effective he could do: in France 'Monsieur Bonaparte' *was* the law. One sees the justice of Marx's sneer at him as *petit bourgeois*; he was to die virtuous, unable to learn the lesson that the revolutionary reformer who will not countenance recourse to violence, has no real alternative but to submit to violence.

I do not intend to spend time on *Justice prosecuted by the Church*: it is a passionate and polemical defence of *De la Justice* and of its author's right in publishing it, but it contains nothing which is not to be found in the book it defended.

By the end of October Brussels was finally decided on. Proudhon had come to terms with Lebègue who agreed to regular payments against delivery, of any MSS which he liked to produce. Euphrasie sold up their home in the Rue de l'Enfer. By the time she and the children arrived, early in November, Proudhon had found rooms for them and bought a few sticks of furniture. There had been much rather acrimonious correspondence between them about their furniture: Proudhon wanted to sell all they had in the house or, if possible, to rent it to the incoming tenant. Euphrasie wanted to keep it all and bring it to Brussels which could be done by hiring an entire train-wagon; or, if she could not do that, at least she must keep their big double-bed. She made such a fuss about this bed that Proudhon complained to Gouvernet that he had no idea there was a religion of beds. She had, as usual, to give away but made it clear that she did not trust him to choose the right furniture for the new home, and certainly not to get good value for their money.

Though the decision to settle had been taken, Proudhon did not feel secure. There was an established practice whereby political refugees, Karl Marx among others, were driven from one liberal country of refuge to another at the 'request' of powerful neighbouring autocrats. If the French Emperor took it into his head to bully the Belgian government, they were unlikely to dare to protect Proudhon; he had already made arrangements in advance for a remoter exile.[10]

In the event, no pressure was put upon the Belgian government to expel him; it was enough that this ultra-Frenchman was denied the land he loved and this was assured when, in the summer of 1859, the French government proclaimed an amnesty extended to all those convicted of breaches of the press laws. Only one such convict was excluded by name: P-J. Proudhon.

The home which Proudhon had found for his family in Brussels was a half-house in the Rue du Conseil in the Ixelles suburb, with a good market conveniently close, and a school which Catherine was sent to. The rent was 372 francs a year, much less than their rent in the Rue de l'Enfer; and there were friends living in the same suburb, Madier-Montjou and other exiles, Proudhon's very warm-hearted new Belgian friends the Delhasses, and his old acquaintance Karl Grün.

But for Euphrasie there was the usual problem: she could not possibly feel at ease with women of education and fashion like Madame Delhasse, however gentle they were with her, and she had never been capable of sharing her husband's interests – a fact which was, of course, one of his reasons for marrying her; in Paris this did not matter much, she had her family and their friends. But in Brussels she felt cut off from all society. She could not complain of the house and her money went further in the Ixelles market than in Paris, but she mourned her old furniture, detested the utility furniture which Proudhon had bought, and must, I think, have been distressed and offended by the separate bedrooms which Proudhon now insisted on. But her real difficulty in settling down was that she was a Parisienne to the very bone: take her a mile from the boulevards, and she was *dépaysée*, lost and sad; and her temper suffered.

Early in 1859 Proudhon was again very seriously ill: it was called a recurrence of cholera but was perhaps some kind of influenza complicated by gastro-enteritis and asthma. Having to nurse her husband in that alien and unsympathetic place depressed Euphrasie to the point of despair. She was saved only by her obstinate belief, which irritated and distressed Proudhon who was incapable of blinking at the truth, that it would soon be possible for them to return to Paris.

Proudhon recovered some measure of health in the spring of 1859 but by the summer's end was in such a state of exhaustion that he would have to have a rest and a change. As always when he was sick he yearned for the air of woods and mountains; he went to Spa, in the Belgian Ardennes, where the Delhasses had a country house: Delhasse, by the way, was a rich man, a socialist, and a writer well-known in Belgium although scarcely outside it. Euphrasie remained at home with the children, but was to have her turn when Proudhon returned: she was to take the little girls to Paris for a fortnight.

Proudhon, as always when he was away from her, wrote to Euphrasie almost every day. In one of his letters he describes his first visit to *La Rédoute*, Spa's then world-famous casino or kursaal; he was offended to the bottom of his virtuous soul by the luxury of the *toilettes* flaunted by the *lorettes*[11] who flocked to Spa to prey upon the rich male visitors; and by the gambling. He had seen one man lose fifty *louis d'or* on the turn of a card, and another win 900 francs at a short sitting. I suppose that he tasted, even if he did not 'take' the waters; he says nothing about that. Most of his time was spent in walking in the wooded hills; and as always the country, and the mountain air, were his best medicine.

Back in Brussels before the end of September, he was worried and irritated by his wife's obstinacy in believing that he could, if he would, take advantage of the amnesty and return to France without danger. She seemed unable to believe that a specific exception had been made in his case, a fact which he had checked with the Ministry. Almost his last word to her as he saw her and the children off at the railway station, excepting for a dispute over a lost five-franc piece, was to put that idea out of her mind. He wrote to her every day during her absence, letters full of complicated commissions and messages and instructions. Her most important task was to call on Garnier and collect 500 francs; she could draw on it but was to bring back as much as possible as he was very short of money and there would soon be the quarter's rent and Catherine's school bill to pay. He received a letter from her; and then one from Theodore Piégard which greatly displeased him: he replied not to Theodore, but to Euphrasie:

Theodore's letter contains a word which displeases me and makes it clear that in Paris they persist in believing that if I do not profit by the amnesty the fault is my own. Theodore tells me not to be pig-headed. Yet you know very well what the Minister's intentions are in my case: you should also know that not for the world would I expose myself to having to squabble with the imperial legal gentry over my freedom, and then have to go running to the emperor. I am angry at all this tittle-tattle which only aggravates your own regrets and irritates me. No, I tell you, I will not return under such conditions. As for you, if living in Belgium is too disagreeable for you, I have told you already that I will not have you making a martyr of yourself, and we must so contrive matters that you stay where you are. I will see that neither you nor the children want for anything, and go on alone to whatever fate has in store for me.

NOTES TO CHAPTER TEN

1. The argument which follows is reinforced by the fact that, in custom and common speech, right is more honourable than left, presumably because of the predominance of the right hand over the left in work. It must be mortifying to socialists that, as a consequence of a mere accident of seating arrangements in the Constituent Assembly of the French Revolution, the conservatives were on the more honourable side, and the radicals for ever labelled 'left'.

2. In the Ottoman Empire, there was only one free man, the Sultan; all the others, from the Grand Vizier downwards, were virtually slaves, just as every man in the USSR is virtually a slave of the state whose will is the only law.

3. As far as I know he could not have read Stirner's *The Ego and his own* because he could not read German.
4. See, *eg*, Kropotkin's *Mutual Aid*.
5. Another foresight: Darwin's *Origin of Species*, with its implication that the individual animal is so constituted as to have to take the survival of his species into account, was not published, and then only in English which Proudhon could not read, until 1859.
6. A curious coincidence of views with some of Proudhon's will be found in a pamphlet, author unknown but possible Kritias, date *c.* 425 BC, quoted by A. R. Burn in his *Pelican History of Greece*. The passage in which Athenian democracy is being explained to strangers, reads: 'Anyone who wishes to can speak [at the Assembly] – any low type, and devises what is best – for himself and his like. [The Athenians] realise that his uneducated low cunning and loyalty produce better results than a gentleman's virtue and wisdom and disloyalty. A city run so may not be ideal but that is how to preserve a democracy. *The people do not want a well-organized city with themselves in subjection, but freedom and power. Disorder is a minor consideration: what you consider disorder is the very foundation of the people's strength and freedom.*' The italics are mine.
7. The book, of course, did not contain 'news'; this charge was simply a legal formula taken from the law controlling the press.
8. Wicked conduct, of course, ran counter to the theory of virtue innate in 'science and conscience'. But wealth and power corrupt, so that virtue is only to be found in the common people.
9. The attempted assassination, 14 January 1858, did more damage to a British than to Napoleon's government, resulting in the resignation of Lord Palmerston.
10. Letter to Bonnon, 27 October. He does not say where but he probably had Geneva in mind. The Swiss did not allow themselves to be bullied. He could, of course, like other Frenchmen including the most distinguished scholar of the Second Empire, Hippolyte Taine, have found asylum in England, but it would not have crossed his mind to live in a land where French was not spoken, France was hated and despised, and property was arrogantly triumphant.
11. *Lorette*: high-class whores. The name is from the *quartier* centred on Notre Dame de Lorette, notorious as a place for picking up prostitutes.

War and Peace and Poverty

TOWARDS THE SECOND HALF of 1859 Proudhon was completing the revision of *De la Justice* for the projected second edition, writing a new work
to be called *La Guerre et la Paix*, and also working on half a dozen more
immediately gainful but otherwise less important commissions. These
exacting tasks were however interrupted when Euphrasie, sensibly
ignoring that rather ill-tempered and self-pitying epistolatory outburst
to the effect that if she could not bear Belgium she had better stay in
France, returned to Brussels in mid-October. There must thereafter
have been moments when Proudhon, much as he liked to have his family
about him, almost wished that his wife had taken him at his word: both
little girls were in the throes of scarlet-fever and two days after their
arrival, with both of them still in bed, Euphrasie herself was stricken
down by such paralysing rheumatic pains in all her joints that she was
forced to take to her bed, could not, in fact, stand.

For three weeks Proudhon had to put aside his pen and become
housekeeper, cook and sick-nurse to his three invalids; and this while
suffering acute anxiety about the household's shortage of money and the
severity of Stephanie's illness; he adored the child, she was certainly his
favourite, and he had to watch her struggle for her life and very nearly
lose her hold on it.

By the time the two children were out of danger and Euphrasie on her
feet again – one suspects that her pains may have been at least in part
psychosomatic – Proudhon was exhausted and there was not a penny in
the house. He was forced to swallow his pride and ask Garnier for
another, this time scarcely justifiable, 500 francs advance; he received it
by return of post. Although the Proudhons in Brussels were never
brought quite so low as were the Marxs in London, for the bum-bailiffs
never actually seized their furniture and sold them up, this was only
thanks to the prompt and unfailing generosity of Garnier. He was by no
means sure of ever getting his money back, although Proudhon never
doubted that his books would earn all that he ever owed his publisher,
and more. That confidence was soon to suffer a cruel blow.

As soon as he could Proudhon returned to his task of preparing the
revised version of *De la Justice* for publication. This was the work which
carried most of his hopes, both for his reputation and for his solvency. At

the same time he was putting the finishing touches to *La Guerre et la Paix*, his philosophical account of the nature of war. And it was while he was engaged in this task that one of his numerous foreign admirers came to visit him, the Russian novelist Tolstoy. The Russian himself possessed strong leanings towards anarchist thinking, and the discussions he had with Proudhon over a period of days in April 1860 left a profound impression on him and – incidentally – provided him with the title of his next major work, *War and Peace*. Proudhon for his part commented that none of the many Russians who had visited him struck him so forcibly as an individual as did Tolstoy.

Proudhon was now working all hours. In addition to the two books already mentioned he was also preparing – rather surprisingly it might seem – an essay on taxation. This grew almost into the dimensions of another book and was, Proudhon claimed, 'the first time to my knowledge that a complete and rigorously deduced theory of taxation has been produced'. Needless to say this theory was firmly set in a Mutualist context. What moved him to write *Théorie de l'Impôt* was a competition announced by the Swiss canton of Vaud, and a prize of 1200 francs that was being offered to the winner. It could well be that in his present straits it was this sum of money which attracted Proudhon more deeply than the theme of the essay.

Meanwhile further domestic tragedies beset him. In May 1860 his brother Charles and his cousin Melchior both died. The death of his blacksmith brother particularly grieved him, even though, he told Rolland,

I expected his death for several years. Nevertheless it afflicts me, or rather renews my regrets when I think that he, my father, my mother, all my family, counted on me, that they expected some little well-being from me, and that, through my socialist impulses, I placed myself outside the conditions of success, outside the communion of fortune.

In the late summer of 1860 Proudhon, suffering again from his catarrhal complaint and his headaches, and on the point of collapse, went once more to Spa, this time with Chaudez. Although his health rapidly improved away from his desk and family, and in the mountain air, it seems to have been his fate always to receive bad news while he was in Spa: this time it was that Garnier would not publish the new edition of *De la Justice*. To do so would have been to expose himself and his printer to another heavy fine and another term in prison. In the first place the news was a financial disaster, though a suspended one, for if Garnier could not publish him, how was he to repay those considerable advances? He still had his Belgian publisher, Lebègue, who was already paying him for other MSS as fast as he could deliver the work: but if the French police banned the book from the largest francophone market, then its sale would be very limited. Publication of the new *De la Justice* under Garnier's imprint might, had the police let the book pass this time, have meant a respite from work, the possibility of a rest during which he might really recover his health. There was now no hope of that. Finally, it was deeply depressing for him to face the fact that his book, now being read all over the Continent and even in Russia, could not be read by the only people for whose good opinion he cared a fig.

He returned to Brussels and to work and early in December came the news which might have been expected to compensate, in some measure, for this misfortune. If France could not have his great book, she could at least have its author, for Napoleon had, unsolicited by Proudhon, given him a free pardon and permission to return unconditionally to Paris, exile having purged his offence. Needless to say Euphrasie was over-joyed; but her rejoicings were not of long duration, for Proudhon did not share them. There was, he decided without hesitation, no question of returning home immediately; one day, perhaps, but certainly not for some time.

He had two reasons; there was a third motive which can hardly be called a reason and which was perhaps stronger than the other two combined. In the first place he was ashamed of and disgusted with the state of France, a country now so degraded that he could scarcely contemplate living in it. It would, in fact, be hard to imagine a society – politically anti-liberal, authoritarian and cynical, economically both corrupt and bankrupt, in foreign policy adventurist and opportunist, socially as wretched as ever for the poor, grossly self-indulgent and luxurious for the rich, its religion dominated by narrow-minded and arrogant bigots utterly indifferent to its moral decline provided they received its submission in matters of faith – a society more designed to affront the feelings, offend the reason and rouse the righteous anger of the most virtuous man in Europe. In the second place he had now con-siderable engagements in Brussels, to publishers and editors which, he felt, must be fulfilled before he returned to France. That was obviously not a good reason. There was nothing he was doing in Brussels which could not have been done from Paris. His real motive, I believe, was his special kind of pride, *cudot* again.

Here two short but illuminating anecdotes: when one of his friends who could very well afford it brought presents for the two little girls, while he did not insist on their being returned, he did, that same day, write to the donor and ask him never to do such a thing again. A greeting card and a five-sous sweetmeat would be an acceptable kindness, but anything more was an embarrassment. What he could not afford to give his children, it would be quite wrong for them to have; nor should they be given toys which he had not first approved of. Second anecdote: after a quarrel with Darimon (which I shall come to in its place) and while Proudhon was away from home, Madame Darimon sent Euphrasie a ham, an event duly reported by Catherine in one of the letters she was by then writing to her father on her mother's behalf. Proudhon wrote at once to say they were on no account to eat it; they could hardly return it, he did not wish to go that far, but the ham, which, by the way, they could well have done with, was to be given to an old lady of their acquaintance who was in want.

For such a man to accept a 'pardon' for what had not, in his view, been an offence in the first place, to accept the freedom of his own dear land from the bandit who had seized and raped her – meant having to eat more crow than he could choke down. So, like Madame Darimon's ham, the emperor's freedom was not, indeed, to be thrown back in the donor's face; it was, simply, not to be used. Enough time must elapse before reception of that gift and the taking advantage of it, to show that it was not highly valued.

Just why the emperor had decided to be generous for once to an enemy, and an enemy so *difficile*, is not clear; Proudhon's grand-daughter, Madame Henneguy, was of the opinion that prince Napoleon, Proudhon's old colleague on the Mountain side of the Assembly, had persuaded his cousin to relent. His arguments would have been that it ill-became the imperial Bonaparte regime to keep in banishment and subject to arrest a thinker of European reputation; that it was unwise to incur odium by excluding from France a Frenchman with enormous influence over the working-class whose support might be needed again as the bourgeoisie got more and more out of hand; and that, in any case, Proudhon was a sick man from whom nothing was now to be feared, and one who, moreover, was quite as much at odds with the conventional left-wing opposition, as with the imperial government.

*   *   *   *   *

In 1861, while Proudhon was trying to finish his *Théorie de l'Impôt* (it did eventually win first prize), Lebègue published *La Guerre et la Paix, Recherches sur le principe et la constitution du droit des gens*, War and Peace, An Enquiry into the principles and constitution of the law of nations.

Once again what is called the paradoxical quality of Proudhon's thinking, and which is really that kind of very rare, clear, open-eyed analysis, based on perception unclouded by taught *cliché*, partisan prejudice, or preconceived idea, resulted in the book being received with outraged indignation. Then as now you simply cannot massacre people's sacred cows, especially if they happen to be of a liberal buff colour, or a pinkish red, without being called a murrain. A work whose theme was that the mission of the 19th century was to put an end to war and to militarism was taken by the critics, may they be forgiven, as a panegyric of war.

From an ultra-libertarian, deeming property and the state to be the great enemies of mankind, the critics expected an outright and downright condemnation of war. Startlingly, the first part of *War and Peace*, war studied at length and in detail, historically and philosophically is a paean in praise of war.

War is divine; like religion, like justice, it is a fact of moral, rather than merely physical or passional, life. It is primordial, an essence of the life and productive work of man in societies, deeply rooted in the conscience of mankind and an element in all our relationships. Since the dawn of history it has been in war that the highest faculties and qualities of man have found expression. An inspiration and often an expression of religion, from it can be derived poetry, the fine arts, political economy, the whole range of human rights, chivalry, nobility and the arts of government. It calls forth heroism, abnegation, self-sacrifice for others or for great causes; is the occasion of mercy, the beginning of discipline, of regulation, of order and of comradeship, of invention and technological progress. By war morality is restored, nations regenerated, codes of law guaranteed, justice establishes its rule, and liberty its warranties. War has been the making of man and the very idea 'peace' without the idea 'war', is a nullity.

War, then, is one of the great, dominating myths by which we live; let no man calumniate it, for as yet no man has understood it. Tactics and strategy, yes; the noise of battle and the dreadful suffering of war's victims, yes; but what of its innerness, what of its 'high morality'? For war, like time and space, like the good, the true and the beautiful, is an attribute of mind, a law of the spirit, a condition of our being. War terrible? War immoral?

To maintain a great cause by heroic combat in which the honour of the belligerents and the conviction of righteousness are equal on both sides, and to do so at the risk of giving and receiving death – what is so terrible about that? And where, above all, is the immorality? Death is the crown of life: how can man, being a creature moral, intelligent and free, find a nobler end?

War is divine right in its plastic expression and as such the creator of royalty. But arms, the military spirit, are equally the makers of democracy: the citizen in full enjoyment of liberty is he who has the right to bear arms for the republic.[1] Moreover, what is the recognition of the right of the majority, but a recognition of the right of superior strength, and therefore of the right to use force?[2]

Out of war comes law: what would civilization have been without the Roman conquests, that is without Roman law? What Christianity without Charlemagne's pact with the Papacy? Napoleon was as great a legislator and codifier as he was a warrior.

What emerges from some hundreds of pages of argument based on historical exposition and philosophical criticism is the vital importance of what Proudhon calls antagonism – what we, I think, would call aggressiveness, and what Arnold Toynbee saw[3] as 'challenge and response'. Proudhon sees this antagonism as essential to the maintenance of standards not only of industry but of morality, purity and generosity; of quality in the arts and sciences and scholarship. He seems to have in mind the social value of the desire to excel and be admired for it, rather than mere commercial push and competition. For, in his examples, he is harsh with the young United States republic which, already reproducing all the vices of the Old World, has, for want of an *antagonist* and because its immense resources make life too easy, produced nothing worthwhile in the arts, sciences and learning, and has contributed nothing to religion or philosophy.

Proudhon here exhibits his great weakness: his exclusive Gallicism. He read Latin, Greek and Hebrew, but knew no modern language except French, and even for his beloved Germans was dependant on translators. America had by 1860 already contributed generously to the sum of mankind's achievements, but it is tolerably certain that he had never heard of Melville, Longfellow, Beecher Stowe, Hawthorne, Thoreau – with whom he would have had so much in common – Prescott, Motley, Holmes.

At all events, having given war its due, Proudhon reassures us: he, too, will conclude against it. Not that it is a matter of abolishing it; war will, inevitably, transform itself, if only because we have become unworthy of it.

'The state, *par excellence*, of any organized being, the proper expression of life and health, is action ...' Physical action on the material environment, or intellectual action on the moral and spiritual environment. It follows that an environment, a non-ego which resists and contradicts the ego, is an essential condition of action. So action is striving; to act is to combat, and in combat the highest qualities of mind and spirit are evoked. The sum of those qualities is, in a word, virtue.

A part of the resisting, contradicting environment is other people, so strife between people is inevitable, and that is well because out of that strife in all its forms comes the complex of social relations and transactions of which law, liberty, morality and politics are derivatives: it is the battle which generates the peace-treaty.

War and Peace, which the vulgar see as mutually exclusive states, are the alternating conditions of the life of all peoples; each evokes the other, is defined in terms of the other as a reciprocal; each complements the other, they sustain each other like the inverse, adequate and inseparable terms of an antinomy.

That being so, arguments about what is lost or gained by war are irrelevant; all or nothing, war and peace are the two sides of one coin. Perhaps one can put it otherwise: if a pendulum swings east it must swing west. 'All that which constitutes our moral and intellectual capital, our civilization, our glory, is created and develops in the alternation of the flaming action of war and the obscure incubation of peace. War might say to Peace, "I sow the seed; thou, sister, watereth it; God gives the burgeoning."'

This truth is terrible: the enormous strides in, for example, electronics and aviation and medicine which *seemed* to be made during the Second World War, 'incubated' during the preceding peace, were hatched by the heat of war. The same is true of the immense social advances of the 1940s and 1950s. Peace incubated and war hatched the Russian Revolution of 1917; peace prepared and war realized the United States' emancipation of the slaves; peace conceived but war gave birth to the states of Ireland and Israel.

Very well; all this does not mean that we must go on accepting war; as Proudhon presently reveals, social progress has made it inappropriate; and the degeneracy of morals, the loss of virtue, have made it too hideous to be tolerated, have, in fact, deformed and degraded it. But can we, therefore, abolish it? If it turns out to be absolutely of our essence, the best we can hope to do is to render it less terrible by making and keeping the rules of war; if, on examination, it turns out to be not of our essence, then abolition is possible. In other words, is war a condition of social health, or is it, rather, a symptom of social disease?

If you can contrive to strip that transcendent fanaticism, that cult of armed force ... of its moral and ideal attributes; if you can deprive war of the prestige which makes it the pivot of poetry, the source of political organization and justice, then indeed you may hope to abolish it.

Proudhon then sets out to do that, by analysing and expressing the myth in terms of a logical statement.

*　　*　　*　　*　　*

Proudhon points out that ordinary people have no doubt that strength has a right to use force; that if might be not always right, yet there is a right in might. And, as he has already argued, might is not mere brute force, it contains at least an element of right, and it can and does make law, establish rights. Unlike other animals,[4] man in his fighting aspires to make of physical superiority an obligation on others to submit; of victory, evidence of right and reason which justifies and imposes that obligation.

Philosophers, on the other hand, deny that might is or can be right. Here it is necessary to keep one's mind very clear and be sure of what Proudhon means; he is not saying simply that right can sometimes be served by might; he is saying that might is of itself and essence, right, as will presently be made still clearer. Having examined and criticized the case of the philosophers, he dismisses it; they are obviously wrong and the common man is obviously right, for he senses even if he does not know that from the doctrine that might is right can be derived the whole range of human rights, and therefore all law; and the dismal failure of every philosopher from Hobbes to Hegel to demonstrate the contrary is good evidence of what is, in any case, manifest in the behaviour of nations.

In short, the right to use force is one of our natural rights, derivative of natural law; thus there is nothing wrong or immoral about, for example, the institution of duelling, provided the duel be honourable and honourably fought, *and not fraudulent*, by which he means not used selfishly or wantonly or for a base purpose such as gain. This is important, for the same condition applies to war. So, then, every free man has a natural right to use force, and honourable superior force used honourably is in itself right. But as it is inexpedient to use force in society, and unnecessary because other means of righting wrongs exist, the citizens cede this right to the prince, that is to the state, which is thus vested by its citizens with the sole right to wage war.[5]

War being a means of sustaining a right, victory is a judgement; and

being the most efficacious of all judgements because sustained by righteous might, must be considered as judicially valid. But, as in duelling,
there are conditions. Since war gives expression to an organic law of
societies – in Marxist terminology, to that 'historical necessity' which
Proudhon discovered, and Marx either borrowed or rediscovered a
decade later – a victory which runs against the grain of historical
evolution, being 'fraudulent', will be null and void, ephemeral and, in
due course, reversed and punished.

Here I can cite only a few of Proudhon's examples of fraudulent
victories. Spain, that is Castille and Aragon, by the forcible expulsion of
the Moors and Jews, and by the rape of Mexico and Peru was brought
swiftly to decline, ruin and degeneracy. France's fraudulent victories in
Algeria and in Italy would be 'punished'. They were, but not until nearly
a century later. I think that Proudhon would have pointed to the victory
of the British in India, and certainly to that of the Nazis in Europe, as
'fraudulent'; and those of the United States in South East Asia, reversed
in the 1970s, clearly come under the same head. If a war be fought in
defiance of the law of armed force, be dishonourable, be in breach of rules
which are not arbitrary but derive from the nature and object of war as a
right, then, '... the victories are no better than odious dragooning of the
adversary, and the victors no better than execrable charlatans, sooner or
later to be chastised by the very strength which they have abused.'

'A method of fighting which resulted in the victory going to the
weaker, and so wiping out the advantage of might, would be an offence
against the law of nations and therefore a felony.' This sounds outrageous but Proudhon has not yet defined what, in this context, he means
by *might*; meanwhile, suppose what very nearly happened, to have
happened and the Nazis to have been first with the A-bomb ...

What, in Proudhon's context, is meant by the might which is right?
When, for reasons which are attributable to the pressure of the environment on the 'ego' of a nation, peoples go to war so that one of them shall
give law and order and gods to the rest and substitute them for endemic
petty warfare, it is right that that people which is not only physically the
strongest, but which is the liveliest, keenest, has best developed its native
genius, organized its strength, mastered the arts of law and politics,
should win dominion, though it cost a blood-letting. Shrink delicately
though we may from so bloody a judgement, it is the only rational,
honourable and legitimate judgement. For the strength of a people is not
only in its numbers and the health and strength of its citizens; it is also in
the faculties of the spirit, courage, virtue, discipline; in the wealth, that is

economic strength acquired by those qualities and in its productive capacity.

But how are the strong to be distinguished from the weak excepting in combat requiring the belligerents to deploy all their physical, moral and intellectual energy, civic virtue, their scientific, industrial and even artistic skills? *La raison du plus fort*, the rightness of the mightiest in those qualities tested in war, gives their measure. The victory they procure is victory deserved, unless, its lawfulness debilitated by an evil cause, it is 'fraudulent'. If there be anything which debilitates the lawfulness of using force, then it is a 'false' victory in which the vanquished are not justly defeated, but are cheated.

In the century which has passed since Proudhon was writing in that vein, we have learned otherwise: war has become utterly base and the only sanction which can restrict the causes for which it is waged, and regulate its forms, is terror balanced by counter-terror. Since war became 'total' any talk of what Proudhon called *guerre loyale* is nonsense. But Proudhon did foresee that this might come to pass and foresaw also the state of mind and spirit which could bring it to pass.

* * * * *

The first, universal and always pressing cause of war, in whatever manner and for whatever motive it breaks out, is the same as that which drives nations to hive-off colonies, to seek land and outlets for their surplus population. It is want of subsistence or, in more technical language, the breakdown of the economic equilibrium ... In the last analysis the original cause of all wars is Pauperism.

Pauperism is the word Proudhon uses to avoid using the word poverty, for which he has a different application. The productive power of a people can never equal its power of consumption. The truth of this becomes obvious if you realize that the power of consumption could be roughly measured by multiplying the population of the nation in question by the annual consumption of the richest man in it. And since distribution is carried out very unequally, certain evils are inevitable: there exists a universal and chronic state of crisis uneasiness; apparently opulent societies are really indigent. So everyone is affected by a state of pauperism, the capitalist living on rents and dividends as well as the proletarian whose sole support is one pair of hands.

If that be pauperism, what is poverty? Poverty is the natural, inevitable and unchangeable state of man once he passes the primitive stage. In the primitive stage man's numbers are so small and nature so bountiful that man's state is *abundance*. Poverty is that state in which a man procures by work the wherewithal to sustain body and soul, neither more nor less. 'Poverty is the true providence of mankind' and it is good and right that it should be so: 'Man's condition on earth is work and poverty; his vocation learning and justice; the first of his virtues, temperance.'

But surely applied science enables us to multiply production? It does indeed, it already has: but as population grows to match production, we are no better off. We can augment the wealth of societies by three means: by so educating the minds and tastes of the workers that we create for them new needs which they supply by more work; by so improving the means and organization of production that we contrive the leisure in which the workers can learn; and by the suppression of parasitism, that is of *aubaines* (see Chapter 4).

But even the augmentation thus achieved does not alter our state of poverty. The new needs entailing greater and more diverse consumption which must be supplied by production, that is by more work, Man is still, 'procuring by work the wherewithal to sustain body and soul', the definition of poverty. The only difference is that body and soul have become more demanding.

Only if it be recognized and freely accepted that man's estate is poverty thus defined, can a just, free and self-respecting society be established. Pauperism is produced by the rejection of this truth and the foolish and dangerous preference for the illusion of riches. The GNP of France in 1860 was such that, evenly distributed, it would suffice to give every household of four persons in the land a daily income of 3 francs 50 centimes which procures the means to sustain body and soul at a decent level. In practice a majority of Frenchmen have less than that, 87.5 centimes *per diem*, millions have only 25 centimes, while a minority have from twice to over 10,000 times as much.[6] The worst consequence of this is that each man believes that he, too, can be rich; riches reproduce the primitive condition, abundance.

Man believes in what is called *fortune* ... By the very fact that he has to produce what he consumes, he regards the accumulation of riches as his goal, and ardently pursues it. The example of some who have enriched themselves makes him believe that what has been done by some can be done by all. He would regard it as a contradiction in nature and an injustice of providence, if it were otherwise ... To pile up riches, to make money, has everywhere become a maxim of both morality and of governments.

All this is based on an illusion: the belief is as irrational as the notion of squaring the circle, but economists and governments are very careful not to say so. The collective production can in no circumstances and by no means exceed the sum of all the man-days of work in a given society. The unit to reckon in is one man-day's work. Now the productive capacity of one man cannot exceed his demand for consumption at the level technically possible in his time, by a significant amount. The effect of the illusion that there is a way out of this trap is to raise appetites, make the poor as well as the rich greedy and intemperate; and with appetite being inevitably disappointed, there follows bitter disillusionment, hatred of society, industrial strife, crime, revolution and war.

The truth of these observations is obscured in our own time by the feeling that we are richer than our ancestors were, at least in the advanced industrial nations, because we have more things. But it is notorious that however hard we work to produce we cannot escape from Proudhonian poverty excepting into pauperism, manifest in the colossal debts contracted by borrowing against future production at crippling rates of interest and entailing continuous inflation, in repeated financial crises, in unemployment, in industrial strife. The truth is even more apparent if we apply Proudhon's thinking on a world-wide scale; the rich industrial nations are only rich at the expense of the millions who die annually of starvation and the hundreds of millions which only just escape doing so: in other words, global pauperism. Moreover, supposing an equal distribution of the world's GNP carried out globally, it is very doubtful if we should even rise as high, in our standard of living, as Proudhonian poverty if only because a very large part of our productive capacity is absorbed in the production of the superfluous instead of the necessary, another symptom of pauperism. We are, slowly, awakening to the truth of our condition: it is now quite impossible, given our resources in raw materials and energy, to raise the living standard of the world's population to that of a middle-class American family.

That pauperism gives rise to revolution is obvious and is 'natural'. But how comes it about that proletariats turn not only on the parasites, that is the proprietors of *aubaines* and the governments which protect them, but can be persuaded to turn and rend each other? To simplify and coarsen Proudhon's answer: because the people join their masters in an effort to cure pauperism[6] by means of loot and pillage. The apparent *political* causes of war, or even real ones mask the true, the underlying economic cause. Moreover, war serves governments in another way, by directing the fury of the people living in miserable pauperism, or in relative pauperism, away from themselves and their parasite protégés, on to the foreigner; which is where the ancient and deep-rooted war myth, degraded to a confidence trick, comes in useful.

Pillage and loot begin in such simple operations as raiding the enemy's farms to steal his crops and the robbery of goods and money in conquered territory, and become more and more sophisticated, taking the form, for example, of war indemnities. Spain conquered her American empire for gold and slaves while contriving to believe that she did it for God; the British conquest of India was in defence of the right to exploit the Indians by trade, the trade of the East India Company. The United States' war with Mexico was a land-grab; the expansion eastward of imperial Russia was a means of consuming surplus serf-power and at the same time robbing weaker people of their land and liberty, and exploiting them. Napoleon looted all Europe for many years. Hitler and his Nazis were a product of the Allies' attempt to loot Germany by means of war indemnities and of the worsening of Pauperism following the breakdown of capitalism in 1929.

So pillage, as a means of trying to redress the economic balance at home, though invariably and inevitably failing, is a prime cause of war: Proudhon even foresaw a very sophisticated form of pillage in the future: pillage by the creation of jobs-for-the-boys and through industrial investment in conquered countries (dollar-imperialism); and in the creation of what we should now call military-industrial complexes, whereby the state and the capitalists in partnership pillage their own citizens.

* * * * *

In short, war, formerly justifiable, has disgraced itself and if, in the social and economic conditions of the second half of the 19th century, we persist in using it as if its great and creative myth had not been discredited by our abuse of it, it will inevitably degenerate into an exercise in mutual terrorization. For the practice of war cannot but reflect the spirit of the age in which it is being waged. If that spirit be base, the war will be basely fought.

The spirit of rapine and greed is the true characteristic of the modern epoch: the poor exploit the rich, the workers their employers, the tenant his landlord, the company promoter his shareholders, no less than the capitalist exploits and puts pressure on the industrialist, the industrialist his workers, and the landlord his tenants. And there is another way in which this antagonism is expressed, in the matter of taxation: the poor want the rich to pay it all in the form of sumptuary taxes, graded income-tax, estate duties, wealth taxes and taxes on unearned income. The rich seek to cast all burden onto the poor in the form of taxes on consumption.

Such a regime cannot continue: it is selfishness, dishonesty, greed, and contempt for our fellow men and for all principle, raised to the level of a maxim, and then deified. In these conditions a generalized war would be no better than 'a reversion to the most atrocious cannibalism'. All war will become a social war. Where politics is dominated by economics 'the jurisdiction of strength is abrogated'. You cannot solve economic problems by bloodshed. 'War, as an expression of creative antagonism, had for its purpose the complete, absolute and manifest triumph of justice; in a word, civilization.' But war had become impotent, was now doing what it had to do badly. It had therefore become necessary to transform it, and this would be possible because, in any case, the destiny of war has always been self-transformation into peace.

Consider the generations of 'rights': right of might begat right of war which begat law of nations which begat political rights which begat civil rights which begat economic rights.

So the ultimate generation is Economic Rights; that means the accomplishment of all that Proudhon has been writing and working for since the publication of *What is Property?* At the economic level, Mutualism, a complex of federated industries owned and managed by their workers and, of course, abolition of interest, rents and dividends – *aubaines*; at the political level, confederations of confederated democratic mini-states.[7] Neither statesmen nor philosophers can bring about this revolution which will transform the expression of antagonism from war into work.

'Peace signed at the sword-point is never more than a truce; the peace elaborated by a council of economists and Quakers would be merely laughable.' Only toiling mankind is capable of having done with war by creating a just economic equilibrium, by accepting the poverty which is man's estate, and is so well-expressed in the Stoic maxim *Sustine et abstine*.

NOTES TO CHAPTER ELEVEN

1. The right of every free man to weapons is implicit in the American way of life and so strongly is this felt that the feeling probably constitutes the greatest obstacle encountered by reformers and the police in their efforts to make the sale of weapons more difficult. In Switzerland the citizen of military age, liable to be called to the colours, keeps his army rifle at home, usually, in my experience, among the walking-sticks and umbrellas. Denial, or oppressive restriction, of the right to own weapons is of course, evidence of the state's fear and distrust of its own citizens, and as such, an offence to liberty.

2. Manifest in language: law-en*force*ment, police *force*, etc.

3. *A Study of History.*

4. Zoology was not as advanced in his day as in ours: most fights between animals end not in death or even serious injury, but in acceptance of defeat by the belligerent whom combat shows to be the weaker.

5. I have reservations about this and have explained why in *Terrorists and Terrorism* (1975): in my opinion, the citizen retains a right to repudiate that treaty unilaterally: Aquinas, Milton and John Locke agree with me.

6. Proudhon's prime example of Pauperism in the 1860s is England: England has at one and the same time by far the largest private fortunes, by far the greatest accumulation of capital, and by far the most atrocious degraded pauperism. She has devoured the Irish and Scotch *plebs* but cannot feed her own. The French philosopher, historian and art critic, Hippolyte Taine, who spent some time in England a few years later, was shocked and horrified by the degraded condition of the English poor. Proudhon points out that it was just the pauperism of England which generated her enormous military budget, to pay for the colossal fleet necessary to protect a commerce conducted on her own terms, and, where possible, imposed by the threat of force, all over the world.

7. *Du Principe Fédératif* was to be published two years later but had long been in Proudhon's mind.

Return to Paris and *Du Principe Fédératif*

IN THE EVENT it was the best part of two years after the emperor's pardon before Proudhon condescended to return to France. Time and again during those twenty-two months he found reasons for staying on in Brussels, until – as it would seem – he was taking an almost pig-headed delight in belittling imperial 'generosity'. The publication of *La Guerre et la Paix* in May 1861 provoked mixed comment: the apparent contradictions contained within it bemused and infuriated many of his left-wing supporters who felt he had written a panegyric of war instead of condemning it, while his customary enemies on the right used the book as a pretext for a predictable attack on the man. However, the book sold well, made him some money – much needed – and aroused the controversy which it had been one of Proudhon's aims to stimulate.

Meanwhile he remained outside France and heard these rumblings only from a distance. In August Proudhon travelled with his family to Germany, journeying down the Rhine by steamer to Cologne. He was interested to study the Rhine as one of the so-called 'natural frontiers' whose existence he had always questioned: but his mood was jaded. He found Germany boringly like France – though he liked the beer. Travel in general he claimed to be a bore too, and an expensive bore at that, and at the end of the month he returned gratefully to Belgium to continue his writings.

Increasingly the daily events of his life had become secondary to the work in hand. With his health deteriorating, Proudhon may have sensed that he did not have all that much time left, and that there was still much to be accomplished. Late in 1861 he was working on a book intended to expose the reactionary character of Polish nationalism, a book which he never published presumably because he had no wish to offend his friends Herzen, Bakunin, or Edmond; neither, with the Polish rebellion breaking out in 1863, did he want to stab the Poles in the back. He was also working on *Théorie de la Propriété*, a return to the theme which had made his name in 1840 with the publication of *Qu'est-ce que la Propriété?* It seems a more conservative book than the former: instead of attacking the concept of property he is now at some pains to justify it, at least such property as safeguards the freedom of the working-man. He places his faith in Mutualism and in associations of free credit to prevent private and state abuses of property. The general tone is softer than it was, and yet there are passages in which the old fire is kindled anew. 'Away with the old patrician, greedy and pitiless, away with the insolent baron, the grasping bourgeois and the hard peasant! Such people are odious to me; I can neither love nor see them.'

In August 1862 he returned again to Spa for his health, staying with Delhasse. Euphrasie would have liked to join him, but Proudhon considered it too expensive; moreover, he wrote to her,

... we should look like down-and-outs. Those who come to Spa are either aristocrats or parasites on the rich, either rogues or whores. It is all a flaunting of insolent luxury, in the presence of which a modest household is out of place. I, with my wide flat hat, heavy shoes and turned-down collar, can go where I like, because I am 53 and Monsieur Proudhon. But a lady and a young lady, that's different. ...

The tetchiness of his manner towards Euphrasie continued, and on 11 August he wrote criticizing her for accepting a dinner invitation which would involve making a new acquaintance when they had too many already. Catherine's spelling also attracted his wagging finger.

What finally drove Proudhon back to Paris after his extended period of self-exile was, in the end, no particular longing to see his native land but the impossibility of his situation in Belgium. Proudhon was contributing articles to a Brussels periodical *L'Office de Publicité*, one of which got misinterpreted as advocating the annexation of Belgium by France. This was the very last thing Proudhon actually intended, but not surprisingly there was hostile reaction in the Belgian press, and angry demonstrations outside his house. What Proudhon actually wrote was an attack, with all the energy still at his command, on the idea of the unification of Italy, whether as a republic which Mazzini was trying to create or as the constitutional monarchy of Victor Emmanuel and Cavour. Italy, as seven small nations, could be the ideal testing ground for his federalist ideas (see below): let the seven Italian states, each justified as it was by ethnic and geographical integrity, link themselves by mutual contract in a loose federation; but a central Italian government – No! Nationalism is by its nature aggressive, ambitious, militaristic and therefore tyrannical and pernicious. God knows, he turned out to be right about that.

In Proudhon's view the unification of Italy was as absurd as the suggestion, say, to expand France in order to include areas of Europe once ruled by Charlemagne, including of course Belgium. But what he intended as an ironical absurdity was interpreted literally by sections of the Belgian press, though how they managed it, heavens knows. At all events it was in an attempt to explain just what he did mean that Proudhon decided to undertake the writing of *Du Principe Fédératif*. And on 17 September, with hostile Belgian crowds at his back, he left for Paris.

The following night Proudhon was in the Hôtel de la Paix, Montmartre, and wrote to Euphrasie who was still in Brussels that for once he was not short of money. Three days later his daughter Catherine wrote for her mother (as she now did customarily) about the distressing things the Brussels papers were saying about him, to which Proudhon replied that Euphrasie was to ignore them: '... they are rumour-mongers who, by stupidity and sometimes by ill-nature, are capable of making those who pay attention to them die of anxiety.' While waiting for Euphrasie and his daughters to join him in Paris Proudhon paid visits to numerous old friends and colleagues, among them Chaudez and Rolland. He planned to settle in Passy, but Euphrasie wrote objecting that it was too far out of town. He disagreed, pointing out that it was a mere thirty-five minutes from the centre – 'quite convenient for Euphrasie's theatre evenings'. And that was that: he prepared to move to Passy. By the end of the month he was hard at work writing *Du Principe Fédératif*, and had also sent to press his reply to the Belgian newspapers, a volume entitled *La Fédération et l'Unité en Italie* which unexpectedly sold more than 12,000 copies in the first four months after publication and brought Proudhon back into the centre of Parisian debate. In early October he found an agreeable set of rooms at No. 10, Grand Rue, Passy, where he continued to work on *Du Principe Fédératif* until, on 25 October he departed for Brussels and at last brought his entire family back to France and to Paris. His wife and daughters were ill and exhausted from the journey, and Proudhon himself suffering from the severe headaches that were to linger throughout the winter and herald the final onset of illness which dogged him for the last two years of his life. 'I am frightfully exhausted,' he told his friend Darimon in January 1863; 'my head feels as big as a barrel.' All the same he had finished *Du Principe*, and in February it was published.

*   *   *   *   *

Du Principe Fédératif et de la Nécessité de Reconstituer le Parti de la Révolution was the full title of this book in which the federative principle is put forward as the only effective solution to the key problem of social and political organization: reconciliation of authority and liberty. Proudhon distinguishes these last as the two spirits of government; both are ideals, never wholly realized, each tainting the other to a greater or lesser extent. Authority finds expression in one of two forms of government: monarchy or communism. Liberty, too, is expressed in one of two forms, democracy or anarchy. Then we have the terms defined: monarchy is the government of all by one; communism is the government of all by all; anarchy is the government of each by each; and democracy the government of all by each.

By monarchy it is clear that he means absolute monarchy; by democracy he does *not* mean parliamentary government with a limited suffrage which was the state of affairs in France and Britain when he was writing. For Proudhon, democracy was understood in the sense of the Greek derivation of the word: government by the *demos*, the people. So, when an overwhelming majority of the French people universally enfranchised made Louis-Napoleon Bonaparte emperor by plebiscite, that was democracy. So too when the Roman people gave Caesar power to overthrow the republic. In a monarchy the state is the monarch. He incarnates the whole of society in his person; his bureaucracy's duty and loyalty is to him and is, therefore the very strength of the authoritarian form of government. A democracy, however, is endangered immediately functionaries specialized in social and political administration are introduced: for the bureaucrats' loyalty is to the state, not to the people, since the state is their own creature.

The working people in any society, having nothing to lose, seek to subordinate authority to liberty; whereas the burgesses, Proudhon's proprietors, having much to lose, seek to subordinate liberty to authority which reciprocates by protecting them. But, paradoxically, when the struggle between the two classes is joined, these positions are reversed. The people find themselves a chief under whom class-differences will be abolished: Caesar finds his advantage, the plebs theirs, in an alliance against the patricians; the French people, by an enormous majority in the plebiscite, make Louis-Napoleon their Caesar in an alliance against the bourgeoisie. The bourgeoisie, on the other hand, tends to set up a more or less liberal constitutional monarchy on the basis of a suffrage limited by property qualifications. Thus the party of liberty and equality sets up an absolute dictatorship, while the party of authority creates a regime which retains a measure of liberty.

Here is the paradox as Proudhon expresses it:

The people, by the very reason of their inferiority and distress, will always compose the army of liberty and progress. . . . But by reason of their ignorance, the primitiveness of their instincts, the urgency of their needs and the impatience of their wishes, they incline to summary forms of authority. What the people seek is not legal guarantees of which they have no conception and no opinion of their power; not a careful balance of forces or combinations of civil devices ... They seek a leader whose word they trust, whose intentions are known to them, and whom they believe devoted to their interests; to him they give unlimited authority and irresistible power. The people, esteeming right what the leader deems expedient, care nothing for forms, see no use in imposing limitations and conditions on the tenants of power. Suspicious, prompt to calumniate, incapable of methodical discussion, all they have faith in is the will of a man, their hope is in him, their trust in his creatures ... They expect nothing and hope for nothing from the only principles which could save them; they do not have the religion of ideas.[1]

This is the judgement of the only great leader of the mid-19th century socialist movement (excepting Weitling) who came from and had first-hand knowledge of the working-class. It is chiefly in *The Federative Principle* that his sour opinion of his own class intrudes. He was to repent, and used his dying breath to dictate a statement of faith in their political capacity. Bearing in mind that deathbed repentance, and his much earlier plea that his fellow-proletarians be given through education the chance to realize their potential, his judgement has all the harshness of a stern father's:

Left to itself or led by its tribunes, the multitude never founded anything. The multitude looks over its shoulder; it forms no traditions, achieves no continuity of ideas, has no thought which could acquire the force of law ... To the multitude politics means only intrigue; government empty promises and brute force, justice vindictiveness, and liberty the freedom to set up idols which, on the morrow, it overthrows. The advent of the Democracy ushers in a period of retrogression which would bring the nation and the state to ruin, if it did not avoid that fate by putting the revolution into reverse.

Despite all of which Proudhon detects a social and political evolution in the direction of liberty at the expense of authority, in that the contractual element gains ground against the authoritarian. And it to this element that we should give our support, paying close attention to ensure that the social-political contract is the outcome of a hard bargain driven by the citizen with the state. The citizen must be certain that he receives from the state at least the equivalent of what he sacrifices to it, and must retain all his liberty, sovereignty and initiative, less only that part of them given up to obtain the special object of the contract, which the state must guarantee. 'Thus drafted and understood, the social contract is what I call a federation.' There is a more specific definition:

Federation, from the Latin *foedus*, a pact, contract, treaty, convention or alliance, is a convention by which one or several heads of family, one or several municipalities (*communes*), one or several groups of *communes* or states, undertake, reciprocally and equally, obligation towards each other for one or several particular objects, the care of and responsibility for which then falls exclusively on the delegates to the federation.

It is of the essence of the Proudhonian federation contract that when entering into it, the contracting parties undertaking equivalent and reciprocal obligations towards each other, each reserves to himself a greater measure of rights, of liberty, authority and property than he concedes to the federal authority: the citizen remains master of and in his own house, restricting his rights only in so far as it is necessary to avoid encroaching on those of others in his parish or *commune*. The *commune* is self-governing through the assembly of citizens or their delegates, but it vests the county federal authority with certain powers which it thus surrenders. The county, again self-governing through the assembly of delegates from the federated *communes*, vests the federal authority of the national federation of counties, with powers which it surrenders. So the federation of counties, or regions is the confederation into which the erstwhile sovereign state has been transformed; and it may, in its turn, enter into federative contracts with other such confederations.

Under all existing social contracts the citizen gives up a greater measure of freedom and authority than the part he reserves: he has an excess, often burdensome, of obligations to the state, owes it too much duty, retains too little individual initiative. Proudhon might be describing the state of affairs in a modern communist or fascist state when he says: 'Any engagement albeit mutual and equal, which requires of the associates the whole of their efforts, leaves nothing to their independence and dedicates them wholly to the association, is an excessive engagement and repugnant to the man and the citizen.' In the federative social contract he proposes, the reverse is the case: it is the citizen who retains more power over himself than he cedes.

In other words, the state as we know it is an evil of which we must rid ourselves lest it devour us, a conclusion which, of course, had been reached by Godwin, Tom Paine and Shelley long since, Godwin calling the state 'that brute engine' and attributing to it all vice and crime. Nor were they the only ones. Here is Ralph Waldo Emerson: 'Every actual State is corrupt. Good men must not obey the laws too well ... Wild liberty develops iron conscience. Want of liberty, by strengthening law and decorum, stupefies conscience.' And here is Thoreau, writing in

1849, 'That government is best which governs least ... carried out it finally amounts to this which I also believe, that government is best which governs not at all.... Government is at best an expedient; but most governments are usually and all governments are sometimes inexpedient.'[2]

However, it was Proudhon alone who discovered what, if an optimum allowance of liberty is to be reconciled with an expedient measure of order, must be the form of social organization. Moreover, this form which would rid us of the scourge of political government, he believed to be based on laws as 'natural' as the physical laws of the universe.

What are to be the powers of the federal authority? In a sense, none: it has no law-courts, no police, no economic power whatsoever, and its soldiers are the very citizens who are its masters. An authority charged with seeing that the terms of a contract are carried out can never overpower the constituent contracting parties for it is literally an executive confined to carrying out orders, and strictly supervised. It must never be forgotten that the moment a bureaucracy is given an inch it takes an ell; and the moment it exceeds its mandate, becomes tyrannical. Proudhon pointed to Switzerland as a model. In our sense of the word there is no Swiss government, but an assembly of delegates (*not* representatives) from the cantons keeping a very jealous eye on an executive with very restricted powers. Moreover, in this confederation there are three distinct 'races' or 'nationalities' speaking three different languages.

By the constitution of the Confederation, its objects are to defend the confederates against the foreigner; and to defend their liberties and rights at home. The cantons are sovereign (Article 3) exercising all those powers other than those ceded to the federal authority. By Article 4 the Confederation guarantees the territory and sovereignty of the cantons, and the rights and liberties of their peoples. As Proudhon says, a confederation is not a state: it is an agency created by the constituent sovereign states for the execution in common of certain services which each state has relinquished and which thus become federal attributions. He sees no prospect whatever of the great European powers forming a confederation, for the very principle of their being is contrary to it: they would have to relinquish a measure of sovereignty, whereas their nature is to command without compromise. Here, the implication is that the revolution must first come within each 'empire'.

The federative contract is designed to avoid, on the one hand, an excess of liberty leading to chaos; on the other, an excess of authority leading to oppression and poverty. The confederal authority may, indeed should, initiate movement and may thereafter supervise it, but it may not manage or control it. 'If, from time to time, it takes a hand itself, it is only by way of starting something and setting an example.' It must then withdraw, leaving the operation of the new service to the local authorities and the citizens.

It will be remembered that in 1848 Proudhon, as a *député*, called for state intervention in setting up national banks, secondary credit institutions, insurance agencies, and railways. He now recalls this, explaining, '... but it was no part of my idea that having accomplished its creative work the state should continue for ever to be banker, underwriter and carrier.' His profound distrust of the state is manifest in his practical suggestions for a means of bringing confederations into existence. First, small or moderate-sized regional and respectively sovereign groups should be formed and associated in federations. In our own time we might think in terms of Scotland, Wales, Northumbria, East Anglia, Brittany, Navarre, Franche Comté, Piedmont, Sicily, Bavaria, etc. The administration within each sovereign mini-state is based on a rigorous separation of powers, equally rigorous delimitation of organs. Nothing divisible is to be left undivided. Instead of the state applying to the citizens, the citizens apply to the state the axiom: divide and rule. Everything the administration does must be done by the blazing light of publicity and under the firm control of the citizens. There must be no question of absorbing the federated local authorities in the regional authority, or the federated regional authorities in the confederal authority. The role of that central authority must be reduced to one of initiation, surveillance and guarantee, and all its orders must be subject to veto by each of the federated regions and carried out only by agents of those regions, never by the central authority's own agents.

All this Proudhon calls political rationalism, of which the great enemy is political idealism:

The people in the miasma of popular opinion conceives of itself as of some gigantic and mysterious Being; and everything in common speech seems designed to maintain its indivisible unity: thus, is it called The People, The Nation, The Multitude, The Masses; it is The Sovereign, The Legislator; it is Power, Dominion, Fatherland, State. It has its Convocations, its Ballots, its Assizes, its Demonstrations, its Pronouncements, its Plebiscites, its Direct Legislation, sometimes its Judgements and even Executions; its Oracles, and its thundering Voice of God. The more aware it becomes that it is innumerable, irresistible, immense, the greater its horror of divisions, rifts, minorities. Its ideal, its most delectable dream, is unity, identity, uniformity, density. It damns what might divide up its power, cut up its mass, and create within it diversity, plurality and divergence, as an affront to its Majesty.[3]

Out of these feelings develops the unitarian centralized state; and although that state take the form of a constitutional, liberal democracy, its very existence as an administrative machine with enormous powers constitutes a terrible danger. For *its political nature depends upon the will directing it*; and that, of course, is the 'brute engine' which Godwin pointed to as the source of all evil. Proudhon says:

Liberal today under a liberal government, it will tomorrow become the formidable engine of a usurping despot. It is a perpetual temptation to the executive power, a perpetual threat to the people's liberties ... No rights, individual or collective, can be sure of a future. ... Centralization might, then, be called the disarming of a nation for the profit of its government ...

Quite apart from the examples of Mussolini, Hitler, and Stalin it has become apparent since the Second World War that United States Presidents can and do make use of the Federal administrative machine in a way which makes a mockery of democracy. But in a Proudhonian confederation, instead of the executive being armed with the strength of the whole against the parts, the parts are armed with their combined strength against abuse of the central power.

Inevitably, with Proudhon, politics is secondary to economics: no federative arrangement of the kind he envisages could survive if there are in its economy permanent causes of dissolution. For as long as society is divided into two mutually hostile classes, the federated state will degenerate, if the proletariat wins, into a 'unitary democracy' (which we should call a people's republic, that is a bureaucratic dictatorship) or, if the bourgeoisie wins, into a constitutional monarchy or parliamentary republic. He did not foresee fascism, that is capitalist dictatorship. So the first problem to be solved is economic; and the solution – rise of Mutualism and abolition of *aubaines* – is there in his earlier writings.

*　　*　　*　　*　　*

The substance of the second part of *Du Principe Fédératif* is a critique of the unitarian or centralized state. Proudhon shows the French Revolution wiping out the last traces of regionalism and provincial independence; and the masters of the Paris mob making themselves masters of all France and treating any inclination towards local autonomy or of *l'esprit de clocher* – parish-pump politics – as treason.

In any unitarian state democracy is a fraud; in such a state the people worship the idol 'France' or the idol 'England'; thus the people can be used to oppress the people, and dissidents, progressives, minorities of whatever kind become 'traitors'. 'The democracy represents itself as liberal, republican, even socialist; the democracy deceives itself. It has never understood the revolutionary triad, Liberty–Equality–Fraternity, which in 1848 as in 1793 was for ever on its lips. . . . Its definitive motto is one word, UNITY.'

Liberty: inviolability of person and home; inviolability of all municipal, corporative and industrial rights and freedoms; guarantee of all legal forms; protection of innocence and free defence. So hopelessly at variance with unity are all these that in 1848 it was the democracy which instituted courts martial, domiciliary visits, which filled the prisons, decreed the state of siege, and transported workers without trial. For, in its devotion to the monolithic idol, the nation, the democracy holds very cheap the rights of individuals, liberty and the law.

Socialism: 'Freedom of trade and industry' – *ie* no state interference of any kind – 'mutuality of assurance, reciprocity of credit, equalization of taxation, equality of riches and remuneration, worker participation in the risks of the industrial enterprises they control, and inviolability of all family rights including inheritance.'

All these, again, are incompatible with the centralized state. For one thing the people's democracy always inclines to communism which is the economic equivalent of political unity, and it conceives of equality only in those terms – an astonishing foresight, that. The democracy demands a whole range of measures which are incompatible with socialism as defined by Proudhon: graded and sumptuary taxation, welfare institutions, nationalized industry, national savings banks, national assistance boards, in short 'all the paraphernalia of pauperism and the drab livery of *la misère*'. I leave that word in French because we translate both *pauvreté* and *misère* by one word, poverty, by which Proudhon meant, as we have seen, something else and admirable. The democracy hates anything smacking of independence and self-reliance: it hates piece-work, treats the notion of free credit with contempt, and favours death duties which, by demolishing family estates, concentrates all wealth in the hands of the state. As for the prospect of a people of educated workers knowing their own minds, it is the very nightmare of the democracy.

At the time when *Du Principe Fédératif* was being written Italy was in the process of unification: in 1858 at Plombières Napoleon III and Cavour had agreed to make Italy a federation of seven states but the Piedmontese and the House of Savoy were determined on a centralized constitutional monarchy. It was therefore natural that, in his advocacy of the federative principle and denunciation of the tyrant central state, Proudhon should draw most of his examples from the Italian case. And one of his most important points is the close connection between the only meaningful 'nationality', and geography, geology and meteorology. In Italy he distinguishes seven 'races' of men in seven regions with their own soil and climate which have shaped the manners and customs of the inhabitants.[4]

Italy is federal by the constitution of her territory; by the diversity of her inhabitants; in the nature of her genius; in her mores; in her history. She is federal in all her being and has been since all eternity ... And by federation you will make her as many times free as you give her independent states.[5]

Not in the book under examination, but in Proudhon's *Justice* (see Chapter 10), the same objections are raised to the unification of the Germanies, a unification which was to have the most appalling consequences for the German people and the world at large. From that same book I borrow the so-called *Little Political Catechism* to quote from, for its clear definition of Proudhonian federalism:

Q: Who are the natural allies of the revolution?
A: All who suffer oppression and exploitation: let the revolution appear and the whole world will welcome it with open arms.
Q: What do you think of the European balance of power?
A: It was the glorious idea of Henri Quatre to which only the revolution can give its true form. It is universal federalism, supreme guarantee of all liberties and all rights and which will, without soldiers or priests, replace Christian feudal society.
Q: Federalism is not much liked in France. Could you not put your idea in other terms?
A: To change the name of a thing is to compromise with error. Say what you like about Jacobin prudence, the true obstacle to despotism is federative union. How did the kings of Macedonia become masters of Greece? By having themselves declared chiefs of the Amphictyony, that is by substituting themselves for the confederation of the Hellenic peoples. Why, after the fall of the Roman Empire, was Catholic Europe unable to reform as a single State? Because the master-thought of the invading barbarians was independence which is the negation of unity. ... Federalism is the political form natural to humanity.
Q: In that federation, what becomes of nationality?
A: The more completely the federative principle be applied, the more firmly will nationality be assured. But it's a far cry from recognizing the nationalities to the restoration of those which have become pointless, not to say dangerous.

Why this shying away from using his federative principle to gratify the aspirations of Polish, Hungarian, Irish and other nationalisms? Marx saw in nationalism, whatever its political colour, a road to social revolution. Proudhon believed that the loudest advocates of the various nationalisms were pushing their causes as a means of evading the economic and social revolution. He probably had in mind the, to him, highly suspect English support of the unification of Italy. England was, after all, the capital of pauperism, the most ruthless exploiter, short of slavery, of the working-class. Moreover, a nationalist revolution was necessarily wholly political; the sole outcome of a merely political revolution is the substitution of one tyranny for another. Nevertheless, in this reservation he is guilty of the sin of which he once accused the economist Rossi: not following his own argument to its logical conclusion.

Du Principe Fédératif is summed up in a single paragraph by Proudhon himself:

In a Confederation the units which compose the body politic are not individuals, citizens or subjects; they are groups determined in the first instance by nature whose average size does not exceed that of a population gathered together in a territory of a few hundred square leagues. These groups are themselves little States, democratically organized under federal protection, whose units are the heads of households, or citizens.

To quote him again: *Voilà tout le système.*

NOTES TO CHAPTER TWELVE

1. Montesquieu, in *L'Esprit des Lois*, said democracy can survive only if it practises virtue. Otherwise '. . . la republique n'est qu'une dépouille et sa force n'est plus que le pouvoir de quelques citoyens et la licence de tous'.
2. Emerson and Thoreau quoted in George Woodcock, *Anarchism*, 1963.
3. This phenomenon, so pernicious for liberty, is studied in depth in Elias Canetti, *Crowds and Power*, English translation 1962.
4. I discussed this concept at length in *Soil and Civilization*, 1952 reissued 1976.
5. This argument is expanded to book length in Proudhon's pamphlet *La Fédération et l'Unité en Italie*, 1862.

THIRTEEN

Art and Women

DU PRINCIPE FÉDÉRATIF was an immediate success, in spite of the muddle Proudhon acknowledged the book to be. 'I tell myself that the contents will perhaps save the form.' In fact within three weeks of publication in February 1863, 6,000 copies had been sold, and it was reprinting.

By 1863 Louis-Napoleon was climbing down from his dictatorial perch, opposition in the Corps Législatif was more open and even the press began to stretch its wings. Proudhon was keen to return to journalism, and in the same month as the publication of *Du Principe* he wrote to the Minister of the Interior seeking permission to bring out a weekly under the title *Fédération*. However, it was refused. In the same month, again, Proudhon and a group of friends began to campaign for a new party of 'Young Democracy' which proposed abstention from all parliamentary political action in the forthcoming elections, the aim being to undermine the strength of the ruling regime and prepare the way for federalism. To this end a committee of abstention was set up in Paris, and another in Bordeaux; and in April Proudhon set out his arguments in a pamphlet entitled *Les Démocrates Assermentés et les Réfractaires*.

Proudhon had held, and continued to hold, that the working-class should attain to revolution not by political action but by economic means only.[1] But some groups of workers, even his own followers, were of the opinion that the workers must have their own representatives in parliament, devoted to their interests; and in May 1863 three Mutualists stood as candidates – unsuccessfully. Proudhon believed this to be a mistake, and his instinct was sound. Working-class interests are not and cannot be assimilated with those of the bourgeoisie and the old 'nationalist' parties. An MP, a *député*, has to represent all his constituents and cannot therefore be devoted to the interests of the working-class. In our own time this has been shown very clearly in the clashes between Labour Governments and the TUC; and between MPs and their local constituency parties.

This was a theme Proudhon was to take up in the last of his books, completed on his deathbed, *De la Capacité Politique des Classes Ouvrières*.

Meanwhile Proudhon, rapidly failing in health, was turning his hand to an ever-wider variety of topics. He published some essays on literary copyright under the title *Les Majorats Littéraires*; he was planning a book on the role of women; he was putting down further thoughts about property; and he was turning his attention for the first time to the theme of the visual arts.

As so often with Proudhon, this book on the visual arts blossomed from a small seed. The idea for it was sown by his friend, the painter Gustave Courbet, as the result of a public scandal caused by one of the latter's works (as I describe later). Courbet and Proudhon had known one another for many years – in fact the painter had been one of the friends who had welcomed Proudhon on his release from jail in 1852. Both men came from the same region of France, Courbet having been born (in 1819) at Ornans, a few miles from Besançon, and attended Proudhon's old school, the *Collège Royale*. Superficially Courbet was as unlike Proudhon as could be imagined: he was a bluff, earthy, extrovert with roaring sensual appetites and loved holding the stage in any company. But beneath this hearty exterior Courbet was a deeply sensitive man who possessed strong socialist leanings and a raw instinct for politics which, later in his life, was to make him an active participant in the Paris Commune of 1871, and to land him in Proudhon's old prison of Sainte-Pélagie for his part in blowing up the column in the Place Vendôme erected in honour of Napoleon I.

In fact it was the call of like to like which drew Courbet to Proudhon and made Proudhon his friend. No doubt the older man's influence hardened the democratic and social strain in Courbet's thinking, but he had certainly come to some Proudhonian conclusions before the two men met. It was surely as much the instinct which distinguishes a dangerous social enemy, as dislike of his painting, which made his fellow artists detest him, and almost the whole body of art-critics and art journalists damn him as a vulgar and boastful *arriviste* who was not even a competent artist. True, those who were really fit to judge, knew better, but they were few: Eugène Delacroix, commenting on the 1855 Salon jury's rejection of Courbet's *The Painter's Studio* recorded, 'I could not tear myself away from this scene. In refusing this work they have refused one of the most remarkable pictures of modern times.'

Courbet compounded his crime against art, as the classicists and romantics of the Academy saw it, by denying the artistic Commandments. When, in 1862, he opened his studio to pupils, young painters dissatisfied with the teaching at the Beaux-Arts, he uttered a manifesto of the kind calculated to infuriate the art establishment but, by the way, bound to appeal strongly to Proudhon:

> I cannot teach my art nor the art of any school, since I deny that art can be taught or, in other words, I claim that art is entirely individual and is for each artist only the talent resulting from his own inspiration and his own study of tradition. To this I add that in my opinion art or talent in an artist can be no more than a means of applying his own personal abilities to the ideas and objects of the period in which he lives.

This, of course, was tantamount to dismissing with a shrug the whole art of David, of Ingres, but also of Delacroix and the romantic school. For the idealists, whether of the neo-classical schools of David or Ingres, or of the romantic school, painting meant almost anything but picturing contemporary life with penetrating and interpretive insight instead of imaginative embellishment.[2] The artist's duty was to refine and beautify, to show heroes as noble, women as lovely, historical events not as they were but as they should have been if noble sentiment prevailed. He must even import his vision of an antiquity which, of course, never was, into his treatment of today, with the result that modern military adventurers are turned into absurdly noble Caesars. Set aside the display of technical accomplishment in the manipulation of forms, colours and composition, and what you are left with is rhetoric, a kind of propaganda for false values.

The art of Ingres, now grown rich and famous and a Senator by its practice, and even the art of Delacroix, was nothing if not gentlemanly; and God knows Courbet was no gentleman, but a red-faced, rustic roisterer with a taste for noisy practical jokes, the life and soul of beer-swilling parties at the Brasserie Andler where he entertained Daumier, Corot, Monet, Baudelaire, Daudet, Gambetta and anyone who liked to listen, with both his nonsense and his sense. That *brasserie* became the GHQ of the realist movement, though to Courbet himself the label meant nothing in particular:

> The name of realist has been thrust on me as the name romantic was thrust on the artists of 1830. Names have never at any time given any idea of the things they stand for; if this were not so, the works would be superfluous. I will not discuss the propriety or impropriety of a designation which nobody, it is to be hoped, is under any compulsion to understand properly, but will confine myself to a few words of explanation so that I may put a stop to misunderstandings. I have studied, without bias or prejudice the art of the ancients and the art of the moderns. I have attempted neither to imitate the one nor copy the other. Nor have I striven for the vain and empty goal of art for art's sake. I have simply tried, by searching the records of traditional knowledge to arrive at a reasoned and

independent consciousness of my own individuality. To know in order to do, such is my wish. To translate the manners, the ideas, and the outward appearance of my age as I perceived them, in a word to create living art, such was my aim.[3]

In 1863 Courbet sent in to the Salon a picture, *Retour de la Conférence*. It would probably have been rejected as offensive by the jury in any case although by then Courbet was someone to be reckoned with; but in the event orders from the Ministry of the Interior, issued on the initiative of the police, left the jury no choice, for which, no doubt, they were thankful. The picture showed a group of drunken priests at the foot of an old oak-tree and near a shrine, while the seven deadly sins, dressed as clergy, and led by Hypocrisy, file past; the scene was set in a pretty landscape and was being observed by a peasant with a sardonic expression.

Courbet's purpose, as understood by Proudhon, will presently appear. His enemies said that he sought notoriety and relished rejection in his repeated outraging of received taste and decent feeling. To which he answered that classicists and romantics alike, that is all idealist artists, by misconceiving the mission of art, degraded and depraved it with their cult of art for art's sake and their betrayal of real values.

Proudhon seized upon the chance to defend his friend; and, at the same time, to state his whole life's case in new terms. But perhaps this was his primary motive.

*   *   *   *   *

Proudhon's apology for Courbet, the book entitled *Du Principe de l'Art et de sa Destination Sociale* develops into a study of the nature and purpose of art; and, characteristically, having demonstrated that the terms idealism and realism are meaningless without each other and are naturally reconciled in equilibrium, he reveals in realism the art of the revolution, and identifies Courbet's *The Stonebreakers* as the first successful 'socialist' work of art.

Proudhon carries on his enquiry in the spirit of one who, on his own confession, knows nothing of art. He has had a great deal of pleasure from, and has given a great deal of thought to, the masterpieces of painting, sculpture and music. But, as one of the common people, the ordinary men who, as taxpayers, have to support the arts whether they wish to or not, he wants to know what it is *for*? As for qualifications, he is, he says, a man of *entendement*, that is of sense, judgement, understanding: 'And it seems to me that the faculties of taste and understanding supplement each other, supplying each other's shortcomings. On those grounds, the efforts I have made to understand the rules of art and to make for myself rules of judgement may be of some small interest.'

Being Proudhon he begins at the beginning and it is necessary to bear with him from that beginning or the force of his argument is lost. He finds the origins of art in two manifestations: that sense of surprise, admiration and wonder which makes us seek to draw other people's attention to what seems to us curious and beautiful, and to share our feeling; and the drive to embellish ourselves and thus make ourselves more attractive and impressive. The child who makes herself a crown of flowers, the woman who makes herself a necklace of sea-shells, the warrior who makes himself more terrible by donning a bear-skin, are all artists. Every significant act of our lives is 'enveloped in art'. He depicts the chieftain who, by refining and enriching and ornamenting his speech, and by making his gait more solemn, his bearing more stately, shows himself an artist – and that to excellent purpose for 'urbanity or politeness is hitherto the most positive and most precious of all art's effects'.

Next he identifies in all men a *sentiment*, feeling, 'a vibration or resonance of the soul' which we experience at the aspect of certain things, as a sixth sense separate and distinct from the others; this is the aesthetic sense. The artist is that man who has the drive and acquires the skill to make the feeling he experiences pass from his own soul into the souls of other men. But the actual development of art has another cause: in response to the basic urge following the aesthetic experience, men seek to make *themselves*, in their own persons, beautiful, noble, glorious; so the arts receive a powerful impulsion from self-esteem, self-respect and pride. Finally, out of the combined action of these two causes develops the faculty of imitation, which we use as a means of fixing and so possessing the ephemeral or remote.

Modern psychology would find this wanting in a whole dimension of motivation but I seek to reveal only what went on in Proudhon's mind. In 1860 Freud was only four years old. What, however, I do find singular in a thinker who derived all philosophy from common sense and who had such respect for the native 'science and conscience' of the common working-man, is that he seems to have had no intimation of the origins of art in work, of painting as the practical magic of the hunter seeking to bring about an event by depicting it;[4] or of music in the work-chants which promote smooth collaboration. This is the more curious in that he does have the insight to reject utterly the idealist (whether in David, Ingres or Delacroix) view of beauty as a pure concept of the mind. No; beauty is real, is objective, is simply the order, symmetry, balance, proportion, harmony, correct function, of the thing observed and, ultimately, of the whole universe. Here, Proudhon seems to have intimations of functionalism.

Proudhonian 'beauty' is, or so it seems to me, that aspect of Proudhonian 'justice' which appeals to the aesthetic sense. What the artist communicates to us as interpreter of what we fail to understand for ourselves, or often even to see for ourselves, is – I say so, not Proudhon in so many words – justice made visible, made audible, made tangible, by the painter, the composer, the sculptor. And those metaphysicians – now it is Proudhon speaking for himself – who have held the concept 'beauty' to be a creation of the human mind, are misled: they have taken a faculty of perception of the real for a faculty of creation of the ideal. For the blind, light does not exist: are we to conclude that it is an ideal concept? No, of course: and Proudhon insists – reinforcing my suggestion that for him justice and beauty were two aspects of the same thing – that so objective is the quality we call beauty that its presence can, as a rule, be taken as evidence of the excellence, the potential, the constitutional soundness of the object or being the word is applied to.

Yet he does not give to the arts a place in the very front rank of human activities. It is not the equal of philosophy:

The role of art is that of an auxiliary; art is a faculty more feminine than virile, predestined to obedience, and whose highest flights, whose progress, must in the last analysis, be governed by the scientific and juridicial development of mankind. Left to itself, art can do no more than turn in upon itself, or run in circles, having, of itself, no direction.

Since, as Proudhon insists, we have an aesthetic sense, or *puissance de l'art*, art potential, and since a faculty is inconceivable without an object, what is that object? It is the ideal, but – see below for what he means by it – an ideal inseparable from the real and which cannot, as the idealisms of Ingres or Delacroix do, falsify the real. To prove this assertion he invokes photography, at that time a very young craft. Take a raw sirloin of beef or leg of mutton and photograph it: what you have is the image of a bit of dead animal, produced by a natural agency, light, acting on a chemical by means of a machine. 'What, in this case, is there to rouse the aesthetic sense, and where's the ideal?' Yet it is certain that this work of realism is *not* devoid of the ideal element and is *not* incapable of rousing the aesthetic sense. Now, for joints of raw meat, substitute flowers, a child at play, and this truth becomes more manifest: that the images created by 'an artist without awareness, absolutely insensible to beauty or ugliness ...' to wit, daylight working through a lens, will give you pleasure.

So there can be no separation of the ideal from the real. Plato, indeed, held that ideas, the eternal types of all created things, that is ideals, existed before creation, in the mind of God. But who, Proudhon asks, today believes in Platonic theosophy? Who, indeed? Feuerbach had disposed of it once and for all, though it is not clear that Proudhon was aware of that; and had he been, I can hear him claiming that the German philosopher's work had been supererogatory because the common man knew perfectly well in his 'science and conscience' that the ideas of things inhere in the things they express, and nowhere else. *In the beginning was the Word*. Rubbish; in the beginning was the Thing.

However, the artist is not a camera, and if he were there would be no point in him: why go and listen to a man who can imitate a nightingale when, simply by sitting up late, you can hear the bird itself? So, either the artist is committed to developing the idea of things, the ideal, the essence, or he is superfluous. Here Proudhon, always incapable of resisting an aside into Greek grammar, defines the word *ideal*: it expresses an object considered in its pure essence and generality, excluding realization, variety and empirical accident; which being so, an ideal indicates, 'a generality, not a reality, the contrary of an observable individual, and consequently antithetical to the real.' In other words it is the perfection, the absolute of the thing observed.

'A rose is a rose is a rose,' is Gertrude Stein's expression of an ideal: and *Rosa canina, Rosa moyesii* are nature's, 'Zepherine Drouin' or 'Peace' the rose-breeder's, attempt to attain that ideal with a real flower. That is my own interpolation. Proudhon preferred geometry. The 'ideal' or 'absolute' point has position but no magnitude, so that since the smallest point we can depict in practice has magnitude, we can imagine but cannot depict a point. But we should be guilty of bad geometry, bad mechanics, bad industrial work, bad art, if we fail to get as near to this ideal as we can. In short, the ideal has no material existence. Reinforce the argument, again from geometry: a straight line is the shortest distance between two points: the points have no magnitude and the line has length but no other dimension. I, you, can imagine a line, but we cannot draw it since it is an ideal.

An ideal having no material existence, it cannot be painted: in other words, the artist is, whatever his fashion, willy-nilly, a realist. Idealism,

in art, can only be realism falsified; realism cannot but strive to reveal the
ideal.

*   *   *   *   *

Proudhon reads a great deal, and all of it of evil portent, into the
French Revolution's adoption of Hellenistic art forms, fashions, and a
declamatory style as imagined by romantic authors. The Revolution was
'swaddled from its cradle in the formulae of an artificial and alien
aesthetic'. That was one of the reasons for the drift into tyranny: the
Revolution was not seen for what it was, but for what a disordered
idealistic imagination misconceived it to be.

Never was more sensibility (aesthesia) affected, and never in any matter of such
weight and moment was there so much mere play-acting. From the opening of
the States General until 9 Thermidor, every man became an actor. Never was
taste more false, eloquence less natural, artistic and literary inspiration so void.
The only original productions of that troubled time, in the matter of art and style,
were the *Carmagnole*, the *Ça ira*, the oaths of *Père Duchêne*, the tricolour flag, and
the guillotine ... The *Marseillaise* is no better than an amplification of empty
rhetoric, like one of Vergiaud's or Robespierre's harangues.

Comes Napoleon; with liberty lost, art and literature are silent.
Roused at the Restoration, they begin the great debate between clas-
sicals and romantics, the former convinced that to abandon the great
traditions of Greece and Rome and the Renaissance would be retro-
gressive, and the latter that art's duty was now to give expression to
nationalism, to energy, to variety and movement. As always, Proudhon's
mind works towards reconciliation, synthesis. He resolves the contradiction between the schools by applying his theory of mankind's progress in
communion. The complete artist can no longer be a classical or a
romantic. 'The complete artist is that man who, knowing how to com-
bine all the elements, all the data of art, all concepts of the ideal, and
rising superior to all tradition, best succeeds in being of his place and
time.'

This synthesis had not been accomplished: true, weary of strife,
both sides have fallen silent and have begun quietly to borrow from
each other. Hence, a new decadence, accompanied by pornography (by
which he meant nudes lasciviously posed)[5]: those 'tacit transactions'
between the two schools are, like doctrinarianism in politics (his word for
the constitutional parliamentary democracy of the middle class), an
hypocrisy.

Examining the work of David, Ingres, Delacroix, Vernet, Robert and others, he sees men of talent producing *sottises et impuissances*; men who see across centuries, frequent the invisible world, inhabit the supernatural, make Shakespeare's heroes pose for them; and who are blind to and incapable of understanding what is happening all about them. And out of this 'confusion and irrationality' he sees saving realism being born, which brings him back to Courbet, taking, as his first demonstration, that painter's *Paysans de Flagey*. Here there is no pose, no flattery, not the least suspicion of idealisation such as even Rembrandt was guilty of in, for example, his *Ronde de Nuit*. But we must not let the truth and simplicity of the work lead us to accuse the artist of offering us a dageurreotype; beneath the 'vulgar realism' you will find a depth of observation, '... which is, to my mind, the real point of art'.

And Proudhon tells us then what he, himself, finds in the picture, giving us the history, character, condition and circumstances of every figure in it. Courbet has given us the very essence of the Franc-Comtois peasantry, of the country-folk of all France, of the French people, thirty or forty years after the revolution. The picture reveals *and interprets* provincial, rural France, with all its uncertain temper, positive mind, simple speech, gentle passions, unemphatic style and down-to-earth thoughts, just as remote, in its respect for rank and position and the social order, from democracy as from demagogy. With its decided pre-ference for the ordinary, familiar ways, it is also remote from idealistic exaltations, happiest when the old honest mediocrity under a temperate authority can be preserved, that *juste-milieu* which, alas, repeatedly betrays the men who cling to it.

In short, Courbet's painting is an authentic, contemporary social document. Of course the critics damned it while admiring the painter's skill, when it was shown at the Salon of 1850–1. Where were the ele-gance, the nobility of art? Fellow-artists of the old schools were even angrier than the critics, and what had Courbet to say to them? 'You claim to paint Charlemagne, Caesar, Jesus Christ Himself. Would you know how to paint a portrait of your own father?'

Proudhon rejects out of hand the precious notion of art as purely intuitive, unaware of itself, avoiding reason. The twin sources of the ideal as essence are 'science and conscience'. The painter must be thoughtful, must study, must be a researcher. Courbet and the realist painters are not only aware, not only men of intellect, they dare also to be social critics. Thus, Courbet's *The Stonebreakers*, alas destroyed in the bombing of Dresden, is the first successful *socialist* work of art.[6] Those two poor workmen, one old and past hoping, the other young and with nothing to hope for, breaking stone at a bleak roadside tell the whole story of the tragic failure of our industrial capitalist society. While daily inventing more and more marvellous machines it is incapable of emancipating and raising up those of the poor who, numbering at least 6 million in France alone, must still toil for a starvation wage at the most painful and repugnant tasks. And that social impotence of the industrial capitalist society, which Courbet has forced us to face, is general. For what is even the better-paid machine-minder, machine-operator, but a serf to the machines he serves, and their proprietors?

*   *   *   *   *

When Proudhon took up the defence of Courbet's *Retour de la Con-férence*, he must have been moved by the parallel with his own case, if he cast his mind back to the fate of *What is Property?* and its sequel, *Warning to the Proprietors*. For, as I have said, it was on the initiative of the police and the Ministry of the Interior that the picture was rejected by the Salon judges of 1863, in much the same spirit of authoritarian oppression. Courbet was held guilty of gross impiety, outrage against religious morality, and stirring up contempt for a whole class of public functionaries in the exercise of their duties.

As for those artists and art-critics who were only too pleased to see the police doing their dirty work for them, they were damning a picture which they were utterly incapable of understanding. Courbet, says Proudhon, was not trying to make the clergy look ridiculous and disgraceful by depicting them as drunkards; that would have been a commonplace jibe far beneath his genius. His purpose was 'to reveal the utter powerlessness of religious discipline, that is to say of idealist thinking, to maintain the clergy in the way of that severe virtue demanded of them'. The picture is, then, a statement of a modern, a scientific, a revolutionary discovery:

The priest, to his undoing, is, like the artists of the Classical and Romantic schools, a worshipper of an ideal and of the absolute; he is not its promoter; he is not the master of his idea or of the impressions it makes on him; he is its slave, and that reduces him to a moral poverty which, sooner or later, leads to a shameful fall.

Just as the priest's dogma obliges him to deny the virtue of man and deny the efficacy of conscience, so the artist of the idealist schools denies the beauty of man as he is; just as the priest puts all his faith in divine grace, so the idealist artist puts all his faith in inspiration, and both deny the value of reflection.

Courbet and the realists are demonstrating that the principle of virtue is in ourselves and requires only the services of two auxiliaries to be made manifest, work and study. These artists are, in short, true men of the Revolution, who have discovered and accepted the social 'destination' of art.

Proudhon never finished *Du Principe de l'Art*, and on his deathbed he sent Courbet a message through their mutual friend the Franc-Comtois novelist Max Buchon, expressing his regrets. Courbet himself assisted with the task of preparing it for publication after the philosopher's death.

*   *   *   *   *

Until very near to death, Proudhon did not allow his ailing body to deny him the single unfailing satisfaction in his life, the power to work. There was nevertheless a debilitating sense of failure at the prospect of the enormous volume of unfinished works, of notes for more works, with which his rooms were crammed: he began to know that he would never accomplish what he had set himself to do. He was desperately tired, his periods of restoration to energy became fewer and shorter; and he confessed to at least one friend that when he looked upon the state of France and faced the knowledge that his own powers were declining, he would, had he a little money put by to leave his daughters, be glad to die.

Another of the works which he was never to finish, and which exists only as one-third of a draft manuscript and a mass of notes for the rest, does him no credit at all, but must, since it exposes an aspect of his character and nature hitherto only partially revealed, be glanced at: *La Pornocratie, ou les femmes dans les temps modernes*.[7]

In *De la Justice* he had developed certain ideas touching the place of women in society, derived from two sources within himself. The first was his puritanism, which for him was simply a manifestation of justice in the sense he gave the word in his great book. The second was his search for a social unit to be the basic component of society, so stable and so firmly founded on what he conceived to be the highest and noblest manifestation of mind and spirit, justice revealed by conscience, that it would make possible his just society, that is a society without political government, without police, and without laws.

That social unit was not simply the free and just man, but the androgynous couple. The bond uniting the man and woman composing it was not love, in the sense of *eros*, which was a manifestation of the lower, animal side of man's nature, useful as a means of bringing the sexes together for the propagation of the species, but on no account to be given more than biological importance. No, the bond was *absolute devotion*: devotion of the man to the physical, intellectual and moral *beauty* of woman; and of the woman to the physical, intellectual and moral *strength* of man; and of both to their union, and to the rearing in beauty and strength of their girl and boy children respectively.

In other words, the basic social unit was the family as a concrete manifestation of virtue; and because, in the absence of political, social, economic, religious and legal authority, it had to be ruggedly strong and bound together in the steel bands of conscience aware of justice, Proudhon excluded divorce as rigorously as did the Catholic Church which he had come to hate. Moreover, he excluded sexual freedom, especially for women. Just as he held that the doctrine of art for art's sake could produce nothing but worthless works, so he held that the equally fashionable doctrine, among the emancipated (in his vocabulary it was a term of abuse), of love for love's sake, was simply prostitution, a corrupting trading of pleasure for pleasure.

He saw the component man and woman of his married couple as equal in devotion, equally respectable for their different merits, but not otherwise equal. He identified man as maker, woman as user; man as producer, woman as consumer; man as thinking mind, woman as feeling heart. But because of his positive, energetic, initiatory role, and his superior physical and intellectual strength, both based on verifiable physical facts – larger muscles and a heavier brain – man must always be superior to the woman, as three is to two.

Proudhon's flat denial that woman, given equal education, could be man's equal in achievement; his insistence that every man must be unquestioned master in his own house; his denial of sexual freedom and of divorce roused the anger of a number of women, writers with the learning and skill to answer him. They belonged to that stratum of Parisian society which he labelled 'the pornocracy': the women, and those men who abetted them, who demanded, and had in some cases, George Sand for example, taken, absolute sexual as well as intellectual freedom. Two of the women of talent who published pamphlets provoked by *De la Justice*, roused his fury to such a pitch that he was driven to write *La Pornocratie* as a rejoinder addressed specifically to them. They compounded the felony of being self-emancipated women by also being Saint-Simonian socialists; and by accusing him of seeking in *De la Justice*, an Absolute, whereas an important purpose of the book had been to demonstrate that no Absolute is possible.

One of the worst offences on which his female opponents fastened was that of making beauty the supreme female attribute, as he made strength the supreme male attribute. They were reacting, as the Women's Liberation movement of today reacts, against the idea of woman as primarily a sexual object, not a person but a body. This was a misunderstanding of his meaning:

Beauty – and let us not forget that I am speaking of beauty as of strength from every point of view, physical, intellectual and moral – is not a nullity; the correlative of strength it is a virtue, a power, an I-know-not-what of which it is easier to point out the action than define the essence.... Beauty in women is more efficacious than strength in men, given that, as a rule, beauty leads strength...

The woman who failed to realize this, and who demanded emancipation, that is to be not a sweet and gentle creature guiding male strength by means of the physical, mental and moral beauty proper to her, but a person on a par with man in all respects, had lost 'her soul's health'. For emancipation must bring about the degradation of marriage, ruin the institution of the family, and so, by the way, deprive Proudhon of the only building-blocks with which he could erect his just society.

Proudhon's extraordinary power of unprejudiced thinking completely failed him when it came to women: two of the anecdotes he uses in the book will serve to reveal this. He says that he once knew the wife of a purveyor of military substitutes at a time when those poor wretches were an article of trade, who, when her husband was away, herself undertook the physical examination of the 'merchandise', necessary to ensure that they would pass the army medical examination.[8] She was a decent, honest woman, quite above suspicion of *galanterie*: 'The substitutes were not men, to her, but simply cannon-fodder ...' Yet, Proudhon insists, what man could approach her without disgust? Clearly, a woman physician would have been an object of horror.

Then, there were those peasant girls he had known as a boy who, in their father's absence, would take the bull to the cow and do what was necessary: 'What those rustic virgins did with their hands is indescribable.' And, of course, it denatured them as women.

He allowed that a woman might be a teacher, even a writer within wifely and matronly limits; but an orator, never. He approved of the provision in the Code which denied to a woman all rights in matters of money and business, unless she had paternal or marital authorization. He had the extreme religious puritan's attitude to actresses: they were all practitioners of that abomination, free love; and a father who took his wife and daughters to the play, was abetting prostitution. Euphrasie had had to put her foot down very firmly to be allowed her favourite pleasure; Proudhon did not accompany her to the theatre.

What of the woman who, having a talent, prefers a career as artist, writer or philosopher before marriage, or who only marries on condition that she remain free of her husband's control in the matter of her work?

By the very fact that a woman, on the pretext that she has a vocation for religion, philosophy, art or love, emancipates herself in her heart, steps out of her sex, seeks to equal men and enjoy male prerogatives, it comes about that instead of producing a work of philosophy, a poem, a masterpiece of art, by which alone her ambition could be justified, she is dominated by a single thought which, from that moment, never leaves her and which takes, in her, the place of genius and idea: this thought is that in all things, reason, strength, talent, woman is man's equal; and that if, whether inside the family or out in society, she does not hold an equal place with man, it is because it is denied her by iniquitous force. As for equality in the matter of the senses, its inevitable consequences are free love, condemnation of marriage, condemnation of womanhood, jealousy and secret hatred of men, and, to crown the system, inextinguishable lechery; such, invariably, is the philosophy of the emancipated woman.

Every illiberal, every cruelly reactionary notion ever used against female emancipation by the most extreme anti-feminist, is to be found in Proudhon's *Pornocratie* or in the notes from which it was to have been completed. 'I do not know which woman it was who was shocked to discover that we men think a woman knows enough if she knows enough to mend our shirts and cook us a steak. I am one of those men.'

NOTES TO CHAPTER THIRTEEN

1. This was a belief which achieved full expression with the anarcho-syndicalists, their theory of the apocalyptic General Strike, and organization of a new society on the basis of the trade unions, in the 1890s.
2. Courbet's letter-heading read 'Maître-Peintre, sans ideal et sans religion'.
3. Quoted by Marcel Zahar in *Gustave Courbet*, London 1950. It is from the Manifesto of the realists published by Courbet when his *Burial at Ornans* and *The Painter's Studio* were refused by the Salon jury.
4. It is true, of course, that Magdalenian painting had yet to be discovered.
5. One wonders which of Courbet's nudes Proudhon had seen.
6. Both 'socialist' and 'realist', Courbet's art has, of course, nothing to do with 'Socialist Realism' which is not realist at all, but, like advertising 'art', the crudest manifestation of idealism.
7. Eventually published in 1875.
8. The army would accept substitutes for the young men who were unlucky in the conscription lottery.

FOURTEEN

The Last Word

Despite the Gods, despite everything, I will have the last word.

October 1864

IT IS DISTASTEFUL to realize that during the very period when he was putting together his anti-feminist treatise Proudhon's own dependence on the loyal Euphrasie was increasing daily, and that he could not have written the book at all without her ministrations. It is another of the many paradoxes and contradictions in Proudhon's life that he should have been capable of holding sternly patriarchal views of a woman's role at the same time as writing to his own wife letters of such touching and humble appreciation of her qualities as a human being.

The cold nights are difficult for me, especially when I have to change my underwear and the air of the big room can get at me. Then I need you; and nobody can take your place with me. No doubt you'll say it is egoism which makes me say so. *Mon dieu*, dear wife, there is always a little egoism in all our actions. What, at least, is certain is that ill or not I am attached to my own nest above all things, and that I love you more than ever.

What was the illness which – progressively and with increasing frequency from 1863 – attacked him and sapped his physical strength? All we know are its symptoms: headaches, asthma, catarrh, erysipelas and cholera-like stomach troubles. The winter and spring of 1863/4 – his first in Paris after exile – was the worst period yet for his health, though his intellectual energy remained unimpaired and he was working harder than ever. With the onset of summer his health improved, and in August 1864 Proudhon travelled to his native Doubs mountains, in Franche-Comté, to convalesce. He always loved mountains, and as an asthmatic undoubtedly felt better in mountain air. He stayed at St Hippolyte with the brothers of Dr Briot who were prosperous tanners, and from here he wrote letters to Euphrasie (including the one just quoted) describing his enjoyment of the scenery, the expeditions he was planning into the mountains, the various Jura wines he has been drinking on his walking-trips, and his plans for the whole family to spend the next summer in Franche-Comté.

In September he was in Besançon where he paid a visit to his old friend the scholar Weiss, who was now eighty-six, and Proudhon described the meeting in a letter to Euphrasie. 'Dear M. Weiss, here is one of your prodigals come asking permission to embrace you.' Weiss took him, weeping, into his arms. 'You are my spiritual father,' Proudhon went on, 'and in my eyes you are the last incarnation of the 18th century. May you live to understand that, for my part, I am one of the incarnations of the 19th.' He was indeed.

From Franche-Comté he travelled to Dampierre to consult and stay with Dr Maguet who was not satisfied with Proudhon's health. The philosopher was extremely weak, he was ageing rapidly and his hair was falling out. He was exceedingly thin, wasting away. On 14 September he returned to Passy, his health deteriorating gravely, and before long he was forced to take to his bed. In spite of illness Proudhon forced himself to keep a rigid timetable of work, every day from seven in the morning until midday. He was engaged on his final book, determined to complete it even though by November he was too weak to hold a pen and was forced to leave the writing of the last chapter to Chaudey.[1] This was based on a conversation of several hours between the two during which Chaudey took notes. By the end of the month he knew that his doctors were concealing the truth – that he was dying. Proudhon lingered on, just alive, into the New Year, and at two in the morning of 19 January 1865, he died. Euphrasie was with him – Euphrasie, so belittled and so loved, to whom Proudhon had said on being asked if he would like to see a priest before he died, 'I shall confess to you'.

The last book Proudhon was struggling to complete between September and December of 1864 was, like much of his work, the outcome of a particular political event of the day. Early in 1864 a group of Mutualist workers from Paris and Rouen, led by Henri Tolain and Charles Limousin, later to be the leaders of the Proudhonian faction of the First International, published a manifesto, to be known thereafter as the Manifesto of the Sixty, arguing that because Deputies did not and could not really represent all their constituents, but in practice represented bourgeois interests in general, or special interests, the workers must have worker-Deputies in parliament, men devoted to the interests of the working-class. Tolain, Limousin, and others chosen as delegates, called to see Proudhon and to consult him about this assertion, and to put a number of questions to him. His last book, *De la Capacité Politique des Classes Ouvrières*, is Proudhon's answer to those questions, and is in fact addressed on the title page to *Several workmen of Paris and Rouen who had consulted the author touching the elections*.

In the first place, Proudhon insisted that the working-class must on no account take any part in parliamentary government: for, if they did, their

representatives would be obliged to abide by its rules. Only total repudiation of the whole system would confer on the working-class the right to
take another way. There were a score of reasons why this was so, but one
of them was supreme: there is an inhibiting incompatibility between the
workers' aspirations and the middle-class democratic system, however
liberal. If the revolution was to proceed along the course of historical
necessity to the point of optimum freedom for all men, then the very first
thing to be done was to identify and understand the *idea* on which *la
democratie ouvrière*, the workers' democracy, must be based.

Proudhon was not taking up a new stance in his advocacy of abstention from the 1864 election; he was merely reiterating what he had said
before the 1863 election. The results of that one appeared to be such a
blow to the emperor's own party, such a boost for the opposition parties,
that, as Proudhon recorded:

You heard it on all sides – that Paris was rousing from her torpor, had for the past
three weeks been coming back to political life, felt herself stirring, revived and
animated by a breath of revolutionary air. Aha! cried the self-appointed leaders
of this movement, here is no longer the new and monotonous and wearisome
Paris of M. Haussmann, with its rectilinear boulevards, gigantic mansions,
magnificent but deserted embankments, and its sad river now bearing on its
stream nothing but stone and sand; with its railway-stations which, replacing the
gates of the old city, have destroyed its *raison d'être*; with its squares, its new
theatres, new barracks, its macadam, its legions of sweepers and its frightful
dust; a city peopled by English, Germans, Dutch, Americans, Arabs and
Russians, so cosmopolitan that one wonders where the natives have gone to. No,
the Paris of the good old days has been restored to us; or was it only its ghost
which appeared by the light of the stars at the whispered cry of *Vive la liberté*!

In the Paris constituencies 235,000 votes were cast, 153,000 of them for
the 'democratic' opposition party which got everyone of its candidates
in. Proudhon had not been among those rejoicing: all that would happen
would be that the triumphant 'liberals' would now strive to put the clock
back and restore a constitutional republic or monarchy, accomplishing
absolutely nothing of the least interest to the working-class. On that
night (1 June 1863) there had been an eclipse of the moon and as the
election results became known there were cries of 'Despotism eclipsed by
liberty!' from the winning side, while the losers muttered that what had
been eclipsed was Parisian good sense. Proudhon's view was that whatever had been eclipsed it was certainly not the imperial craftiness: a
slightly stronger but still helpless opposition gave the regime a misleading look of democratic respectability. The rural vote for the
emperor's party predictably swamped the urban vote against it; some

revolutionary steam had been given a safety valve. By analysing the voting statistics for 1851, 1857 and 1863 Proudhon came up with a very interesting explanation of the 1863 result: in the earlier elections the working-class vote had simply been withheld in the cities; it was that vote which had reversed the position in the same cities. But the workers who had gone to the polls this time were not fools: they were not voting for the bourgeois opposition to the imperial autocracy; they were voting against their own Elect of the 1851 plebiscite. At last conscious of its power, the proletariat was using it. But Proudhon warned, both in the summer of 1863, and again when the elections of 1864 confirmed the 1863 results, against the illusion that anything useful had been accomplished.

*   *   *   *   *

Proudhon examined, in his book, the three systems more or less well-adapted to the new industrial civilization, which the workers might, as the coming dominant class, adopt as the expression of their democracy. Against both communism, with its inevitable destruction of liberty and responsibility and self-respect, and against social democracy in a mixed economy with its inevitable pauperization (welfare) he repeated the arguments of his earlier works.

There remained Mutualism: the working-class must make it what it was destined to be, mankind's solution to the social-economic problem of organizing society; and it was emerging already from the 'science and conscience' of the working-class. Mutuality, reciprocity, exchange, justice: these are to be substituted for authority, community, charity. Society becomes a system of mutually balancing free forces in which every man is assured of enjoying the same rights on condition of fulfilling the same obligations.

Of all the examples of how Mutualism would work in practice, Proudhon's application of it to insurance is the easiest to follow. He begins by pointing out that insurance companies make very large profits: dividends to shareholders of 50 per cent are common and 100 per cent not unusual, 150 per cent not unheard of. These dividends are a levy on the insured, that is they are theft justified by risk. In a Mutualist society every man underwrites every other man's risks *pro rata* with the valuation he sets upon his own. Each underwrites all in the measure that he is underwritten by all. This insurance is simply a part of the reciprocal undertaking or contract which is the basis of Mutualism.

In 1860 it had been proposed and debated that either the state should take over all insurance; or that it should offer national insurance to the citizens in competition with the insurance companies. Proudhon rejected this without hesitation: what, he asks, is the point of exchanging exploitation by capitalists for exploitation by the state? Mutual insurance was the only sound answer; and he calculated that whereas current fire–accident–theft premium rates were of the order of .40 francs per cent, under the mutualist system they would be of the order of .15 francs per cent – the cost of administration.

Now see how mutualism applies in the matter of remuneration of labour – wages, salaries and fees: a day's work = a day's work; utility = utility; function = function; service pays for service, and a product for a product where costs of materials and labour are equal.

A rich man wants me to go to work as his valet. Says I to myself, there's no such thing as a stupid trade, there are only stupid people, and care of another man's person is more than a work of utility, it's an act of charity placing the servant morally above the served. So, as I've no intention of being humiliated, I make a condition on which I will undertake the service: that the man who wants me as his body servant pay me half his income. Anything less and we lose fraternity, equality, mutuality; we no longer compose a democratic society, but a society of aristocrats and flunkeys.

Proudhon himself raises an objection: it is true that whether he be an unskilled labourer or a surgeon, muck-forking peasant or a physicist, a machine-minder or a managing director, a man using his skill and strength with all his heart can do no more than a day's work in a day; and therefore, morally, there can be no question but that a day's work equals a day's work. But nor can it be denied that some functions are more difficult, require more intelligence, strength, application, moral fibre, than others. In other words, function does not equal function, and this should be recognized in remuneration differentials.

An earlier French philosopher, Blaise Pascal, conceived of mankind as a single, undying person who accumulated in himself all the knowledge, successively realized all the ideas, and accomplished all the kinds of progress conceived by men. Proudhon applied this concept to political economy: Giant Society with his countless brains and hands works all the industries, produces all the wealth. How, by what rule, are we to award more or less merit, more or less payment, to this, that or the other of his component parts? I am here reminded of Aesop's fable in which the body's members revolting against the endless toil of filling that greedy fellow Stomach with food, go on strike, with obvious results. Proudhon says – concede the point that all men of goodwill, regardless of capacity and function, are morally equal; set aside altogether the factor of moral worth and dignity, and consider man simply in terms of economic action, as worker-producer: capacity and faculty differentials are not infinite, they are not only limited but small.

Here is the demonstration of that assertion: although the average man does not exist, the concept is useful. Suppose that in terms of mind, we set the level marked 'common sense' as average. Suppose, further, that in terms of body, we state the output of strength of an average man on an average diet, as we could, in horsepower (today, we should do it in wattage). Now, the extremes above and below those average levels are small: a man with the strength of three men would be a Hercules, one in ten million; and a man with 'enough brains for three' a demi-god.

From this point Proudhon goes on to argue that the output of a day's work in any trade, industry or profession, by a man of average strength, skill, intelligence, age and health, in value-equivalent of goods or services, can be estimated or even measured. I have a reservation about opinion-value, that is the value put on the work of the artist, poet, novelist, actor, singer, dancer, by opinion or fashion; but let that pass. Since it is expedient to recognize exceptional capacity in exceptional importance of function or difficulty of function, let it be rewarded above average; but only within the measure that capacity really can, in nature, be above average. This leads to the conclusion that remuneration differentials might be as three to one; no higher.

What of the people below the line? Two Proudhonian principles are here involved: a day's work equals a day's work; but it is dangerous and pernicious to ignore the natural and universal principle of justice in its Proudhonian sense of functional rightness. Since we have conceded that it is expedient to reward superior capacity with above average remuneration, we must – since mutualism excludes pauperization by welfare – concede that below average capacity be rewarded below average. But it will be recalled that in his earlier writing Proudhon had argued that political economy must be concerned to rectify the inequalities of 'innate property' – physical and mental endowment at birth. In practice, what you do is to set a minimum wage based on what is required to secure a decent subsistence in terms of food, clothing, shelter and opportunity. Mutualism, excluding welfarism, has to tolerate poverty; but not degrading poverty.

The effect of mutualism on commerce is to remove the element of *agiotage*, under which heading Proudhon includes speculation in all its forms, exorbitant profit, and exorbitant salary. Why is it, he asks, that among nearly all civilized peoples trade, more especially retail trade, has been held in contempt? The answer is that an element of dishonesty, even of perfidy, has always and everywhere been inherent in it. This can be eliminated if the object of trade becomes the sale of goods as cheaply as possible and to the greatest benefit of all.

The most obvious solution to the problem of retail distribution on those terms, is the consumers' cooperative: but Proudhon insists that this obvious solution is the wrong one, almost as wrong as the solution of the capitalist chain-store. Because, if men are not to decay, they must always be left with the greatest possible measure of freedom and take full responsibility. Retail trade should be left to the small shop-keeper dependent for his livelihood on his own judgement and his own integrity. There are other reasons why Proudhon makes this surprising choice, which I shall come to presently.

The first condition for fair trading is consistent and continuous publication of such statistics as the volume of supplies of all commodities, raw material prices, labour costs, and forecasts and estimates of harvests and manufactured goods. Consider the problem of the distribution of a major commodity: wheat. In a Mutualist economy, we begin with an average cost of production worked out from the figures from as many years as possible. This is adopted as the standard production cost, and we will suppose it to be 18, including of course, the farmer's own labour cost. The selling price of wheat will then be 19 or 20, according to the harvest. The farmer's revenue will then be between 5.50 and 10 per cent of what he is paid for his wheat, the actual percentage depending partly on the weather in a given season and place, and partly on the farmer's skill and efficiency. Suppose a bad harvest with the total yield down by 10 per cent below standard: then the price is allowed to rise proportionately all along the line, so that the hardship of a bad harvest is shared equally by producer, processor and consumer. Suppose the opposite case, a bumper harvest; then the price is allowed to fall, again proportionately, and society buys and stores the surplus above requirement.

This system eliminates the commodity broker, and therefore his *aubaine* levied on the bread; and, more important, it eliminates commodity speculation. Proudhon is quite fair even to such parasites as commodity brokers: in an unrestricted 'market' economy, that is an economy of every man for himself and the devil take the hindermost, parasitism, deception, corruption and gambling are inevitable. But because the mere dealer-speculator is not the creator of any utility, he gets his living by levying tribute on our subsistence.

Mutualism will cure this leprosy not by means of a network of penalties more or less judicious and nearly always vain; nor by restraint on freedom of trade, a cure worse than the disease; but by treating commerce like insurance, I mean by giving it all the requisite public guarantees & so bringing it into the Mutualist fold.

Thus the risks and the benefits of trade are shared by all in the community by means of a complex of reciprocal undertakings which together compose the social contract. The market is retained but it is disciplined. Good Mutualists are as well aware as anyone of the uses of the law of supply and demand; they require only that its application be made just by the publication of supply statistics kept constantly up-to-date; of needs, means and cost-of-living statistics; and of honest breakdowns of production costs. Then, prevision of and provision for all eventualities: these take the form of agreements between producers, traders and consumers on minimum and maximum profit margins. These are the kinds of measures by means of which Proudhon seeks to discipline the market forces: within the restraints set by reciprocal contract entered into *en pleine connaissance de cause*, the benefits of competition are not lost, and business still goes to the most skilful, diligent and honest traders.

The whole system was designed to eliminate the most undesirable of the flaws in conventional socialism, in a word, dependence; and from capitalism also its most undesirable element, *agiotage*, speculation. No man receives a wage, a salary or a dividend; every man receives his revenue either as payment for what he has produced – the great industry becomes a multi-headed and multi-handed artisan – or as a fee for service. But to get his revenue he has to compete, to strive always to do his best lest he fall to that level below which society, out of respect for the undeniable fact that innate property is unequal, or in other words that some men and women are born handicapped, will allow no human being to fall. What Proudhon thus guards and preserves are the two qualities which make a man wholly human, neither a beast of toil degraded by pauperism, nor a machine scarcely more respectable than the metal one he serves: liberty, and responsibility.

*   *   *   *   *

Housing: Proudhon never changed his opinion that ideally every family should own their own house and a piece of land on which to grow their vegetables and fruit. Mutualist economic forces, or perhaps I should say, the economic forces generated by Mutualism, eliminate the large landowner, and, of course, speculation in land-values. The owner retains the right to sell, but at a price which is stabilized by those same forces, so that property values can rise only by the worth of real improvements (see Mutual Credit, below). But there is a difficulty: in great cities it could be very difficult to ensure that every family owns its own home; living accommodation for rent – and therefore, landlords – are necessary. Here Proudhon offers two solutions: the municipality as landlord, the one we have since adopted in Britain; or, much better, building-workers bound into companies by Mutualist contracts, build, own and maintain blocks of apartments, and are remunerated by rents. But these rents are composed of only two elements: long-term amortization of building costs; payment for maintenance service. The element of *aubaine*, profit over and above a fair return for materials and labour, being eliminated, rents are low enough to fall within the terms of the Mutualist contract.

*   *   *   *   *

The accomplishment of Mutualist housing, as of Mutualist commerce, and of Mutualist industry and agriculture, depends, since the private capitalist is being eliminated as a costly and oppressive parasite, and the state is the ultra-capitalist, on mutual credit. Here we have to bear in mind that all economic transactions whatsoever are simply an exchange of goods and services, and that, excepting as tokens, as bus-tickets, money has nothing whatever to do with it. (Mankind had almost everywhere created and sustained an elaborate complex of economic activity long before money was invented.) It is easier for the poet to pay his train fare, his water-rates, or to buy his bread and his beer with a token of the value of his book of poems, than by tearing out and handing across the counter a page from that book. If the seller of what he wants does not happen to like poetry, he might refuse the offered value, whereas he will accept it readily enough if it is a token exchangeable for something he does want. But money, whether shells, salt ingots or coins, is permissive of evil the moment it is treated as a commodity which can be bought and sold. This flaw has been overlooked because the early forms of money, including gold and silver, were, indeed, commodities; the promissory note, that is paper money, is not. The money-hoarder and lender-at-interest, is as surely a parasite as a louse or a leech on your body, sucking its provision of blood from your circulation; or, for example, a water supply engineer taking advantage of his job to draw off from the public supply water to irrigate his private garden.

Credit, says Proudhon, is from the Latin *credo*, I believe or confide, and was originally an accommodation granted against a man's word. He rebukes those working people who consider a demand for a gauge or security to cover a loan, an insult. The mutual credit banker will require sound security or collateral, just like his capitalist opposite number; what he will not require is interest. In the field of mercantile credit two categories are considered, bill discounting, and investment capital advances. Interest is at once the most burdensome shackle hampering labour, and the most intolerable levy endured by the consumer. The last year for which figures were available to him when he was writing the book was 1857: in that year the Bank of France alone – without counting the numerous private banks – bled the nation's money stream of 640 millions, giving no value, no 'utility' in exchange. One consequence is permanent inflation: the price of everything has to increase by a percentage equal to whatever percentage 640 million represents of the GNP. Also grossly inflationary is bill discounting at between 6 and 9 per cent, described as 'a tribute we kindly pay for the use of our currency'. The mutual credit system is as simple as the mutual insurance system: all accommodate each and each all at a rate which would simply cover the costs of administration.

The same applies to investment capital: what is it that is invested in any material project? Three things only – raw materials; labour, skilled and unskilled; and energy. In order to assemble and organize these a token of value exchange for goods and services is a convenience, in fact a necessity. Money is the usual one; but it makes no sense at all to have to *buy* it at 5, 10, 15 per cent above its face value. The mutual credit bank simply manages the circulation of money, charging only the actual cost of doing so, probably about a ½ per cent. It is, however, as Proudhon pointed out, extremely difficult to persuade people to realize what money really is instead of taking it for what we have been persuaded to believe it is.

Proudhon, being Proudhon, reminds his reader that Jesus Christ, generalizing the Mosaic prohibition of taking interest on money from a fellow Israelite, forbade the lending or borrowing of money at interest: it is written in the Vulgate, *Mutuum date, nihil inde sperantes*. What I dare say he did not know is that Moslem law also frowns on this practice if the Koranic prohibition of *ribâ* means what it appears to mean; indeed, Moslem law goes further, for the Believer is enjoined to abstain from making aleatory contracts which would seem to make the whole capitalist system unacceptable.[2]

The object of mutual banking, then, is to put an end to three insufferable evils: the continuous violation of economic 'justice'; the ever-growing levy in the form of interest on the national wealth for nil return; the growth of a progressively corrupting parasitism: 'We pay tribute to ignorance, to chance, to gambling, to speculation, to monopoly, and to charlatanism & advertising ... Economic justice and economic law are everywhere violated, and everywhere that violation entails a subtraction from the common wealth at our expense.'[3]

*   *   *   *   *

It has already been noted that Proudhon condemned consumer cooperatives and chain stores, and wanted retailing left to small, independent and responsible shop-keepers, a class for whom he had great respect. The shop-keeper, he says, has to be intelligent, well-informed, a source of reliable information for his customers touching supplies, prices, new lines; he has to be zealous and honest. Once the speculative element has been removed from retail trade by the Mutualist guarantees and the shop-keeper, saved by mutual credit, is freed from the burdens of interest paid to banks and rent to landlords, he can afford to be as honest as he would wish to be. This approach to retailing has one very great advantage socially: it reconciles the *petite bourgeoisie* and the proletariat:

No question of depriving any man of the place he has made for himself in society; it is simply a matter of restoring to labour and to probity that which capitalism deprives them of by its levies, by reduction of interest on money, and of rents; by cheap and easy bill-discounting; by the elimination of parasitism, extirpation of speculation, reduction in all transport costs,[4] fair equation of values, higher education for the working-classes, definitive preponderance of labour over capital, and a just measure of recognition afforded to talent and function. All this will augment the general well-being by ensuring economic security; will avoid the ruin and bankruptcy of small businesses by introducing certitude into all transactions; will prevent the spoliation of society by the accumulation of large fortunes without real and legitimate foundation; in a word, will put an end to all the anomalies and perturbations which sound analysis has always identified as the chronic causes of poverty and proletarianization.

*   *   *   *   *

Mutualism eliminates conventional politics: the political centre is everywhere, the circumference nowhere. Each group or variety of population, identified by ethnic, linguistic and geographical integrity, is master of its territory. Proudhon would, today, be very favourable to the Scottish, Welsh, Breton, Basque, Catalan and all other separatist movements. While he lay dying and dictating the notes on the basis of which Chaudey was to complete this last book, the American Civil War was raging: Proudhon declared that there was no justice, but only political expediency, in Monsieur Lincoln's determination to deny, by force, the right of the South to secede.

'Each and every city . . .' here the word is used in the sense *polis* not the sense *urbs*, 'reciprocally guaranteed by its neighbour cities, is queen of the circle defined by the radius of its influence. Unity is no longer legally defined by anything more than the promises, undertakings and guarantees given to each other by the diverse sovereign groups.' And here he repeats all the principal arguments of *Du Principe Fédératif*. In order to accomplish the new order of society the working-class, to which that task is entrusted by history, should avoid recourse to violent revolution. The steady and ever quickening growth of Mutualist association causing the shrinking and withering away of capitalism, and all economic power being then in the hands of the productive workers, they would be in a position to demolish what remained of the centralized state, and replace it with the decentralized federation of Mutualist sovereign 'cities'. And it was for these reasons that he would not countenance participation by the workers in the bourgeois democracy: does the Protestant go to Mass? No. Does the Catholic go to the Protestant sermonizing? No. And the working-class voter has no business in the church of bourgeois politics.

*   *   *   *   *

Was Proudhon, as he lay dying, deceiving himself when he claimed to see *la democratie ouvrière* composed of economic Mutualism and political federalism, clearly emerging from the 'science and conscience' of the working-class? In the long term, was there no future for either capitalism combined with constitutional parliamentary systems, or for the 'centralizing autocracy' of communism? We have, since his last words were written, endured a century of both: a century during which the Four Horsemen of the Apocalypse have ridden all mankind under their hooves. We know now that we must indeed have a new order, or perish. That order is much slower to emerge from the science and conscience of our kind than Proudhon foresaw, perhaps because he did not foretell – who did? – the enormously greater power to repress and destroy which advanced technology put into the hands of central governments determined to survive, to keep their power and their privileges. Millions more starve, millions more cower under the lash of authority, there are petty Caesars, more cruel and strutting juntas, more corrupt cabals, than ever before in the history of humanity. It is reasonable to suppose that these evils are in a very large measure the logical consequences of our continued toleration of authority.

NOTES TO CHAPTER FOURTEEN

1. See Chaudey's preface to the first and second editions of *De La Capacité Politique*, Brussels 1865 and 1868.
2. But see Rodinson, M. in *Islam et Capitalisme*, Paris, 1966.
3. The substance of this part of *De La Capacité Politique* was first published in Proudhon's *Organization du Credit et de la Circulation* in 1848.
4. Proudhon believed, apart from the generally beneficent effect of a Mutualist approach, that by the thorough exploitation of waterways transport freight rates could be cut by as much as 80 per cent. This was based on his experience at Gauthiers.

Index

Aberdeen, George Hamilton, fourth earl of, and Guizot, 104

absolute, the, 201–3; and the concept 'ideal', 270; and women, 272

absolutism, based on Divine Right, 218

Academie des Sciences Morales, 47; and *Qu'est-ce la Propriété?*, 53

Ackermann, Paul, 33; friend of Pr., 29, 30–1, 34, 64; and Fallot, 35n13

agiotage (commercial arbitrariness), 192, 280–2

Agoult, Marie de Flavigny comtesse d', *History of 1848*, 107

agriculture, nationalization, 7, 189–90

air, Comte/Pr. and its appropriation, 41, 42

Algeria, 141, 196

alienation, 85

anarchism, its meaning for Pr., 46–7, 59; and 1848 revolution, 101; strife in Bolshevik Russia, 174; negation of the Absolute, 203; role of militarism in achieving revolutionary justice, 218; solution of social questions by absolute liberty, 218; use of violence in imposing authority, 218; definition, 252

Anarchist movement, vii; beginnings, 32–3; and Napoleon III's *coup d'état*, 96; newspaper, 106; and February Revolution, 108; Pr./Marx differences, 143n3; socialist hostility, 173

anarcho-syndicalists, apocalyptic General Strike, 274n1

anticlericalism, 16–17, 62

Arago, Dominique François, 126; and National Workshops, 130

art, Pr.'s book on visual arts, 262; Courbet and, 262–3; neo-classical and romantic schools, 263, 268; rated below philosophy, 266; and socialism, 269–70; Pr. and 'art for art's sake', 272

Athenians, explain democracy to strangers, 233n6

aubaines (unearned increments), 45, 68, 129, 136, 142, 182, 244, 245, 257, 281, 283

Austria, and Swiss dispute over Jesuits, 100–1; economic slump, 101

authority, Pr. as its enemy, 12, 32, 41, 87, 91, 150, 184; source in God, 87, 89, 193; destroyed by 'harmonization of economic tensions', 185; universally

corrupting, 185–6; incompatible with liberty and equality, 186; instanced in statute justice, 193; no right to judge and punish, 194; reconciliation with liberty, 251–2; forms of expression, 252; results of its continued toleration, 287

Babeuf, 'Gracchus' (François-Émile), 123, 185; Society of Equals, 2

Bakunin, Mikhail, vii; Russian anarchist, 1, 6, 75, 120, 174, 218, 249; disciple of Pr., 170; exiled in Paris, 170

banks, nationalization, 188

Barbès, Armand, revolutionary leader, 123, 125, 129, 144n15; and Polish nationalism, 128, 133; imprisonment, 133

Barrot, Odillon, 104, 159, 161; and February Revolution, 108, 109, 111, 112–13, 114; and a Regency, 115

Bastide, Jules, 134

Baudelaire, Charles, *La Tribune Nationale*, 120

Bedeau, General, and February Revolution, 114–15

Belgium, 101, 124; accepts Pr. as political exile, 226, 230; misunderstanding over article in *L'Office de Publicité*, 250–1

Bellet, Charles, 229

Benda, Julien, and God as the common enemy *(Le Trahison des Clercs)*, 99n19

Bentham, Jeremy, Utilitarian, 4

Bergier, Father, *Dictionnaire Theologique*, 25; *Elements Primitifs des Langues* (additional essay by Pr.), 20

Bergmann, philologist, 33; and Pr., 29, 34, 37–8, 49, 210, 224; dedicatory preface to *De la Création de l'Ordre*, 61

Berruyer, *Histoire du Peuple de Dieu*, 35n17

Berryer, and Legitimist opposition, 105

Besançon, birthplace of Pr., 9, 10, 18, 28, 79, 211; Collège Royale, 13–15, 17, 67, 262; Académie *pensioners*, 19, 20, 28–31, 36; annual essay prize, 31–3, 36; bans sale of *Célébration du Dimanche*, 33; and *Qu'est-ce que la Propriété?*, 49, 52; trial of Pr., 56–9

Beslay, Charles, 152, 225; imprisonment, 167

186; his organizational plan, 142–3; right of self-defence, 194; no need of a Church-based ethic, 218; equated with the State in communism, 218; and idea of contract, 219–20; ways of augmenting its wealth, 244

Society of the Seasons, 123

Spain, 104; militant working classes, vii; fraudulent victories, 242, 246

Spanish Civil War, communist/anarchist hatred, 174

Spence, Thomas, *Administering the Landed Estate of the Nation*, 2

Stakhanov, Comrade, 86

Stalin, Josef, bureaucratic monster-tyrant, 7, 46; re-establishes the State, 88, 257; freezes state capitalist era, 141; end result of Revolution, 184; ruthless policy, 199n3; and the clergy, 200n13; calls halt to the Revolution, 203

state, the, 2–3, 6, 7; and taxation, 40, 45; Pr.'s proposed substitutes, 46, 59, 69; as thief, 46, 143; communist delusions, 85–6; no help to poorer classes, 87; root of all evil, 87; replaces God and Providence, 88–9, 186; arch-enemy of liberty, 174; Pr. and its abolition, 183; enemy of revolution, 193; right to use force, 241, 248n5; pillages its own citizens, 246; distrust of, 256; Pr.'s incompatibilities under unitarian model, 257–8

Stein, Gertrude, 267

Stendhal, 54, 111; *La Chartreuse de Parme*, 65n4; *Lucien Leuwen*, 6, 51, 65n4, 103, 117nn3, 4, 206

Stirner, Max, *The Ego and His Own*, 35n14, 233n3

Suard, Jean-Baptiste, Académie *pensions*, 19, 20, 28–31, 36

Sue, Eugène, republican, 178

Switzerland, civil war over expulsion of Jesuits, 100; right to bear arms, 247n1; constitution, 255

Syndicalism, 4

Taine, Hippolyte, asylum in England, 233; and English poor, 248n6

talents, *see* innate properties

taxation, 82, 86–7, 246; why do the rich pay more?, 39–40, 86

Thiers, Louis Adolphe, 104, 107, 213; and

February Revolution, 109, 111–12, 113, 114; and 'June days' insurrection, 134; and Finance Committee, 135; and Pr.'s arguments, 136, 137

Third Republic, National Assembly, 143n1

Thompson, William, 91

Thoreau, Henry, 260n2; on government, 254–5

Tissot, James Joseph, 60

Tolain, Henri, Mutualist, 276

Tolstoy, Leo, 16, 235

Toynbee, Arnold, 239

trade, 43–4, 281–2, 285

trade unions, 1, 6, 51; bourgeois antagonism, 18; legalized in Britain, 67

Trotsky, Léon, and anarchism, 174

unemployment, Pr.'s philosophy of poverty, 129, 143n7; assumed worthless idlers, 129–30; 'coals-in-the-bath' syndrome, 130; remedies proposed, 130, 143n9; and Pr., 138

United States, 39; slave-owning democracy, 184; a crime to be without visible means of support, 194; results of lack of an *antagonist*, 239; emancipation of slaves, 240; fraudulent victories, 242, 246; right to bear arms, 247n1; undemocratic presidential actions, 257

usury, 188, 284, 287n2

Utilitarianism, 4

utility, Pr. and, 82–3, 84, 86

USSR, substitutes state for private capitalism, 84–5; deifies the State, 88; Bolshevik suppression of anarchism, 175; a 'crime' to criticize the Party, 193–4; and revolutionary impetus, 199n3

value, concept of, 82

Vasbenter, business manager *Le Peuple*, 152; imprisonment, 155, 172

Verheyden, Director of Public Security, 226

Vernier, Pierre, 268

Viard and Fauvety, editors, 96–7

Vivien, Minister of Justice, 146, 149, 151

Le Voix du Peuple, backed by Herzen, 169–70; mocks the Prince President, 171, 173; defamed by other papers, 173–5; article 'Vive l'Empereur', 176–7; extinction, 179, 180

Voltaire, François Marie Arouet de, 103